Total Relationship Marketing

The Chartered Institute of Marketing/Butterworth-Heinemann Marketing Series is the most comprehensive, widely used and important collection of books in marketing and sales currently available worldwide.

As the CIM's official publishers, Butterworth-Heinemann develops, produces and publishes the complete series in association with the CIM. We aim to provide definitive marketing books for students and practitioners that promote excellence in marketing education and practice.

The series titles are written by CIM senior examiners and leading marketing educators for professionals, students and those studying the CIM's Certificate, Advanced Certificate and Postgraduate Diploma courses. Now firmly established, these titles provide practical study support to CIM and other marketing students and to practitioners at all levels.

The Chartered
Institute of Marketing

Formed in 1911, The Chartered Institute of Marketing is now the largest professional marketing management body in the world with over 60,000 members located worldwide. Its primary objectives are focused on the development of awareness and understanding of marketing throughout UK industry and commerce and in the raising of standards of professionalism in the education, training and practice of this key business discipline.

This book is dedicated to the future of our daughters Charlotte and Madelene

Total Relationship Marketing

Evert Gummesson

From the 4Ps – product, price, promotion, place – of traditional marketing management to the 30Rs – the thirty relationships – of the new marketing paradigm

Published in association with the Chartered Institute of Marketing

BUTTERWORTH
HEINEMANN

OXFORD AUCKLAND BOSTON JOHANNESBURG MELBOURNE NEW DELHI

Butterworth-Heinemann
Linacre House, Jordan Hill, Oxford OX2 8DP
225 Wildwood Avenue, Woburn, MA 01801-2041
A division of Reed Educational and Professional Publishing Ltd

℞ A member of the Reed Elsevier plc group

First published 1999
Reprinted 1999

British Library Cataloguing in Publication Data
Gummesson, Evert, 1936–
    Total relationship marketing: from the 4Ps – product, price, promotion, place –
    of traditional marketing management to the 30Rs – the thirty relationships –
    of the new marketing paradigm
    1. Relationship marketing 2. Marketing – Management
    I. Title
    658.8

Library of Congress Cataloguing in Publication Data
Gummesson, Evert, 1936–
    Total relationship marketing: from the 4Ps of traditional marketing
    management to the 30Rs of the new marketing paradigm / Evert Gummesson
    p. cm.
    Includes bibliographical references and index
    1. Relationship marketing. I. Title
    HF5415.55.G86 1999
    658.8'12–dc21   99–25381
                                                                        CIP

ISBN 0 7506 4463 X

Typeset by Avocet Typeset, Brill, Aylesbury, Bucks
Printed and bound in Great Britain by Bath Press, Bath

FOR EVERY TITLE THAT WE PUBLISH, BUTTERWORTH-HEINEMANN
WILL PAY FOR BTCV TO PLANT AND CARE FOR A TREE.

Contents

Figures and tables

Figures

Tables

Preface and acknowledgments

Relationship marketing (RM) is a challenge to established marketing management theory and practice. Although RM has had an international breakthrough during the 1990s, the perceptions of RM go far apart. This book presents my contribution, expressed as *total relationship marketing (TRM)* with the thirty relationships of marketing, the 30Rs, in its core.

It started in 1968 when hired by a large international management consulting firm. Reality made me brutally aware of the consultants' dependency on networks of long-term relationships. In 1982 I participated in the American Marketing Association (AMA) Conference on Services Marketing. Before flying back, a few restful days in the Everglades of Florida inspired me to see the resemblance between services marketing and the European network approach to industrial marketing. My first sketch of a new concept of marketing based on relationships, networks, and interaction, was born.

What I understood intuitively then took fifteen years to deepen and communicate. I first presented the ideas at the EMAC (European Marketing Academy) annual conference in Grenoble, France, in 1983, and later at an AMA conference in the US. The audiences were not overly excited. The response from The First Nordic Meeting on Service Management in Helsinki, Finland, was better; I even remember one participant who was enthusiastic. But neither the time, nor my thoughts and my way of presenting them, felt sufficiently mature.

Many have contributed to the development of RM and many have given me an opportunity to test and elaborate my TRM concept. I would like to mention some people, organizations and events in particular; many more are found in the quotations and references of this book. Their reactions to TRM cover a wide range from almost embarrassing praise to warnings that I am way out of line. I have listened and tried to understand, but I have the responsibility – as well as the prerogative – to decide what to use and what to reject.

Among the many companies who took an early interest in TRM ideas are Ericsson, ABB and Volvo. The tentative ideas were published in a report by the Marketing Technology Center (MTC, a Swedish Foundation for linking academe with the business world) and, in 1987, *The Journal of Long Range Planning* and its editor Bernard Taylor accepted a revised version of the report for publication.

TRM then consisted of nine relationships. In 1992, Management Centre Europe invited me to address business executives in Paris, and Christer Engléus of Informationskollegiet asked me to speak to a large audience in Stockholm. The relationships had expanded to twenty-two. Other important opportunities during the 1990s were the series of International Colloquia in Relationship Marketing; the annual conferences of EMAC and its recently born cousin ANZMAC (Australia and New Zealand Marketing Academy); the conferences at Humboldt-Universität, Berlin, and University College Dublin, Ireland. The ideas have been tried and developed in numerous presentations for students, academic researchers, business people, and government representatives in Europe, North America, Australia, and New Zealand.

In annual lectures at Stockholm University, meetings and correspondence, Philip Kotler has offered insightful views. I have had lively debates with George Fisk, Emory University, and Shelby Hunt, Texas Tech University. As RM has partly evolved from services marketing, service management and quality, many researchers from these areas have influenced me. Among them are Christian Grönroos, Kaj Storbacka and Uolevi Lehtinen and many other faculty members of the Swedish School of Economics and Business Administration and Tampere University, both in Finland; Bo Edvardsson and his staff at The Service Research Center (CTF), University of Karlstad, Sweden; Len Berry, Texas A&M University, and Parsu Parasuraman, University of Miami, who were early in emphasizing RM in services marketing; Eb Scheuing at St John's University, New York, and consultants and authors Pat Townsend and Joan Gebhardt, particularly through the bi-annual Quality in Services (QUIS) symposium and the International Service Quality Association (ISQA); and Johnny Lindström with his staff at the Swedish Institute for Quality (SIQ) and the Swedish Quality Award has helped to make business see the interdependency between quality and marketing.

Many others have generously given me opportunity to speak and write about RM or through their dedicated work become sources of inspiration. Among those in the UK are Martin Christopher, Adrian Payne and other faculty members of the Cranfield School of Management, and David Ballantyne (now at Monash University, Melbourne), themselves authors of successful books on RM; Bob Johnston, Warwick Business School, editor of the *International Journal of Service Industry Management*; Michael Baker, Michael Thomas, Andy Lowe, Mike Saren and Nikos Tzokas, University of Strathclyde, and Douglas Brownlie, University of Stirling; Keith Blois, University of Oxford; Colin Armistead, University of Bournemouth; Richard Teare, Oxford Brookes University, editor of the *International Journal of Contemporary Hospitality Management*; in Ireland Tony Cunningham and Liam Glynn, University College Dublin; in Sydney, Australia, Louise Young, UTS and Ian Wilkinson, UWS Nepean; in New Zealand Rod Brodie and Richard Brookes, University of Auckland, Brendan Gray, University of Otago, and Jay Kandampully, Lincoln University; in Canada and Montreal, Ulrike de Brentani and Michèle Paulin, Concordia University, and Ronald Ferguson, and at University of Calgary, Nicole Coviello; in the US, Steve Brown and Mary Jo

Bitner, Arizona State University, in connection with service research and an AMA Faculty Consortium; Jag Sheth and Atul Parvatiyar, Emory University, Atlanta; Roland Rust and his staff at Vanderbilt University, Nashville; and David Bejou, Texas A&M. Others are Latin American enthusiasts and crusaders Jackie Pels, Universidad Torcuato di Tella, Buenos Aires, Argentina, and Javier Reynoso, ITESM, Monterrey, Mexico; Johan Olaisen and Tor Wallin Andreassen, Norwegian School of Management (BI), Oslo; Willem Verbeke, Erasmus University, the Netherlands, who drew my attention to the conflict between RM and hypercompetition; and Anton Meyer, Ludwig-Maximilians-Universitat, Munich, and Brigitte Pfeiffer, who gave me the privilege of addressing the German Marketing Association at its Marketing-Tag.

Among others who provided me with material and comments and otherwise supported me, I would like to mention my colleague Bo Hedberg and PhD students Tony Apéria, Maria Frostling-Henningson, Richard Gatarsky and Henrik Uggla, Stockholm University, and also students of its Marketing Academy; Björn Wolrath, Leif Edvinsson and Kjell Ängelid, Skandia; Göran Liljegren, MTC; Kazimierz Rogozinski, Academia Ekonomiczna, Poznan, Poland; Åke Ortmark, business reporter, author and TV personality; long-time friend and marketing strategist Carl-Gunnar Thor; and Caroline Monthelie, Loyalty Partners.

Through his intellect and friendship, Barney Glaser, together with Anselm Strauss the originator of grounded theory, has enhanced my theoretical and methodological sensitivity as well as given me courage to pursue my own research strategy. Within its spirit I consider all research a temporary stop – it is search and re-search and re-search in a never-ending journey. Knowledge development in practical work in learning organizations as well as scholarly research can only humbly report progress and should not boast about conclusive results. RM will not only be the object of development for the coming decades but also of controversies and competition between professors, consultants, and authors.

Evert Gummesson
Stockholm University, School of Business
S-10691 Stockholm, Sweden
e-mail: eg@fek.su.se

Introduction

The purpose of this book is to contribute to a more realistic approach to marketing management. It addresses the question: 'What do you learn if you look at marketing as relationships, networks and interaction, and what can you do with this knowledge?' This way of approaching marketing is referred to as relationship marketing (RM). It further introduces the concept of total relationship marketing (TRM), the broadest and most comprehensive framework of RM that has so far been designed.

The book has been written for all those who want to develop their knowledge of marketing – practitioners, students, and academic researchers. As marketing management permeates every activity in today's business – and not only the marketing and sales departments – this book will be of particular interest to top executives and managers of all types of functions.

The book defines thirty relationships prevalent in business. After the concept of RM is introduced in Chapter 1, these relationships are covered in detail in Chapters 2 to 5. Chapter 6 is about financial aspects, including return on relationships (ROR), Chapter 7 deals with RM and the imaginary organization as well as the significance of RM for the market economy, and Chapter 8 covers theories and experiences that have influenced my RM concept. The book concludes with Chapter 9 advocating that RM is a paradigm shift in marketing.

The structure of the book, particularly the presentation of 30Rs, is, in a sense, encyclopedic – a hypertext in modern terminology – which gives readers the option to look up what they are interested in without having to read every page in sequence from cover to cover.

Evert Gummesson
Stockholm, May 1999

Rethinking marketing

In Chapter 1 the concept of relationship marketing, RM, is introduced. Certain basics of marketing are treated together with the significance of common sense, the ability to see marketing from different perspectives – through the 'relationship eye-glasses' – and to adjust to a paradigm shift in marketing. The chapter ends with an overview of general characteristics of relationships and a summary of the thirty relationships of RM – the 30Rs – and a definition of total relationship marketing.

What is relationship marketing?

My definition of relationship marketing, RM, is as follows:

> Relationship marketing is marketing seen as relationships, networks and interaction.

Relationships require at least two parties who are in contact with each other. The basic relationship of marketing is that between a supplier and a customer (Figure 1.1).

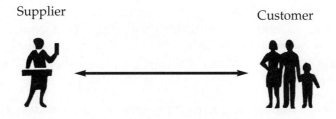

Figure 1.1 The basic marketing relationship

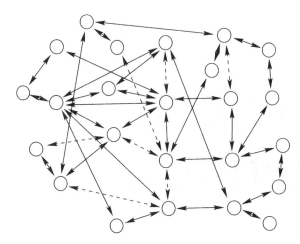

Figure 1.2 A network of relationships

A *network* is a set of relationships which can grow into enormously complex patterns. The graphic pattern of a network of relationships is shown in Figure 1.2. In the relationships, the simple dyad as well as the complex networks, the parties enter into active contact with each other. This is called *interaction*.

Two experiences in particular drew my attention to the importance of relationships in marketing.

The first dates back to 1968. Just hired by a large international management consulting firm, I was assigned to sell the services of a group of consultants. My knowledge of marketing was based on textbooks used in business school education and practical experience as a marketing manager of consumer goods. I was taken by surprise when realizing that the consulting company did little or nothing that the books prescribed. No explicit marketing strategy, no marketing organization, no marketing planning, no marketing research, no sales force, no advertising, no public relations.

Should the fresh consultant tell the CEO the bad news – that they were doing everything wrong – followed by the good news: I'm here to set it right? There was a disturbing fact, though. The company was making a profit and expanding. It must be doing something right.

Through observation and advice from senior colleagues – one had worked for fourteen years as consultant to the same large corporation – I learnt that one thing in particular mattered beside the professional knowledge: The network of relationships that the individual consultants belonged to through professional achievements, birth, or membership. And furthermore, relationships were equally important internally when consultants were selected by their colleagues to staff new assignments.

> Creating and maintaining a network of relationships – outside as well as inside the company – constituted the core marketing of the consulting firm.

Another significant experience occurred twelve years later while working for Ericsson. The then CEO, Bjorn Svedberg, commissioned an assignment with the following words: 'Evert, explain to us what we are actually doing in our marketing and selling!' A supplier of telecom equipment and systems worldwide, Ericsson is currently best known for its market leadership in cellular telephony. Each sale was large, complex, high tech and long term. A major marketing strategy – although it was not officially perceived as such – was the creation and maintenance of long-term relationships with a few large telecom administrations, as well as the cultivation of relationships with research institutions, own suppliers, government agencies, politicians, banks, investors, the media and others. The relationships concerned many people in several tiers and functions within the customers' organizations and also within Ericsson's own organization.

> Ericsson's success was based on a combination of state-of-the-art technology and a well-developed network of relationships.

These two experiences taught me a very obvious and common sense lesson: When your current real world experience clashes with your previous experience and received theories, rethink! Simply put:

> When – after careful scrutiny – you find that the terrain differs from your map, trust the terrain and your own judgement!

A consulting company is a service operation, marketing solely to other organizations, not to consumers. Ericsson is a combination of manufacturing and services, primarily involved in business-to-business marketing but increasingly dependent on consumer marketing. Although the frameworks presented in marketing books claimed to be universally valid, they dealt with consumer goods marketing: cola drinks, painkillers, cookies and cars. Contrary to common belief, consumer goods marketing is the smallest part of all marketing; services marketing and business marketing account for the major share. The books did not include services, and only marginally included business marketing. There was not a word about relationships – and there still is very little! The textbooks diverted the mind from substantive and significant issues.

Today, relationship marketing is beginning to provide a framework for such marketing situations as described by the two experiences. But its applicability has also invaded consumer goods. Relationship marketing is becoming a general marketing approach. It offers a paradigm shift in marketing. Here are some more examples of the variety of marketing situations in which relationships are crucial:

■ At the Royal Orchid Sheraton Hotel in Bangkok, Thailand, all staff on the Executive Floor address each guest by name. They are also expected to quickly learn the guests' habits and preferences and to relate to them in a warm and welcoming manner.

■ Christer, who runs the locally well-known and highly esteemed Ulla Winbladh Inn,

Stockholm, Sweden, is always present and has an apartment above the restaurant. He keeps a close watch on guests and employees and senses the atmosphere, making sure that everything runs smoothly. He knows many of the guests and makes them personally welcome. 'You must like your guests,' he says. 'If you don't, the job is impossible.'

■ Instead of letting a large number of suppliers fight for contracts at lowest price, companies increasingly choose to develop intimate relationships with a limited number of suppliers. In the 1990s, Motorola cut the number of suppliers by 70 per cent, 3M by 64 per cent and Ford by 45 per cent. Information technology (IT) can facilitate the creation of close customer–supplier networks. An extreme example is Procter & Gamble, the world's largest producer of packaged consumer goods, who has joined forces with Wal-Mart, the world's largest retailer. They have set up an information system which coordinates online the production and delivery of the goods with the sales in the stores.

■ Resources are increasingly being built through networks of cooperating companies. In the early 1990s, IBM had formed alliances with several of its major customers, competitors and suppliers. Some of the most important were Toshiba (joint factory in Japan for colour screens), Mitsubishi (selling IBM mainframes in Japan under its own name), Intel (joint development of chips), Apple (joint development of operative systems and technology for the integration of sound, data, graphics and video), Lotus (IBM being an agent for Lotus software), Sears (joint ownership of Prodigy, software for home shopping), and Siemens (joint development of chips). Furthermore, IBM North America cooperated with some 4000 companies.[1]

■ Danish industrialist Maersk McKinney Møller mixes with kings and queens, presidents, government members, and the world's most powerful business leaders. As a personal friend of Thomas Watson, he served for many years as the only non-American on the board of directors of IBM. His personal and social relationships on a mega level – his 'non-market networks' – make it possible for him to direct conditions in the market in his favour. These people are socially empowered to influence regulations, provide financial assistance, bypass gatekeepers, and expedite bureaucratic procedures.

These examples give glimpses of the significance of relationships, networks and interaction, through personal contact and IT, at grass roots and government level, in small local businesses and global giants, and in diverse types of countries and cultures.

It is important that the guests enjoy the Royal Orchid Sheraton and the Ulla Winbladh and keep coming back. Long-term customer relationships are created with loyal consumers who speak well of the hotel and the inn to friends and acquaintances. They epitomize customer retention, referrals and word of mouth which are sometimes presented as the sole purpose of RM.

But RM reaches further than that. One example showed that it can be efficient for companies to have few or even a single supplier and to have few customers.

---

[1] Based on a *Fortune* article (Kirkpatrick, 1992, p. 120).

Collaboration becomes a key marketing strategy. By linking their order and delivery systems, they cement sustaining relationships; the relationships become part of their organizations' structural capital. Transaction costs are kept down as selling, purchasing and invoicing become streamlined.

Not even global giants like American IBM, Japanese Toshiba and German Siemens, can develop, manufacture and market their products and services on their own. They enter into alliances with customers, competitors, distributors and others to gain time and cost advantages and to access markets. The corporations add to each other's resources for the benefit of all stakeholders.

In the last example, relationships are formed on a level above the market proper. Certain conditions have to be fulfilled to allow presence in the market. Royalty, politicians, ambassadors, government officials, and others are engaged to create these conditions. It happens on a mega level where friendship and political support play a decisive role for marketing success.

The book is about these and other relationships. The relationships will be listed, described, analysed, illustrated and discussed. RM is not just another bag of tricks to capture customers, it offers a wide range of conditions for more efficient management and marketing – and opportunities of making money. This will be elaborated on throughout the book.

Society is a network of relationships – and so is business!

Relationships are in the core of human behaviour. If we dissolve the social networks of relationships, we dissolve society and the earth is left with a bunch of hermits. In that case no marketing is needed for two reasons. The short-term reason is that hermits live alone. They breed their own sheep for wool, cheese, and meat; they grow their own vegetables; and they tailor their own clothes. They do not need mobile telephones because there is no one to call. No market exists.

The long-term reason is that the human race will be extinct after one generation. But if it is true that nature has a genetic urge for multiplication, couples and families will spring up and the atomistic world of individuals will turn into a growing network of relationships.

As citizens and family members we are surrounded by relationships in our daily lives. We have relationships at work, with neighbours, with stores and other providers. Driving a car is a complex social interaction with other drivers in a network of roads.

People have girlfriends or boyfriends, go steady, marry, have an affair, divorce. Many have used matrimony as a metaphor for business relationships: to enter into marriage with a customer or to divorce a supplier. 'Business dancing' has been suggested as another metaphor.[2] Dancing is a dynamic relationship. You can invite somebody to dance with you. It can be a smooth waltz, but you can also step on

---

[2] Wilkinson and Young (1994).

your partner's toes. Peters[3] makes it even more dramatic: 'Today's global economic dance is no Strauss waltz. It's break dancing accompanied by street rap. The effective firm is much more like carnival in Rio than a pyramid along the Nile'.

Relationships are central for business people. Craftsmen exchange services with other craftsmen whom they know and trust. The first thing I heard about business was that you need to be well-connected, and that it helps to have relatives in high places and to belong to the right clubs. People who knew each other did business and then the seller wined and dined the buyer. As individuals, we voluntarily enter formal relationships through associations. Rotary, for example, brings people together from different trades and professions. The Rotarians get to know each other – not to do business through the association, that is prohibited – and business relationships are facilitated by the friendship that develops among the members.

Marketing and business are subsets or properties of society. In practice, relationships, networks and interaction have been at the core of business since time immemorial.

Relationships have certainly not gone unnoticed by business people. For example, Ericsson has expanded and remodelled its network for 120 years. The sad story is that relationships have too long gone unnoticed in research and education. Does the current interest in RM imply that marketing theorists are getting closer to marketing reality? Are we beginning to discern the marketing content of Japanese keiretsus, Chinese guanxies, global ethnic networks, the British school-tie, trade between friends, loyalty to the local pub, and so on? Marketing theory has not invented these phenomena, practice has. Some practitioners have lived them, others have not. A book can draw your attention to relationships by adding them to the map, making them visible.

Relationships between customers and suppliers are the ground for all marketing. Within the current marketing management mode of thinking much of marketing is reduced to impersonal exchange through mass promotion and mass distribution. The manufacturer offers products and services via an intermediary and the consumer offers money. The manufacturer and even the retailer are no more than trademarks, they may even be totally anonymous to the consumer, who in turn is just a statistic. This approach to marketing does not comply with the reality of society.

In contrast, the prime focus of RM is on the *individual*, on the segment of one. It's one-to-one marketing.[4] But focus is also on groups of like-minded people, *affinity groups*. The group members share a common interest, they want a relationship with the supplier, its products and services, and even with each other. Golfers, environmentalists, computer freaks, and Harley-Davidson owners belong here. They form *communities*.

---

[3] Peters (1992, p. 17).
[4] Peppers and Rogers (1993, 1997).

The roots of RM

During the industrial era, mass manufacturing of standardized goods gave birth to mass marketing and mass distribution. During this brief period of our history, marketing theory and education evolved around consumer goods marketing. Services and business-to-business marketing – where relationships were also central during the industrial era – were disregarded.

Research and practice in marketing during the past twenty years points particularly to the significance of relationships, networks, and interaction. Literature on RM is emerging at an exponential rate in many languages. With certain exceptions, the literature is mostly narrow, characterized by treating single issues in RM such as consumer loyalty, databases for smarter direct marketing, call centres, or customer clubs.

These are all valuable bits and pieces, but they lack a coherent framework. My RM concept – total relationship marketing – is influenced by several areas of marketing: traditional marketing and sales management and the marketing mix (the 4Ps of product, price, promotion and place); services marketing; and the network approach to industrial/business marketing. It is also inspired by total quality management, TQM. The core of the contemporary TQM concept is customer perceived quality and customer satisfaction – which is also the core of the marketing concept. Together with an overview of different RM approaches and definitions, these contributions are further discussed in Chapter 8.

A pivotal question for every manager is: Does RM pay? The answer is that RM offers a road to improved customer retention, but also long-term relationships with vendors, competitors, governments, the media and others. When used with skill, RM leads to enhanced revenue, reduced cost and improved financial performance. What we currently know about *return on relationships* (ROR) and its measurement will be presented in Chapter 6.

Furthermore, marketing needs its own organization and a place in the organization of a corporation. RM is not happening in a vacuum, it is mirroring other events in the business world, among them trends in organizational structures. When organization is discussed in the following chapters, it is treated as a network of relationships and referred to as *virtual organizations*, or with another term: *imaginary organizations*. Hedberg et al. state: 'While "virtual", to our taste, takes us to the world of technologies, "imaginary" carries more flavour from the world of humanities.'[5]

---

[5] Hedberg, Dahlgren, Hansson and Olve (1997, p. 13). Imaginary organizations is the designation for a major research programme at Stockholm University School of Business. See also Davidow and Malone (1992).

Basic values of marketing

The 'new' IBM says it will reap greater rewards from long-lasting relationships with customers; Sony Thailand says that it is going from excessive mass marketing to RM; and banks everywhere claim that they pursue strategies to strengthen the relationships to customers.

Management thinker Peter Drucker said somewhere that 'the problem with good ideas is that they quickly degenerate into hard work'. There is invariably a gap between ideas and action. The gap can be caused by lack of implementation skills and stamina, but also by difficulties of grasping the essentials. There may be a lack of data, or inability to put data together in a meaningful pattern or map – 'theories' – which facilitate decisions and actions. The difficulties are caused by at least four 'random variables': customers; competitors; the general economy; and technology change. None of these and their interdependence can be predicted with accuracy.

The gap is also caused by marketers who have not internalized marketing values. Drucker is often referred to as the first to formulate the *marketing concept* in a classic management book from 1954: 'Marketing...is the whole business seen from the point of view of its final result, that is, from the customer's point of view'.[6]

The essence of the marketing concept is understanding customer needs and wants. If a company offers goods and services that satisfy needs and create value for the customer, customer satisfaction and the right customer perceived quality, the company stands the best chance of success. This is in opposition to *production orientation* according to which the customer is obliged to buy what is available, or not buy at all. It is typical of markets with a shortage of goods and services, and markets of centrally planned economies, but also of complacent industries in wealthy market economies such as the USA.

The marketing concept is popularly expressed as *customer in focus*. This has become a widespread slogan, understood and implemented only by a few of those who express it. They may just perceive it as a fad which it is timely to confess to, or yet another smart trick to trap the consumer. The customer in focus values have not killed the old ones, just pushed them into a corner from which they make recurring efforts to break out.

In order to implement a customer in focus strategy, *marketing management* should be broadened into *marketing-oriented company management*. Since the early 1970s, I have made a distinction between the *marketing and sales department* and the *marketing and sales function* in order to emphasize that marketing and sales are more than just the activities of specialized departments. They are functions that must permeate the whole organization, not least the minds and actions of management. This is an old thought which has turned out to be enormously difficult to convey and implement. In companies I successfully use the terms *full-time mar-*

---

[6] Drucker (1954, p. 36). For a discussion on the past and future of marketing, see Baker (1995a, 1995b).

keters (FTMs) and *part-time marketers* (PTMs) to stress that everybody, irrespective of task and expertise, influences customer relationships either full-time or part-time. Marketing management in this sense requires marketing-orientation of the whole of the company, that is, marketing-oriented management.

> I propose that inadequate basic values and their accompanying procedures – the wrong paradigm – is the biggest obstacle to success in marketing. If marketers and top management do not understand and accept relationship values as a natural vantage point, there will be no positive effect of RM.

Fundamental values in RM are:

■ *Long-term collaboration and win–win.* The core values of RM are found in its emphasis on *collaboration and the creation of mutual value.* It includes viewing suppliers, customers and others as *partners* rather than *opposite parties.* In 1976, Michael Baker in the UK suggested that marketing be defined as 'mutually satisfying exchange relationships'. RM should be more of *win–win* than *win–lose,* more of a *plus sum game* than a *zero sum game.* In a plus sum game, the parties increase value for each other, in a zero sum game what one gains is the loss of another. A constructive attitude is expected by all those involved and all should find the relationship meaningful. If these conditions are fulfilled, the relationships may become long term and sustaining. For a supplier, it is important to retain existing customers, a fact which is increasingly being stressed. Extending the *duration* of the relationship becomes a major marketing goal. Too much emphasis has been put on the acquisition of new customers and too little on caring for existing customers. RM encourages *customer retention* and discourages *customer defection;* it encourages *retention marketing* first and *attraction marketing* – getting new customers – second.

■ *Recognizing that all parties be active.* As RM represents a new marketing paradigm and the beginnings of a new theory, it should not be mixed up with *relationship selling*[7] which represents the supplier perspective and does not put the customer and an interactive relationship in focus. In relationship selling, the initiative comes from the salesperson and depends on '…how well the relationship is managed by the seller'.[8] Relationship quality and a long-term relationship in that sense become the consumer's trust in the salesperson based on the salesperson's present and past performance.[9] But the initiative to action cannot be left to a supplier or a single party of a network; everyone in a network can, and should, be active. Contrary to the mythology of marketing, the supplier is not necessarily the active party. In business marketing customers initiate innovation and force suppliers to change their products or services. Consumers suggest improvements but have a tough time getting lethargic and complacent suppliers and

---

[7] Sheth (1994).
[8] Levitt (1983, p. 111).
[9] Crosby, Evans and Cowles (1990).

legislators to listen. In services marketing consumers are often both producers and 'project leaders', whereas the role of the provider is limited to offering an arena.

■ *Relationship and service values instead of bureaucratic-legal values.* Bureaucratic-legal values are characterized by rigidity; legal jargon; application of dysfunctional laws and regulations; a focus on internal routines; belief in the supplier as the expert and the customer as ignorant; more interest in rituals than in results; and the customer being a cost and a residual of the system. Customers are masses and statistical averages, not individuals; customers generate cost; and it is important to win over the customer in a dispute. These values historically dominate governments and their agencies. Its representatives have previously disclaimed marketing, but the international wave of privatization, deregulation and demand for competition as well as the failure of the command economies, have forced a change. RM is a valid concept for public organizations as well, and an understanding of how marketing could be applied to public bodies to the benefit of the consumer/citizen is growing. Unfortunately bureaucratic-legal values are also common in private companies. RM requires different values based on relationships and services to the customer. These values establish that all customers are individuals and different in certain respects; that the outcome is the only thing that counts; that customers are the source of revenue and should be in focus; and that the supplier's task is to create value for the customer.[10]

With these values, RM may stand out as a naively idyllic and benign agenda. RM requires more ethical behaviour than traditional marketing. But all business people do not base their activities on RM values as presented here. Competition means winning over somebody, even destroying others, showing who is the biggest, the best, and the wealthiest. Short-term greed often overrules long-term survival. For some, this fight has a value in itself. One of the strategies in the world of *hypercompetition* is called 'simultaneous and sequential strategic thrusts' defined as '...a series of actions designed to stun or confuse competitors, disrupting the status quo to create new advantages and erode those of the competitors'. Furthermore these thrusts '...are used by hypercompetitive firms to harass, paralyse, induce error, or block competitors'.[11] The values of hypercompetition run contrary to RM values.

Although collaboration is the core property of RM, my RM concept holds that *both competition and collaboration are essential in a functioning market economy.* Traditional marketing is prejudiced in favour of the benefits of competition. It sees collaboration as inhibiting the forces of the market. The misunderstanding is obvious among those politicians and business leaders who advocate competition as a cure-all for society's problems, a counter-reaction to the socialistic advocacy for central planning and regulations.

---

[10] See Gummesson (1993, pp. 40–2).
[11] D'Aveni (1994, p. 34).

RM versus transaction marketing

RM is often presented as the opposite to *transaction marketing*, the one-shot deal.[12] In transaction marketing, the fact that a customer has bought a product does not forecast the probability for a new purchase, not even if a series of purchases have been made. A customer may repeatedly use the same supplier because of high switching costs, but without feeling committed to the supplier or wanting to enter a closer relationship. Transactions lack history and memory and they don't get sentimental.

In RM, loyalty – especially customer loyalty – is emphasized. In the 'loyalty ladder'[13] the lowest rung is the contact with a *prospect* who hopefully turns into a *customer* and a first purchase. Recurrent customers are *clients*; those have come back and a long-term relationship is in the making. In the next stages the client becomes a *supporter* and finally an *advocate* for the supplier.

Transaction marketing has no ambition to climb the loyalty ladder. Still it is often a realistic and functional option. A purchase can concern standardized goods at lowest price within a specified delivery time and grade of quality. Such deals are made, for example, on metals exchanges. A consumer may only buy a home on a single or a few occasions in a lifetime and rarely has surgery on the appendix more than once. IT offers new alternatives and can facilitate the consumer's search for the lowest price of a branded product. Through the deregulation of telecom services, the customer can choose the operator with the lowest rate at a specific hour to a specific destination.

But even a one-shot deal can mean deep interactive relationships. If a company builds a new office, the interaction with the builder and a network of providers may be intense for a year or two. The company may not build another office for the next few decades. If you have surgery and stay in a hospital, the interaction will be intense and painfully intimate, but both parties hope that the relationship shall be superfluous as the wound heals.

In order to conceptually incorporate transaction marketing in RM, it can be seen as the zero point of the *RM scale*. The scope of the relationships can then be enhanced until a customer and a supplier are practically the same organization.[14] No doubt we were misled by authoritarian neoclassical economics in which markets are made up of standardized goods and anonymous masses who behave according to simplistic and distinct laws. Only the *price relationship* exists, and I call that the *zero relationship* on the RM scale.

The fact that this book is about RM and advocates relationships as essential in marketing does not imply a religious belief in relationships as a magic panacea. On the contrary, we know that human relationships can be a source of insur-

---

[12] See Jackson (1985a, 1985b) who treats marketing and RM in the business-to-business context.
[13] Christopher, Payne and Ballantyne (1991, p. 22).
[14] See also Grönroos' 'marketing strategy continuum' (1990, pp. 144–8), and a further elboration of this scale in Lehtinen, Hankimaa and Mittilä (1994).

mountable hassle as well as of unlimited joy. But we cannot live without them. The larger share of world literature and entertainment deal with relationships between adults, parent and child, police and crook, and not least between the players in a business venture. The oil tycoon JR of the soap opera *Dallas* stands out as an international role model for greed-driven manipulation of all types of relationships, be it oil contracts, politics, or family matters.

A relationship should not be retained if it works badly. Long-term relationships and customer care are not the same as admitting customers to the geriatric ward of the supplier, attaching them to the bed and keeping them on life support. Relationships should not necessarily be broken just because there is a conflict, however. They can often be restored and improved or they may be the best option for the parties despite a conflict. The beginning of a relationship is often romantic and passionate. It is when the passion phase fades that the real work of building a relationship starts.

Jackson[15] succinctly states a commonsense RM strategy: 'Relationship marketing...can be extremely successful where it is appropriate – but it can also be costly and ineffective if it is not. Conversely, transaction marketing...can be profitable and successful where it is appropriate but a serious mistake where it is not.'

Common sense and experience

Running a company revolves around two eternal themes: *Make sure you have something to offer* and *make sure you sell it at a price that is higher than your costs.*

It is a matter of common sense. The issue is how to make it happen. Common sense, sound judgement, instinct, intuition, and wisdom are stressed in the handbook-type marketing literature; in the scholarly literature they are often treated with contempt. I feel inspired by the way common sense is defined in *Brewer's Dictionary of Phrase & Fable* from 1870:

> Common sense does not mean that good sense which is
> common...but the point where all five senses meet, supposed to be
> the seat of the soul, where it judges what is presented by the
> senses and decides the mode of action.

Let us widen the five senses to include experience, intelligence, emotions (today even referred to as 'emotional intelligence',[16] masculine and feminine instincts, and extrasensory perception if we have it. The complexity of today's markets and organizations, the gradually more advanced technology, and the differentiation of goods and services, conceal the obvious and we get lost in a maze. Companies

---

[15] Jackson (1985a, p. xi). See also Dwyer, Shurr and Oh (1987); Anderson and Narus (1991); and Paulin, Perrien and Ferguson (1997).
[16] Goleman (1995).

grow and employees cannot overview the meaning of their job. We must go 'back to basics', or 'forward to basics' as it is not a matter of regressing to a past society but of adapting to the present and the future. When Scandinavian Airlines, SAS, commenced its turnaround in the early 1980s, one of the instruments was 'smile courses'.[17] Among other things, people were taught that it is important to smile to customers; they will then like you more than if you look gloomy and disinterested. Common sense and sound judgement had to be reinstated. They had got lost in the red tape and standardized mass production of the industrial society. Nordstrom, an exceptionally successful US chain of department stores, says in its *Employee Handbook* under the heading 'Nordstrom Rules': 'Rule No. 1: Use your good judgement in all situations', and adds: 'There will be no additional rules.'

Many have stressed 'management by walking around', leadership through presence where and when it happens. The concept 'rapid reconnaissance' is used in science and refers to the scientist's need to quickly assess a situation or a problem.[18]

This does not mean that theories are dead. It only means that we must enhance our ability to utilize *both* systematic analysis *and* personal experience and insights.

The rules of the marketing game are rewritten through political events and changes in values, consumption patterns and technology. Marketing reality requires living with complexity, paradoxes, uncertainty, ambiguity, and instability. Many markets are perceived as chaotic, but chaos holds opportunities for those who can see them and use them better than the competition. Chaos is not chaotic *per se*, there is order in chaos[19] but we fail to see the underlying pattern. It was an uncertain venture when, for more than a hundred years, European companies took their new products to South America. Many of these ventures succeeded and spawned today's global corporations. Currently, the former Soviet Union nations are chaotic markets holding a gigantic potential; Hong Kong – the epitome of capitalism – has become part of communist China; the Asian economies are shattered; and membership of the North American Free Trade Agreement (Nafta) or the European Union (EU) offers new conditions. We may wish to reduce uncertainty, but the market economy is built on dynamic change, which is only partially predictable.

What do we see through the relationship eye-glasses?

We need new approaches that reflect today's markets and help us find our way in these markets. There is no general marketing theory that makes us see everything at the same time. New categories, concepts, models and theories work as lenses

---

[17] Carlzon (1987).

[18] Patton (1990, p. 134) mentions this as a research strategy in social sciences when a qualitative, inductive approach is deployed.

[19] Prigogene and Stengers (1985).

through which we perceive the world. If the lenses are wrongly curved, the world will look blurry. If they are tinted, it may look sunny when in fact it is cloudy. Certain lenses improve our vision at close range, others at a distance. As marketing is a complex field, a single pair of glasses is not suffient. There are bifocals that allow two perspectives, but we need more than two. This book offers the *relationship eye-glasses*. If we look through these glasses we can only see relationships, networks and interaction. RM is about what you see through these glasses.

New concepts, models and theories can very well be the emperor's new clothes and only the innocent child dares says the obvious: 'But he doesn't have anything on!' I have, however, come to the conclusion that RM provides a new costume which is both visible and tangible. RM offers more common sense in marketing, and it makes important phenomena visible in the confusing world in which marketers search for meaning. It is then up to the readers to try RM on their own reality and draw their own conclusions. If marketing executives or sales people either get a feeling of *déjà vu*, or are made aware of something they might already have sensed or even used but were unable to articulate, it means that the text is close to reality and has validity.

My conclusion is that a radically new thinking in marketing – a paradigm shift – is necessary.[20] But it is not enough to think in new ways to claim a paradigm shift; it must also materialize in action.[21] Research and experience have contributed with general properties of relationships which can help us understand and evaluate individual aspects of relationships and networks. These properties are presented in the next section. An overview of the thirty specific relationships which I have found applicable in marketing-oriented management follows.

General properties of relationships, networks and interaction

In studies of relationships, networks and interaction, a series of general properties have emerged. In the network approach of industrial marketing a distinction is made between three types of connections which together form a business-to-business relationship between buyers and sellers:[22]

1 *Activity links* embrace activities of a technical, administrative and marketing kind.
2 *Resource ties* include exchanging and sharing resources which are both tangible such as machines, and intangible such as knowledge.
3 *Actor bonds* are created by people who interact and exert influence on each other and form opinions about each other.

---

[20] For criticism against the value of RM, see Blois (1996); Bliemel and Eggert (1997); Brodie *et al.* (1997); Mattsson (1997); Möller and Halinen-Kaila (1998); and Snehota and Söderlund (1998).
[21] RM as a tool for implementation is treated by Gummesson (1998).
[22] Håkansson and Snehota (1995).

The interaction can also be approached as a hierarchy where *activities* (lowest level) together form *episodes* which form *sequences* which form *relationships*. The relationships constitute the *partner base*, the organization's total network.[23] *Relationscapes* has been suggested as a designation for all the relationships that are included in a network.[24] These relationships may be active and visible; they could also be invisibly embedded in the network by being passive and unobtrusive, yet still be influential.

It is also feasible to list the properties or dimensions which a party may perceive in a relationship. In a study of service consumers as many as forty-five properties were identified.[25]

The general classifications and properties of relationships can be useful in RM for decision making and planning. In the next four chapters where thirty relationships, the 30Rs, are presented, applications of these properties will be continuously examined.

The following sections will summarize important general properties of commercial relationships.[26]

Collaboration

Collaboration has already been claimed to be the fundamental property of relationships between suppliers and customers, competitors, consultants, government agencies and others. The collaboration can be linked to a single deal or be continuous. The degree of collaboration could be combined with the degree of competition.[27] A situation with little competition and little collaboration between two or more companies can be a good start for expanded collaboration. A high degree of collaboration and a low degree of competition provide a base for a long-term and harmonious relationship. Relationships can also thrive in a situation of both extensive collaboration and competition. If the collaborative part is insignificant and competition takes over, it becomes imperative to either divest in the relationship or to consciously work for a reinforced relationship.

Commitment, dependency and importance

If a relationship is important, we are dependent on it and we must then commit ourselves to making it work. If a delivery is delayed, a whole factory or construction site may stop, particularly if they are part of a just-in-time (JIT) produc-

---

[23] Holmlund (1997).

[24] Strandvik and Törnroos (1997).

[25] Ward, Frew and Caldow (1997).

[26] The summary in this section primarily draws on research within the network approach; see references in Chapter 8. It is also inspired by studies within sociology and psychology; see Granovetter (1973, 1985); Bossevein (1976) and Scott (1991).

[27] According to Wilkinson and Young (1994).

tion system. Dependency is dramatically obvious when emergencies occur, for example when an ambulance or fire-fighters are needed. There are also daily and trivial dependencies on the telephone, the newspaper, and public transport to and from work. In services marketing, three levels of dependency and commitment have been proposed.[28] On Level 1, customers are primarily attracted by low prices. The effect of this attraction quickly fades away if the competition also lowers its prices. Level 1 is often easy to copy. On Level 2, the relationship has deepened. There is no longer just a price relationship but also a communication with the customer that may consist of face-to-face contact or personally addressed direct mail. Level 3 adds a structural dimension which means that the parties have pooled resources and are therefore highly committed to making the relationship work. The Procter & Gamble and Wal-Mart production-sales-delivery system is such an example.

Trust, risk and uncertainty

The success of closer collaboration between customer and supplier is often credited to trust. Consumers can trust an airline, a plumber or a doctor, but also a certain brand. A company can have a trusting relationship with a bank which facilitates credit decisions. Management consultants live on their clients' trust for them; to 'objectively' measure their performance is usually not feasible or meaningful. Individual lawyers and accountants can be important to a person and they must be available when needed; the client may not want to turn to other professionals, even if they work in the same firm. Often we only know partially what we are buying – we do it on trust – for example, when our dentist performs root canal surgery. We only know the value of an insurance policy when a claim is made; we have probably not quite understood the fine print and legal conditions of our home insurance or retirement plan. This ignorance creates uncertainty. Alliances represent a great risk; there may be arguments, one party may pick the other party's brain without giving anything in return. The degree and significance of trust varies widely between cultures and nations.[29]

Power

The amount of power in a relationship is only rarely symmetrical, meaning that each party has the same power. An asymmetrical relationship means that one party is weaker and may feel used, but the relationship can still be functional if there is no better alternative for the weaker party. It can also be perceived as unfair and at the first opportunity the weaker party exits. Patients with toothache are left to the discretion of dentists and their willingness to serve them; they may be left at the mercy of an emergency clinic where patients must wait long hours.

---

[28] Berry and Parasuraman (1991, pp. 136–42).
[29] See Fukuyama (1995).

The symmetry of power can change. A company in a booming market may be short of components and the supplier has the power, but when the market turns downward the customer can negotiate cuts in prices and delivery times. To use one's position to the extreme is detrimental to a sustaining relationship; a certain amount of goodwill and helpfulness is demanded from all parties.

Longevity

It has been stressed that the long-term relationship is a pillar of RM. This is in opposition to transaction marketing which is characterized by single deals and customer promiscuity. The concepts of duration, retention and defection have been defined above. A long-term relationship can be more effective for all parties especially if it takes a long time to build the relationships, a common case in industrial marketing. Switching costs may be high and no relationship should be broken because of negligence or lack of interest. The parties learn how to handle the relationship and utilize it to their benefit. Sometimes it is rational to break a relationship. It may have become obsolete or lost its zest. For example, it is reasonable to change advertising agency at times in order to stimulate creativity.

Frequency, regularity and intensity

Certain relationships are frequently and regularly active, such as travel to and from work or bank transactions. Following a fixed timetable, which is part of a long-term contract, the Swedish railways transport rolls of paper from Sweden to newspaper printers in London every day. Other relationships are rare, such as engaging a funeral parlour or estate agent, but loyalty to a specific provider can still be strong. Education can require an intense relationship during several years, heart surgery an intense relationship during a few days. The relationship to a convenience store can be sustaining and frequent, but not particularly intense.

Closeness and remoteness

Closeness can be physical, mental or emotional. The physical proximity facilitates mental and emotional contact. Companies that want to do business in a foreign country often have to be continuously present in order to obtain credibility. Cultural differences exist between countries and ethnic and religious groups may build mental distance despite physical closeness. Certain relationships become truely personal, especially if you meet often and even associate privately. Others are remote in the sense that the conduits are machines and IT, such as ATMs and internet banks. Closeness strengthens the feeling of security. The majority of relationships thrive on tacit understanding between parties and only a minority are regulated in contracts and much. Consumers are often far away from manufacturers who must rely on distance information through intermediaries, such as reports from market research insitutes.

Formality, informality, and openness

Commercial relationships are usually more informal than formal. As consumers we rarely have a contract or any other written obligation, but there are exceptions. As members of a golf club we have consented to abide to strict rules and we cannot usually just move to another club; to be effective a retirement plan may force us to stick to the same insurance or financial company and the payments and contracts are formal and regulated. If we break the rules we may be punished or even be dropped as customers. The better we know the people in a small store, the more informal the relationship may be. They may let us in after opening hours or give us credit if we have left our purse at home. In industrial marketing informality is an absolute necessity as a supplement to formal agreements. Problems are solved over the telephone and the parties trust each other. Negotiations and exchange of information may occur at the golf course or in a hotel bar, sometimes leading to major deals with long-term effects. The formal aspects must be heeded, however. One such aspect is the degree of openness. For example, how much are we obliged to reveal to the other parties concerning our own cost and revenue?

Routinization

A common complaint in marriages is the lack of romance and excitement; after a period of passion the relationship turns into routine. Although it sounds dull, routine procedures may be conditional for efficiency and cost effectiveness, both in commercial and marital relationships. Banking today is routinized through computers and telephones, and the days when you went to your local branch office and were greeted by a bank teller with whom you had a chat, may be counted. Even if you think you telephone your local bank branch, a digital switch will select a free line to a customer service department, which can be located anywhere in the country. In industrial marketing, routines are established for deliveries and both the customer and the supplier follow rituals and standard procedures. However, customers also abandon suppliers who show no interest in them. So there is a trade-off between routines and standard procedures for speed and low cost, and the feeling that the relationships develop and live.

Content

The content of a business relationship is traditionally described as economic exchange. One party provides goods and services and the other provides money; streams of goods or services go in one direction and financial streams go the other. In this sense marketing is exchange. In new marketing and management theory, the relationship is increasingly seen as interaction and joint value creation. The content of a relationship is often knowledge and information. This is a rationale for alliances, for example, for product development or for a hotel to join a room reservation network. This way a company 'can become bigger without growing'. Coordination and utilization of resources for manufacturing and distribution can be important. For example, competing newspapers who share a printing plant and the distribution to subscribers in order to slash costs.

Personal and social properties

These are age, sex, profession, education, personality type, geographical and social mobility as well as personal traits such as lust for power, or an ability to create trust and confidence. Charm, charisma, personal vibrations and chemistry belong here, all phenomena that are difficult to analyse but which we recognize when we encounter them. In social network analysis, efforts are made to identify patterns of relationships – cliques, clusters, blocks. The analysis offers matrices and descriptions of structures of personal relationships. The sociogram is a graphical technique to show patterns of relationships between individuals. Relationships can be of the first degree concerning friends, of the second degree concerning friends of friends, of the third degree, etc. The relationships can be direct or can be arranged through a mediator.

It is often asked which properties are the most important. The idea is to be Pareto optimal and to zoom in on the properties that account for the lion's share of the benefits of RM. Collaboration must always be in the core of a relationship. Some claim that power is always decisive, others that commitment and trust are the key.[30] Most of the properties are fuzzy entities which overlap in several respects.

Rankings are often misleading as the importance of a property is relative to a specific situation. For example, if trust is taken for granted in a specific business culture, it is only when trust is abused that the property stands out as pivotal. Something else is needed, such as superior social contact or a formal contract.

The general properties of relationships can contribute to the evaluation of a relationship and its development or liquidation. But they cannot alone serve as a basis for marketing decision-making, planning, and execution. Even if each of them highlights an interesting phenomenon, they must be put into context. I have therefore chosen to define types of relationships which are composed of many properties and which can be recognized in the management of marketing.

The 30Rs of RM – introductory specification of thirty relationships

The philosophy of RM and the examples have to be converted into tangible relationships that can become part of a company's marketing planning. This has been done by defining thirty relationships – the 30Rs. These are listed and briefly char-

---

[30] About power see, for example, Thorelli (1986, p. 38); about commitment and trust, see Morgan and Hunt (1994).

acterized in Table 1.1. With the exception of the first relationship – R1 – The relationship between a supplier and a customer, which is the foundation of marketing – the Rs are not in ranking order. Their significance varies between companies and markets. In reading the text, keep the vantage points of RM in mind by posing the question: If we view marketing through the relationship eye-glasses, what do we see and how do we use what we see?

The relationships are grouped in the following way. The first two types are *market relationships*. These are relationships between suppliers, customers, competitors and others who operate in the market. They constitute the basis for marketing, they are externally oriented and apply to the market proper. Some of them concern relationships to both consumers and other organizations, others are focused on either consumers or they are *inter*organizational relationships. The market relationships are:

- *Classic market relationships*. (R1–R3). The classic market relationships are the *supplier–customer dyad*, the *triad of supplier–customer–competitor*, and the *physical distribution network*, which are treated extensively in general marketing theory.
- *Special market relationships* (R4–R17). They represent certain aspects of the classic relationships, such as the *interaction in the service encounter* or the *customer as member of a loyalty programme*.

Table 1.1 The thirty relationships of RM – the 30Rs

Classic market relationships (Chapter 2)

R1   The classic dyad – the relationship between the supplier and the customer
      This is the parent relationship of marketing, the ultimate exchange of value which constitutes the basis of business.

R2   The classic triad – the drama of the customer–supplier–competitor triangle
      Competition is a central ingredient of the market economy. In competition there are relationships between three parties: between the customer and the current supplier, between the customer and the supplier's competitors, and between competitors.

R3   The classic network – distribution channels
      The traditional physical distribution and the modern channel management including goods, services, people and information, consists of a network of relationships.

Special market relationships (Chapter 3)

R4   Relationships via full-time marketers (FTMs) and part-time marketers (PTMs)
      Those who work in marketing and sales departments – the FTMs – are professional relationship makers. All others, who perform other main functions but yet influence customer relationships directly or indirectly, are PTMs. There are also contributing FTMs and PTMs outside the organization.

R5   The service encounter – interaction between the customer and the service provider
      Production and delivery of services involve the customer in an interactive relationship with the service provider, often referred to as the moment of truth.

Table 1.1 The thirty relationships of RM – the 30Rs (*continued*)

R6 The many-headed customer and the many-headed supplier
Marketing to other organizations – industrial marketing or business marketing – often means contacts between many individuals from the supplier's and the customer's organization.

R7 The relationship to the customer's customer
A condition for success is often the understanding of the customer's customer, and what suppliers can do to help their customers become successful.

R8 The close versus the distant relationship
In mass marketing, the closeness to the customer is lost and the relationship becomes distant, based on surveys, statistics and written reports.

R9 The relationship to the dissatisfied customer
The dissatisfied customer perceives a special type of relationship, more intense than the normal situation, and often badly managed by the provider. The way of handling a complaint – the recovery – can determine the quality of the future relationship.

R10 The monopoly relationship: the customer or supplier as prisoners
When competition is inhibited, the customer may be at the mercy of the supplier – or the other way around. One of them becomes prisoner.

R11 The customer as 'member'
In order to create a long-term sustaining relationship, it has become increasingly common to enlist customers as members of various loyalty programmes.

R12 The electronic relationship
Information technology – telecom, computers, TV – are elements of all types of marketing today and they form new types of relationships.

R13 Parasocial relationships – relationships to symbols and objects
Relationships do not only exist concerning people and physical phenomena, but also to mental images and symbols such as brand names and corporate identities.

R14 The non-commercial relationship
This is a relationship between the public sector and citizens/customers, but it also includes voluntary organizations and other activities outside of the profit-based and monetarized economy, such as those performed in families.

R15 The green relationship
Environmental and health issues have slowly but gradually increased in importance and are creating a new type of customer relationship through legislation, the voice of opinion-leading consumers, changing behaviour of consumers and an extension of the customer–supplier relationship to encompass a recycling process.

R16 The law-based relationship
A relationship to a customer is sometimes founded primarily on legal contracts and the threat of litigation.

R17 The criminal network
Organized crime is built on tight and often impermeable networks guided by an illegal business mission. They exist around the world and are apparently growing but are not observed in marketing theory. These networks can disturb the functioning of a whole market or industry.

Table 1.1 The thirty relationships of RM – the 30Rs (*continued*)

Mega relationships (Chapter 4)

R18   Personal and social networks
      Personal and social networks often determine business networks. In some cultures even, business is solely conducted between friends and friends-of-friends.

R19   Mega marketing – the real 'customer' is not always found in the marketplace
      In certain instances, relationships must be sought with governments, legislators, influential individuals, and others, in order to make marketing feasible on an operational level.

R20   Alliances change the market mechanisms
      Alliances mean closer relationships and collaboration between companies. Thus competition is partly curbed, but collaboration is necessary to make the market economy work.

R21   The knowledge relationship
      Knowledge can be the most strategic and critical resource and 'knowledge acquisition' is often the rationale for alliances.

R22   Mega alliances change the basic conditions for marketing
      EU (the European Union) and NAFTA (the North America Free Trade Agreement) are examples of alliances above the single company and industry. They exist on government and supranational levels.

R23   The mass media relationship
      The media can be supportive or damaging to marketing and they are particularly influential in forming public opinion. The relationship to media is crucial for the way media will handle an issue.

Nano relationships (Chapter 5)

R24   Market mechanisms are brought inside the company
      By introducing profit centres in an organization, a market inside the company is created and internal as well as external relationships of a new kind emerge.

R25   Internal customer relationship
      The dependency between the different tiers and departments in a company is seen as a process consisting of relationships between internal customers and internal suppliers.

R26   Quality providing a relationship between operations management and marketing
      The modern quality concept has built a bridge between design, manufacturing and other technology-based activities and marketing. It considers the company's internal relationships as well as its relationships to the customers.

R27   Internal marketing: relationships with the 'employee market'
      Internal marketing can be seen as part of RM as it gives indirect and necessary support to the relationships with external customers.

R28   The two-dimensional matrix relationship
      Organizational matrices are frequent in large corporations, and above all they are found in the relationships between product management and sales.

R29   The relationship to external providers of marketing services
      External providers reinforce the marketing function by supplying a series of services, such as those offered by advertising agencies and market research institutes, but also in the area of sales and distribution.

R30   The owner and financier relationship
      Owners and other financiers partly determine the conditions under which a marketing function can operate. The relationship to them influences the marketing strategy.

The next two types are *non-market relationships* which indirectly influence the efficiency of market relationships:

- *Mega relationships* (R18–R23) exist above the market relationships. They provide a platform for market relationships and concern the economy and society in general. Among these are *mega marketing* (lobbying, public opinion and political power), *mega alliances* (such as the NAFTA, setting a new stage for marketing in North America), and *social relationships* (such as friendship and ethnic bonds).
- *Nano relationships* (R24–R30) are found below the market relationships, that is relationships inside an organization *(intra*organizational relationships). All internal activities influence the externally bound relationships. Examples of nano relationships are the *relationships between internal customers*, and *between internal markets* that arise as a consequence of the increasing use of independent profit centres, divisions and business areas inside organizations. The boundary between the externally and the internally directed relationships is sometimes fuzzy; it is a matter of emphasis. For example, the physical distribution network (R3) is part of a logistics flow, concerning internal as well as external customers.

In her book *From Tin Soldiers to Russian Dolls*, Vandermerwe (1993) uses the metaphor of tin soldiers and wooden dolls to describe the management of an emerging service society. The tin soldiers, who represent an obsolete management paradigm based on strict army hierarchy, are neatly placed in rows; they follow orders and regulations. The dolls represent the new paradigm of the network or imaginary organization. A Russian doll is composed of dolls enclosed in each other and mutually dependent in a never-ending series. The book inspired me to draw 'the relationship doll' to provide an illustration to the logic of RM and its organizational dependency (Figure 1.3). It shows layers of relationships which are connected but are of different character.

The two dolls in the middle represent the market relationships. The nano relationships are the hub and together with the mega relationships – the outer dolls – they constitute the necessary conditions for market relationships. The metaphor points to connections and dependencies that must be considered when a company organizes its marketing. The doll becomes a symbol of the imaginary organization where the borderline between organization, market and society is not as clear as in traditional organization theory and economics.

Total relationship marketing

The concept of total relationship marketing sums up what has been briefly presented in this chapter, and what will be explicated in more detail in the remainder of the book. It is defined in the following way:

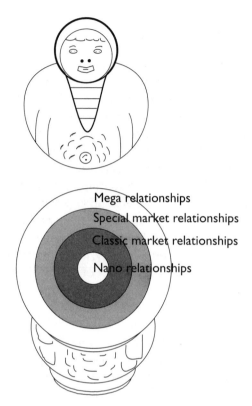

Figure 1.3 RM as a Russian doll, 'the relationship doll'. The metaphor of the Russian doll is inspired by Sandra Vandermerwe and is used with the permission of the author. (Source: Vandermerwe, 1993)

Total relationship marketing (TRM) is marketing based on relationships, networks and interaction, recognizing that marketing is embedded in the total management of the networks of the selling organization, the market and society. It is directed to long-term win–win relationships with individual customers, and value is jointly created between the parties involved. It transcends the boundaries between special-ist functions and disciplines. It is made tangible through the thirty market, mega and nano relationships, the 30Rs.

Therefore, total relationship marketing represents a paradigm shift in market-ing.

Chapter 2

Classic market relationships

The first three relationships are marketing classics although here they are observed through the relationship eye-glasses. The relationship between the customer and the supplier (R1) – the classic dyad – constitutes the foundation for commercial exchange and interaction; it is the parent relationship of marketing. It is supplemented by a third force, competition, which is a necessary element of a market economy; the relationship between a customer, its present supplier, and the supplier's competitors constitute the classic triad (R2). Physical distribution has always been central in marketing. It has broadened into channel management and here it is viewed as a network of relationships, the classic network of marketing (R3).

Relationship 1 The classic dyad – the relationship between the supplier and the customer

The relationship between the one who sells something and the one who buys something forms the *classic dyad of marketing, a two-party relationship.* This is the *parent relationship of marketing.*

The two interacting parties are a *supplier* and a *customer.* Customer usually means *external customer.* The notion of the *internal customer* has become widely accepted and is defined as one of the nano relationships (R25).

The supplier is the *seller,* and the seller can be represented by a *salesperson,* whose task is personal selling. In the latter meaning there is a face-to-face relationship or a relationship via letter, telephone, fax, internet, or other media.

In individual market relationships a customer interacts with another individual who is a salesperson, or another employee of the selling organization.

Market relationships also exist between companies, industries, regions, countries, and groups of countries. When the selling situation is more extensive and complex, the selling activity turns into *negotiations.* The salesperson becomes a *negotiator* and the negotiations are often handled by a team from either side.

The concept of *interactive marketing* – in contrast to *traditional* or *mass marketing* – broadens the view on personal selling.[1] It puts emphasis on the significance of interaction beween the two parties. It further tells that relationships of importance for selling are often not handled by salespeople but by other employees who enter into personal contact with the customers. This is the case with frontline employees of a service provider and those who participate in major deals in industrial marketing.

Caring for existing customers used to be second to *attracting new customers*. The salesperson who acquired new customers was dynamic, while the guy who 'just' took care of old customers was considered old and tired and frightened of the new. Today, *keeping, caring for, and developing existing relationships*, is given priority. The strategy is: Court your own customers before you start courting somebody else's customers.

A rationale for investing in existing customers is that customers are increasingly being perceived as the scarce resource of a business; another is that getting new customers is costly. Consequently long-term and stable relationships come in focus. Berry[2] defines RM as 'attracting, maintaining and...enhancing customer relationships'; the number one priority of marketing being 'to protect the customer base'. Attracting new customers is only the first stage in the marketing process, not the final stage. The second stage – to establish a sustaining business relationship – is the most demanding part of marketing.

The terms *retention marketing* and *zero defection*[3] emphasize the relationship to existing customers. The latter term is paraphrasing the 'zero defects' quality strategy. This strategy says that a company should continuously improve its quality and deliver defect-free goods and services. Zero defection means a defect-free relationship, reducing the loss of customers to zero. This strategy does not imply that customers should be kept at all cost. If a customer has no need for our offering or the customer will remain unprofitable, defection should be encouraged. There should be an ongoing *customer migration*; customers *immigrate* to us, or *emigrate* from us to other suppliers. This is a freedom factor in a market economy. What the zero defection strategy really says is that customers should not leave because of disinterest from the supplier, late delivery, sloppy service, or wrong pricing.

A key question is: To what extent is it profitable to keep a relationship, and when should we accept that a purchase is just a one-shot deal? Among marketers we often hear that it is five to ten times as expensive to make a new customer than to keep an old customer. I do not know how well this is proven, but it has become a buzz axiom.

---

[1] See further Grönroos (1990, pp. 140–2).
[2] Berry (1983, p. 25).
[3] The term 'zero defection' is taken from Reichheld and Sasser (1990).

A salesperson adage says that 'real selling isn't making sales but making customers'. This strategy has been taught at sales courses as a practical experience. It is more uncertain how many understand and live the strategy. Carl Sewell in Dallas, the world's most successful Cadillac dealer, has understood and follows the advice. To him, selling cars is creating a lifelong relationship to each individual customer. He estimates that each customer is worth US$332,000. That is what a Cadillac customer is expected to spend on purchasing and servicing cars during a lifetime. As one measure to strengthen the relationship, Sewell keeps the auto repair shops open on Saturdays and evenings. He explains his relationship credo as follows:[4]

- 'If you're good to your customers, they'll keep coming back because they like you.
- If they like you, they'll spend more money.
- If they spend more money, you want to treat them better.
- If you treat them better, they'll keep coming back and the circle starts again.'

It is hard to argue this credo, it is common sense.

A major question is whether it is possible to create a relationship if you have thousands or even millions of customers as can be the case, particularly in consumer marketing. Is not mass marketing through advertising and supermarket distribution the only possibility? In mass marketing, the customer is anonymous. The contact through 'mass communication' is *indirect, impersonal,* and *one-way.* In fact, it is deceptive to call it communication, which should be a two-way street.[5] At best it is *information* at worst it is barely *noise.*

In the rationalistic mode of the Western industrialized world, the cost of keeping personal relationships are too high, especially if the product or service is cheap or exposed to price competition. Therefore, relationships are made mechanical, which is possible by means of large-scale mass marketing, supermarkets and self-service. Personal relationships are substituted for packages which carry product and price information, and the consumers themselves fill trolleys and bags with goods.

The transfer from an individual relationship to a mass relationship offers many intermediary forms. The notion of *customized mass marketing* may appear an oxymoron but is an increasingly viable marketing strategy.

Marketing attempts to create an impression of a personal relationship to customers even if the supplier does not know the customers or even meet them. It is a *pseudo-personal relationship,* but, all the same, it could be an efficient one. There are, however, quality differences in the personal relationships between a family doctor and a patient, or a restaurant keeper and a regular dinner guest, and the relationship between a consumer and a newspaper advertisement or a poster in the subway.

---

[4] Sewell (1990, p. xviii).
[5] Edfeldt (1993, p. 100).

> ## Case study
>
> Slater Menswear in Glasgow, is an example of customized mass marketing. It is the world's largest men's store and the entrance displays a diploma from the *Guinness Book of Records* to prove this. The store guarantees at least 12,000 suits in stock (including well-known fashion brands) and a price level 25 to 50 per cent lower than in the average store. As a customer you are quickly attended to by a sales assistant who is helpful but leaves you alone if you prefer to look around on your own. You can turn to any sales assistant, they do not seem to protect you against their colleagues. They advise you on colour and fit. Measurements for changes are taken immediately, are offered without extra cost, and are ready the next day or, if you are pressed for time, within an hour or less. If you are from oversees, they complete the documents for a sales tax refund and they do it without you asking for it. The documents must be signed by Customs when you leave the country and then sent to an address, but Slater has already given you an addressed envelope with a stamp. If you wish, the refund goes onto your credit card so you do not have to bother about foreign cheques and excessive bank fees in your home country. Everything is smooth, quick and easy. It is large scale, but the personal service is high. It is difficult to leave Slater without buying. According to owner Paul Slater, one explanation for the low prices is the purchasing and payment policy:[6] 'We buy large amounts from the manufacturers and pay them within three to five days of delivery, allowing us to pass on discounts to our customers. Experience has shown that we are very easy to deal with and we have succeeded in building up very successful relationships with some of the large fashion houses over the years, Slater creates a positive relationship to vendors as they are not spoilt with speedy payment. This in turn makes Slater more competitive to consumers. However, low price is not enough; the staff also quickly establish a relationship with the customer.

Direct marketing has long worked with personally addressed letters to enhance the impression of a close relationship.[7] Computers can repeat the name of the customer in the text of the letter and the order card. The tone can be personal: 'Dear Mr Smith: You have been selected...'. *Reader's Digest* was early in deploying this technique in a large-scale international operation for individualized direct mail.[8] In the middle of the 1960s this was a sensation, but was frowned upon by many companies and advertising agencies. Even if most consumers intellectually understood that the letter was not genuinely personal, the individualized letter increased the response rate dramatically.

---

[6] The quotation is from an advertisement for Slater Mensware.
[7] Blomqvist, Dahl and Haeger (1993) paricularly stress the usefulness of direct marketing for RM.

Case study

Reader's Digest established advanced relationships with the subscribers of the magazine at its start in 1922 by using the customer base for direct mail. Seventy-five years later the monthly magazine is printed in seventeen languages and has twenty-eight million subscribers. When the operations were broadened to books and music, its address list – the customer base – became their most valuable asset. The new products were sold to existing magazine subscribers through personally addressed letters. The mailing lists were divided into segments: subscriber, subscriber and buyer of one (two...) books, subscriber and buyer of one (two...) music albums, and other combinations. It turned out that the more products a consumer had bought, the higher the probability that he or she would buy yet another product. The long-term relationship between *Reader's Digest* and the consumer determined future sales. It was clearly established in sophisticated statistical tests that sociodemographic variables for segmentation, such as age, sex and income – which are routinely recommended in marketing textbooks – added no value whatsoever.

Hanna Andersson is a mail-order children's clothing business in Portland, Oregon. One way to keep in touch with customers and make loyalty rewarding is their Hannadowns concept. According to their mail-order catalogue: 'When your kids outgrow their Hanna clothes, send them back to me in good used condition, and I'll reserve your credit for 20 per cent of the purchase price. That's a real head start on your next order! Meanwhile we'll donate your clothes to kids in need, where they'll become favorites all over again.' Other mail-order operations such as L.L. Bean and Land's End are now showing that individual relationships to consumers are possible not only all over the American continent, but also to European and Japanese consumers.

In Europe, the leading Norwegian insurance company Storebrand has implemented a comprehensive programme to establish a correct and complete customer database. For an insurance company it is a production necessity to keep records. The novelty is that the database is now actively used for marketing and the maintenance of closer and long-term relationships; marketing and production have entered wedlock. Through the database, the company can identify each individual's needs for insurance and target customized offerings to each of its 900,000 customers. Getting the customer database in order was found to be a mammoth undertaking. The base contained a high error rate, including people who died long ago. The oldest 'customer' who still received mail died the same year as Napoleon Bonaparte, which was in 1821. Talk about caring for old customers![9]

Direct marketing is increasingly using the telephone and media other than

---

[8] For the history of the *Reader's Digest*, see Heidenry (1993).

mail;[10] that is the reason for changing the name from direct mail. *Telemarketing* has become a major industry. For example, Teleperformance, an international telemarketing service, claims that 70 per cent of marketing and sales communication is handled by telephone; that a telephone contact is five to ten times as efficient as mail contact; and is often as effective as a face-to-face visit but costs five times less. Although the toll-free 800 number was opened in the United States in 1967 it took until the 1980s for companies to realize its potential for a dialogue with consumers. Today all 800 numbers are taken and a new series, 888 numbers, has been opened. In most other countries similar telephone services are quite recent.

The establishment of an accurate and useful database has been made possible through IT. But IT takes you nowhere unless you direct your efforts to RM and manage them properly. At the Ritz-Carlton hotels each employee is trained to note a guest's likes and dislikes. The data are entered in a computer database which includes the guest history of Ritz-Carlton's 240,000 repeat customers: credit card number, corporate rates, previous hotel visits, non-smoker, etc. It is a practical measure that creates a bond with the guest. It smooths the interaction between the customer and hotel staff at reservations, check-in and check-out, and it helps to make each visit a memorable visit. The disadvantage of impersonal treatment caused by large-scale operations is partly offset, and IT, in combination with personal customer contact, makes relationship maintenance efficient.

In a market economy, a company must make a profit to survive. Excellent relationships with customers is no goal in itself; productivity in marketing must be kept up. Sales staff and others who negotiate deals must know how to close a deal within a reasonable time and with reasonable prices. The customers must offer a reasonable profit potential. For example, Storebrand found that 100,000 of its customers were not reasonably profitable. Some qualities of the horse salesmen and the poker player are needed but must be weighed against the ability to cement long-term, professional and trusting relationships with customers. Short-term greed is not a viable RM strategy.

The supplier gives *promises* to the customer.[11] The customer reciprocates by promising to pay. Promises create expectations which must be met for the relationship to sustain; it is a part of business ethics which makes both parties trust one another. A trusting relationship is rational as it reduces red tape and the risk for litigation. A European businessman long settled in Japan, has portrayed the Japanese business relationship as follows:[12] 'The Japanese customer demands personal contact with his suppliers. He does not buy on the basis of sales letters, catalogues, brochures and the like. He wants to speak to the seller.... . These per-

---

[9] According to Alfred Bakken, Vice President Storebrand.
[10] See Rapp and Collins (1995).
[11] See further Calonius (1987).
[12] Delaryd (1989, p. 25).

sonal promises must of course later be confirmed in a written document, but this is usually very brief. It is of primary importance that the buyer has contact with one particular person at the selling company, one who feels totally responsible for the contract... . The human being plays the lead role – not long and complicated contracts on paper.'

For small businesses – and most of them do not want to grow – the relationships can be a goal *per se* for the owners. In a study of small hotels in Scotland[13] it turned out that the 'familial unit' – the nuclear family, relatives, friends, regular customers, employees, suppliers – came first and the hotel second. The network and the interaction was a personal goal, a lifestyle which was beyond financial goals. This attitude and behaviour is poorly considered in economic theory where the supplier is expected to rationally pursue economic self-interest, usually meaning growth and maximization of net income.

Person-to-person contact with consumers is common especially when selling expensive and complex products like cars, homes, and retirement plans. In other service-producing operations like small stores, hotels, restaurants and schools, the personal interaction can also be extensive. Sales to households via the telephone or door-to-door, has decreased in many countries but is important in others. The milkman is an institution in the UK; in the Netherlands the retailer brings a whole store in his van. From its start, Electrolux based its success on selling vacuum cleaners door-to-door. Their most successful salesman sold 14,000 cleaners during his career. He made an average of five per day; three is enough to bring the salesperson into the star class.[14] He points to the importance of the minute details in the interaction with the customer:

- You have twenty seconds to develop a positive contact.
- Do not ring one long demanding signal but two short, merry signals.
- Stand back five feet from the door and a little to the side so that the customer must open the door completely.
- Shake hands with the customer to improve contact.

Systematic work with these and other details, together with continuous learning and testing have a decisive influence in situations where the salesperson must quickly establish a relationship.

The transition from person-to-person contact to person-to-machine contact has reduced the personal relationships in areas where they used to be ubiquitous. Banking is a current example where the dealings with a bank teller are replaced by an automated teller machine (ATM), a telephone, or a computer. The social interaction has transformed into electronic interaction which involves a radical shift in the bank–customer relationships (see R5, the service encounter and R12, the electronic relationship).

---

[13] Lowe (1988).
[14] From an interview with Ove Sjögren (Ohlson, 1994).

Identifying marketing's parent relationship is not enough and R1 can be divided into several special types of market relationships. R1 only shows the tip of the iceberg whereas the 30R approach attempts to show the whole iceberg. Marketing is also dependent on the supporting nano and mega relationships. The following relationships highlight interaction between parties in networks of relationships and different facets of the interaction process.

Relationship 2 The classic triad – the drama of the customer–supplier–competitor triangle

A cornerstone of the market economy is the presence of several suppliers in each market. Competition arises, consisting of a triad of players: the *customer*, the *customer's present supplier*, and *competing suppliers*.

The treatment of competiton in this section assumes a RM perspective; it is not an orthodox overview.

There is extensive literature on competition. Particularly the books by Porter have drawn the attention of marketers to competition during the 1980s.[15] At the same time as the interest for RM is growing, the interest in competition is growing. The well-established recommendation to create a sustainable competitive advantage through product differentiation, lowest cost, or niche marketing, is being challenged. Competition increasingly seems to turn into *hypercompetition*, a state of flux and warfare. Hypercompetition is intense, fast, and thrives on continuous disruption of competitive advantages, both one's own and those of competitors. A strong player in the market is one with superior ability to manoeuvre in constant turmoil.[16]

In market economies, competition is hailed as the driver of economic evolution and a necessary condition for wealth. This is a traditional view advocated by the business community, and also by governments in countries where *deregulation* and *privatization* have become forceful strategies.

However, the 'capitalist' societies are *mixed economies* in which market forces and regulations have entered into wedlock. In totally unregulated markets many destructive forces set in: only a few may be able to obtain the necessities of life; price competition may become cut-throat with streams of bankruptcies; quality may be impaired and dangerous products will be sold freely; and powerful corporations offset competition. The opposite extreme – total regulation – leads to rigidity. There is no general formula that tells us in what proportions freedom and regulation should be mixed. Every market and period have to find their own specific solution.

---

[15] Porter (1980, 1985, 1990); see also Hamel and Prahalad (1994); Hunt and Morgan (1995); and Moore (1996).
[16] See D'Aveni (1994) and Verbeke and Peelen (1996).

Competition is desirable whenever it is efficient, but it is certainly no panacea. Through competition, relationships are formed between customers and many possible suppliers. It gives rise to types of relationships other than a monopoly (see R10). The customer is given a choice, and a supplier can never be sure to have the customer in its pocket. Nor can a customer be sure to have a supplier in his or her pocket.

In its idealized and theoretical form, the market functions through the 'invisible hand' provided by supply and demand and refereed by competition and price. Every moment millions of purchasing and selling decisions are made, and millions of activitites are performed by individuals, and, today, also by computers. These decisions and activites are accumulated and – according to neoclassical economics – strive in the direction of a *long-term market equilibrium*.

I propose a pendant to market equilibrium, namely *marketing equilibrium* composed of three forces: *competition; collaboration;* and *regulations/institutions*. My thesis is that:

> the focus on collaboration is the most important contribution from RM, with an impact on both marketing management and economics, and that collaboration in a market economy needs to be treated with the same attention and respect as competition.

But collaboration will not be efficient without the other two forces. In order for regulations, through government resolutions, laws, and rules, to operate in practice, *institutions* are needed. Institutions inform, facilitate execution, and check obedience. They can range from very formal institutions like the courts and the tax authorities to religious creed, family values, accepted practice, moral codes, professional ethics, and a shared, tacit understanding of good manners. Although both collaboration and regulations/institutions are mentioned in the marketing literature, they are not in its core and they are often treated as impediments to competition.

Even if RM puts emphasis on collaboration, I would like to see RM as the synthesis between competition, collaboration, and regulations/institutions (Figure 2.1). The issue is which combination of these three forces will best contribute to an optimal and dynamic balance – a marketing equilibrium – in each specific situation.

The global wave of privatization and deregulation is a reaction to markets that have become stifled. The bureaucratic–legal values lead to a misguided interference by politicians and an unreal belief in centralized control of society. Inadequate and obsolete formal regulations/institutions are allowed to rule.

Deregulation does not mean abandoning all regulations. It is a search for more adequate laws and institutions which are supportive to constructive forces of society and hold back destructive forces. In fact it is not deregulation but

Figure 2.1 The three forces of the market economy which together can create marketing equilibrium

re-regulation. Since the beginning of the 1980s this has been a leading strategy around the world.

Collaboration, hypercompetition, privatization, and re-regulation create new relationships between customers, their current suppliers, competitors, and other parts of society. How these relationships should be handled we only know to a limited degree today. For example, the re-regulation of the financial sector caused chaos in many countries.

The extreme belief in the automatic blessings of competition is just as naive as the dream of the total, planned economy where 'experts' with the 'right' knowledge and armed with regulations and institutions survey a country's economy and through 'facts' and 'analysis' engineer an equilibrium in a completely integrated system. There is no known market that has functioned without regulations and institutions, nor one that functions without competition and collaboration. In the former Soviet Union and its colonies where the socialist extreme – the total regulation of the market – was replaced by the capitalist extreme – completely free competition – the outcome is chaos, poverty, injustice, bribery, and violence. 'Good institutions' that support economic activity are required, both the formal ones and those inherent in the informal, collective consciousness of a people.

There are necessary elements of the market economy that competition and the free market forces do not master. They can be worded in two paradoxes. The first paradox says: *Regulations are needed to secure that free competion will not be curbed.* In spite of all the sweet talk about competition, every individual company or industry prefers to be spared the hazards of competition; on the other hand they consider it essential for other companies and industries. The second paradox says:

The goal of competition is to get rid of competition. Being competitive means that a company attempts to reduce the influence of other suppliers through various activities, among them barriers to entry and disruptive hustle and bustle.

Regulations therefore are not the same as restrictions. They can also be dynamic influences by forcing slow companies to take action, for example to declare the content of their products, and to make environmental considerations. The EU is designing institutions and regulations, among others' courts to handle discrimination and contract disputes. It is a formidable task as both differences in national politics, tradition, language, culture, and legal premises are being thrown into a melting-pot. Whether a dinosaurian bureaucracy – big, with a small brain and in reality extinct – is being born in the EU 'capital' Brussels, Belgium, or whether the EU is succeeding in constructing institutions that make markets more functional, is yet to be seen.

One of the winners of the 1993 Nobel Prize in the Economic Sciences, Douglass C. North, has studied the significance of institutions and regulations in a market economy. In his Nobel Lecture, North (1993) proposed that the study of economic development 'ignored the incentive structure embodied in institutions [and] it contained two erroneous asumptions: one that institutions do not matter and two that time does not matter'.

North continued: 'Institutions form the incentive structure of the society and…are the underlying determinant of economic performance.' Being an economic historian with a longer time perspective than marketers, he claims that it takes 500 to 600 years to implant a functioning institutional framework in a society; it is the outcome of the collective consciousness of a people. The possibilites of creating 'instant capitalism' are consequently no more than daydreams which many African countries and Russia have verified.

There are signs that the interest in collaboration is gaining ground not only in real business life but also in marketing theory. Alderson[17] long ago complained about the the economists' lack of interest in cooperation: 'Cooperation is as prevalent in economic activity as competition… . Marketing cries out for a theory of cooperation to match the theory of competition.' Solomon[18] says that 'business life, unlike life in the mythological jungle, is first of all fundamentally cooperative'. According to Mattsson and Lundgren[19] 'competition and collaboration are not antipodes but two different dimensions, one being a condition for the other'. Brandenburger and Nalebuff (1996) introduce the term 'co-opetition', a combination of cooperation and competition; Doz and Hamel (1998) stress 'co-option' and cospecialization as the primary reasons for partnering. Gray points to collaboration as a solution to the multi-party problem and says: 'Despite powerful incentives to collaborate, our capacity to do so is underdeveloped.[20]

---

[17] Alderson (1965, p. 239).
[18] Solomon (1992, p. 26).
[19] Mattsson and Lundgren (1992–93, p. 9).
[20] Gray (1989, p. 54).

In the same spirit Senge, in his treatise on learning organizations and the need for dialogue says:[21] 'Interestingly, the practice of dialogue has been preserved in many 'primitive' cultures...but it has been almost completely lost to modern society. Today, the principles and practices of dialogue are being rediscovered and put into a contemporary context.' The word dialogue comes from the Greek and literally means 'thinking together'.

A company's result and behaviour may be more dependent on its partners in long-term relationships than how it is positioned to competitors or mass markets. Viewing the company and its market as part of a network is central in RM. Consequently the classic triad of a buyer, a supplier and a few competitors is naive: *These three parties represent networks and the competition occurs between networks of firms rather than between individual firms* .[22]

Neoclassical economics is based on the existence of anonymous mass markets, while in reality these markets are far from anonymous. In industrial marketing each customer and each competitor is often personally known. In consumer marketing this is also true, for example, restaurant owners' relationships to loyal guests, and the dentists' relationships with their patients. Consumer goods can be bought and sold on a scale ranging from total anonymity to the consumer and the retailer being buddies. Retail outlets may be small and intimate or be huge 'hypermarkets' that resemble the impersonal and standardized assembly line of a factory.

Competition usually refers to rivalry between suppliers. In times of shortage there is competition also between buyers, and buyers have to court sellers by queuing, appealing to personal relationships, exerting pressure and power, or paying under the table. In many countries housing, higher education, legal services, day care, and health care are in short supply – and for some strange reason these shortages are accepted as inevitable. In a similar vein the offical institutions of the Soviet Union accepted that soap, bread, and cars were scarce commodities. In the former East Germany the waiting time for the Trabant car was twelve years before the Berlin wall was knocked down. And the Trabant was obsolete and expensive, was reputed to cause throat and breathing disorders, and had a highly variable manufacturing quality.

If networks of relationships become completely stable over the long term, true competition ceases to exist. A new supplier stands little chance to enter the market, the door is locked. This is not new but it still seems to come as a surprise to marketing theory and it is not acknowledged in economic theory except as an anomaly. Arndt wrote about locked and domesticated markets: 'To an increasing degree, transactions are occurring in "internal" markets within the framework of long-term relationships, not on an ad hoc basis'[23]. Collaboration sometimes knocks out competition. and marketing becomes a political game.[24]

---

[21] Senge (1990, p. 10).
[22] Thorelli (1986).
[23] Arndt (1979, p. 69).
[24] See Arndt (1983); and Stern and Reve (1980).

In Japan – where long-term relationships are institutionlized in the culture – it happens that a new supplier gets an order from a customer and the regular supplier may perceive this as a failure in his relationships with the old customer. It is not necessarily a failure, the customer just wants to stimulate competition and make sure the regular supplier stays alert: Don't take me for granted! Japanese companies use more than one bank to secure excellence in service and to create an incentive for banks to be continuously interested in their customers.[25]

TQM does not specifically consider competition, but the vantage point is to be 'world class' or 'best in class' in order to survive. *Benchmarking* refers to a comparison with the *very best* – not the average or the mediocre. It requires comparison, not only with competitors but with best practice in whatever company or industry it can be found.

Competitive bidding is demanded by law in certain instances, above all when government agencies purchase goods and services. A purpose of the bidding procedure is to make markets mechanical and impersonal. Tenders must be delivered before a specified hour and competitors are expected to submit their bids independently. This does not always work in practice. The building and construction industry lives with continuous bidding contests. From time to time, however, secret cartels are uncovered where competitors have split the market and design bids to help an elected 'colleague' win a contract. Industrial espionage in order to learn about competitor bids is not uncommon. Bribes exist: pleasure trips; parties with 'hostesses'; help to build a summer house; and lots of other ingenious variants. However, bids are not always rational. They tend to get stuck on price comparisons as price is the easiest variable to measure. Service, quality and not least security, trust, commitment, joint development, and flexibility – which are in the core of long-term relationships – are difficult to pinpoint in simple short-term indicators.

At the same time, it is common that a supplier gets a first order in competition and if this order is successful new orders will follow through negotiations without a bidding procedure. The first order is often not profitable but a precursor to future profits. Competition in its entirely free and price-based version may cause excessive *switching costs* (costs to change to another supplier) as well as excessive *transaction costs* (costs of handling the purchase and the sale).

Blumberg has pointed out that the strength of the market economy – competition and the profit incentive – encourages fraud.[26] It pays to cheat! He calls this the *paradox of the market economy*. Everybody is familiar with this from jobs and private consumption, but it is swept under the carpet in marketing theory. The official image is idealized: competition as the driver to create customer satisfaction and in its wake profitability and long-term success. Customers are asked about the quality they get, but their knowledge is limited. In 1271 St Thomas Aquinas stated

---

[25] Based on Delaryd (1989, pp. 30 and 98ff).

[26] Blumberg's (1989) study is based on 700 essays written by sociology students who had worked in different industries. From their job experience they have told about systematic methods to swindle their customers.

that it takes great knowledge to assess quality and that most consumers lack this knowledge. This is just as true today, maybe even more true as the complexity of society and its offerings has grown. A cynic is reputed to have said: 'Customers are not as stupid as you think. They are much more stupid.' Maybe this is not just a cynicism but is sometimes true and is explored by suppliers. For example, prices are sometimes raised before a sale and then reduced – '25 per cent off!' – meaning the same price as before the raise; some taxi-drivers tamper with meters; and some suppliers exploit customer stress, confusion and helplessness.

Can good customer relationships emerge in spite of such behaviour? Yes, it seems so to a degree as customers, especially consumers, must buy on trust. If the consumers believe they have been given the right product or the correct service they feel satisfied. Or they lower their expectations and accept the imperfections of life; they become 'happy slaves'.

The current dramatic changes in the telecom market provide an example of the efforts to strive toward marketing equilibrium. Deregulation – or rather re-regulation – has made it possible for telecoms to expand beyond national markets. But they can hardly do it on their own. Telecoms from Italy, the Netherlands, Sweden and Switzerland have formed the Unisource alliance. British Telecom has joined forces with MCI Communications, the second largest operator of international telecommunications in the USA. GTE, one of the largest telecoms in the USA, is both competitor, customer and supplier to AT&T. GTE buys equipment from AT&T, competes with AT&T on certain telephone lines, but sells access to local lines to AT&T. In the early 1980s, with reference to the antitrust laws, the then dominating telecom in the USA, Bell, was broken up into seven regional operators, the Baby Bells. The purpose was to stimulate competition. AT&T is prohibited by law to acquire stock in the Baby Bells. But AT&T has acquired the largest operating company in mobile telephony, McCaw. With the help of its cellular technology, AT&T can bypass the regional and local operators and the assistance of the Baby Bells is no longer required.

The examples show ongoing efforts to find a marketing equilibrium. When telecoms companies experience restrictions from regulations, they attempt to (legally) circumvent these by creating new networks through alliances or utilizing new technology. Competition thus takes new forms and the effects of existing regulations are nullified; re-regulations become imperative, and so forth.

Could it be that hypercompetition is the real driver of the upsurging interest in RM, that there is a need to neutralize the effects of increasingly faster, more fierce and ruthless rivalry? When competition becomes hypercompetition, perhaps collaboration must become *hypercollaboration*?

Relationship 3 The classic network – distribution channels

Physical distribution is the most obvious network in marketing; it constitutes a classic network. Distribution networks are numerous, complex, and interwoven.

Sometimes they are efficient and fast, following the shortest path to market. Sometimes they are slow, inefficient and replete with detours and broken chains. As consumers we are surrounded by them. We are unpaid workers in the distribution networks when we shop for food, walk to the postbox with a letter, or drive our car to work.

When traditional marketing literature deals with distribution, its domain is physical distribution of consumer goods, although a major share of distribution concerns industrial goods as part of business-to-business marketing.[27]

However, the networks of the distribution channels distribute not only *goods* but also *services*, *people* and *information*, often in combination.

The distribution system for consumer retailing is a service network. Its core mission is to make goods conveniently available. The system is supported by services other than the actual goods distribution such as location and parking facilities. These goods distribution channels are well developed in most countries and industries, but there are exceptions. At the time of the dissolution of the Soviet Union, the state was unable to organize the distribution of a loaf of bread. Waiting lines were part of daily life in Moscow and eventually you needed an ID to be allowed to buy bread. It was not the lack of grain that prevented the supply of bread, but the lack of functioning networks.

The relationships between the parties in the distribution network vary for many reasons. If a store is part of a chain, the producer often sells to central buyers. The goods are sent to a central warehouse or regional warehouses, or direct to the store. Many intermediaries can influence the deals in the supply chain. The goods are eventually bought by consumers. If a household consists of several individuals, it becomes an organization and the family members play different roles in a similar way as in organizational buying. All actors in the distribution chain – except the last one, the consumer – are both buyers and sellers.

If a few chains in the daily goods distribution are big and powerful the relationships between the producer and the central buyers become predominant. The producers risk having no relationship with consumers and cannot monitor the changes that take place in attitudes and buying and consumption behaviour. The producers try to compensate for this through market surveys and visits to stores whereas retailers link consumer to the stores through cards and membership (see R11).

Producers can circumvent the traditional wholesaler–retailer networks through telemarketing, mail order, and the opportunities that are increasingly offered by TV, personal computers, modems, the internet and World Wide Web. Companies can set up chains of one-product shops. Factory outlets – each selling their own brand at substantially reduced prices – began to gather in outlet villages during

---

[27] An overview of distribution channels is found in Stern, El-Ansary and Coughlan (1996). On distribution in business marketing, see Gadde (1994). There is an emerging interest to view distribution from an RM perspective; see e.g. Weitz and Jap, (1995) and Pelton, Strutton and Lumpkin (1997).

the 1990s. In 1997, the Great Western Designer Outlet Village with some hundred stores was opened in Swindon, UK, including such well-known brands as Laura Ashley, Levi's, Nike, Tie Rack, and Timberland. Network marketing is a system for marketing goods and services which is usually based on contacts with friends and friends-of-friends. Multi-level marketing (MLM) offers a network of collaborating one-man firms who support each other: 'You are in business for yourself, but not by yourself.[28] Often these firms are operated out of the owner's home at minimal overhead and investment[29]. Tupperware is an example of successful party selling of household goods. You cannot really get closer to the customer. When recruiting new salespeople, Tupperware says: 'More than Just Parties. The location is never a problem. Perhaps you would prefer a demonstration during a lunch hour or after work. Maybe you'd like to invite a few friends for coffee at a nearby restaurant...'

Distribution of goods is *per se* a service – which may seem confusing – but services as the focal point for distribution are put on hold in the literature. In reality, services are the core of a great part of today's distribution systems. Examples are the services provided by restaurants, insurance companies, hairdressers, consultants, electric power companies, water suppliers, telecoms, stock and metals exchanges. Important, but often badly managed consumer services, are repair and maintenance of homes and household equipment. Internal services in organizations are not treated.

If services are viewed as activities, often interactive between customer and provider, it is the availability of these potential activities – the service distribution infrastructure – which makes marketing possible. Such examples are the network of post offices, post boxes, and the postal deliveries. Post offices were early global network builders. Through bureaucracy and monopoly, they long lagged in adjusting to contemporary society. Under pressure from deregulation and competition, mail services have undergone changes. Two examples of innovators are Federal Express and DHL, both started by students around 1970. Federal Express has a hub and spokes system which means that all mail is flown to Memphis, Tennessee, where it is assorted during the night and delivered the next morning. DHL uses Brussels, Belgium, as its main hub in Europe. Both have aircraft of their own and pick up and deliver with their own vans. The mail is marked with a bar code and can be traced quickly. Time of delivery is guaranteed and many ancillary services have been developed to facilitate distribution from the perspective of the two customer groups, the senders and the receivers.

Distribution of people and information are also services, for example being able to travel by train but also to call Amtrak for information on train departure,

---

[28] Hawkins (1991, p. 8).
[29] Serious MLM should not be mixed up with the type of pyramid selling where a company persuades independent salespeople to buy big parcels of goods which they in turn sell to others who sell to others and so forth, in each instance at a cost plus price. These pyramids have sometimes just become a gamble with most of the participants as losers.

arrival and fares. The role of a forwarder is to direct goods through a transport network. Whereas goods must be lifted and stored, people usually walk themselves or drive their own cars. Consumers are feeders to an institutionalized system, as when they walk endless concourses at airports, carrying heavy luggage. Transportation is seldom associated with do-it-yourself but it may be the largest do-it-yourself system in existence. Travelling – including tourism, conventions, business travel, hotels and other facilities – is among the fastest growing industries. Travelling consists of fragmented components, centred around a transportation technique such as aviation. Gradually, the understanding for more integrated systems has emerged – the seamless service – where the customer is in focus and not the technique or tradition. As SAS advertised: 'We used to fly aircraft. We now fly people.' Packaged vacation tours have assembled the pieces of the trip and the stay in order to make holidays hassle-free.

Different means of transportation are increasingly being perceived as complementary rather than competitive. Fast railroads connect city centres with airports. In Sweden, the domestic and international airline redesigned malfunctioning ground transportation to and from airports, and implemented a functioning system despite the disinterest from local transport companies; the fight for the air passenger at one stage was not in the air but on the ground. The reconstructed Union Station in Washington, DC, which was ready in 1988, is an example of how different transport techniques meet in symbiosis: train; bus; taxi; rental car; and closeness to the national airport via the subway. The station is also a service centre with restaurants, shops, and movie theatres; banquets are even held on the main station floor. Travellers are still inconvenienced by transfers from one means of transportation to another.

Excellence in after-sales services in business marketing is an antecedent to future sales and is often a matter of distribution of people. On the world market, exporting companies often have difficulties in the distribution of service people; keeping them on the spot it is often judged to be too costly. To fly out personnel for troubleshooting can work in certain markets but not in others. In Japan it is considered unsatisfactory; it is too slow and the personal relationships become shallow.[30]

Distribution of speech and data via electronic media are not part of the distribution systems as they are presented in marketing theory. The electronic relationship has many unique properties and is treated as a separate relationship (R12). Physical and electronic distribution supplement each other. By converting physical transportation into electronic transportation, the speed can be accelerated, for example a letter being replaced by fax or internet transmission. On the other hand, it will probably not be feasible to fax parcels or people unless the IT-based virtual reality and cyberspace machinery can act as a surrogate for actual physical presence.

The concept of *logistics* concerns the flow of goods, all the way from the extrac-

---

[30] Delaryd (1989, p. 73ff).

tion of raw material, manufacturing of components and assembly, to finished goods in the store and their arrival at households. The goods flow is accompanied by an information flow via documents and computer transmissions. Logistics cuts across functional and hierarchical borders. The idea of logistics is in tune with the efforts to organize along processes instead of functions. The consumer's transport of goods to their homes and their treatment of the goods is also part of the logistics flow. Increasingly, environmental laws require recycling, which is why logistics are stretched even further (see R15).

Logistics require a holistic understanding of a business operation. It is a matter of making processes more effective, so that manufacturing and delivery are performed straighter and faster and on time, keeping costs and capital employed down. The slower the logistic process, the more capital is tied up and the longer the time before the customer pays. Logistics is also a marketing strategy, one strategic decision concerning the scope of the suppliers' offerings: Should the supplier offer a complete systems solution or a partial solution, or enter into alliance with other companies who provide elements of the system?

Kiichiro Toyoda, founder of Toyota Motor Company, coined the concept *just-in-time* (JIT) as early as in the 1930s. The emphasis was on the just, meaning that only just what was absolutely necessary should be done, and this should be done at just the right time.[31] JIT is usually presented with the emphasis on the time, meaning that ordered goods should arrive at exactly the right time, neither after, nor before. 'Just' and 'time' are equally important in distribution. They contribute to a harmonious flow. The Toyota factory stops after thirty minutes if scheduled deliveries of components do not arrive. In comparison, the traditional auto factory strategy was to order large quantities of components and store them for several weeks.

Logistics and JIT influence quality, productivity and profitability. They establish a regular and close relationships between supplier and customer. They must make plans together and connect their systems into a fluid process which requires investment and continuous maintenance and improvements. It becomes a partnership, an alliance, rather than a supplier–customer relationship. The earlier strategy for organizational buyers was to use multiple suppliers and to play them against each other and press prices. The trend has gradually turned in the direction of fewer and closer supplier relationships, with less weight on price and competition and more on collaboration. During the 1990s, Sundstrand in Germany has gone from 550 suppliers to 120; Ford in the USA from 6000 to 2000; and McDonald's from 175 suppliers of beef in the USA to only five. During 1992, IKEA decided to cut the number of subcontractors in Northern Europe from 400 to 300. The company demanded cost reductions of 15 per cent from the remaining suppliers, but also offered assistance with the implementation of the reductions. One of the issues was the closing of a central warehouse and introducing JIT deliveries direct from a factory to the furniture stores.

---

[31] Helling (1992, p. 28); see also Womack, Jones and Roos (1990).

Although JIT is usually discussed for goods delivery, it is equally applicable on services, people, and information. As services are partly produced and consumed simultaneously, they must be produced when needed. Extreme examples are emergency services performed by the police and paramedics.

Waiting lines have not been particularly investigated in marketing. From a customer point of view I would like to propose the following definition: *A waiting line is an inventory of customers waiting to be served*. A waiting line contributes no 'value-added', only 'value-reduced'. A service delivery system stores capacity to perform services, but the services themselves must be delivered JIT; they cannot be stored in a ready-to-use shape.[32]

T50, the huge project run by ABB to reduce cycle time, is an example of time-based management or speed management. T50 means reducing cycle times by an average of 50 per cent. Kotler (1997) talks about 'turbomarketing' which means both reducing development and delivery times, and getting the products established faster on the market.

Distribution networks are often locked by those who have established themselves in the networks. It may be difficult or costly to set up a new network. Although US companies have a competitve advantage on the Japanese market concerning lifestyle and youth products – Coca-Cola is the most popular soda, McDonald's the most popular fast-food chain, Disneyland the most popular theme park – they have difficulties in getting into the Japanese distribution networks.

Remarkably enough, foreign companies have some privileges in the Japanese financial market. But also there, entry into distribution systems can be hard. Citibank, aiming for the private customer market, has had difficulties in getting access to a sufficient number of networks of ATMs. Foreign insurance companies are kept out of the distribution network for car insurance, as this is sold through car retailers. The distribution of cars is blocked because most car retailing is owned by the manufacturers and therefore only offers one brand.

Keiretsus have made up impermeable networks, based both on regulations, cross ownership between members of the network, and social and personal relationships. Habits change, however. In the wake of globalization, catalogue sales by Land's End and L.L. Bean direct from the US are gaining market share in Japan. Internet shopping will shake up national, locked distribution networks.

Looking at channels through the relationship eye-glasses, we see networks and partnerships in which processes between manufacturers, service producers, intermediaries and customers are being integrated. This requires trust more than power-based control mechanisms, contracts and formal vertical integration. Although most literature does not particularly stress it, relationship building has been salient in many channels. Negotiations between manufacturers and retail chains often have a strong social content where personal relationships and trust, joy and enthusiasm are crucial ingredients.

---

[32] Waiting lines are treated in queue theory but primarily from a short-term cost perspective.

Collaboration in distribution networks is a requisite for success:[33] 'Marketing channels cannot function without sustained cooperation in which each party knows what to expect from his opposite number'. A current example of this is *efficient consumer response* (ECR). Consumer goods manufacturers enter into partnership with retailers. In collaboration they try to reach consumers with the right product line in order to increase revenue and slash cost. This leads on to *category management*, to handle categories of products linked to specific consumer needs and consumption behaviour. One category could be 'breakfast'. Managing this category means arranging products in a retail outlet around the breakfast need, not around the type of product. The breakfast category can consequently include yoghurt, fruit, jam, bread and cereals.

In summary, by looking at distribution channels and channel management in the light of RM, we are provided with a different focus:

■ Distribution literature sets the headlights on consumer goods and less on industrial goods and there is not even a candle to shed light on the distribution of services, people and information. All these exist in combinations, although one of them can be the core object of the distribution while the others are ancillary.

■ Distribution becomes a value enhancing service in which goods are just one component. The RM focus is on the total offering and the customer's combination of components and interaction with providers and others.

■ RM sees distribution as a complex network of interactive relationships rather than a sequential channel.

---

[33] Alderson (1965, pp. 239–58; quotation from p. 239).

Chapter 3

Special market relationships

Chapter 2 presented classic marketing issues interpreted through the relationship eye-glasses. This chapter deals with special market relationships. They are of course all rooted in R1, the parent relationship of marketing, and they may have a direct or an indirect connection to the two other classics. The focus of the relationship eye-glasses, however, allows us to see other aspects of marketing, those which do not stand out well in the general marketing management approach but are of current significance for marketing success (R4–R15).

Relationship 4 Relationships via full-time marketers (FTMs) and part-time marketers (PTMs)

Marketing cannot survive in isolation from other functions. This has been pointed out in Chapter 1 and in the treatment of logistics and JIT in R3. Marketing management theory does not specifically address the dependency between functions, although many have over the years pointed to the inadequacy of functional silos. In practice, the marketing function is spread throughout the firm and the marketing and sales departments may even play a limited role in the total marketing effort. Perhaps there is not even a marketing and sales department. Instead, each and everyone is involved in marketing. This may be perceived as an organizational dilemma, but should be seen as a possibility to enhance marketing resources.

We can identify two types of marketers: *full-time marketers* (FTMs), and *part-time marketers* (PTMs). These are not only found within a company but also in its environment. They are defined as follows (Figure 3.1):

Full-time marketers (FTMs) are those who are hired for working with marketing and the sales task. Part-time marketers (PTMs) are all others in the company and those in its environment that influence the company's marketing.

Role as marketer / Resources	Internal	External
Full-time marketer, FTM	Marketing and sales staff	Distributors, advertising agencies, etc.
Part-time marketer, PTM	All those who are not FTMs	Customers, investors, media, etc.

Figure 3.1 Internal and external FTMs and PTMs

FTMs are found in *the marketing and sales departments* and among *external providers of marketing services*. Outsourcing of services has increased in recent years and these services are reinforcements to the marketing function. Distributors offer transportation, wholesaling and retailing services, all strategic and crucial for success in marketing. The marketing function also engages external professionals such as advertising agencies, market research institutes, and management consultants (see R29). At the time these providers are engaged, they can be viewed as FTMs for their client company.

Sales people are professional contact people who build relationships; they are FTMs. But they can never make it on their own. *FTMs cannot be at the right place at the right time with the right customer contact and right knowledge, but the PTMs can!* Unsuccessful marketing is not solely to blame on the marketing and sales departments, but also on the marketing function as a whole and its lack of integration with other functions.

The distinction between FTMs and PTMs has extensive consequences for the approach to marketing. It makes it legitimate and imperative for everyone to influence customer relationships.

Two cases will be shown, one from manufacturing, and one from services. The first concerns the marketing organization of a large manufacturing company which sells primarily to other companies and government agencies (Figure 3.2).

FTMs are found in the marketing and sales departments and in the group of reinforcing specialists; PTMs in the other boxes:

■ *Management* spends time on designing marketing strategies, negotiating major contracts, and entertaining VIP visitors.

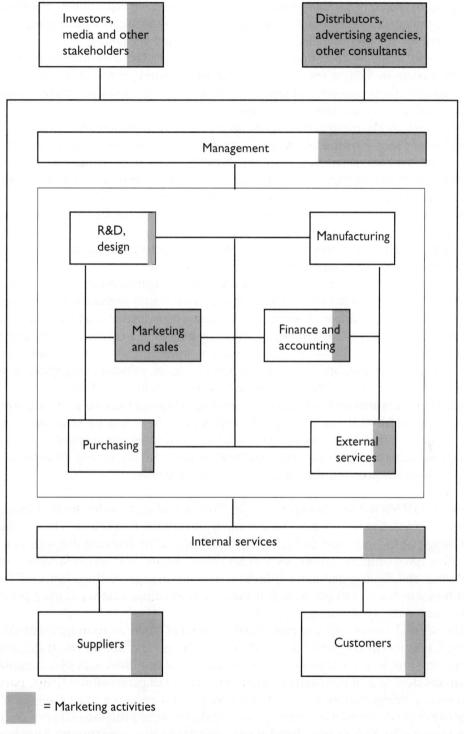

Figure 3.2 Principal components of the marketing function of a manufacturer of industrial equipment

- *Product development,* including R&D, design, and engineering departments, has to understand the needs of customers, design quality into the specifications and blueprints, and prepare for the user-friendly operation of the finished equipment.
- *Production,* including operations management and manufacturing, influences customer relationships by fulfilling specifications (production quality) and keeping delivery times. Organizational customers visit plants for inspection to get a first-hand impression of a potential supplier but also for continuous quality assurance.
- *Purchasing* affects customer relations as the end supplier has the responsibility of equipment sold – irrespective of who manufactured single components – and for outsourced services connected with the product. Even if an independent transport company causes damages to the goods and is formally responsible and the supplier declines responsibility, such incidents will damage customer–supplier relationships.
- *Finance* is often an important – sometimes *the* determining factor in major deals – especially for major customers in strained financial circumstances. Those customers may be forced to buy from a supplier who offers an attractive financial solution rather than looking at the quality of the equipment or services.
- *External services* are important as facilitators and as augmentations of the equipment. They contribute to differentiation and uniqueness, and ultimately competitiveness. There are a large number of services connected with industrial equipment, both *before-sales services* (such as custom design, solutions offered in a tender, and demonstration of equipment), and *after-sales services* (such as installation, training and education of customer personnel, operations support, updating of software, emergency support, and maintenance), and *general services* such as the telephone exchange.
- *Internal services* shall be supportive to marketing. They must not be 'administrative routines' or rituals that rigidly adhere to regulations; they must be sensitive to needs. Among the internal services are secretarial services, computer services, legal services, canteen services, health services, and services from the accounting department such as handling invoices and the sales people's travel expenses.

These are PTMs *within* the organization. The case also includes several groups of *external PTMs. Customers* may be the most important marketers. They influence the image of the supplier and they can recommend or criticize the supplier. Our *suppliers* have opinions about us and let others know, and so do *investors, media,* and *other stakeholders and opinion leaders.* The advantage of the external PTMs is that they are not on our pay roll, but the disadvantage is that we cannot prescribe what they will say about us.

The second case concerns professional services such as management consultants, CPAs (certified public accountants), lawyers, and architects. It is common for professionals to see themselves as producers of qualified services, negotiating contracts during a limited part of their time. In small professional firms, partners and senior professionals are PTMs and they often perceive marketing as a nuisance that steals time from 'productive' work. In large professional service firms, there is usually also a specialized marketing and sales department. This department has to include experienced professionals who have a gut feeling for the

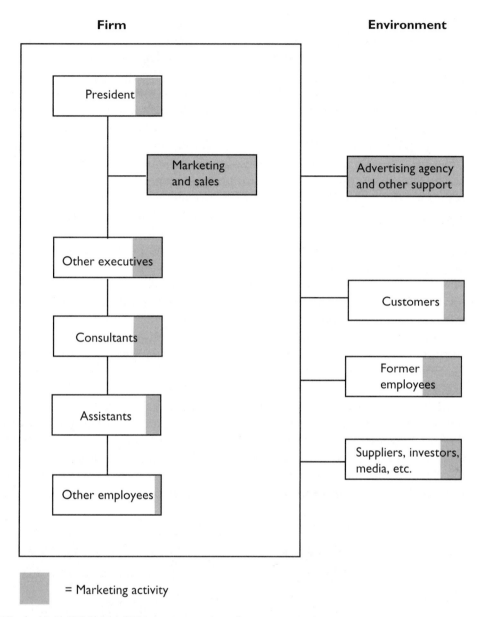

Figure 3.3 FTMs and PTMs in a consulting firm

service delivery process. In order to get leads and introductions to prospective clients and information about competitors, the department has to draw on the skills and contacts of those professionals and assistants who are carrying out assignments and have inside knowledge from the field. They also have to rely heavily on the professionals creating long-term relationships with clients leading to extended assignments. The marketing and sales departments, if they exist, are populated by FTMs, while other employees are PTMs (Figure 3.3).

Just as in the case of the manufacturing firms, there are external marketers. Present and former clients are instrumental in enhancing or degrading the image of the professional service firm. But above all *former employees* become influential PTMs. Consultants who take up positions in existing or potential client companies will buy consulting services in the future. It is therefore essential that 'beautiful exits' are offered so that departing consultants are treated well and leave gracefully, keeping a positive relationship with their former employer. Remarkably enough, many consulting firms behave naively from a marketing point of view, and make it difficult for employees to leave or to start their own business. The employer considers the consultants as owned assets and want to be compensated for damages. Other consulting firms see departures as part of their marketing strategy. The management consulting firm McKinsey with over 4000 employees in thirty-five countries, is such an example. In their recruitment brochure, they present the opportunities for consultants both to make a career inside and outside the firm. When consultants leave they are offered membership in an alumni association, become subscribers of a newsletter and are invited to various events: 'McKinsey keeps in active contact with its alumni. Wherever they go, there remains a strong bond between McKinsey and its alumni, with most people maintaining close personal and professional relationships for a lifetime'.[1] There are consulting firms who get half or more of their assignments from former employees; they have become the most valuable marketers although they are unpaid PTMs.

The PTM concept dissolves the boundaries for marketing responsibilities to embrace not only the marketing and sales departments (and probably never did in successful companies). The job of creating and maintaining market relationships is being shared between the professional FTMs and the ubiquitous 'amateurs', the PTMs. The network of contacts inside the firm, the formal and the informal, the professional and the social, become part of the marketing function.

> Everybody is either an FTM or a PTM. Those employees who do not influence the relationships to customers full time or part time, directly or indirectly, are redundant.

Relationship 5 The service encounter – interaction between the customer and the service provider

The emerging understanding of the unique properties of services has given new meaning to relationships and interaction. Marketing embraces not only the cus-

---

[1] The quotation is from a recruitment brochure for McKinsey (1991, p. 14).

tomers' contacts with sales staff but all types of contacts with the service provider's personnel and equipment during the production and delivery of the service. We can talk about *interactive marketing* but also about *interactive service development, production* and *delivery. The provider and the customer create value together.* The marketing that takes place during the interaction is often the most important, sometimes the only marketing the service provider does. Although FTMs are central to many service companies, the PTMs account for the major share of customer contact.

The interaction between customer and provider is referred to as the *service encounter*, or in popular management jargon the *moment of truth*.[2] The following interactive relationships can be defined in the service encounter, as seen from a customer perspective (Figure 3.4):

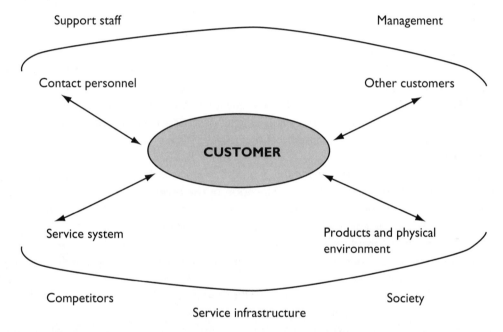

Figure 3.4 Interactive service production and marketing from the customer perspective. (Source: Gummesson, 1993; pp. 106–108)

---

[2] The concept ' moments of truth' was introduced by Normann in the 1970s (see Normann, 1991, pp. 16–17) as a metaphor for the encounter between services contact staff and a customer, borrowed from bullfighting. Like when the matador confronts the bull: 'It is the skill, the motivation and the tools employed by the firm's representative and the expectations and behaviour of the client which together will create the service delivery process.' Together with the slogan 'Customer in focus!' moments of truth reached global fame through former Scandinavian Airlines CEO Jan Carlzon (1987). In another interpretation the metaphor stands out as macabre, but not an untrue one. The critical encounter between the matador and the bull, when one of them shall die or at least outsmart the other, is sometimes a realistic description of the service encounter. To pierce the bull with a sword and kill him, or to be tossed on his horns, however, is obviously incompatible with the philosophy of RM.

- *Interaction between the provider's contact personnel (the front line) and the customer.* This can be the contact between the doctor and a patient, an advertising agency's account manager and a marketing manager, or a flight attendant and a passenger. Only if the customer cooperates during the production of the service – the patient take the prescribed medication, the marketing manager briefs the advertising agency properly, or the passenger appears at the gate on time – will the quality of production and delivery be secured. The customer becomes a co-producer and this gives rise to a different type of relationship between customer and service provider than the relationship between a customer and a manufacturer. Most customers, particularly consumers, never participate in the work in a factory, but they participate as labourers in the 'service factory'.

- *Customer-to-customer interaction.* The customers partly produce the service together if the provider offers the right system, environment, and personnel. An obvious example is the dance club. In order for its core service – dancing – to be produced, the guests must dance with each other. The provider can only make sure that the arena for interaction is inviting. Customers who wait in line or listen to a concert interact and influence the production of a service. When a city or country's team win a major championship, streets will be blocked with enthusiastic fans who celebrate the event and this is an essential part of the service quality of the event. Unfortunately, sports games increasingly attract hooligans and trigger destructive emotions leading to vandalism; a limited group of customers can ruin the quality of the service for the other customers.

- *Interaction between the customer and the provider's products and physical environment.* One example is the supermarket where the location of the products, the way in which they are exposed, the layout of the store, and the convenience of the parking will affect the customer's behaviour and their relationships to the store. The marketing director of a hamburger chain considered the most important people in his marketing department to be six architects. They designed the physical surroundings – the buildings, signs, tables, colours, music – which all add to the relationships with customers in the service factory of the fast-food restaurant. The staff are scarce and the physical environment, the 'servicescape',[3] becomes more prominent for the customer.

- *Interaction between the customer and the provider's service system.* This interaction between human beings and systems is just as important as between people, for example between man and banking systems (manual service or ATMs), or a taxpayer and the tax system. The system should be customer friendly and educational in its construction or the customers will not function well and will perceive their relationship with the provider as less satisfactory. Unfriendly systems scare customers away.

In the view of Cova,[4] the northern approaches to RM (Northern Europe, North America) advocate organized and tightly controlled customer interaction in clearly designed systems and servicescapes. The purpose is 'user value', a no-

---

[3] A term used by Bitner (1990).
[4] Cova (1997, a quotation from p. 663).

surprise service that complies with customer expectations. In contrast, the Latin School sees products and services as carriers of 'linking value', getting people together in communities where they can express individual needs as well as tribal identity. The service provider, then, should offer 'wilderness servicescapes',[5] which '...reintroduce recesses, corners and curves, fuzziness, enabling people to meet, to get together in a part-open and part-closed space that favours community encounters...' with opportunites for '...micro-events, incidents and happenings...'. The customer-to-customer interaction becomes especially pivotal, outweighing much of what is commonly referred to as superior service quality such as short waiting time and predictable delivery.

Four roles for 'personnel' can be discerned which together shape the production and delivery system. Considering their role as co-producers, the customers should be treated as members of the service providing organization, as part-time employees. *Contact staff* (the front line) consists of those who have the immediate contact with the customer. The *support staff* are found behind the line of visibility (backstage); these employees are not visible to the customer but are in interaction with the front line. Furthermore, there is *management*. By focusing on each of these roles separately it is possible to see the service encounter from different perspectives.[6] Finally, the relationships are influenced by the *competition*, and by *society in general*, such as the *service infrastructure* (for example, the availability of IT capacity).

If these roles are strictly assigned to employees and never rotate, a major problem arises. Those who never meet an external customer get no opportunity to confront customer behaviour and needs. This lack of experience makes employees hallucinate and develop phantom images of customers. It does not result in empathy. Technology can change the relationship between the provider and the customer with ensuing consequences for marketing. Banks have gradually moved their relationship from face-to-face to a *faceless relationship* via cash machines and electronic banking. Instead of going to the bank to pick up cash we go to ATMs. Bank cards connected to a credit or debit system allow you to withdraw money outside the branch office of another bank than the one where your salary is deposited or where you have your mortgage. Therefore you may not even notice at what bank you are withdrawing your money. Little personal contact will be left with the bank. The only contact person who can charm you or scare you off is represented by a call centre telephone voice, the one that happens to be available when you telephone. It means that if you need to telephone several times to settle an issue you can be sent off to different people each time. These people are rarely empowered or enabled to complete more than standarized machine-like tasks. The relationship has become mechanically neutral, even sterile. The service encounter

---

[5] According to Price, Arnould and Tierney (1996).

[6] For a discussion on different perspectives of relationships in a service organisation and the roles of the individual, see Gummesson (1993, pp. 94–112). See also the discussion on contextual matrices in the same source (pp. 108–10).

has moved from the bank office – the money retail store – to the street, the telephone, the computer, and a standardized 'human' voice.

During the service production and delivery, the interaction process offers marketing and sales opportunities – *points-of-marketing.* Good service encounters encourage the customer to speak well of the provider and eventually to become valuable PTMs. These points-of-marketing can occur in all the encounters between the customer and the provider's organization. A viable strategy in services is to establish the points which make an impact on the customers' relationship to the company and decide how to best handle them in order to cement the relationships and improve retention.

If the interaction works well, customer perceived quality will increase. The customer's *style of participation* – behaviour, lifestyle, mood – becomes important. It is particularly important in *the intensive phase* which embraces the interaction with the customer during the production of the core service.[7] The provider's ability to design and produce the service and its production/delivery system is equally crucial. The job of the customer must be deliberately matched with the job of the provider. This has led to *service design*, manifested in such techniques as service blueprinting and service mapping.[8] These are techniques for making drawings and specifications of a service. Considering that services consist of activities, the drawings resemble flow charts over the process during which the service is produced and consumed, and the organizational structure and the systems which are engaged in the process. What is new and differentiates the traditional administrative flow chart from the service drawing is the fact that the customer's behaviour and perception provide the vantage point, not the producer's systems and organizational structure.

The relationships between the consumer and the provider can be of different character. The following ten bonds have been found.[9] The first five – legal, financial, technological, geographic, and time-based – can be controlled by the provider and it can be difficult for the consumer to leave the relationship. If you have your mortgage with one bank, legal and financial dependencies are there, maybe also geographical. The remaining five bonds – knowledge-based, social, cultural, ideological, and psychological – are primarily tied to the personalities of the consumers and their perceptions of the provider.[10]

I once learnt about the doctor–patient model in which the doctor–patient relationship is '...the voluntary and trusting submission of the patient for treatment, and the essentially prescribing role of the doctor'.[11] The doctor establishes the

---

[7] Participation style and intensive phase are concepts taken from Lehtinen (1985).

[8] See Shostack (1981); and Kingman-Brundage, George and Bowen (1985).

[9] Liljander and Strandvik (1995).

[10] Although studies routinely compare differences between male and female views and behaviour, it is only recently that gender is entering research in marketing on a relational and more fundamental level; see Palmer and Bejou (1995).

[11] Cang (1976, p. 4).

patient's symptoms and prescribes a therapy and the patient follows the doctor's orders. It is a stereotype interpretation that doctors are know-all experts and patients are ignorant amateurs. It is a highly asymmetrical relationship with all the power on the doctor's side. A close look at the roots of the word 'patient' in an encyclopaedia also uncovers a bundle of obsolete, bureaucratic-legal values. A patient is a miserable creature, passively undergoing treatment, suffering, waiting, and not complaining. The reverse is also possible in service encounters if the customer bullies the staff.

These types of relationships do not develop quality in its commonly used sense. Quality is the outcome of interaction between equal parties, where each party contributes with his or her knowledge and activities. The doctor represents a competence for setting a diagnosis and recommending a remedy. The patients have knowledge about themselves and motivation to contribute to the right outcome quality, that is, eventually to become well or at least improve their health. The Ritz-Carlton Hotel Company, a chain of twenty-seven hotels with headquarters in Atlanta, Georgia, won the Baldrige Quality Award in 1992.[12] Its credo is 'We Are Ladies and Gentlemen, Serving Ladies and Gentlemen'. It proposes that the hotel staff and the guests are equals and both have a role in the service production. This is very different from the roles of master and servant or expert and amateur which still prevail in many service encounters, backed by either or both parties.

Service encounters include people with differences in life situation, demands, social status, age, sex, language, and other physical, cultural, and social aspects. As contacts are often very brief, the parties have little opportunity to develop empathy. One example of a delicate and often irritating interaction in the service encounter is tipping. Shamir (1984) claims that the custom of giving gratuities is actually what differentiates services from goods. He asks: How does tipping influence the relationship between service personnel and customers? How does a service firm, which attempts to standardize services in large scale or multiple operations, handle this tacit, uncontrollable and individualized method of payment? Tipping – which is not dealt with in the services marketing literature but has a significant effect on pricing of many services – is the outcome of economic, social, and psychological elements in the interaction between provider and customer. In the 1933 edition of the *Oxford English Dictionary*, a tip is defined as 'a small present of money given to an inferior, especially to a servant or employee of another, for a service rendered or expected'. Note the word 'inferior'! In some countries, tips were the only 'salary' for the staff. It became related to performance; those who did a good job and were pleasant could earn more. Then, in some countries, a certain percentage gratuity was added automatically to the bill; the customer was forced to pay whether the service was excellent or not. It is not clear for the customer what is included in the price of the service and what is extra

---

[12] The Malcom Baldrige National Quality Award is the prestigious US quality prize which has become a role model for quality prizes throughout the world (see also Chapter 7).

> ## Case study
>
> Two Australian resorts can serve as cases of services high up the interaction inten-
> sity scale. Lizard Island, a reservation in the Great Barrier Reef, has one hotel with
> thirty-two rooms. Its strategy is high quality service and a premium price level. All
> front-line employees address the guests by name. Meals are served at the tables and
> the guests take their time; the dinner offers a five-course menu. The days are filled
> with sports activities, among them snorkelling, diving, and boat excursions. The
> guests interact both with the staff and with each other, but guests who prefer to be
> on their own are left alone. Camp Eden – a health spa off the Australian Gold Coast
> – goes even further up the intensity scale. Thirty guests form a group during one
> week. They all arrive at the same time and in the welcome speech they are informed
> that there are two options:'Either you are here and stick to the programme or you
> are not here.' Apart from health food and physical exercise there is mandatory train-
> ing in emotional development and group relations. A guest's interaction with staff
> and other guests is sometimes so intense that conflicts occur, they may even be
> evoked as part of the service, and there is no chance for a guest to be left alone.

service. A subculture develops in which the employees, the provider, and a whole
service industry, make customers feel uneasy. For many who travel between
countries, tipping is a constant nuisance. You can pay extra everywhere to get rid
of the issue and take the cost as a necessary evil, or you can feel a constant irritation and insecurity. In some service areas and cultures, tipping has degenerated
into organized begging. To me it creates a relationship of disrespect between
contact personnel and me as customer, but it seems to be popular among US
service consumers. Or is the tipping system accepted out of tradition and not
tried for functionality, a sign of the happy slave syndrome? Furthermore, where
does tipping end and become bribes, for example in the relationship with government officials? Or with 'facilitators' in major international purchasing? (see
R17 The criminal relationship).

The intensity of relationships and interaction can vary considerably. The front-
line staff who has continuous but brief contacts with customers – the cashier in
the supermarket or bank, the receptionist and telephone operator, the waiter, the
ticket collector in the cinema – can experience emotional strain. At the Disneyland
Paris hotel New York, I found a poster in my room with Disney's 'Ten Standards
of Excellence'. Number 3 reads: 'We smile. It's contagious. Remember: we create
happiness and memories.' This seems an excellent strategy, but a demanding one.
In all intense or frequent interaction with customers, the strain on personnel is
high. The natural smile can lose its warmth and turn into just showing your teeth.
Many services are concomitant with emotions, insecurity and severe stress for the
customer, for example hospitalization, fear of flying, making certain that the

craftspeople do a proper job in repairing your house, and engaging a lawyer in a divorce case.[13]

> As all corporations which traditionally classify themselves as manufacturers also deliver services, and increasingly so, studies of the relationships in 'pure' service organizations are of general interest for marketing management.

Relationship 6 The many-headed customer and the many-headed supplier

When we leave the simple dyad, we quickly enter into increasingly more complex networks. In business marketing – including marketing via wholesalers and retailers – both the customer and the supplier can be many-headed. Companies are made up of individuals, and relationships between companies have to be tied to people in order to become tangible; the company as such is an abstraction (see Chapter 7). A company does not buy and sell, individuals do. IT offers some exceptions and the buying and selling is sometimes delegated to computers; the Procter & Gamble and Wal-Mart examples have already been mentioned. Behind the computers, however, are systems generated and maintained by people.

Models of organizational buying behaviour emerged in the 1960s and 1970s. These models are presented in marketing textbooks and often constitute the ground for the presentation of business marketing. The models have obvious merits and contribute to RM. However, additional approaches are needed in order to understand the game in which goods and services are invented, designed, produced, marketed, and bought.

In the many-headed customer and many-headed supplier relationship people representing a variety of functions and expertise on both sides participate in the marketing and purchasing process (Figure 3.5).

In order to find one's way in such a network, guidance is needed by concepts, systematic studies, long-term strategies plus stubborn endurance. Knowledge of the network becomes an asset; an investment in marketing.

The complexity of the network increases if the product consists of high-tech equipment and accompanying services and if the market is global. In this sense, Ericsson is an obvious case. Its products are telephone systems and switches and during the past decade it has become a global market leader in cellular telephony. Its largest customers are telecom operators around the globe. Ericsson has 100,000 employees, and the size of key customers varies, but usually they have some 10,000 employees or are giants like British Telecom with 175,000 people. Both parties, therefore, are large and powerful organizations. A deal concerning a new

---

[13] Goodwin (1996).

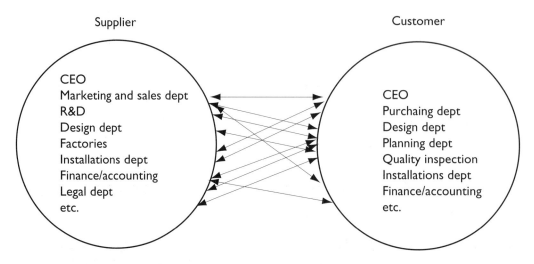

Figure 3.5 Relationships between the many-headed supplier and the many-headed customer

telephone system – which often is a matter of several hundred million US dollars – emerges in stages. Several employees are involved both from the supplier and buyer side. The following stages for such relationships have been discerned and the division in stages of the customer–supplier relationship are based on studies of Ericsson:[14]

1 *Establishing contact and credibility.* If the customer is new, the supplier must start by establishing an initial contact with the customer and create credibility. The first objective is to be considered for tendering. Professional and personal relationships need to be established with key personnel in the buying organization, usually on several organizational tiers and in different functions.
2 *Competitive bidding.* During this stage the tender is made and presented to the customer. The idea behind tendering is to 'let the best man win'. As was discussed in R2 on competition, marketing and purchasing are reduced to an allegedly 'objective' and 'unambiguous' presentation of price, technical quality, and other clearly measurable requirements which have been specified by the buyer. To advance their competitive position, suppliers circumvent the 'rational' bidding procedure; it simply becomes too burdensome. There can be intermittent contacts for clarification of specifications; illegal means through facilitating payments may be tried (R17); mega relationships with lobbying activities can play a role (R19); and so can the formation of alliances (R20).
3 *Evaluation.* Usually the law demands that evaluation of tenders must be made without contact between the bidders and buyers. However, efforts to circumvent the rules of the bidding procedure can become even more elaborate and initiate further manoeuvring than at the bidding stage.

---

[14] The division in stages of the customer–supplier relationships are based on studies of Ericsson (Gummesson, 1984).

4 *Contract.* This may be preceded by a 'letter of intent', which is a declaration that the customer is inclined to buy from the supplier. The design of the formal contract may require final negotiations and the complete deal can consist of several subcontracts.

5 *Planning, engineering, and market adaptation.* Provided the contract is landed, this stage embraces planning the execution of the contract and fitting the equipment to an individual customer's specific technical requirements. It means an ongoing relationship between Ericsson personnel and customer personnel.

6 *Production.* The relationship continues, partly with other people involved. Quality inspectors from the buyer may show up without appointment to check quality levels, to make certain that delivery dates will be kept, and to prevent problems with potential delays before they become acute.

7 *Delivery and installation.* Deliveries are made during a long period of time, sometimes several years. There is collaboration between the installation team of Ericsson and the customer's employees to make certain that the equipment and systems function according to requirements. Only when an 'acceptance test' has been completed, does the customer take over the responsibility.

8 *After sales.* In this stage the supplier must make sure that the customer is satisfied. If not, problems must be cleared up. These can be technical, but can also concern, for example, payment. This stage is an opportunity for further sales. If relationships are successfully cemented, future business will follow. The next contract goes through the same stages as before but often in a much simplified form. The buyer may not ask for bids from others, and the evaluation of the offering from the supplier is negotiated without direct competition albeit with the threat of potential competition.

9 *Conclusions and evaluation.* It is desirable to reflect over a completed deal and learn for the future, both what was good and bad. Unexpectedly, and almost in shock, Ericsson lost a prestigious deal with the national telecom of Norway. ITT, a then major competitor, won. In retrospect it was clear that Ericsson neglected to establish credibility on the mega level, among politicians and the general public, while ITT devoted considerable resources for this. ITT had hired a public relations firm and one of its tasks was to design the final bid to communicate properly, and not just become a technical document. Ericsson took for granted that its reputation in Norway was superior to that of other suppliers. An analogous pattern of events had occurred in Mexico a couple of years before, but organizational learning had not taken place as the same individuals were not in involved in both deals.

During these stages, Ericsson is represented by individual members of management, sales engineers, designers, operations management staff, educators (to train customer employees to use new equipment), financial officers, lawyers, and others. Some of these come from corporate headquarters, others from local subsidiaries. On the customer side, relationships are established with individuals from management, technical departments, planners, financial officers, lawyers, installations people, and those who receive education from Ericsson. The marketing and the whole production process become a joint project; the parties are producing value together. Both professional and social interaction is essential on these occasions.

Figure 3.6 shows a case of a complex network of relationships where the key players were Atlas Copco, an allied supplier, and a customer in Ecuador. Atlas sells equipment for drilling to be used in the construction of, for example, tunnels, and its ally represents the building and construction industry. Liljegren[15] has made a thorough analysis of the relationships and interactions in this deal. He speaks about the complex networks of relationships to the internal organization of the customer as 'customer-in-customer relationship'. Within Atlas, there were three units who wanted to deliver the whole or part of the equipment. The allied partner had three units that considered themselves in charge of the whole or part of the deal. Some thirty diagrams were used to show how the network of relationships changed during the negotiation process. Figure 3.6 shows three of these: an early stage, a middle stage, and the final stage.

It is a recurrent problem in sales management how many headed a relationship should be. The prevailing strategy of reducing the number of suppliers and integrating their activities more closely requires organizational adaptations. The organization on either side must facilitate the processes of a smooth, ongoing partnership.

Key account management[16] is a concept to provide just that, as it is specifically geared to the management of relationships with strategic customers. The concept raises a series of questions, none of them new or with a simple and general answer. Should a supplier who sells different products use different sales people for these, even if those employees who do the purchasing in the customer organization are the same? A company may have several different product lines which are somehow related, but which are bought by different people in the customer organization. An insurance company can sell retirement plans, life insurance, and fire insurance. Retirement plans and life insurance for employees may be bought by a financial or human resource department or the individual employee, while fire insurance is bought by the property management department. A management consulting company might offer many types of services – company audits, cost reduction, quality management systems, market research, executive search – and the purchases are decentralized to the users of the services. The consultants who sold the first assignment may wish to continue, since they have established relationships and trust. Another individual consultant may consider himself or herself to have excellent contacts in the company through other channels. Selling to a customer's head office may be handled by one of the offices of the consulting company. The sales to a subsidiary in another district could be handled by the first office or by the office where the subsidiary is situated. We are confronting an eternal dilemma: Who 'owns' a relationship?

R6 shows the necessity to think in terms of networks of relationships in business-to-business marketing. Up-to-date knowledge of the networks and an ability to interact and manage in these networks become the foundation for marketing strategy.

---

[15] Liljegren (1988, pp. 244 and 250).
[16] McDonald, Millman and Rogers (1997).

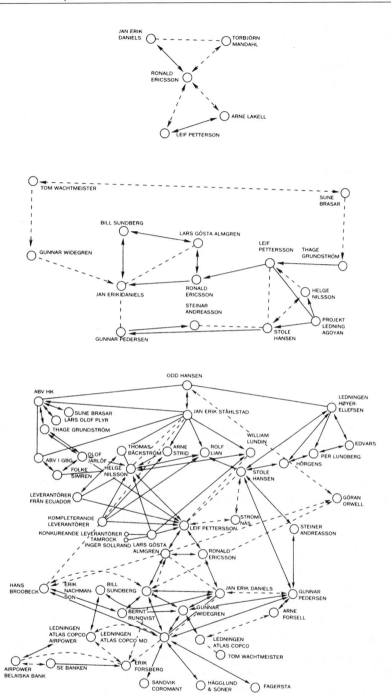

Figure 3.6 Networks of relationships. The figure shows three stages in negotiations between Atlas Copco, an allied partner, and a buyer in Ecuador. The lines mean——— regular and active relationship; - - - - - existing relationship which is irregular and passive new relationship. (Source: Liljegren, 1988; pp. 174, 243 and 255; reproduced with permission of the author)

Relationship 7 The relationship to the customer's customer

In business-to-business marketing customers are using received deliveries as input to deliveries to their customers. It can be the same product, which is sold onward, or a delivery, which goes into further manufacturing or assembly; it can be equipment or facilitating goods and services such as office supplies or security services.

Every supplier has a relationship to the customer's customer. It is there even if it is indirect and not recognized. Many products pass through several stages before they reach the end user. The stages can represent different companies, more or less related to each other. Iron ore becomes steel and then sheet steel which become components which are assembled into a car which is then sold to a consumer. In between there can be different types of distributors. This creates a dilemma: who is the customer and whose needs and specifications should be satisfied?

The dilemma has been expressed in the following way: 'It is also possible that the properties sought by the customer may not be the same, or may even be at odds with those properties required by the user further downstream. In this respect the injunction to match the product not only to the needs of the immediate client, but also to those of the user further downstream is worth recording even if this is difficult to achieve in practice'.[17] Sometimes a new product may be neutral to the intermediary, but of special value to the end-user. Should a supplier then turn directly to the end-user? This may seem rational but at the same time it means a disturbance in the relationships to the middlemen who feel that their positions are threatened. The intermediaries in turn may protect their business by withholding information and blocking personal contact between the manufacturer and the user. If the trade is international the distance grows not only physically but also culturally through differences in language and legislation.

The suppliers can choose their mission to be 'helping customers to do business with their customers'. They must then understand the customer's customer. They must understand that if a delivery does not arrive on time, the workers and the machines in the customer's factory will be idle, and the customer's customer is put in the same predicament. Chain reactions occur which may not be obvious to the first supplier in the chain. This was pointed out in R3 in connection with physical distribution, logistics, and JIT.

Ericsson must understand how telephone subscribers think and feel, as their direct customers, the telcom operating companies are only middlemen. The question is what type of relationship they should establish with their customer's customer. Ericsson's long-time strategy was not to interfere with the subscribers' behaviour or problems for fear of disturbing the relationship to the telecoms. Unfortunately, most of these were state monopolies, and several of them did not feel they should put the subscriber, above all not the household or the small firm, in focus.

---

[17] Smith and Laage-Hellman (1992, p. 47).

The importance of understanding the customer's customer is also imperative when it comes to consumer goods and retailing. A brewery uses the distinction between customers (wholesalers, retailers, restaurants) and consumers (the beer drinkers). In retail chains, the central buyers for these chains have been endowed with power over the manufacturers. They are intermediaries between manufacturers and consumers and they are closer to the consumers than the manufacturer is. The manufacturer risks not knowing enough about customer needs and behaviour and how these change. They lose the opportunity for customer interaction. To mitigate the power of the intermediaries, manufacturers take marketing action toward consumers by means of image and brand advertising and sales promotion in stores. Their representatives travel to the stores to inform, deliver promotion material, help to fill shelves, and offer samples to consumers. ECR has already been mentioned as a strategy to create a mutually beneficial partnership between manufacturer and retailer.

Today, ordering is increasingly computerized and online with suppliers. Manufacturers also do their own consumer research, for example through consumer panels who meet regularly to discuss tastes, fragrances, or new products.

In the previously mentioned study of Atlas Copco,[18] it turned out that changes with the customer's customer influenced the delivery of drilling equipment from Atlas to the construction and building industry. Atlas' customers had local and regional governments as well as factories and estate owners among their customers. Their projects varied over the years from increased production of housing, roads and bridges during the 1970s to more individual homes and large international projects at the end of the 1970s to repair and maintenance during the 1980s. Atlas had to keep track of these changes and if possible predict them.

Figure 3.7 is a generalized model of customer–supplier relationships as an endless chain. 'Company∞' signifies an undetermined number of relationships embedded in a more complex network. In order to recognize the multiple-chain relationships two more companies have been added before the consumer, the end-user, is reached.

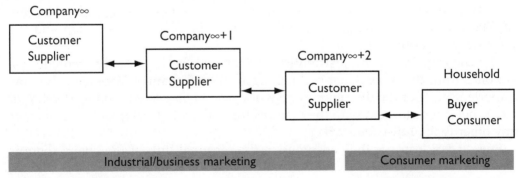

Figure 3.7 Customer–supplier–consumer relationships as a never-ending chain

---

[18] Liljegren (1988, pp. 399–401).

The relationship between Company∞+1 and Company∞+2 develops between a supplier and a customer, where the customer is an organization which resells a product as is, or after using it in manufacturing. This is business marketing. Company∞+2 must protect the relationship both to its supplier and the consumer. This is natural if we see companies as members of networks where everything that happens in the network can influence everything else. If not, the contact will be adversarial and the goal of either party becomes that of outsmarting and pushing the other for short-term profit. Companies begin to change this attitude and see suppliers as partners in a win–win relationship. AT&T talks about 'vendor relationship',[19] Philips about 'co-makership'. The term 'reverse marketing' has been coined for upstream marketing, directed to suppliers, as an addition to the ordinary downstream, customer-directed marketing. The supplier relationship is particularly crucial in times of shortage, for example during a boom.

The relationships between Company∞+2 and the buyer and consumer must also be considered by Company∞+1. The consumer constitutes the terminal point of a supply chain. We are now in the transition phase from business marketing to consumer marketing, characterized by the fact that the customer is the consumer and not a supplier to someone else. The buyer and consumer can be the same person, but in a household they can be different people. If one person buys food which the whole family and the dog eats, there is an in-household supplier–consumer relationship.

In RM, two-way relationships are emphasized, while in mass marketing relationships are primarily one way. Consumers also have an active relationship to suppliers. The notion of the seller being the aggressive party and the buyer the passive party is erroneous. Just as often an organizational buyer or consumer is the active and aggressive party; the initiative can go both directions. Consumers wish to have pleasant relationships to their retailer, gas station, hairdresser, and doctor. In times of ample supply of goods, the relationships can be dependent on a store or gas station having a courteous staff, be located in a good spot, and having a system that is known by the customer. With doctors is can be different. Through the relationship it becomes easier to get an appointment; the doctor already knows much about the consumer who can count on being well taken care of. The consumer's behaviour becomes part of the service production and the interaction determines the quality.

The construction of the distribution channel can be used to differentiate one supplier from the other. Channel management and channel leadership become important parts of the distribution network. The management and leadership of a channel can be located with the manufacturer, the wholesaler, or the retailer, or any other type of distributor.[20]

Even if you can see the consumer as the terminal link of the chain, there is

---

[19] This and the following terms are quoted from Payne (1993, p. 34).
[20] The importance of distribution channels in a network are treated by Stern, El-Ansary and Coughlan (1996).

Case study

To a consumer it is not always obvious who the supplier is. A consumer needed a new toilet. A plumber was contacted to deliver and install it. He bought the equipment from a well-known manufacturer. The toilet did not work after installation. It leaked when flushed, and the lid could hardly be lifted. When telephoning the plumber, he referred to the manufacturer as the one responsible for the guarantee, but with whom the consumer had not had any contact whatsoever. When contacting the manufacturer – a large, anonymous and disinterested organization – they told the consumer to wait for a fortnight. They considered it only natural that the bathroom was out of order for two weeks! The consumer called a member of his Rotary club – the local club is a network of members with different professions – who was president of one of the major plumbing firms and asked for advice. 'Call the head of the division and refer to me,' he said 'we are one of their biggest customers.' After several calls – the division manager was not too keen on consumer contact – he finally answered. Just as uninterested he tried to get out of it, but afraid of disturbing his relationship with the consumer's Rotary friend, he promised to fix it. All the same it took two days. The consumer felt he was the customer of the plumber whereas the plumber felt he was only an intermediary without responsibility and without customers. The manufacturer was not prepared to handle consumer relationships. Needless to say, they both lost one customer for good.

reason to point to R3 (the distribution and logistics relationship) and R15 (the green relationship) in which the fact is considered that production–consumption are increasingly viewed as an ecological cycle. Then there is no terminal point; the manufacturer or distributor becomes liable for closing the circle and recycling the product.

It is easy to lose sight of the relationships to the customer's customer or not even make an effort to look one step beyond. The relationship is there whether you care to acknowledge it or not. As our customers live by their customers, it is an intelligent marketing strategy to help our customers help satisfy their customers.

Relationship 8 The close versus the distant relationship

Both marketing literature and managers can give the impression that market surveys and research techniques, particularly the use of quantification and statis-

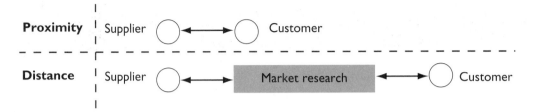

Figure 3.8 The physical proximity to the customer versus the distant relationship via market research reports

tical formulas, provide first-class knowledge about customers and the effect of marketing activities. Closeness to the customer seems to be of little significance.

In my view it is the other way around: *The interaction with customers is the single most important source of marketing knowledge and the cry for more market research is often a sign of failure.* Top management and marketing executives often have such limited contact with customers and the front line that they do not understand what is going on in the minds of customers and competitors. They are forced to hire someone to ask their customers for help and to make historical reconstructions. History is reported in seductive multi-media presentations where the design of coloured graphs, animations and music offer an illusion of knowledge. In reality they drive into the future with a steady glance in a dimmed rear-view mirror.

This was the bad side of market research. It might have sent shock waves through the minds of some readers. Sometimes market research techniques are required as certain data are difficult to access in the daily operations. Market research, with the use of approved techniques, is a supplement to the knowledge which comes naturally through customer relationships, interaction and active reflection but it is not the prime source of marketing knowledge.

The basic problem is *access* to customers, competitors, and others. The relationship to the customer can be *close* or *distant*. The close relationship is *direct* and *personal*. The distant relationship is *indirect* and *impersonal* with market survey reports as intermediaries (Figure 3.8).

The current trend goes in both directions: increased distance knowledge and increased knowledge through proximity to the customer. This is not an oxymoron. It is simply that the interest in the customer has grown dramatically in marketing practice; in the marketing textbooks it has always been there. This is of course commendable. However, market research and the techniques that are used are a consequence of the mass manufacturing and mass marketing of the industrial era. In current and future society with more customized production and marketing, mass marketing research techniques – in which individual differences are concealed and evened out – should not play the star part.

In search of access, I have found it essential to discriminate between *understanding at first hand* via personal experience and involvement, and *understanding at second hand* via intermediaries.[21] 'Experiencing customers' – through discussion, observation, participation, working at the front line, and continuous reflection – renders deeper understanding than can be reached through research performed, reported, and interpreted by others. Mass marketing largely builds on second-hand understanding and recommendations based on the interpretations of intermediaries. This is sometimes advantageous, because an outsider to the firm or the industry may see things in a new light. But it can only be supplementary. Despite the fact that techniques for market research are becoming more sophisticated, for example in search of the multiple characteristics of lifestyles, it is difficult to present valid and useful studies of consumers and the cause and effect of behaviour. Proximity, the pulse, the richness of variation – it is all degraded to standardized statements and simplistic conclusions. The customer becomes an average, a number, a percentage and sometimes even a couple of decimals. The personal relationship has turned into a *statistical relationship*.

Everything cannot be experienced, as access to the customer or the data is sometimes physically and mentally barred. This is true for certain quantitative data as answers to questions such as:

- How many customers prefer our service to that of competitors?
- How much of a specific product do they buy from us as compared to how much they spend on the product in total?
- How often do they go to the theatre?

Certain parts of marketing operations are difficult to review through presence and interaction. The closeness to the customer deteriorates when a company grows and gets thousands or millions of customers. At least, it may seem so. Small companies can get their knowledge about the customer through close relationships, but only if they are sensitive to the knowledge. This is true for stores as well as hotels and factories. R6 defined relationships between many-headed customers and many-headed suppliers. Representatives of both parties have close contact on several levels and build knowledge about one another. Alliances between suppliers and customers are often formed with the purpose of facilitating knowledge transfer (see R21, the knowledge relationship).

In hotel rooms, we find questionnaires asking guests to assess the hotel and its services. They could have a function, provided that the guests fill them out and the hotel does use the responses. Seldom do these forms tell you more than how much the hotel values your views and nothing about what they intend to do with them. I often make a list of things I am not satisfied with, but I rarely tell the hotel management. They do not give the impression that they really want to know and the risk of standing out as an odd grumbler holds me back. Despite the physical proximity that exists between a hotel guest and the staff, the mental proximity is not present and the 'communication' is left to a questionnaire.

---

[21] The concepts access, understanding, and preunderstanding are treated in Gummesson (1999).

Ingvar Kamprad, the founder and owner of IKEA, has 130 giant furniture stores in twenty-eight countries. These receive 120 million visits from shoppers in a year. As long as the stores were few, the management could keep in close touch with customers and personnel. The management of each separate store can uphold this contact, whereas international corporate headquarters in practice cannot. In order to compensate for the relationship difficulty, 'anti-bureaucrat weeks' were introduced. During these weeks, staff from the corporate head office work in the stores. In an interview, Kamprad said that he does not trust statistics or reports; he wants to be directly confronted with reality.

Hyatt Hotels send their bosses to 'In-Touch Days' and on one day per year head office is closed for all, including the CEO. Top managers work as janitors, cleaners and in other hands-on jobs. This is excellent *per se*, but a single day or week is short for the day-to-day reality to get under your skin. As an IKEA executive said: 'You are just a guest to reality.'[22]

The old expression 'all business is local' also concerns today's global society. Joshua Tetley in the UK controls some thousand pubs. In order to strengthen the personal relationship to the consumer, the '100 Club' was established. Eligible for membership were personnel who knew the name and habits of a minimum of 100 guests. A misgiving was expressed that no one would qualify for membership, but the outcome was staggering. 250 employees knew the names of 500 customers or more; fifty could address 1000 customers by name; and the champion could address 2000 customers.[23]

The Italian Benetton family, merchants of branded fashion clothes and accessories, has 6400 franchized shops in some hundred countries. Its founder, Luciano Benetton, travels to the stores to exercise leadership and collect his own impressions; as do 200 of his staff. Furthermore, the Benetton shops are part of an online computer network, which enables global monitoring of current sales. This is both a close and distant relationship, based on both personal contact, utilization of state-of-the-art IT, and streamlined logistics.

Instead of measuring customer relationships at a distance, a company could engage the customers in interactive improvement and development work. Marriott Hotels collaborated with business travellers in the design of the motel chain Courtyard. When the Swedish Railroads launched the long distance rapid train service X2000, the introduction was a six-month test period and this was explained in the advertising. Business travellers were offered free tickets to make them test the train as an alternative to flying. The railroads dared not let the train travel at full speed in the beginning as it put high demands on the rail network and safety precautions. A railroad operation is a closed network and all train movements, such as delays, affect all other trains. Personal interviews were made on board the train with a sample of passengers, and questionnaires were distributed to all passengers.

---

[22] The data on IKEA are based on documents and a presentation by Pelle Zandén (1992).
[23] According to Tetley's Personnel Director, Terry Lunn (1990).

The staff was selected for those with the capacity of listening, observing and suggesting improvements. The train crew convened before departure and after arrival to plan and assess the journey. They also had regular meetings with management. The 'product manager' of this particular train service also travelled on the train several times per week. Taken together, the railway company deployed both the personal face-to-face relationship and systematic, standardized, and continuous information as support. Moreover, the interactive research became a way of engaging and influencing the customers – it became an important part of the promotion.

The examples show that it is possible to keep close contact with the front line – both staff and customers – even if the operations are large scale. The real impediment is not size, it is soiled relationship eye-glasses and lack of innovation. Supplementary input from other sources such as the deployment of market research techniques can add to the knowledge.

Social and psychic distance are key concepts in RM. The further we are apart the greater the risk for misunderstandings. This can be particularly disturbing in international trade where not only physical distance but also culture and language raise obstacles.[24] If customers are kept at arm's length and are only percentages and anonymous masses, you do not apply the same ethical standards as if you are close to the customer. Anthropological studies have given rise to the hypothesis that honesty in exchange relationships is inversely related to the social distance.[25] Studies of fraud show that staff do not feel as much hesitation to cheat an anonymous customer as they would a person they know and meet. Blumberg sums up his conclusions in the following way: 'The injury done to others is often impersonal… . People die in automobiles far from those who have designed them. Smokers die quietly far from those who manufacture and advertise cigarettes…in a large bureaucratic organization people abandon their role as full moral human beings'.[26]

Management and personnel can hide in large organizations and systems, and rarely have to take direct responsibility for the relationship to the customer. Through size and distance, large scale promotes inferior ethics and inferior relationships. However, the distance can be reduced in many ways and several of the 30Rs concern the reduction of social and mental distances.

My conclusion is unequivocal:

> You can only understand customers by regularly meeting them, training your empathy, and reflecting over your observations.

---

[24] Hallén and Widersheim-Paul (1979).
[25] Czepiel (1990).
[26] Blumberg (1989, pp. 106–9).

Relationship 9 The relationship to the dissatisfied customer

When customers are dissatisfied with the relationship with their present supplier, they have the following options:[27]

- *Exit* – The customers leave for a competitor, or stop buying the goods or services temporarily or permanently.
- *Voice* – The customers speak their mind and demand correction.
- *Loyalty* – The customers remain loyal for lack of alternative suppliers or prohibitive switching costs, inertia, ideological reasons and others, at least within limits.

All these options are used by customers. The feelings behind them, however, are largely a black box to suppliers. When British Airways commenced its quality improvement programme in the 1980s they were surprised by the reaction from customers: 'Recovery was the term we coined to describe a very frequently repeated concern: if something goes wrong, as it often does, will anybody make a special effort to set it right? Will someone go out of his or her way to make amends to the customer? Does anybody make an effort to offset the negative effects of the screw-up? Does anyone even know how to deliver a simple apology?'.[28]

Recovery is more than settling a claim, it is the restoration and strengthening of a long-term relationship. The course of action must be constructive, not just mechanical or routine. *Complaint management* is becoming a discipline of its own.

In the spirit of modern quality management, a zero-defects strategy – always doing it right the first time – should be pursued. Errors will occur despite the strategy, particularly in service production. A positive way of dealing with the error must be designed into the customer relationship. In brief: 'Combine ultra-reliability with excellent recovery'.[29] The conclusion builds on research which says that 'reliability' is the central quality dimension – the product should not break, the train should leave on time, the customer must be able to trust the hotel room reservation.

An often suggested strategy, particularly in the USA and Japan, is 'customer delight', not only meeting customer expectations but giving a little extra. Applied to complaints management it would mean being generous, overcompensating the customer. It is a delicate balancing act between giving just enough and giving too little or too much. To add to the dilemma, customers have individual and changing expectations and demands. A study of Norwegian consumers indicated that it was not necessary to delight customers in order to regain their confidence and loyalty.[30] The requirement was compensation for actual cost, ascertaining that the

---

[27] According to Hirschman (1970).
[28] Albrecht and Zemke (1985, p. 34).
[29] Berry (1989, p. 27).
[30] Andreassen (1997, p. 209–13).

customer perceived the treatment as fair. The study further showed that single negative experiences – properly settled – did not make customers defect.

Two cases from a study of critical incidents in the relationship between consumers of retail banking may serve as illustrations to alternative treatment of dissatisfaction:[31]

1 A customer wanted to withdraw money from an ATM but only received a fraction of the amount. The customer telephoned the bank who promised to make an instant investigation. Service staff were sent to the ATM and they noted that banknotes were stuck in the machine. The incident has not impaired the relationship with the bank as the bank took the customer seriously and quickly solved the problem.

2 A man and a woman had standing orders for payments coupled with their accounts. They later opened a new account together and informed the bank that the standing orders now should be charged to their joint account. The woman later received a letter which claimed she had overdrawn on her account and that continued overdrafts would ruin any possibility of future loans. She concluded that the bank erroneously had proceeded to withdraw money from her old account and told the bank so. The bank clerk promised to correct the mistake, but nothing happened. After further contacts with the clerk and with others in the bank no correction was made. The customer lost her trust in the bank and transferred to another bank; she 'didn't want to nag any more'.

In the first case the bank acted correctly although not with any particular generosity. In both cases, the banks caused the customer costs, trouble and insecurity; in the second case maybe even sleepless nights and depression. The demonstration of social, mental, and physical distance – a tradition of many bank managers and clerks to shield themselves from mismanaged relationships – obstructs the application of RM. From the bank perspective the customer is a free utility. When banks charge for their services, they should naturally pay 'fees' when they cause customers extra work. The production of bank services is an interaction where the customer does most of the job. If the customer has power over the bank by being a major corporation, the customer can influence the conditions and 'voice' compensation. In many places today, the bank culture is so uniformly uncooperative that 'exit' is no actual alternative for consumers or small firms; the grass is not greener elsewhere.

The inability to understand the customers' lack of power in a relationship when a bank has failed, when passengers miss their connection, or when a hospital gives a patient the wrong therapy, is no less than tragic. Most of us have encountered situations of this kind. Why do they arise? I have never been able to grasp why the same mistakes must be repeated over and over again, so that eventually you believe that is the way it must be. Nor have I been able to reconcile with it. Is it incompetence, deficient systems, indifference, lack of empathy, arrogance? I am

---

[31] From Olsen (1992, p. 369) who reports 272 critical incidents in his study.

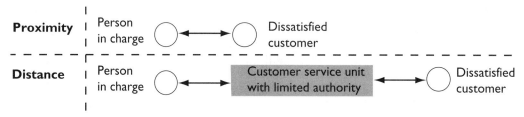

Figure 3.9 Alternative relationships to the dissatisfied customer

inclined to conclude that all of these explanations have validity.

Usually members of the front-line staff cannot correct mistakes themselves as these are designed into the goods, services, systems, organization, and resources. Therefore, management should promote both vertical interaction between the layers of the hierarchy and horizontal interaction between departments and functions (see further R25). From the quality awards that have now been introduced around the world, it is obvious that quality can never be made certain unless the whole organization is geared toward quality. According to one of the best-known quality crusaders, Edwards Deming (1986), the operating staff can only correct a small percentage of defects; the majority are built into the systems and organizational structure.

In the same way as in R8 – the close versus the distant relationship – dissatisfaction can be handled through direct contact with decision-makers or indirectly through middlemen (Figure 3.9). Companies have established customer service departments and call centres to handle customer relationships, concerning service, information, and complaints. The ability of a member of a call centre to relate to dissatisfied customers is strongly dependent on personality, but also on the organizational culture. Sometimes call centres are outsourced to telemarketing companies. If their contact staff have been both empowered and enabled to solve complaints when and where they arise, disputes can be settled quickly and smoothly. Unfortunately, at the same customer department you can encounter anything from empathic employees who graciously set things right to hibernating Soviet commissars.

There can be several reasons for establishing a customer service department.[32] One is to unload people in the organization from continuous disturbances caused by calls or letters from customers. Another is to keep customers at arm's length, a third to get away by stalling. At the same time as a customer service department is established, a natural access opportunity between customers and managers is abolished. The good intentions of proactive complaint management turns into a vicious circle. Customer service staff can experience difficulties with their internal relationships to support staff, such as middle managers. The experience and knowledge that piles up at customer service may never reach the bosses; if cus-

---

[32] See further Fornell and Wernerfelt (1988); and Fornell and Westbrook (1984).

tomer service employees become too obtrusive in their efforts to get internal response, they may get in trouble. The messengers of bad news risk getting their career paths blocked.

The Baldrige Quality Award lists complaint management as a special 'area':[33]

> The principal issue is prompt and effective resolution of complaints, including recovery of customer confidence. However, the Area also addresses how the company learns from complaints and ensures that production/delivery process employees receive information needed to eliminate the causes of complaints. Effective elimination of the causes of complaints involves aggregation of complaint information from all sources for evaluation and use throughout the company. The complaint management process might include analysis and priority setting for improvement projects based upon potential cost impact of complaints, taking into account customer retention related to resolution effectiveness.

It is imperative to separate what is right from strictly legal considerations and technicalities, and what is right from a long-term relationship perspective. If a customer has bought machinery and made modifications, which in turn cause disturbances, the supplier is probably not legally responsible to repair the machinery. In Japan and many other countries, the correct relationship strategy is often to offer assistance to the buyer without charge. The production manager who initiated the modifications may be criticized by his superiors. He comes out of this predicament if the supplier takes the blame. As a consequence 'he owes you one', which opens up for future deliveries. It is not a matter of the repair cost, it is a matter of investment in long-term relationships. It is an RM cost, not a manufacturing cost.[34]

Being both employees and consumers, many of us have noticed that a customer complaint resolved well creates a solid relationship, sometimes even better than it was before the incident. There are companies that do not take performance too seriously, but are very prone to settle disputes in a generous way. There are even stories about companies which deliberately make mistakes just to be able to show how good they are at correcting them. I am not sure, however, that is a commendable marketing strategy.

Frequently, the customer does not know whom to talk to. The person who receives the complaint is often badly trained, has low status in the organization, and little chance of contacts higher up in the hierarchy. Silly replies and explanations should therefore not in the first place be attributed to front-line staff but to their president and top managers. Furthermore, consumers in many cultures are too timid to ask for recovery. Japanese consumers raise their voices, although

---

[33] Malcolm Baldrige (1997, Area 3.2, p. 23).
[34] The Japanese example is taken from Delaryd (1989, p. 69).

politely, and the supplier makes apologies. The important thing is to restore trust, or the Japanese customer will be quick to inform authorities and others.

In her report on trends, Popcorn claims that the vigilante consumer who takes personal action, is a new and growing phenomenon in the USA: 'For years, consumers couldn't see the man at the top of the corporate ladder. Now we want him out front, and held accountable'.[35] Apart from directly criminal operations, the worst sinners are found in the government sector. Officials have been able to hide behind locked doors, lawyers, and stalling tactics. This seems to be changing, but only slowly.

Offering a guarantee is a way of preventing customer dissatisfaction. Richard Chase, professor at the University of Southern California, Los Angeles, has introduced a course guarantee. The students who were not satisfied were promised $250 plus reimbursement of course material expenses. During the first years of its existence no student has evoked the guarantee. Guarantees in services, however, are scarce even though they have been more attended to during the past few years. Warranties for goods have been there a long time, even if they often imply extensive extra work for the customer. The fact that there is a guarantee can exert pressure on a company to do a better job as evoking the guarantee is an indicator of failure.

Unfortunately, it is often inconvenient for customers to use a guarantee. A good guarantee shall fulfil the following requirements:[36]

- be unconditional and free of the fine print in legalese, and not make exceptions for everything of importance;
- in clear and simple terms state what the customer needs to know;
- focus on customer needs;
- be meaningful both to the customer and the supplier;
- easy to evoke;
- the customer should not have to beg for its implementation.

The customer and the supplier front-line personnel face a particularly loaded moment of truth when a customer is dissatisfied, be it for goods or services. According to one study, a customer whose complaints have not been solved well will tell ten to twenty people; one who gets well treated will tell only five.[37] This shows the merciless revenge that can be taken by dissatisfied customers in their role of PTMs, and the value of the satisfied PTMs. Furthermore, it is claimed that research shows that few consumers raise their voice when dissatisfied. On the other hand, they punish the supplier by exiting, now or later.

Initially, the options of exit, voice, and loyalty were quoted. In the spirit of RM I would like to add a fourth option – *collaboration*. The parties solve a problem

---

[35] Popcorn (1992, p. 69ff).
[36] This is based on Heskett, Sasser and Hart (1990, pp. 89–90). They solely deal with service guarantees but the same guidelines seem applicable to goods, too.
[37] TARP (1986, p. 50).

together – in interaction – with the purpose of creating joint value out of the current situation. It has already been advocated that collaboration is the most significant contribution from RM to general marketing.

Relationship 10 The monopoly relationship – the customer or supplier as prisoners

This section is about *monopoly* and how monopoly affects the relationship to customers, suppliers, and other interacting parties. Economic theory talks about monopoly when there is only one supplier, and *monopsony* when there is only one customer.[38] The term monoply will be used here to denote any party who has power over another in a relationship; monopoly is accepted jargon for power and power misuse. It is an asymmetrical relationship, where one party has unlimited, or almost unlimited, control over the other party.

The causes for pursuing a monopoly strategy are manifold: can be caused by lack of empathy between the parties in a network; one party's desire to dominate over the other and misuse power; short-term greed; or simply the adherence to a taken-for-granted tradition.

I would like to introduce the concept *power organization* for a company or public agency that has power, either as a traditional monopoly, or by being in a relationship where the customer or any other party is in practice imprisoned. Monopolies can, however, be both benevolent and predatory. A series of examples will show different types of monopolies.

We are involved in more monopoly relationships than we are aware of. In several of the 30Rs abuse has been brought to the fore leading to captivity instead of freedom. Table 3.1 features a sample of these.

A subcontractor can be in the palm of a single customer. The customer demands reports of the subcontractor's costs, and the price is set by the customer. The subcontractor's business becomes customer controlled, most evident in a JIT system. When IKEA demanded a price cut from suppliers by 15 per cent, suppliers had two choices: comply and face a challenge, or go bust. Finding a new large customer in a recession is next to impossible but the demand from the buyer may be an incentive to cut fat out of the organization and its processes. Power can be used constructively for a symbiotic rather than a parasitic relationship. By being dependent on a big and responsible customer, the small supplier enjoys a certain security and stability. A big customer can also be dependent on continuous delivery. If the switching-costs are sizeable, a small supplier has power. This is particularly so if the companies are structurally dependent after having integrated their systems and product or service development, or if the supplier offers a unique strategic component or service.

---

[38] Monopoly, and monopsony come from Greek 'monos', alone; 'polein', sell; and 'opsonein', buying food.

Table 3.1 Examples of power organization effects on relationships.

R9 The relationship to the dissatisfied customer	A product or service fails and the supplier makes it difficult for the consumer to evoke the warranty
R11 The customer as 'member'	It can be expensive for the customer to change supplier (high switching cost) through negative pricing (penalty for leaving).
R16 The law-based relationship	Legal technicalities are misused; the power organization dictates 'justice'.
R18 Personal and social networks	Can require unwanted social adaptation, but not being in the network can make business impossible.
R20 Alliances	Alliances can create power industries where every supplier behaves uniformly and no genuine alternative remains for the customers.
R22 Megaalliances	Misgivings that the EU will force small member countries to accept rules and activities that impair their economy.

'Power corrupts,' says a well-known adage. Corruption in business is usually associated with *financial corruption*, that those in power are paid unofficially or enjoy freebies. The 'nomenklatura' of former communist countries – the upper class of the classless society – was corrupt in this way and a large number of them survive today in the new economies retaining similar or even better privileges.

There is also *mental corruption* in which you imprison both others and yourself. Morgan's (1997) metaphor of the company as a psychic prison can be transferred to the customer's and supplier's propensity to handcuff themselves. The American auto industry became inmates of its own escape-proof cells built on its historical record of success. When the small car arrived – first the German Volkswagen and later Japanese cars – the auto industry could not absorb the information or adjust to the new competition. It did not understand the small car concept. It did not want to understand the combination of improved quality and lower price of the Japanese car. When consumerist Ralph Nader suspected General Motors' Chevrolet Corvair to be defectively designed and that this was the cause of hitherto unexplained accidents, the manufacturers did not listen and examine the suspicion. They knew. In industry conventions, the car-makers determined that such accidents were caused by 'driver error', a catch-all concept for unexplained events that was erroneously perceived as an explanation. The design could simply not be deficient.[39]

Public agencies can only plead the prerogative of making authoritarian deci-

---

[39] Nader (1965).

sions when such power is called for and adds value to society and its citizens; only then should they be allowed to act as power organizations. Those who travel by air, are often imprisoned by airport authorities and sometimes by airlines. An airport authority must have full and undisputed authority in air traffic control. But it should not impose this power on services in general. Authorities embrace bureaucratic–legal values which are in direct confrontation with RM. An airline has a certain market share protection through 'slots', these are the permits to traffic the airport at certain times. If they have concessions and the attractiveness of the destination is growing – like Brussels because of the EU headquarters – airlines will continue to get more passengers, irrespective of the quality of their services.

If you have installed oil heating in your house, you are forced to buy oil. The installation is so costly that the sacrifice in money, time, and trouble provides an insurmountable switching cost. Same thing if you have your mortgage in a bank and a long-term contract, or if you live in a place with no choice of convenience stores. Hotels in Northern Europe usually include a self-service buffet breakfast in the room price. In some countries this is rare; premium prices are asked; the customer has to wait to be seated; wait for service; and be expected to enjoy somebody else's idea of a standardized breakfast. The breakfast customer is treated as a prisoner. Remarkably enough a majority of guests succumb to this treatment, probably being under the impression that this is the way it must be.

It is possible to order, for example, theatre tickets by giving your credit card number over the telephone. As no ID and no signature are required, it opens up the possibilities for fraud at the same time as it is convenient for both the theatre and the customer. When credit card companies try to create relationships with customers through the legal system (see further R16) by utilizing force and the customer's lack of power, they become power organizations. They cannot constructively exploit the benefits of RM. Such behaviour is not only unethical, it represents a stupid marketing strategy.

Official monopolies are not the same as real monopolies. Nor is the presence of several suppliers a guarantee for absence of power organizations. If all companies in an industry belong to alliances, social networks, and trade associations they become power organizations, even if they seem to compete. Together they constitute *power industries*. From the customer's point of view, there is no actual competition when the suppliers are primarily protecting each other. There is no choice, everybody is as good or bad as the other. The relationship between the competitors has then become too collaborative, they have become colleagues instead of rivals. They meet in the industry association to unite against the ugly customers, authorities, and other 'threats'.

Many successful upstarts have clashed with the accepted practices of the trade, set up by an established power industry. In its early days, IKEA was perceived as a threat to the traditional furniture stores and as it turned out rightly so. The reaction, however, was less appropriate. Instead of improving themselves, the members of the industry used the hyper competition strategy to harass manufacturers and threaten to blacklist them if they delivered to IKEA. Eventually, IKEA had to turn to suppliers behind the Iron Curtain, which proved to be a brilliant strategy and still is. Finland has kept IKEA out for thirty years through the lobbying of the local retailers. BBBK, a pest control company in the United States was frowned upon by the industry when it introduced unconditional guarantees. The establishment of the trade had monopolized truth and functionality.

Within some areas of expertise, competition is curbed with reference to 'scientific requirements' and 'scientific evidence'. We can call these *expert monopolies* protected by *expert power*. Within these restrictions, they can do a lot of good in certain areas. It is when they believe that their expertise is the one and only approach and they begin to fight competition based on rival approaches and new developments, that they become a menace to the free market. Health care is an obvious case. The medical establishment and its perception of what science is puts limitations on the development of medicine. This is sometimes for the benefit of customers and citizens, sometimes not. For example, ordinary patients and practising dentists have observed and suspected that fillings, primarily amalgam based on poisonous mercury, could cause severe disorders. In many countries this is stamped as nonsense by the representatives of dental research and assigned to mental problems; the patients are referred to psychiatrists. The reason is 'lack of scientific evidence', a declaration so devastating that consumers and practising dentists are knocked out. Lack of scientific evidence, however, only means that nothing has been discovered through the application of routine and narrowly delimited research techniques, not that an observation is untrue. More innovative and adequate research techniques could show different results. 'Truth' had become the monopoly of a power industry. Until 1997, with reference to 'science' and legal technicalities, a united power industry claimed that cigarette smoking did not cause lung cancer and was not addictive.

When the Consumer Cooperative was founded in 1844 in Rochdale, England, the customer was truly a prisoner. The factory owners ran the stores, set the prices, and let the workers buy on credit. As long as the workers were in debt to factory owners, they could not leave their jobs, they were imprisoned. The co-op released the prisoners.

In the cases where a company has a real monopoly, it can disregard customers. Monopolies therefore become complacent, fat, and lazy. There can be exceptions, however, provided that customer-oriented values prevail. In some countries – among them Finland, Norway, and Sweden – spirits, wine, and strong beer are only sold in state-owned monopoly stores. The purpose is to keep excessive drinking down. The Swedish retail monopoly on alcohol has a demanding mission: lower the consumption of alcohol by promoting sounder drinking habits, develop a taste for wine at the expense of hard liquor, and offer an attractive product line in high-quality and high-productivity stores. How much of the alcohol consumption that goes beside the monopoly is difficult to assess; a monopoly is rarely absolute. Buying alcohol in other countries or at tax-free stores at airports and on ferries are options for the traveller; private production may be illegal but is carried out all the same.

If competition grows because of deregulation, the arrival of substitutes, or the product loses its flair, the monopoly must either adjust or close down its operation. Public agencies often have a monopoly and react in different ways, sometimes by adjusting to new conditions, sometimes by demanding more protective legislation, sometimes by support from ideologies or politicians.

According to the original bureaucratic–legal values, it is a virtue to be inaccessible. Personal contact is replaced by impersonal 'systems contact'. People should have positions, be easy to substitute, go by the book, and handle each case 'objectively'. This, in practice, only works for extremely simple and standardized matters. A more customer-oriented approach has been introduced in some niches of the public sector. After having been a dirty word, marketing has gained acceptance, and has in some cases even become a fashionable buzz word. Government organizations and authorities have been forced to obtain revenue from other sources than taxes, which requires marketing. Unfortunately, they often mistake marketing for colourful advertisements, glossy brochures, and a fancy logo, and do not introduce a changed mode of operations with the customer and citizen in focus.

Organizations also have *internal monopolies.* Forrester succinctly expressed this more than thirty years ago:[40]

> On a national level monopolies are forbidden because of their stultifying influence on economic efficiency. Yet within corporations monopolies are often created in the name of presumed efficiency and are defended as avoiding duplications efforts. For most activities the economies of scale are not as great as commonly supposed...It should be a principle...that every type of...service must exist in multiple. No person is limited to a single source for his needs. No person is dependent on a single user of his output.

A rationale for the decentralized organization is to provide profit centres with the choice between insourcing and outsourcing (see R24).

In conclusion, a power organization and power industry can lock an economy into a permanent marketing disequilibrium. Sometimes, though, monopolies and unrestricted power are required for security and human reasons. In general, however, the market economy works best when there is an ongoing search to balance competition, collaboration, and regulations/institutions.

Relationship 11 The customer as 'member'

If you buy a Harley-Davidson, the king of motorcycles, you become a member of Harley Owners' Group, HOG, with 360,000 members, spread around the globe in

---

[40] Quoted from Forrester (1993).

1000 local chapters. The club offers insurance, emergency assistance, contests, magazines, and most important the opportunity to make friends and hit the road with other Harley fans.

HOG is an example of a growing marketing strategy: 'membership' for commercial purposes. Membership usually means being a member of an association for idealistic reasons, personal development, sports, and leisure activities. *Genuine membership* is non-commercial or commercial in a cooperative sense; it is not there primarily for a profit reason. We are also 'members' of a nation or a mega alliance such as the Nafta or EU, but there we are not just customers, we are also *citizens*.

Membership is used commercially to reinforce customer loyalty and to promote long-term relationships. There are combinations of genuine membership and commercial purposes, for example through affinity cards. Affinity credit cards are issued to members and supporters of a special organization and cause, for example World Wildlife Fund and the protection of endangered species. They require a relationship between a credit-card company, an affinity group that gives the issuer access to their membership list for marketing purposes, and the members. In return the issuer makes payments to the affinity group, the size being dependent on the number of cards issued and the frequency with which they are used.[41]

Membership can be demanding or non-demanding. The customer who wants to visit a 'private' nightclub might be able to enlist at the door, maybe only for a single night. Membership of golf clubs may cost thousands of dollars per year, and there are even exclusive clubs that charge US$100,000 or more. The strategy of subscription is close to membership; you pay as long as you do not cancel your relationship to the telecom provider, the *Wall Street Journal*, or the bank.[42] If everybody can become members with a simple qualification and the relationship is commercial, it is a *pseudo membership*, not a genuine membership.[43]

The following way of classifying pseudo membership has been suggested:[44] *full choice* for the customer (the customer can choose to be in or out, but can use the supplier in either case), *price-driven membership* (offers lower prices), *earned membership* (you must spend a certain amount of money to qualify for benefits), and *access membership* (only members get access to the goods or services). If membership is easy to copy, it loses some or all of its impact on the market. The relationship gets thin with little customer commitment.

The idea behind a cooperative is that the members themselves own and run the operations as an economic and democratic association. The consumer cooperative emerged in the nineteenth century because the retailing, banking and housing

---

[41] See Worthington and Horne (1993).
[42] See Lovelock's (1983) classification of 'membership relationship' and 'no formal relationship'.
[43] Björn Lindvall has drawn my attention to the risk of commercializing genuine membership by appointing the members 'customers'.
[44] Gruen and Ferguson (1994).

industries were mismanaged. In the spirit of the original cooperative idea, the consumers shopped in their own stores and were genuine members. This turned into a pseudo membership when the co-ops grew in size and members became anonymous and lost their individual influence on the stores. The members became just customers and the strong loyalty advantage, which differentiated co-ops from other stores, was lost.

With 130 furniture stores, a growth rate of ten stores a year, activities in twenty-eight countries, and 1500 suppliers of 12,000 different products, IKEA develops and maintains a complex network of relationships. The most intimate relationships between the customers and IKEA are established when customers visit a store. The relationships, however, must be kept alive from a distance. One activity is the yearly mailing of sixty million catalogues. Another is membership in the IKEA Family, which gives benefits such as discounts and pre-sale invitations. In the early 1990s there were two million members in ten countries. Members buy 30 per cent more than non-members and the contact is upheld with five to six letters per year. 'Warehouse clubs' have grown quickly in America.[45] In 1985 sales were $4 billion and had increased to $35 billion in 1992, an annual growth of 25 per cent. The strategy is:

- low price and strictly for members;
- low cost locations but still accessible;
- concentration on the most popular brands;
- 4000 articles instead of 80,000 in a full service store;
- rapid turnover of goods;
- only cash;
- no advertising;
- large packages;
- other cost saving measures.

Sales of fresh food has increased and now account for one fourth. Through acquisitions, four chains have 90 per cent of the market share.

Frequent flyers' loyalty programmes are the technically most advanced attempts to create long-term individual relationships through membership.[46] The member collects points for travelled mileage and can turn these points into free airline tickets. Membership gives access to special check-in facilities, lounges with free meals and newspapers, and availability of various services like fax. British Airways have gone far in customizing meals. On long distance flights, the members of the Executive Club are offered a choice of seven special meals (apart from the standard offer): 'Asian vegetarian, vegetarian (lacto-ovo), vegetarian (non dairy), kosher, Hindu, Muslim, and sea-food.' In addition, there are eleven variants of 'medical meals'.

---

[45] Degan (1992).
[46] The data on the frequent flyers' programmes are primarily taken from Rice (1993).

With its AAdvantage programme, American Airlines were the pioneers in the beginning of the 1980s. Ten years later they had sixteen million members in the United States and the regime had spread to airlines around the world. Today no major carrier can exist without a loyalty programme.

In the USA there are thirty million members in the airlines loyalty programmes, but an assessment have shown that only 15 per cent make use of the benefits. Many become members of several programmes, but the real pros stick to one or maybe two airlines. One of the best relationship strategies has proved to be the upgrading of members to elite status: silver, gold, platinum cards. This gives extra benefits, for example that every mile is counted as two miles if you carry a gold card. The purpose is to increase share of customer, that is the ratio of a customer's total purchases of a specific product or service that goes to a specific supplier.

Members must guard their rights. At some airlines, the points expire after three years, at others they are valid forever, at still others they can only be used on certain dates. At the beginning of the 1990s, American Airlines blocked twenty-six days per annum while United blocked 150. The mileage needed for free tickets varies. Continental offered one free round trip ticket USA–Europe after 35,000 miles (60,000 kilometres) while Delta required double. There can be fine print regulations which confuse the members. If the airline goes bankrupt, there is insurance with Lloyd's to protect the mileage gained. The member can choose to become a mileage donor to, for example, 'Miles for Kids in Need'.

Membership provides a unique opportunity to maintain a database record of each customer with a potential for individual treatment. The use of certain data, however, may conflict with laws on privacy. In applying for the SAS EuroBonus membership you have to sign an agreement to the following: 'SAS will register the information you give in this application and use it as a base for marketing communication. SAS will record when you order a ticket. This is necessary in order to calculate the points that give you the EuroBonus benefits.'

Information about individual customers has been used in the practice of marketing long before the advent of IT, but marketing theory has been preoccupied with averages and masses. USAA in San Antonio, Texas, was founded on insuring motor vehicles of military officers and their families, but their operations have since been broadened. For USAA it is advantageous to insure a homogeneous group, characterized by an economy in good order. Historical statistics, which are the grounds for insurance, offer reliable predictions. The company takes service quality seriously, for instance by calling the customer after a claim has been processed to make certain that they are satisfied.

Trading stamps or gifts, which have long been used to promote loyalty, give little continuous customer information. The pseudo membership and the card offer better opportunities. Argos is a card system in which the consumer collects points for purchases, which can later be used in Argos-associated stores. Any retailer can join the system. In the UK, the retail chains Boots and Sainsbury offer the possibility of collecting points for train and airline tickets.

The value of a customer database can easily be overrated, it is not self-organizing. It offers an opportunity, which demands active management and innovative and systematic utilization. Database marketing is likely to develop continuously during the next decade; it is often presented as the greatest advantage of IT with the opportunities it gives to increase customer retention.

There is no doubt that pseudo membership provides benefits to customers. But it also requires work from the customer. The provider and the customer are co-producers of a win–win relationship although the many and sometimes intricate membership regulations can make customers behave irrationally. For example, upgrading on flights has proven attractive for business people. Instead of arriving just before check-in and boarding time surprisingly many come even two hours before to line up for a possible upgrade. The customer may become imprisoned in a rat race for benefits. Furthermore, being a member in too many commercial clubs makes it difficult to keep track of all the cards, codes, and offerings.

In summary, membership serves the following purposes for the supplier:

1 it helps increase retention and share of customer;
2 it provides more information about customers, and IT makes it possible to build a database of any number of customers, thus replacing blunt mass marketing with targeted communication and customized offerings;
3 if the competition offers membership, an individual supplier may have to join in order to stay in the market.

Relationship 12 The electronic relationship

Electronic relationships are formed through the new media of the 'IT triangle': computers, telecommunications, and television.[47] The IT triangle offers marketing a distant relationship which is more interactive than traditional mass media and the earlier use of electronics. Interactivity and the possibility of quick access and response may also make distant relationships become closer relationships.

Although IT is presented as conveying and processing information in a richer and faster way, it offers primarily media – conduit – and not content. A letter does not improve in content because it is written on a computer or sent via the internet. On the other hand there is a link between content and media. Even if we do not entirely subscribe to Marshall McLuhan's famous thesis that 'the medium is the message', the chosen medium influences the receiver's perception of the content. It partly offers a new context. Davenport (1997) speaks of information *ecology* instead of information *technology*. To become meaningful, he states, data needs a relationship context and consequently computer networks should be designed to manage relationships, not to manage information.

---

[47] The general background material for the electronic raltionship comes from media reports, but also from efforts to put the IT development into more comprehensive context (see Gates 1995; Jakobsson 1995; Vedin 1995; Pattinson and Brown 1996; and Gabbot 1998).

Just like the telephone, the internet is a relationship builder between companies and consumers, between organizations, and inside organizations. The internet is an electronic network of networks of relationships in which we can choose to interact. It is global, has no central locus, no boss, and no owner. It supports the creation of imaginary organizations and the links between market, mega relationships, and nano relationships.

Internet relationships extend to everyone with a computer, a program, and a modem, although restrictions or censorship are possible and are being put in force. *Intranet* is a dedicated application for use inside a corporation; *extranet* is an application for a select group in a company's network of relationships, such as customers, partners and own suppliers. For example, in 1996 Visa connected its employees and partners through intranet and extranet applications, which also provide employee directories, newsletters, cafeteria menus, and other types of internal information. The net stretches beyond the core company to its 19,000 allied banks who handle their cards.

The media are filled with highflying ideas of the revolution of marketing through IT. From computer companies with high stakes in the net – currently Microsoft and Netscape – we are bombarded with 'information' on new opportunities offered by IT. Those who do not join now are out; they will become the outcasts of the information society.

A more pragmatic conclusion is that IT provides an addition to the networks of roads, railroads, waterways, air corridors, and mail services, all indispensable and long-established elements of marketing infrastructure. General national post traffic began in Europe in the seventeenth century and post became international at the beginning of the nineteenth century. The traditional service infrastructure is required for economic development, but it is primarily based on mechanics.

The ancestors of today's IT, the telephone and the telegraph, are a hundred to two hundred years old in the western industrialized world; radio and television transmissions established themselves gradually during the twentieth century. Computers were introduced on a larger scale in business during the 1960s. The breakthrough of the fax came in the late 1980s and the fax took over part of mail services, thus creating a new style of interaction between companies.

In the 1990s, e-mail, the internet, and World Wide Web entered the arena and spawned a new wave of communications. The IT triangle is becoming an integrated system, acquiring an expanding share of marketing infrastructure with the internet and mobile telephones as its fulcrum. Smartcards with built-in electronic chips provide a medium to link the consumer to an electronically based market system.

Contrary to the popular talk about faster and faster development and changes, IT is not an instant revolution, it is a slow evolution. This is corroborated by Microsoft's Bill Gates, who says that companies must view the use of the internet and the web as long-term investment which demands redefined marketing strategies. The internet and the web will not reach their full potential until after ten or twenty years. The profits will not come immediately.

In the mid-1990s, the internet connected fifty million users around the world.

In 2001 the number of users is forecast to rise to half a billion, even to one billion; in 2006 half of the world's population might be connected. Take the numbers for what they are, speculation. IT forecasts are notorious for being inaccurate.

The *physical marketplace* is being replaced by an *electronic marketspace*.[48] Companies become truely imaginary with a minimum of physical walls. They can interact with customers, intermediaries, suppliers and others through an electronic network with no physical contact. The difference between the marketplace and the marketspace can be shown by looking at *content, context,* and *infrastructure*. For example, in a marketspace a car auction offers the cars as information and the actual cars need not be present (content); the auction is on-screen instead of face-to-face (context); and computers, telecom, and a television screen replace the car lot (infrastructure).

We are just in the beginning of utilizing the electronic marketspace. The marketing strategy 'any time, any place'[49] is on its way to become reality by means of electronic relationships. Electronic marketing is not just 'data processing' which was an aid to mass production of information and large-scale storing. Electronic marketing is a means for developing novel and hopefully better marketing strategies. It is a new type of market, which is missing in the typology of markets. Increasingly, a company is an actor in the market only if it is a member of an electronic network. If the farmers in the old days had no stall on the market, they were not part of the network. This marketplace was tangible, just like today's food stores. Now there are global markets where the terminal is the stall and the customer relationship is electronic. The electronic marketspace is everywhere and nowhere; it is interaction through the electronic network of relationships that makes the market.

The electronic marketspace will not make the physical marketplace obsolete. It is rather the proportions that will change. Products are still sold in town centre squares and little corner shops in spite of all the supermarkets and malls. Business travel, predicted to be replaced by telephone conferences and e-mail, has refuted the predictions and gone the opposite direction. Business travel is booming! The same is the case with internet conferences; there are more 'physical' conferences today than ever before. Electronics seem to build up the need for people to meet in the real reality.

Marketing through electronic media can improve relationships in several ways. A customer and a supplier can more easily enter into dialogue. A customer can solicit the opinions of other customers. They can survey offerings from competing suppliers and compare certain price, delivery times, and other conditions. The future executive, salesperson, and maintenance crew become portable nomads dressed in computers, cellphones and fax machines. They have no fixed place of habitation or at least seldom stay there, and you don't need to know where they are when you call them.

---

[48] See Rayport and Sviokla (1994).
[49] Davis (1987, pp. 12–89).

Electronic networks build markets and relationships between suppliers and customers and others in the marketspace. Some specific applications of electronic relationships are given below.

Physical products

A growing application is *home shopping* through computers. Instead of visiting a store, the customer orders from a computer and television. It is online retailing and shopping on the web. The number of commercial domain names being registered are increasing rapidly. The number of potential online buyers in the year of 2000 is estimated at thirty million in America alone. Still however, website retailing usually does not offer much which cannot be found more easily through conventional channels in an urban area. Even if you can browse for a book globally and quickly on a website, it is of little comfort if the physical book distribution system is fragmented, slow and unpredictable. But electronic media as such give birth to new patterns of consumer behaviour and can augment the value of book store services. They can, for example, prompt consumers to give views on books, suggest new books to be sold, and enter into conversation with other customers.

Automatic trade between organizations

Retailers order goods via small portable terminals in their stores, online to warehouses and factories. In R6 (the many-headed customer and the many-headed supplier) is was said that a company does not buy and sell, individuals do. This is not entirely true; computers, too, buy and sell. Through EDI (electronic data interchange) and internet applications documents and logistics can be handled for scheduled repeat deliveries between parties with an established relationship. A network of computers speak to each other over the telephone. An important application is the simplification of public purchasing and consequent slashing of transaction costs. Public procurement is one of the largest markets in most nations and a mammoth market in mega alliances like Nafta and the EU. In established networks between a customer and its approved suppliers, IT handles a purchase through computer interaction. No documents and no human decisions are needed. Furthermore, electronic agents can be directed to search for specified information and alternative sources and present the best buy.

Music and advertising

Muzak, producer of background music for elevators, stores and other applications is using the interactive radio technique for advertising. It has developed an electronic, satellite-based network that connects 1800 stores for sending commercial messages direct into stores. The network can also disseminate information from manufacturers and wholesalers about occasional offerings, such as price reductions on a surplus of fresh food. Consumers have responded and sales have grown rapidly in the stores.[50]

Tickets and reservations

Computerized reservation systems for travel companies have completely changed the relationship to the passengers and created an electronic market-space for travel services. The reservation system Amadeus gives travel agencies direct access to the timetables and seat availability for 350 airlines. An airline ticket today can include rental cars and hotel rooms, all ordered as a package through thirty-nine chains of car rental firms and 18,000 hotels. We have grown used to ATMs for withdrawing cash from bank accounts. We now have also ETMs (electronic ticket machines) in which the customer enters the gate by inserting a card into a machine. United Airlines were first in introducing ticketless travelling for domestic flights. The International Air Transport Association, IATA, has decided that from 1997 the electronic ticket, the e-ticket, will gradually replace the majority of conventional tickets.

Money

In the financial sector – banks, insurance, stock exchanges, brokers, finance and accounting departments, consumer transactions – membership in an electronic network is a *sine qua non*. DIAL, a European insurance company, is an example of efficient administration and marketing through IT. Its insurance for cars and homes is sold via direct mail, telephone or computer, and personal relationships are only required in special cases. The historical date when the London Stock Exchange went electronic (8 March 1987) is referred to as 'the big bang'. The traditional, elderly London City banker and broker dressed in bowler hat, umbrella, and with a Roll-Royce, was replaced by the computerized yuppy dressed in Italian fashion suits, with credit cards and a Porsche. The old boy network of British gentlemen, held together through their fathers' social relationships, the school tie, the club, and title began to lose its grip. Computer knowledge, youth, action, and a stream of financial innovations became the hallmark when the marketplace transformed to marketspace. Difficulties arose for the old broker companies whose previously stable and impermeable networks became redundant. In buying shares, you no longer become the owner of a tangible certificate on paper, it is an intangible 'electronic share ownership' in a 'certificate-less society'. Today the broker relationship is on its way to become a broken relationship altogether. This is so because customers can open accounts with electronic brokerage services and do the trading themselves. It is quicker and cheaper, but it lacks the personal advice and assistance. Through its speed, it is offsetting a

---

[50] According to *Business Week* (Jones, Yang and Warner, 1993).

healthy type of inertia of the traditional system which allowed better control and held back premature reactions.

These were examples of current marketing practices involving electronic relationships. But electronic relationships are not limited to marketing. Henry Ford acquired fame through his declaration that 'everybody can get the colour of the car they want, as long as it is black'. This one-size fits all strategy became a 'truth' in the era of standardization and mass manufacturing, when productivity was maintained through long series of identical products. For many years, we have been able to buy basic cars models with options for colour, air-conditioning, automatic or manual gears, among others. It is a *modular design*, which the computer can handle by combining a large number of standardized modules. It has been given the paradoxical label *mass customization*.[51]

We see how manufacturing, services, delivery, and marketing are integrated into a whole by IT. It leads to direct consequences for market segmentation whose development can be characterized in the following way:

1 Everything was *customized* in the crafts society, often with high technical quality, but expensive for the ordinary consumer. Every *individual* was their own segment.
2 *Mass manufacturing* in the industrial society – *economies of scale* – gave low prices but the same product to everyone with ensuing misfit between the product and individual needs. All individuals belonged to the same segment and they were exposed to *mass marketing*.
3 *Crude segmentation* through the mass marketing of mass manufactured products by means of socio-demographic variables – men/women, children/adults – allowed a limited number of variants.
4 *Refined segmentation* to more subtly defined *niches* according to lifestyle and previous buying behaviour enhanced the possibilities for individual adjustment.
5 *Customized mass production* unites large-scale advantages with individual needs, directed to individuals or communities of consumers with shared needs. We are back to the individual segments of the crafts society but with different technology. Economies of scale also become *economies of scope*.

The circle is closed, but we are not back to square one. The stages take us 'forward to basics', to the individually and community customized offering. The concept of *surgical marketing*[52] suggests among other things that we must make a diagnosis of the current market and be precise in our efforts to reach the right customers with the right offering. We have broadened the scope of options through new production, distribution and promotion techniques. These are not mutually exclusive, rather coexisting supplements. We will still need craftspeople, and PepsiCola will be produced in mass quantities and be partly mass marketed. But

---

[51] Davis (1987, pp. 138–40).
[52] Surgical marketing is a concept used by Frankelius (1997).

the dominance of the industrial mass manufacturing and mass marketing society is broken.

Those who did not grow up with the present electronics may have difficulties in utilizing the potential; there are cognitive and emotional walls to knock down. The CEO of Sony Electronic Publishing Co. may be correct in concluding that when people come home and sit down in front of a television they are only open to interaction with the refrigerator.

There are conspicuous advantages with electronic markets – speed, global reach, access to updated information, and online transactions through charge cards. But electronic markets also provide ample stumbling-blocks: unreliable software and hardware; difficulty to assess the quality of information and the credibility of the other party; insecurity concerning payment; and systems over-load. The internet can be as congested as a Los Angeles freeway. The technological constraints must be overcome and people have to change attitudes and behaviour. IT does not offer a market unless somebody organizes a market and consumers and businesses must be connected to the net and actively explore its potential. The new markets in the electronic marketspace must establish regulations to make collaboration and competition work. They must strive in the direction of marketing equilibrium.

It is easy to get carried away by the prospects of IT; it is difficult to tell the genuine from hype. Whatever is described as the 'truth' in this text on IT applications and their relational content may have been succeeded by a fancier 'truth' when the text goes to print. Looking back we find that IT promises frequently do not come true, do not find widespread application, have a long way to go before they are of any practical use, or quickly become obsolete. Next to the industry of politics, no industry leaves as many unfulfilled promises behind as the computer industry. Its actors announce applications as if they were functioning while in fact they are visions, or simply illusions. Personally I have been talked into a series of silly IT investments both as a manager and consumer.

The use of the electronic marketspace raises a number of fundamental questions. Is a new type of social and commercial relationship being established among people who grow up with the internet? What type of business culture and society do electronic relationships engender? What happens to the high tech–high touch balance? What happens when face-to-face relationships are replaced by electronic relationships, which has been in progress in banking for many years? When home banking has taken over, a bank will only know its customers as transactions and statistics, not as people. How do you make the customer return to your web page when it is so easy to browse from one page to the other? How do we achieve 'return on electronic relationships'? How do you make money from a database, how do you charge, how do you make payment secure? Should you pay a flat rate for an annual subscription of the online updated version of *Encyclopaedia Britannica*, or pay each time you consult its database, or both? And finally, the eternal question for marketers – timing. When is the time ripe to do what?

Whatever the answers to these questions are, IT is changing both market relationships and mega and nano relationships. Electronic relationship have their own specific properties and will shape new markets and new modes of operating a business.

Relationship 13 Parasocial relationships – relationships to symbols and objects

We usually think of relationships as personal and the 30Rs are primarily relationships between people. But there are also *parasocial relationships*,[53] which involve objects, symbols and other less tangible phenomena. Our relationships to corporations, their services, and products are often impersonal but yet important through the *image* they convey to us. These relationships are manifested in the connotations of company names, brands, trade-marks, and well-known business leaders or other people who symbolize a business. Just like a person, a product or a company has a soul, a personality, and a body language. A limousine and French champagne have a different appeal than a taxi and beer. Russian caviar, oysters, and red roses symbolize festivity, romance, and wealth.

Goods and services have certain inherent properties, but just as important are the properties we as individuals or groups allocate to them. Companies, goods, services, and celebrities become surrounded by myths. 'Reality' can be seen as a social construct in which goods and services are consumed for their symbolic meaning. In a broader social context consumption not only includes the relationship between the supplier and the customer, between the customer and the product but also between the supplier and the product.[54] *Positioning* is a strategy for allocating a position – a cell in the consumer's brain – to a product or service in order to make the consumer think of a special brand when a purchase is pending.

According to Linn[55] the *meta product* is 'the whole of the invisible world of perceptions which we link to a branded product'. He proceeds: 'Every object has its metaphysical properties. It is sufficiently strong in symbols like the Christian cross, the David star or the hammer and the sickle for people to sacrifice their lives...' He gives the classic example of the Volkswagen 'Beetle': 'It was so personal that it was almost provocative...people established a relationship to the car. You had to react, it was hard to be indifferent...If we want to see the whole in which the marketed product thrives, we must look more to men and their rela-

---

[53] 'Para is Greek and means 'beside', parasocial relationship then are relationships beside the relationships between individuals. For a discussion of its meaning for RM, see Cowles (1994).
[54] See overview by Saran and Tzokas (1994).
[55] Linn (1985); the quotations are compiled from pp. 9, 26 and 28.

tionship to the products than we do today.' The perceived reality is not constituted by the product and service as independent objects, but by the relationships and interactions between the beholder and the product/service.

DeBono (1992) says that offering *integrated values* is the third stage of a firm's development. It has been preceded by a product-oriented stage when goods were scarce and manufacturing was the overriding issue. In stage two, competition was in focus. Companies are now approaching the third stage, but this stage is still in its infancy.

Taking a closer look at image, brands, and quality, it is easy to find examples when the 'reality' is in the customer's eye, heart, and brain and does not exist in an objective sense. In an essay on pop art and restaurants, its author says:[56] 'There is any number of Pizzeria Napoli around the world and often these are more 'original' than the 'original' in Naples. By the way, is there an original at all? Isn't it so that Pizzeria Napoli rather imitates a popular image of what a pizzeria in Naples should look like? If there is no original, there can't be any copies.'

It is both an opportunity and a risk to use aesthetic gimmicks such as imaginatively designed colour slides, fancy logotypes, glossy brochures, and beautifully decorated premises to make the market believe that you are something you are not. Rationality – that if you cannot live up to your image, customers will unmask you after some time and exit – should not be taken for granted. One example is the cosmetics industry, which can deliver very little of its promises – youth, beauty, happiness, and romance – but the consumer wants to believe it.

In entertainment and culture, mass production is often a goal; the bigger the audience of your show or circulation of your book, the more successful you are. For example, 'The Three Tenors' – Luciano Pavarotti, Placido Domingo and José Carreras – sang at sport stadiums with audiences of up to 60,000 people. Yet there exists a relationship between the opera fans and the tenors. The relationship between the entertainer and the consumer is rarely a personal friendship. Celebrities such as rock groups or sports champions, become symbols of lifestyles, beauty, strength, and smartness. Sometimes an actor's charisma, star quality, visibility, and private life are equally important or much more important to the fans than his or her professional performance. People know them from their appearances but also from news media and gossip columns. The fans can come close to their idols in their imagination. It is a personal relationship for one party, and a mass relationship for the other; the fans 'know' their stars as individuals, but the stars usually know their fans as anonymous audiences. The role and the stage personality are perceived as real, and get mixed up with the private person. The fame of the star can be used to add credibility and popularity to products and services and to boost images.[57]

The strength of the parasocial relationship became blatantly obvious when Diana, Princess of Wales, died in a Paris car accident in 1997. Her beauty, love

---

[56] Nilsson (1993, p. 27).
[57] See further Rein, Kotler and Stoller (1987).

affairs, and care for the less privileged, combined with her own vulnerability, captured the minds of people around the world. They genuinely mourned her as a close friend. Her relationship with the paparazzi and reporters included mutual dependency, but an inability to turn it into win–win relationships.

Rapp and Collins[58] point to new types of brands, *relationship brands*, which bear a resemblance to the parasocial relationship:

> ...with the ability to identify prospects and customers by name and address, learn more about them, and interact with them in an ongoing relationship, a new form of branding is evolving: 'relationship branding'. You no longer simply brand or promote what you sell. You brand and promote the relationship as well.

In a similar vein Duncan and Moriarty offer an RM model claiming that 'communication is the primary integrative element in managing brand relationships,' with brand equity as the goal and core category.[59] A relationship brand has a name, a logo, usually offers membership, is advertised, and includes continuing involvement.

Harley Owners' Group (HOG) has already been presented as an example of a customer club, established to increase customer retention. But it is more than that, it is also a successful relationship brand. Customers do not only have a relationship to the Harley-Davidson brand and its motorcycles. HOG is in itself a brand that represents a relationship to a community of people, an affinity group. Harley owners rarely used their bikes – it was no fun hitting the road on your own – and consequently did not buy more than one motorcycle in their lifetime. With the HOG clubhouses, strategically located in the dealerships, Harley owners consume their product as part of a community. They have not just bought a product, they have joined a group. They further identify with the group through branded Harley merchandise. Incidentally, Harley-Davidson now earns more money on its merchandise than on the motorcycles. And the HOG members are extremely loyal with a 95 per cent repurchase rate. The parasocial relationship to the Harley-Davidson brand has spawned the HOG social relationship.

Monopoly means that the market is ruled by a single supplier. When there is competition, companies differentiate their offerings. One strategy is to achieve a *value monopoly*.[60] There are many cities, paintings, movie directors, cartoons, and awards but only one Venice, one Mona Lisa, one Ingmar Bergman, one Donald Duck, and one Nobel Prize. Patents give a temporary, innovation-based value monopoly. A corporation can dominate its industry, like IBM ruled over the computer industry up until the 1990s. Then Microsoft took over the star role and its president Bill Gates became the symbol for the new and exciting IT future.

---

[58] Rapp and Collins (1985, pp. 197–298) and discussion with Stan Rapp in 1997.
[59] Duncan and Moriarty (1998, p. 1).
[60] DeBono (1992).

The cost of breaking a value monopoly can be so excessive that no competitor will succeed. A handful of such brands are known throughout the world. In the 1990s, among the top ten on the global list were Coca-Cola, Sony, Mercedes, Kodak, Disney, Nestlé, Toyota, McDonald's, IBM, and PepsiCola.[61]

Some brands have become so well-known that they degenerate as brand names and are identified as synonymous with the generic product. 'To Xerox' now means to take copies even if the brand of machine is Canon and Caran d'Ache, the Swiss pencil manufacturer, is used as the word for pencil in Russian. When New Zealand growers launched the kiwi fruit on the world market, it became such a success that other countries began to grow the fruit and profit from its formally unprotected name. The kiwi is a local bird which has become a national symbol; New Zealanders are colloquially called Kiwis. In 1997 the New Zealand grown kiwi was renamed Zespri, a name that research showed to have the desired connotation: fun, energetic, effervescent and nutritious. 'The issue is whether we're going to try and market a superior branded product that captures premium prices and consumer loyalty or trade a generic perishable...' says the chief executive of Zespri International.[62]

An intriguing issue is the ratio between price and the symbolic values of a parasocial relationship. What does it take to break a relationship between a customer and a brand? As it is a commercial relationship, it has a price. In England, the major retail chain Sainsbury introduced a new brand for a cola drink, Classic. The price was set 25 per cent below the price of 'the real thing', Coca-Cola. It soon surpassed the sales of Coca-Cola. In Canada, a similar development occurred when another retailer, Loblaw's, introduced President's Choice.

When Nestlé bought Rowntree-Mackintosh and the brands After Eight, KitKat, and Quality Street, the price exceeded the tangible assets by 300 per cent.[63] The price reveals *brand equity* – the financial value of these brands. It was a purchase of both tangible product values and abstract values. In traditional accounting terms, goodwill is not registered as an asset unless a certain amount of money has been paid for its acquisition. In 1994, the highest valued brands were Coca-Cola (US$36 billion) and Marlboro (US$33 billion); Nescafé was the highest valued European brand (US$11.5 billion).[64]

Companies choose different strategies in building an image and value monopoly:

■ Unilever, one of the world's largest corporations, does not advertise its corporate name to consumers but has invested in strong brand names, such as Cornetto ice-

---

[61] According to a study by Landor Associates, USA, based on 10,000 interviews. The winning brands were distilled from the exposure of 6,000 brands to American, European, and Japanese consumers. Cited from *Time* (Ball, 1991, p. 53).

[62] Based on Teutenberg (1997).

[63] Nilson (1993, p. 154).

[64] Accoding to an assessment made by the consulting firm Interbrand.

cream, Lipton's tea, Surf and Bio Luvil detergents, Lux soap, and Pepsodent toothpaste. All these are well-known convenience goods brands throughout the world.

■ BSN, the third largest producer of branded food in Europe after Nestlé and Unilever, used a different strategy. In 1994, it changed its name to Danone.[65] This was its brand for dairy products and after Coca-Cola the largest brand in the food stores. The company chose to invest in corporate image rather than in brand image. The urgency of a name change was felt; BSN was unknown and in Spain there was a bank with the same name, in the US a textile firm, and in Japan a TV-station.

The established term 'brand' emerges from a product tradition and agriculture; a symbol was burnt into the hide of cattle to mark ownership. It is equally applicable to services, companies, people, or other carriers of symbolic values. The brand can be a word, an acronym, a token, or a graphic design such as a logotype. It can also be a human being whom you do not meet, or who may not even exist. Companies have signed direct mail with genuine-looking, yet fictitious, names and if a consumer has asked for the name on the phone, someone has answered with this name. Tobacco companies use healthy looking beauties and tough cowboys on horseback to spread the blessings of smoking. It is embarrassing both to the manufacturer, the media, consumers, and society in general that some of the best known models have died of lung cancer. The tobacco companies of course want to limit the dissemination of such information and are quite successful in doing so.

Marketing via symbols can be seductively low-key. I should like to introduce the term *subtle marketing*, as opposed to the usual obtrusiveness of television commercials and other types of promotion. One example is the doctor and the 'health and illness industry'. By creating an air of divine powers – the rulers of health and disease, of life and death – medicine has built an almost invincible image. The connotation of the white coat and the characteristics of the hospital environment have become strong symbols, which govern the relationship to the customer and the interaction process. Through laws and membership to associations the industry has monopolized alleged abilities. According to the American Medical Association only members are allowed to claim that they *cure* disease. If others so claim, they will be taken to court. The expert monopoly becomes a reality, a unique and timeless 'patent' supported by a veil of 'scientific' jargon. As no monopoly is free of leaks, alert patients look for alternative treatment and seem to be doing so increasingly.

Finally, there are efforts to handle the parasocial relationships systematically and make them efficient. *Design management*[66] has been suggested as a collective concept for what the company wants to bring to the market and what it stands for, a 'corporate body language'. It is a matter of transforming a consistent mission and culture into symbols, both physical such as buildings and logotypes,

---

[65] The example is taken from the *Economist* (1994, p. 7).
[66] See Svengren (1995, pp. 17–19).

and in action, such as the behaviour of owners and employees. *Brand planning*, based on a long-term vision and research, is another concept for creating a systematic approach around an identity.

The issue of brands and image is not new, but is currently stirring up more interest than ever. By approaching the issue through the relationship eye-glasses, new marketing insights can be generated. We even find relationship brands. There is no doubt that parasocial relationships belong in RM.

Relationship 14 The non-commercial relationship

Marketing is primarily about the commercial part of our economy. It applies to companies that are run on market conditions with profit as the yardstick of success and survival. Economies are also based on non-profit organizations. The public sector, which is mainly a non-commercial service sector, has gradually begun to understand that marketing – in an adjusted form – is necessary. There are also other non-commercial sectors which are poorly described in official statistics, notably the voluntary sector with associations and clubs. And where do households and DIY (do-it-yourself) fit although they are fierce competitors in, for example, care and repair services?

The non-commercial sector has some fundamental properties, which separate it from the commercial sector and give rise to relationships of a partly different character. Pricing belongs here. *In public services, pricing and payment are not part of the same system as production and delivery.* It is often not the same person who pays and benefits from the services. Even if it is, payment and delivery do not coincide in time. Payment can be a general insurance cost via the tax bill, for example against illness, or it can be help to the less privileged, such as unemployed people. The customer – the citizen – does not perceive a tangible connection between price, cost and such public services as health care, education, and police services. Payment – the tax – disappears into a black hole; when you benefit from taxes, the money appears as windfall. The services may easily be perceived as 'free', which from an individual standpoint is true at the time they are needed. This may lead to excess consumption or inability to value the services: 'Those who are offered a free meal do not go to McDonald's, they go to the Ritz'.[67]

In commercial marketing, payment and performance belong to the same system and are largely simultaneous. But even here it can be difficult to see the connection between price and performance if, for example, daddy pays and kids consume.

R5 dealt with the service encounter and the individual's relationship to a service provider. The notion of the service encounter is also applicable to public sector services. Public agencies, however, offer two types of services. One type is services which could also be private and where both private and public alternatives may exist, for example in education and health care.

---

[67] Based on Albinsson-Bruhner (1993).

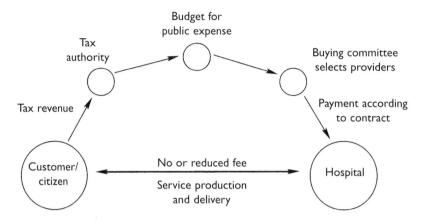

Figure 3.10 The relationship between payment of taxes and public services and the customer/citizen

The other is the authority that public agencies are allowed to exercise. From the individuals' point of view, there is a positive side when authorities assist them. There is also a negative side to contacts with authorities, a *service collison* rather than a service encounter. Authorities provide both services to the community of all individuals, and to the single individual. Some authorities have the monopoly of using force against the individual for the benefit of the whole of society. Those who get arrested or are forced to pay additional taxes are not inclined to see this as a service; the encounter becomes a collision. There is also a collision when authorities fail because of disinterest, inertia, sloppiness, legal technicalities, or red tape. The criminal is let loose and the victim is offered no help, the little guy is harassed while the big crook is left alone. The 'values' of the legal and bureaucratic establishment are often far apart from what citizens perceive as fair.

Figure 3.10 shows one possible pattern of a purchasing procedure for public services, in this case public health care. The service is produced directly between the customer/citizen and the hospital staff. The payment, however, goes via the taxes to a budget for public expense. In this case, hospitals offer their services in competition through bidding, a committee selects the winner, and payment follows a contract.

The terms customer and supplier are now being used in non-commercial operations, too. It is an effort to change the relationship between, for example, the customer/citizen and the tax authority, and to make the tax authority both an *authority* and a *service organization,* not just an authority. The two roles of authority and service provider have been mixed up when publicly owned organizations behave like an authority in instances when they should be performing ordinary services. This attitude has created an unhappy relationship to the customers/citizens and low quality and productivity. By handling service tasks well, however, it becomes easier to exercise authority. The tax agency must ascertain the revenue from taxes. At the same time, the citizens and the companies perform services when they fill in tax forms and deliver money. Laws and regulations are frequently difficult to understand intellectually. They are sometimes ambiguous, and sometimes not even passed before they are supposed to be applied. No wonder that the taxpayer makes mistakes or cheats. A majority of the mistakes can be prevented or smoothly corrected if the authority enters into constructive interaction with the citizen. This requires that the authority informs in a way that is comprehensible to the citizen and is available for consultation. In most countries availability is a major hurdle even if some countries' authorities have realized the need for change of attitude and work procedure.

Unfortunately, many of those employed by authorities do not realize that they are there for the citizens, but believe that the citizens are there to serve them; the organizational culture inverts the roles. The citizens' perceptions of relationships with authorities have been characterized by the French author Anatole France as 'the State is a surly old man behind a window'. A new generation of officals is emerging which will – hopefully, but not without conflict – replace the bureaucratic generation. Even if many changes have taken place, the historically bureaucratic–legal values are still in charge.

It is difficult to draw a line between what types of consumption should be a human right, and what should be the effect of own work and earnings. Much of the political tensions between different economic systems are caused by conflicting opinions about a fair trade-off between rights and own performance.

Public authorities and service agencies increasingly become 'borderline organizations'.[68] They live in a fuzzy zone between public and private, between the non-commercial/tax financed and a competitive market economy. Deregulation and privatization have been international strategies for many years. An airport authority may be state operated. It exercises authority over certain aspects of the airport such as air traffic control and operates services such as parking and tax-free sales.

While the public sector is paid via taxes, the voluntary sector receives its means through donations and unpaid work (to some extent through public funds and taxes, though). According to Drucker the voluntary sector, which he calls the third sector, has been the fastest growing economic sector in the United States; it engages more people than the private and public sectors together.[69] Churches, scouts, and environmental groups such as Greenpeace, belong in the voluntary sector. Their work neither fits the market economy and its price mechanism, nor the taxed-based public sector institutions and the political system. In spite of its size, the voluntary sector becomes a residual in official statistics and is neglected

---

[68] Winai (1988).
[69] Drucker (1989).

by management and marketing theory. It lives on conditions other than the public sector. Its missions have been unnoticed or mismanaged by the private or public sector or they lack the capacity to handle them. Voluntary work is often pioneering, often scorned and actively opposed by the establishment, one example being environmental protection. The third sector has a long tradition and is used to handle many of the issues which were later transferred at least in part to the public sector. We could also add a fourth sector which embraces what we do for ourselves, our family and friends.

The board of directors has a special role in voluntary organizations, namely to be the driver in the collection of funds.[70] This is an additional role from the board in a commercial enterprise or a public agency. An important part is building relationships with donors for fund-raising, or better: *fund development*. The change in terminology is essential for RM. To *develop* funds is more long term and more intimate than to *collect* funds. According to Dudley Hafner, head of the American Heart Association, '...your true potential for growth and development is the donor...someone you want to cultivate and bring along in your programme. Not simply someone to collect this year's contribution from.'

The quotation stresses that long-term relationships must be cultivated through a programme, as compared to the transaction, the occasional gift. One strategy is to engage the donor in actual work in the organization. Hafner continues: 'Someone who pays taxes does not think of himself or herself as getting involved in the welfare programme. But if they become involved in a Salvation Army activity or the Visiting Nurses programme, they *are* involved. They are involved spiritually and they are involved monetarily. That makes a difference.' If an organization consists of members – real members and not pseudo-members – these can be both recipients of the organization's offerings and producers for themselves or for others. This way of looking can be expanded to seeing nations as organizations of 'members', the citizens. To regard members or citizens as customers requires the insight that their role is only partly commercial.

Companies are increasingly developing strategies for their donations by funding long-term projects.[71] This corporate philanthropy aligns self-interest with doing good for society, the companies becoming corporate citizens. Examples of causes are increasing literacy, AIDS prevention, school reforms, and environmental programmes. It does not only include cash but also advice and the use of their technology and human resources.

A large share of the cultural sector is non-commercial. A museum must target its relationships to two groups.[72] One is visitors – in order to reach them, the museum needs intermediaries, like tourism organizations and the media. The second is those who support the operations through contributions, such as corporate sponsors, local government, and grant committees. The third is inward

---

[70] This and the next paragraph based on Drucker (1990); quotations from pp. 85 and 88.
[71] Smith (1994).
[72] Bradford (1991, pp. 93–6).

bound, the organization of the museum and those who propose exhibitions, plan them and implement them. All this is tied together; it is three perspectives of the marketing of a museum.[73]

When I was born, savings banks presented newborn babies with a bank account and a small deposit.[74] When I started school, I received a savings-box, which was emptied regularly under the supervision of the teacher, and the money was deposited in the bank. This was seen as community work without a profit motive. The savings banks had an assignment from society, just like the schools had. Saving was a virtue: 'Save First, Buy Later!' The mission of the savings banks was to give the less privileged a chance to improve their financial situation, go to college, and acquire their own home; and to let small farmers and firms develop their operations. The savers were members and citizens rather than customers. Today, Grameen Bank in Bangladesh with 900 branch offices, has targeted segments, which have no attraction for the traditional banks, namely the poor and women. Every loaner buys a share and becomes an owner.[75]

The non-commercial relationship is ever so important for the commercial economy and the marketing equilibrium. What cannot be handled through market mechanisms must be handled by the public sector and the political system – including setting up adequate regulations and institutions – and by the voluntary sector. Relationships between customers, suppliers and other stakeholders are important all the same, but are of a somewhat different character.

Relationship 15 The green relationship

> Dear Guest: Try to imagine how many tons of towels from all hotels around the world are washed unnecessarily. Think of the enormous amount of detergent and water, which thereby contribute to the strain on the environment. Please note that if you put the towel on the floor it means that you would like it to be replaced. However, if you leave it hanging on the rack it means: I can use it again – and help protect the environment.

This type of message is increasingly found in hotels. It is an instance of a new phenomenon – the green relationship. Hotels are trying to establish a relationship with guests through environmental issues. They want interaction and co-production with the customer. They have found that green issues are not just costs and threats, but also offer opportunities for cost reduction and revenue enhancement.

The green relationship concerns the company's way of handling environment

---

[73] See also Kotler and Andreasen (1992).
[74] This section is primarily based on Hessling (1990).
[75] Yunus (1992).

and health issues in its offerings and the relationships that are created to specific individuals and communities of individuals. Despite the fact that environment and health have been in focus for public debate for decades, it is the object of a new type of relationship to consumers and society.

However, companies as well as governments have been reluctant to take action. 'Our company does not cause pollution! It's fad and fashion among confused idealists and will soon pass! It costs too much! There is lack of scientific evidence! The customer does not want to pay for it! We will lose our competitive edge!' Legislation has often not been enforced and companies have been granted temporary exemptions that have turned permanent. Those who have been appointed responsible for environmental issues at corporations often lack power.

In recent years, the interest has grown and more people are begining to grasp the necessity for action. *Green marketing* is becoming a sub-discipline of marketing.

In the mid-1990s, US consumers spent over US$100 billion on products from companies that they perceive as environmentally and socially progressive.[76] In one study,[77] eighty-four per cent of all Americans considered pollution a serious problem getting worse; 75 per cent that the air was getting more polluted and that 80 per cent of lakes and rivers were more polluted than twenty years ago. The group of 'green consumers' who take an interest in the environment and health is growing. Previously, protests against environmental destruction was most visible in demonstrations and efforts to boycott companies. Consumers 'vote' by their purchases of goods and services and a growing share of 'voters' refuse to buy products which are detrimental to health and the environment. Fifty-four per cent of Americans read the labels on packages to find out if the product was environmentally friendly, and fifty-seven per cent looked for products and packaging made from recycled material. The number of green products has grown. In 1985, they accounted for 0.5 per cent of all new products, in 1989 for 4.5 per cent, and in 1991 for 13.4 per cent.

Figure 3.11 shows green market relationships – to individual consumers and middlemen – and relationships on a mega level, to citizens as a group. Companies sell their goods or services to customer segments or individuals who can be more or less environmentally and health conscious. There are communities of people dedicated to green issues. Children have been inclined to accept the messages and have begun to influence their parents' purchasing habits.[78] Producers of daily goods establish closer relationships to the distribution channels in order to solve environmental problems – not least with packaging – and to explore the sales opportunities provided by the increasing green interest. Investment in good relationships to authorities, environmental organizations, and the media, can be supportive to marketing. During its 150 year history, Church & Dwight in the USA,

---

[76] Entine (1996, p. 31).
[77] The data in this paragraph are quoted from Ottman (1992, pp. 3, 8 and 13).
[78] Ottman (1992, p. 146).

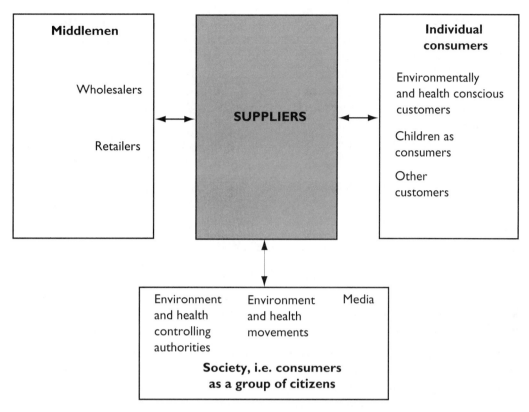

Figure 3.11 The company and its relationships in the green network

makers of Arm & Hammer baking soda, have worked with both the product and its package to make it more environmentally friendly. Its representative says: 'Building coalitions with all stakeholders keeps the company abreast of environmental regulations, issues, debates, technology, and attitudes...[which] results in a dialogue...'.[79]

Companies and consumers alike are in continuous interaction with the environment. The consumer might not notice much of this, as a large share of environmental destruction caused by production and consumption appears with delayed effect and away from the consumer's location. The general environmental destruction which we cannot do much about as individuals, hits back at us as members of a nation, as citizens. The products we consume have an impact on our individual well being. This is very obvious with food, a choice we can partly control. If wrongly combined, it impairs our general health status and immune defence system and causes disorders. We incur costs both directly as consumers and indirectly as citizens.

Marketing as a discipline is primarily dealing with issues of a micro and short-

---

[79] Ottman (1992, p. 146).

term character. Companies endeavour to maintain long-term profitability and survival, but in practice short-term considerations are given priority. Survival this year is a necessary condition for long-term survival. The consumer is often focused on satisfying momentary needs. In a macro perspective and over the long term, both companies and consumers have a responsibility as citizens which is partly in conflict with the individual's immediate self-interest.

Reasons for a delayed breakthrough for green marketing are therefore found in the conflicts between our responsibility as individual consumers, suppliers and citizens. There are *short-term* and *long-term* effects as well as *direct* and *indirect* effects.

Individual consumers

In our role as *individual consumers* we can choose to buy certain goods and services. We demonstrate environmental and health awareness through our consumption habits. This requires that the products we want are available at a reasonable price or the green considerations will become too much of a burden of daily life. One obstacle is the lack of infrastructure such as distribution networks based on ecological considerations. If consumers want to buy organically grown food, they usually find that availability is low, both in stores and restaurants. If consumers want to patronize manufacturers that use recycled material, reliable information is difficult to obtain. Much of what we do as individuals has a direct, predictable, and short-term impact. Indirect and long-term effects are vague and provide weaker incentives.

Suppliers

In our role as *suppliers*, we can choose to produce goods and services as long as we live within the law – or more realistically: do not risk to be discovered or punished – and as long as it pays. Today, environmental costs incurred by companies are passed on to others, or society at large, even to other countries via air and water. Even worse, pollution and the consequent destruction of natural resources has a more general consequence. It is stored in molecules, which are then distributed through the ecological cycle. We get 'molecular rubbish', the invisible rubbish which is ten times the amount of the visible rubbish.[80] In the long run, we cannot dodge payment of these anonymous costs; they will hit us as consumers and citizens.

Citizens

As *citizens* – that is *us*, the same people as those mentioned above but in a different role – it is comfortable to hide in the collectivity of society. We may not see

---

[80] Robèrt (1992).

ecology as our responsibility, and as single individuals we may feel we cannot do much as long as authorities do not take action. This is also a neat excuse for doing nothing. Politicians are squeezed between a will to act on issues which have not matured in public opinion and to become popular and attract votes. The limitations thus set by the level of collective consciousness creates a dilemma.

It would be easier if environmental and health hazards could be identified by mainstream scientific research. In many cases there is overwhelming evidence both from science and common sense observations; no more research is needed. In other cases treating green issues as part of an eco-system requires new scientific mindsets. A current thrilling but equally scaring is the uncontrolled development in genetic engineering. Genetically manipulated food (or 'gene modified food' as suppliers have campaigned for, to make it sound more friendly to consumers and politicians) is already sold and there is a colossal future market. But proper research lags behind and nobody – including the most prominent scientists – can forecast the effects of gene technology. With the profits and stakes involved, it is tempting to modify green issues to greed issues; changing just one tiny letter changes the whole strategy.

Table 3.2 shows that companies are driven by different motives in their environmental considerations. *Law driven firms* heed environmental issues only when forced to by court orders. They often try to escape the issues through massive use of lawyers and stalling techniques. Lobbying organizations have been formed to discredit environmental efforts and to spread disinformation, even demanding free use of nature for the benefit of short-term business profits. No doubt, environmental enthusiasts have sometimes gone too far, not accepting any kind of human interference with nature. The fifteen-mile bridge between Sweden and Denmark has been the object of environmental studies and controversies for decades before the actual construction could start. This has forced the proponents

Table 3.2 Drives of companies to deal with environmental and health issues

Law driven firm	Public relations driven firm	Value driven firm
Defensive strategy	Opportunistic strategy	Offensive strategy
Cost to be avoided	Image enhancement	Basis for revenue
Consumers do not really care	Consumers want it to some extent	Consumers demand it
Resistance	Cosmetic add-on	Inherent in their business mission
Threat	Faddish	Opportunity for sustaining competitive advantage
Let the court decide what is a good citizen	Efforts to be perceived as a good citizen	Genuine desire to be a good citizen

of the bridge to consider – and reconsider – its effects on the flow of the water and the living conditions for fish and organisms. Any change, however, will have some effect on nature and the question is how much is acceptable and how the harm can be reduced.

Public relations driven firms seem to constitute the most prevalent species. For them, green issues are trendy and if consumers seem to want them, firms offer them in order to enhance sales and image. They apply a 'green-washing strategy' rather than implementing fundamental changes. This is in line with the values of the 4P approach with promotion, persuading the customer to view the company in a positive light, a matter of 'information'. A study in the USA showed that 87 per cent of consumers thought that less than half of all companies took environmental issues seriously.[81]

Value driven firms – those who understand and believe – are still a minority. Green products are often manufactured and distributed by voluntary organizations based on personal beliefs and values, such as those of anthroposophs and biodynamic farmers. Some of the companies that have seen the business opportunities in environment and health are Ecover in Belgium, Ben & Jerry's Ice Cream in the USA, and The Body Shop in the UK. More traditional companies have sometimes spent large sums on green programmes and made certain improvements, but the larger share of their operations continue as before. It is hard to uncover if there is, besides the voluntary and idealistic organizations, any commercial enterprises that fully embrace green values, not only in rhetoric but also in action. We would like to believe their claims and some companies have received extraordinary media coverage for promoting green issues.

Particularly in Europe, where consumer and producer cooperatives have large market shares in the food market, one could have expected leadership in green marketing. The explanation may be simple: management never understood that environment and health could be part of a business mission. A survey of advertisements from the period 1950–1985 indicated that companies did not reveal any growing awareness of green opportunities, although the arguments for health increased somewhat during the 1980s.[82]

Environmental aspects are included in the quality awards that now exist around the world. In the *Malcolm Baldrige National Quality Award* in the USA, societal responsibilities, including environmental improvements, appear in several of the criteria. Reference is made to green technology and green manufacturing, health and safety, emission levels, waste stream reductions, by-product use and recycling.[83] According to former Baldrige chief executive Curt Reimann, the importance of environmental issues for the applicant is weighed against a company's potential impact on the environment. Consequently, a producer of chemicals is judged by tougher standards than, for example, a life insurance company.

---

[81] According to *Marketing News* (Schlossberg, 1992).
[82] Feurst (1991).
[83] Malcolm Baldrige Award Criteria (1997, pp. 5, 27 and 30).

Case study

The Body Shop is one of them. Its products seem to sell themselves through unique perceived qualities and consumers constitute the sales force as voluntary PTMs. The company has never advertised but claims to get 10,000 favourable mentions in the media per year. It was founded in 1976 with one store in Brighton, England, and in 1999 there were 1700 stores in forty-six countries. The official strategy is to make both the products and the packaging as environmentally friendly as feasible. They are based on natural ingredients and must not be tested on animals. The Body Shop has introduced a rolling five-year rule in its relationship to the suppliers. Twice a year, suppliers must sign a confirmation that the ingredients or the finished product have not been tested on animals during the past five years. Companies that currently practise animal testing but cease to do so can become suppliers to The Body Shop five years later. Bottles are standard plastic bottles used by pharmacies and consumers can get them refilled. Plastic has been a major problem, and the company has worked systematically to recycle the material; this is now beginning to succeed. Every individual store has an environmental programme, a requirement in the franchise contract. The Body Shop establishes relationships with environmental organizations, among them Amnesty International and Greenpeace. From 1984 – when the company went public on the London Stock Exchange – to 1993 the value of the stock increased by 10,944 per cent. The growth, which has taken place through franchising, is exceptional. Obviously there is no contradiction in marketing green products and running a profitable operation, as has incessantly been claimed by traditional companies.

Its founder and president, Anita Roddick, expresses her business philosophy in the following way:[84]

> …many trading companies are now fighting to clamber on to the bandwagon and are loudly proclaiming their brand-new, shining green products and policies. I would be happier if I thought they were motivated by real concern for the environment.

> …at first media and the politicians…categorized environmentalists as brown sandal freaks with a screw loose. They sneered at them.

> The Body Shop is, and has always been, an unshamedly green company… it was a simple expression of our core values and beliefs, values that are constantly policed by our customers and staff…[85]

---

[84] Roddick (1991, pp. 220–1).

[85] It has been argued by Entine (1996) that there are flaws in the green Body Shop facade, the image being glossier than the reality.

The traditional task of companies is production and marketing, the task of consumers is to consume, and it is the task of local governments to dispose of the rubbish. In an ecological perspective, however, the whole must be considered. Rubbish disposal and recycling must be designed into the product and the delivery systems; it must be a natural part of the logistics. A major share of environmental pollution is directly coupled to daily consumption, how the raw material was produced, how the products were manufactured and transported, and how they are taken care of as rubbish. Sixty to 85 per cent of household waste could be recycled or composted.

In the future, producers will be responsible for their products all the way to scrapping and wasting, which means a role after sales and consumption. The supply chain is extended and the network of relationships with consumers, intermediaries and others changes shape. This will require a dramatic redesign of the logistics of the producers. While only 5 to 10 per cent of packaging is recycled today, 90 to 95 per cent might be a future goal. Car manufacturers have developed systems for recycling. A new model of Mazda was introduced as a cleaner, quieter, and safer car: 'Naturally such a lovely car can be recycled. All metal and 80 per cent of all plastic components can be used again.[86] In the Italian Fiat cars, plastic material is going to be used up to three times. Counting the life expectancy of a car to twenty years, the material will be around for sixty years. Security details such as bumpers are made of new plastic, which will be recycled and used for less critical components. Canon recycles cartridges for copying machines and asks the customer to return them to retailers. For the future, the distribution system needs to be as efficient *from* the customer and retailer as it now is *to* the customer and retailer. Recycling requires new systems and processes, in fact a whole new infrastructure. This strategy is 100 per cent different from the 1960s when throw-away and 'no deposit-no refund' was considered the most efficient production and consumption strategy.

There are signs that a changed and more constructive view on green marketing is slowly coming forth, even if the degree of awareness varies considerably between consumers, industries and countries. In order to break through among consumers, green products have to be as easily accessible as a can of Coca-Cola. Marketers begin to see opportunities, eloquently epitomized in the following words: 'When the boss got green glasses, the red numbers disappeared'.[87]

Relationship 16 The law-based relationship

'When ITT came to the customer for final negotiations and to sign the contract', an international businessman told me, 'the delegation consisted of nine lawyers

---

[86] Advertisement in *Svenska Dagbladet*, 18 January 1992.
[87] Karpesjö (1992, p. 9).

and one engineer. When Ericsson came, they were nine engineers and one lawyer.'

The anecdote uncovers two very different relationships. For one company, it is first and foremost a legal relationship with the courts hovering over the negotiations. For another, it is a professional and even personal relationship focused on technology, with some provision for legal features.[88]

The formal regulations/institutions of the marketing equilibrium are partly found in the law-based relationship. It involves three objectives:

1 *Quality assurance through prevention.* Law for preventive purposes, during negotiations and in contracts, is used to avoid potential misunderstandings and install a certain protection against a party that does not fulfil its obligations. The work of legislators and lawyers then is quality assurance. As in all quality work, prevention should be maximized. If relationships are good, parties usually solve a dispute without taking it to court. Oral and informal agreements where people trust each other are continuously being made in business and are a necessity for the market to operate smoothly.

2 *Quality inspection and solution of disputes.* Prevention is always more effective than measures taken after the problem has arisen, not least if the goal is long-term relationships. The world is not perfect so legal procedures are also needed for quality inspection and rework, as a ground for settling a dispute, and for dealing with outright dishonesty. Misunderstandings can occur, however, if the parties cannot reach an agreement through a benign and constructive effort, they may be forced into a law-based relationship. The outcome of legal procedures can solve a problem, but there are dark sides. Winning a war is not the same as winning the peace; even the winner of a case becomes a loser if the cost of litigation in money, time, and psychic effort, is substantial. The outcome can also be random or controlled by technicalities, obsolete legislation, ruthless smartness of lawyers, and ignorant courts. Unfortunately, sometimes prevention can be an antecedent to a win–lose relationship; the stronger party makes certain that it is exempt of all responsibility and only has rights.

3 *Manipulation.* Law is also used to deliberately trap another party. Within the marketing mix and the 4Ps, law ought to have its own P for the art of using legal technicalities to exploit and fool another party, thus winning a 'victory' over a customer, supplier, ally, or employee. This type of law application is counterproductive to RM and can only function in transaction marketing and situations where the customer, or other party, has little power; it is also unethical. Notorious examples are fine print in contracts, which cannot be understood without the assistance of lawyers and courts. In hypercompetition though, manipulation of the law is part of the ongoing marketing warfare.

The law-based relationship to the customer is partly an indirect relationship. It goes via a 'repair crew' of law firms, prosecutors, courts, juries and judges. They work as intermediaries – wholesalers, retailers, agents – who are distributors of

---

[88] For a discussion of contract law and its transactional and relational qualities, see Macneil (1983, 1985); and Paulin, Perrien and Ferguson (1997).

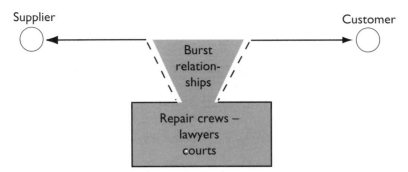

Figure 3.12 The law-based relationship as a substitute for burst social and business relationships

decisions about who is right and who is wrong. They also function as the refuse collectors of broken human relationships; they are expected to clean up where others have littered. The fact that legal institutions have to be activated is a sign of relationship failure (Figure 3.12).

Although rarely mentioned in marketing texts, bankruptcy is a natural ingredient of the market economy. It is a way of tidying up in the marketplace, a Darwinian selection, the survival of the fittest. Through periods of snowballing bankruptcies in many countries, they have become a more obtrusive part of the relationship between supplier and buyer. Suppliers are vulnerable in a customer bankruptcy; little is usually left to pay invoices. Tax authorities and sometimes banks can have preferential right to remaining assets. This is remarkable as banks boast about being professional credit assessors, while a supplier seldom has a chance to foresee the failure of a customer company. A failure has a domino effect; a supplier goes bankrupt because his customer did and he cannot pay his debts to his suppliers, and so forth.

Bankruptcy often leads to legal proceedings where fraud and unethical practice is uncovered. Some bankruptcies are a deliberate and systematic abuse of the legal system and a way of making money. Most failures, however, are not deliberately criminal, but formal mistakes are often made in the confusion that precedes the failure. In either case, bankruptcy leads to law-based interaction.

In the airline business there has been a partial switch from a bureaucratic–legal paradigm to a service and relationship paradigm. It has been a well-known secret that airlines overbook. Promises are given but the airlines do not know if they can deliver. It was quite common that they refused to admit overbooking, blamed the passenger, the airports, or the weather, and disclaimed all responsibility. Today, serious airlines acknowledge overbooking, or 'denied boarding' as they prefer to call it. The financial necessity to overbook has been explained together with the best techniques to make the overbooked passenger satisfied.[89] Some airlines ask for volunteers to give their seats to a traveller with an urgent need to be on the

---

[89] See for example *The SAS Quality Book* (1987).

flight. They promise the volunteer a seat on the next flight and offer a free ticket for a future flight or cash compensation.

The value of a free ticket for a customer usually exceeds by far the cost for the airline. The failure is turned into recovery, a win–win relationship flavoured by customer delight, the little extra, which is often recommended in modern quality management.

From a strict, legal perspective, airlines could probably waive the responsibility or make it burdensome for passengers to claim compensation. Compared to goods transportation, passenger transportation has been neglected by the legislators.[90] Airlines and many others have realized the importance of long-term relationships and understand that legal tricks spoil relationships. Instead, they volunteer to solve problems and the outcome is reinforced relationships.

In 1970, the USA had 355,000 lawyers, in 1984 they had grown to 622,000 and at the turn of the millennium they are estimated to pass one million. In the mid 1980s the USA had twice as many lawyers per capita as the UK, 5 times as many as Germany, and twenty-five times as many as Japan. USA has 5 per cent of the world's population, but 26 per cent of its lawyers according to one source, even 70 per cent according to another source.[91]

All these lawyers must find work. One way is to indulge in more fierce and innovative marketing, in hypercompetition. By tradition or formal regulation, lawyers only got jobs through personal relationships and professional networks. In the USA, the marketing of legal services can be extremely aggressive, both through advertising and personal sales. There are 'ambulance chasers', looking for traffic victims, helping to sue as many parties as possible in the vicinity of the accident. They encourage citizens to sue each other. In some countries lawyers take on cases on speculation and the customer does not take a monetary risk; the lawyer's fee may be a third or half of the settlement if they win. It can therefore pay to speculate in law just like in a lottery. *Frivolous suits* in the USA are a speculation on the imperfections of the law, shortcomings of judges and jury members, and the other party's frailties or lack of power. It is not a matter of who *is* right, it is a matter of who *gets* right. Law can both support security and cause insecurity.

Another strategy of securing the future of the legal profession has the character of megamarketing; by making sure that new legislation is continuously passed, the market keeps expanding. A good political support for the future is the fact that 46 per cent of the members of the US congress and 63 per cent of the senate are lawyers. Going to law school is considered a road to a bright future for students.

The threat of litigation, together with the bureaucracy and complicated interstate regulations in the USA, is a major hurdle experienced by overseas compa-

---

[90] See Sisula-Tulokas (1985).
[91] The numbers are compiled from Hartley (1985, p. 179); Ramsey (1991) and Blumberg (1989, pp. 210–11).

nies. Here are some other examples of legal applications in the US market which show the difficulty for companies used to another type of business culture:[92]

- Electrolux with 30 per cent of its sales in the USA had eight lawyers at its American headquarters dealing with some 400 legal cases. At its international headquarters there were four lawyers dealing with the rest of the world but with no case taken to court for several years.
- Primus-Sievert, makers of camping stoves, terminated its US sales in 1983 after a series of lost cases. Half the premium the company pays for an insurance against damages goes to the 4 per cent of its Canadian sales. This is not because the insurance is needed in Canada but because Americans who buy the stove in Canada or receive it as a gift from Canadians, can sue the manufacturer in US courts.
- According to US law there is a strict product liability. It is enough if a product is present when an accident occurs – not to have caused the accident – to make the manufacturer potentially liable. A Volvo owner in California filled up with contaminated petrol and after a while the engine stopped. The driver parked the car by the kerb and walked across the street when he was hit by another car and broke a leg. He sued Volvo. The strategy is 'Go for the deep pocket'.
- Two of the most publicized instances of punitive damages in the USA concern a doctor and a granny. The doctor managed to get $2 million in compensation for bad paint on his BMW car. A granny, departing from a McDonald's drive-in, spilt hot coffee and burnt herself. For this inconvenience, which would have gone unnoticed in most countries, she was awarded $2.7 million by a court although the amount was later reduced.

These examples sound like fabrications for a comedy soap opera – and they are funny until you discover they are for real. This type of legal action is far away from common sense. A serious and devastating attack on legal and bureaucratic systems – with the striking title *The Death of Common Sense: How Law Is Suffocating America* – is offered by Howard (1994), himself a lawyer. The randomness of the courts' decisions where a jury of lay people are influenced by the sued company being rich, domestic or foreign, and how pitiful the prosecuting party stands out, adds no value to the market or society.

Mass torts, where a large number of customers simultaneously sue a company, are becoming a special type of litigation. When customers experience that a product has been damaging to their health, they have no other chance than to unite. Injuries caused by a herbicide and asbestos fibres had each a quarter of million claimants; Dow Corning and other manufacturers of breast implants had almost half a million claimants.[93] And in June of 1997, the tobacco industry agreed to set aside funds for the victims of smoking, to the amount of $350 billion, that is the staggering sum of three hundred and fifty thousand million dollars!

---

[92] The examples from Electrolux, Primus-Sievert and Volvo, as well as some of the background material for this section is taken from Ramsey (1991).
[93] *Fortune* (Nocera, 1995).

In Japan, contracts are expected to be brief and allow a flexible interpretation. To be forced to go to court is a defeat for all parties. Those who break a business agreement will not be seen as trustworthy in the future and will be excluded from the business community. In US business life it is considered smart to trap counterparts; in Japan a trial has only losers.[94] On the other hand, Japanese business can be ruthless to foreign companies who have to sue them and be persistent to secure, for example, patent rights.

The way legislation has mushroomed in America creates a strained relationship between customers and suppliers, such as between patients and hospitals. Both health insurance and hospital insurance rates rise, in turn burdening the patient's cost. Doctors have to be on guard every moment. There is also a positive side; the insights into the secluded guild of doctors are improved. The USA have gone to a ludicrous extreme and fantasy damages can be awarded to people who are in a legal sense maltreated. In other countries, for example Sweden, you must have robust health in order to survive if you challenge the health and hospital systems; the damages for malpractice are no more than an insult to the consumer.

I can speculate in two explanations for these developments. One is that the bureaucratic–legal values have taken over from common sense and human empathy. The other is that citizens have got so fed up with the treatment they have received as consumers – unfulfilled promises in advertising, low-quality products and services, little or no willingness to settle complaints, monopoly behaviour – that they are now hitting back.

Suing someone is a natural part of marketing in the USA but it is not mentioned in marketing texts. When *Fortune* magazine reports the alliances in the computer industry, one of the properties of relationships could be labelled 'litigation'. Microsoft has strengthened its alliance with Apple by successfully developing software for Macintosh. This has occurred despite the fact that the two corporations are direct competitors in some areas and that Apple has sued Microsoft for theft in connection with Microsoft's launch of Windows software. This is accepted with the motivation that 'This is business. We're not allied with Apple out of love'.[95]

According to Blumberg:[96] 'It is an elementary sociological fact that as the social fabric of society unravels, shared values and norms that once guided behaviour break down and are replaced by formal codes, regulations, and laws. As the sense of community withers further, social conflict intensifies and litigation proliferates as each person seeks advantage at the expense of others.'

New forms for mitigation are sought, however. In the USA, 95 per cent of all cases are solved in the last minute before a trial. Legal systems – or rather a set of loosely linked components – are extremely closed and tied to rituals. One practical solution is a private American company organized around a network of

---

[94] The Japanese examples are based on Delaryd (1989, pp. 57–9).

[95] Michels (1992, p. 8).

[96] Blumberg (1989, p. 209).

2000 retired judges who solve disputes faster and more simply than the courts do.[97]

In a thesis on the significance of contractual law for organizing companies and markets, an article from 1931 by is quoted:[98] '...transactions come in a variety of forms and...a highly legalistic approach can sometimes get in the way of the parties instead of contributing to their purposes. This is especially true where continuity of the exchange relation between the parties is highly valued.' The statement is equally applicable today; it shows that RM as a phenomenon is an old commonsense practice. The author further points out that a transaction which is unambiguously defined in a contract and which is then fulfilled in each and every detail is unusual, and that we deceive ourselves by believing otherwise.

In the spirit of RM, it is more realistic to speak about *relationship contracts* which also include judgement calls, negotiations to solve a problem, an assessment of the long-term consequences for future collaboration, and high ethical standards.

Relationship 17 The criminal network

Organized crime is based on personal relationships in closed networks. It can consist of a global mafia but also of a long-term relationship between a local thief and a fence. The presence of criminal networks impacts the relationships between the triad of suppliers, customers and competitors and impairs the marketing equilibrium. Economic crime disturbs and threatens the functioning of whole economic systems or it can hit single individuals. The networks comprise organizations built on a criminal business mission such as trade in narcotics, fencing and 'protection'. It can also comprise legal trade with goods and services which, behind a respectable facade, is using bribery, murder and threats to get orders. Within legal trade there are also false promises, illegal use of brands, tax fraud, and computer crimes.

This section aims to showing two things. First, networks of relationships are a condition for sustaining criminal business operations. Second, if the good market forces in certain industries or geographical areas are obstructed, the rules of the competitive game are set aside, and the existence for law-abiding businesses is jeopardized.[99]

Obviously the reason for detailing criminal relationships is not to teach unethical and illegal behaviour. The reason is that illegal networks are widespread and that it is important to demonstrate their effect on legal marketing. For the same reason, the University of Buenos Aires introduced courses in the mechanisms of corruption and other illegal procedures.[100]

---

[97] Based on Harper (1993, p. 10).
[98] The quotation from an article by Karl Llewellyn and reproduced by Williamson (1981).
[99] For an overview of economic effects of organized crime, see Gianluca and Peltzman (1995).
[100] From *Time* (May 10, 1993, p. 16).

When monitoring professional journals and news media for organized crime and other illegal acts by companies and governments, I found the subject to be treated daily. It stood out clearly that organized crime and corruption are not limited to a few countries and regions; they are omnipresent although their 'market share' and influence vary. A report[101] on corruption in the world, based on the experience of business people, puts New Zealand, Northern Europe and Canada at the top of countries where corruption is infrequent, while a number of developing countries are at the bottom of the list. In countries with a low rate of domestic corruption, major cases of corruption were reported to surface from multinational companies.

Organized crime is reported through official investigations, research institutes, investigative journalism, and memoirs, and it is a pet theme in novels and entertainment. Scholarly research on organized crime is limited. It is a matter of surveying closed and protected networks; talk about proprietary information! Even if ongoing criminal activity is publicly known, people are frightened of speaking out or taking action. It is both difficult and dangerous to research the area. It can be done through covert action research where researchers infiltrate an organization under disguise. It can also be done through people who have defected and are willing to talk, and through criminal investigators and courtroom proceedings. The story by Italian judge Falcone about his war on organized crime, told just before he was assassinated, has credibility as a report from the inside.[102]

Organized crime builds its operations on a criminal business mission and the illegal marketing is performed through networks. Except for the godfather, no one is supposed to be able to overview the cells and relationships of the network. A family is often in the core and social ties are strong. Telling on someone produces a clear feedback; you are not fired, you are fired at.

The shadow economy of a country – its unofficial economic sector – consists of the black, illegal economy, and of household and voluntary activities which are not registered in the GNP. All statistics of the shadow economy are uncertain but assessments of 10 to 20 per cent of the economies of industrialized countries are often reported in the media. The abandoning of the border checks within the EU and the dissolution of the Soviet empire offer new 'business' opportunities and so do sales taxes, value added taxes, and subsidies which operate within deficient control systems. The turmoil and ignorance of this new situation and gaps and differences in legislation and institutions between countries are taken advantage of.

Illegal trade in narcotics, gambling, and prostitution was assessed to be 1.1 per cent of the US GNP in the mid-1980s.[103] Revenue from the narcotics trade in Europe was estimated to be between US$200 billion (corresponding to the GNP

---

[101] According to a survey by Transparency International, 1998, as reported in the press.

[102] Falcone and Padovani (1991).

[103] According to *Newsweek* (1986) and *Fortune* (Rowan, 1986). The rest of the paragraph is based on continuous media reports.

of the Netherlands) and US$800 billion (the GNP of Italy). The amphetamine exports of the Netherlands are claimed to be bigger today than its well-known trade in tulips and bulbs. Bolivia, Colombia and Peru account for 98 per cent of the world cocaine trade. According to the Italian Mafia prosecutor Caselli, organized crime worldwide had a global revenue of US$700 to 1000 billion in 1996. The narcotics trade alone was estimated at US$500 billion which makes it the second largest industry in the world after arms, but before oil. Another source claims that narcotics amount to 8 per cent of world trade.

Covert price cartels are another type of illegal network. Representatives of the largest companies in some industries meet once or twice a year to fix world market prices and decide on markets and market share. They meet in an airport hotel, different each time, and leave no written records behind. Bidding cartels – competitors that agree on who is going to give the lowest bid and thereby get the order – kill competition in certain areas of the building and construction sector. These illegal forms of RM also occur in companies where everything else is operated according to laws and regulations.

Money laundering is an important part of illegal trade. Black money which can be traced must be turned into white money. If 70 per cent of black money from the drug trade is laundered, US$15 to 60 billion of 'dirty money' will be passed through the international financial systems. Parlour offers the following description of the laundering process and the network, which is required to perform the process, follows a certain pattern.[104] First, the money must be deposited (placement). Then the money is separated from its source by a series of confusing and complex financial transactions which make it hard for accountants and police to trace (layering). Eventually, the money is placed in legitimate funds (integration). He forecasts '…further sophistication of money laundering techniques, greater investment of dirty money into established businesses, further internationalization of money laundering networks and intensified involvement of criminal organizations'.

A disquieting but long-term trend is that legitimate and illegitimate practices are woven together into a fabric of relationships. Invisible power organizations – octopuses stretching out their many arms – are created; they are in a double sense imaginary organizations. Organized crime increasingly seems to establish itself behind respectable fronts, investing in companies on the stock exchanges, using IT and sending their staff on executive training programmes. The illegal becomes even more intangible as some of those who are appointed to fight corruption themselves become members of the criminal network.

The establishment of mega relationships in order to involve people in high places is a necessity for organized crime. It cannot thrive without the support of a network of government officials, police and courts, and specialists such as lawyers, accountants, chemists, and physicians. Crime becomes embedded in the power centres of society. In the Russian parliament, the douma, it has been esti-

---

[104] According to Parlour (1993); quotation from p.66.

mated that 40 per cent of the members have organized crime connections. A seat in the douma is a strategic investment as its members have immunity from the law and cannot be the object of criminal investigation or prosecution.

In order to be competitive, organized crime indulges in a series of most effective acts, such as physical threat, bribery, kidnapping, blackmailing, assault, murder and arson, and legal technicalities are used to obstruct justice. These marketing tools are never mentioned in marketing textbooks. It is hard to tell how frequently they are used, but there is no doubt that they are crucial for marketing 'success'. All the same, organized crime can run into financial difficulties. In 1995, an accumulation of events led to red figures for Italian Mafia organizations. Some four thousand bosses, 'employees', and affiliates were in prison; lawyers' fees skyrocketed, as did the monthly salaries guaranteed by the Mafia to its inactive staff; property had been confiscated by the police; and operations in their most lucrative market – bidding for building and construction contracts – had been halted by the authorities.

'Facilitating payments' can be a euphemism for bribes, but the term also comprises the need for support; it may be a condition for certain types of business. Such payments are usually illegal, but appear under various disguises. It is hard to uncover what is behind certain consulting fees and commissions. The borderline between corruption and legal dealings is unclear and each country has its own laws and customs. The arms contract between Bofors and India became a sensitive issue at the end of the 1980s; government members and officials involved in exercising pressure and facilitating payments were suspected. During the 1990s, corruption among Italian politicians and civil servants has been continuously reported. These have been given *'tangenti'* – kickbacks – which means that to make a buying organization accept a supplier's offer, a percentage of the order sum has to be returned as a personal gift to those who handle the purchase. The Milan scandal showed that *tangenti* were a *sine qua non* to getting orders for building, construction, and service contracts for the subway, airport, railroad, sports stadium, and theatre.[105] In defence of competing suppliers it was established that there was no realistic way of getting an order without facilitating payments.

Organized crime is a challenge to the 'violence monopoly of the state'. One definition of organized crime is 'violence-based private protection operations in conflict with the state violence monopoly'.[106] The inertia of bureaucracy and its red tape, impossible regulations, and a lack of leadership and institutions open up a market for organized crime. When a state cannot handle the protection of citizens, for example against muggings and shop lifting, criminal groups can provide the protection for a fee and do it efficiently. The boundary between legal regimes and authorities and illegal organizations then become subtle. A legal system can be designed in a way that it is next to impossible to do business. Established gangs,

---

105 According to *Wall Street Journal* (Bannon, 1992).
106 Lappalainen (1993).

'*yakuza*', in Japan work more or less overtly. If *yakuzas* are left with their trade – primarily gambling and betting – they help the police to keep other crimes down. They can also be hired for special assignments, such as intimidating competitors or people who refuse to sell a company or a house.[107] In some areas of the world, the majority of small stores and restaurants, are forced to pay for 'protection' in order not to become victims of violence.

Here are some examples of multinational 'corporations', based on a criminal 'business mission' and organized as networks:

- *Italy.* Organized crime in Italy accounts for 2 per cent of GNP.[108] Eighty per cent comes from strictly illegal operations – drugs, car theft, hijacking of trucks and their loads – and the rest from legal activities carried out with illegal methods. The latter often concerns tenders and public contracts. The Italian statistical bureau ISTAT in 1993 estimated illegal crime revenue to US$18 billion with a staff of 170,000, making it the country's fifth largest corporation. Sixty per cent of the money lands on the official financial market. The three largest 'corporations' are *La Mafia* (Sicily), '*Ndrangheta* (Calabria) and *La Camorra* (Naples), all in the south. In the richer and industrialized northern Italy, says a business person, 'you can still say no to corruption, in the south they shoot you'.

- *Russia.*[109] Estimates claim that Russia has up to 5800 crime syndicates, of which 1600 have access to top government, industry and financial circles. As organized crime has taken over an estimated 80 per cent of Russian caviar production, quality has gone down dramatically and prices have been dumped. This can mean that Russian caviar is rapidly losing its image and value monopoly.[110] Soviet organized crime was divided among different 'corporations'. The Krasnodar mafia ruled the tourist trade in the Crimea; there was the Uzbekian cotton mafia and the Azerbedian petrol mafia. A string of organizations had conquered niches of the market, such as fruit and vegetables, collection of customs tariffs, and foreign trade. The political power and organized crime were united in securing privileges for the 'nomenklatura', the communist elite. Today, largely the same people together with trained members of former 'security' organizations constitute the core of organized crime. A particularly profitable service industry during the 1990s is based on prostitution, both in domestic and foreign markets. According to statistics from the Russian Ministry of the Interior, prostitution is Russia's third largest industry after the weapons and drug trade. The largest threat for the creation of a market economy in Russia is probably organized crime and the lack of adequate institutions and regulations.

  Foreign companies that established themselves in Russia and the Baltic states during the 1990s have had to pay special attention to organized crime. In 1994, after its president had been assaulted, Finnish oil giant Neste stopped all investment in Latvia while

---

[107] According to Rossander (1992).
[108] According to the Italian Institute Censis.
[109] Based on Waksberg (1992, 1994).
[110] *International Management* (1994).

waiting for the authorities to guarantee the safety of their employees.[111] The gas stations of Statoil, the major Norwegian oil corporation, were exposed to car bombs. The objective of Statoil was to open forty stations in the Baltic states by 1998. Two security companies have been hired for twenty-four hour surveillance of stations, offices and the residences of key staff. The infiltration of organized crime among authorities has not been confirmed but there are strong suspicions about corruption. For example, both Statoil and Electrolux have been victims of brutally executed tax raids.

■ *Hong Kong,* which is now part of China, has been described as a 'supermarket of crime'.[112] It is estimated to have some fifty criminal 'triads' with at least 100,000 members and these are closely related to other triads in China. 'Triad' here stands for the three elements of life – heaven, earth and human being. The organizations consist of 'a network of shady businessmen and friends in high places'. Just the smuggling of people to America gave a revenue of US$2.4 billion in 1992. Those who run and finance criminal operations such as drug trafficking are often business people, politicians and members of the legal system including the police. For them, it is just one of many types of investment. In Hong Kong it is obviously part of daily business to be exposed to threats unless you pay for 'protection'. Competing triads also collaborate in alliances, for example to facilitate the collection of debts, and outsourcing the heroin distribution in America to the New York mob.

These three countries serve only as examples. Organized crime and corruption are integral parts of every economy. An intriguing fact is that Hong Kong has one of the most flourishing economies in the world, Russia one of the failures, and Italy counts among the wealthy countries. Let us recall Blumberg's (1989) paradox discussed in R2 claiming that the strengths of the market economy – competition and the profit incentive – encourage fraud. In economic theory and its limiting assumptions about market mechanisms, violence is not included. In reality it is different; in some markets violence is the number one marketing tool. Both marketing theory and economics are treating criminal market mechanisms with naivety. Both white collar economic crime and organized violence distort the functionality of the marketplace and obstruct the dynamics of the marketing equilibirum.

A provocative hypothesis – and not a very agreeable one – is that a certain element of illegal action is necessary to make an economy work. Weak governments and inadequate official institutions/regulations, open the market for illegal entrepreneurship. RM, however naively, is based on a belief in win–win not only in individual relationships, but also from a societal perspective.

---

[111] The following example is taken from Paulsen (1994).
[112] From *Time* (Walsh, 1993, pp. 36–41).

Chapter 4

Mega relationships

Chapters 2 and 3 dealt with market relationships, the relationships to suppliers, customers, competitors, and others who operate in the market. This chapter is about mega relationships, located a step above the market relationships, in society in general. The mega relationships (R18–R23) set conditions for market relationships.

Relationship 18 Personal and social networks

In many cultures, business is not conducted with strangers and where business with strangers is accepted, the preference is for people one knows and likes. Even in the age of IT, the personal relationships will be pivotal. They are the most stable part of business life and can even help to mitigate recessions.[1] The formation and maintenance of social networks are important tasks for top management, marketing and sales. Sometimes social networks may even be more important than professional relationships and a supplier's competence.

As Figure 4.1 shows personal relationships and social networks have emerged from different areas of life, and they mostly have another origin than business. It is therefore justified to approach them as mega relationships.

Personal networks – the old boy network, invisible colleges – are locked for non-members. It may be just as appropriate to speak about old girl networks, as those can be strong through family, friendship, ownership, and class bonds, and their power is probably underrated.[2] Gender-based networks have attracted growing attention, particularly as women have formed their own networks against the suspected conspiracy of male networks. Rotary, composed of representatives from different trades and professions, used to be open only to men, but since the end of the 1980s it is also open to women.

It is possible if not always easy to establish new business relationships in the USA, but it is just as easy to break the relationships. In Japan it is difficult to be accepted, but relationships last. *Keiretsu* is the designation for long-term, personal

---

[1] See McKenna (1985).
[2] Kahn and Yoshihara (1994).

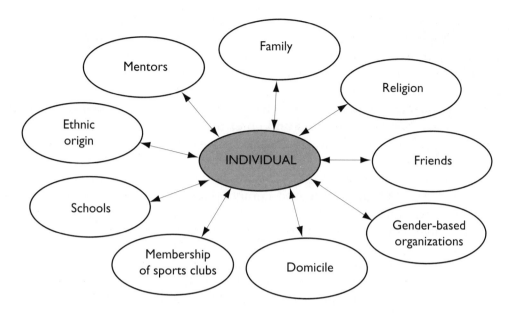

Figure 4.1 Different types of relationships that constitute an individual's social network

and financial relationships between companies. The good side is the potential productivity of a stable relationship, the bad side is that others are locked out. In the six largest *keiretsus*, firms are fifteen times more likely to borrow capital within their own group and three times more likely to trade with members than with outsiders.[3] The president of the US Chamber of Commerce in Japan claimed that *keiretsus*, bidding cartels and personal networks are formidable obstacles for US firms in Japan, whereas Japanese firms in the US do not encounter similar resistance.[4] At the same time, a study concludes that 94 per cent of large multinational corporations established in Japan are doing very well.[5]

According to Nakane:[6]

> In scope and density of personal relationships and in availability, 'school clique' relationships function more effectively than kinship…those educated outside Japan are handicapped in their careers. On the other hand, a foreigner who has been educated in Japan is accepted in the group and can enjoy and make use of in-group feelings…the sharing of experience during the critical period of the teens and twenties has life-long effects.

In Japan, both presidents of large corporations and government organizations

[3] Gerlach (1992, pp. 121 and 144).
[4] From an interview in *Fortune* (Faltermayer 1992).
[5] According to Kahn and Yoshihara (1994).
[6] Nakane (1981, p. 134).

come primarily from the University of Tokyo and some of the other leading universities.[7] Together with corporations, government agencies and politicians, they form a comparatively closed system within which a power elite is produced. Only when there is need to refill the systems, new members are let in. It is common that an official of a public agency, at the age of forty to fifty, transfers to industry and becomes a colleague with his fellow students who entered a business career. In the meantime, their sons grow up and enter the system and social alliances are formed through marriage. Clans and dynasties are established. The German word *'Schicksalverbundenhei'* – to be linked through a common destiny – has been adopted by the Japanese language. An example is found in the Case study below.

Networks based on friendship and family bonds are highly stable but require the members to adhere to tacit regulations/institutions. The team feeling is highly developed in Japan and it is almost a capital punishment to be excluded from the family, company, or university alumni association. It is practically impossible to exist in business if you are out of favour with the group.[8]

The ties to family and friends are grounded in strong feelings and values, not restricted by national boundaries or current domicile. Kotkin (1993) claims that

Case study

Yoshihiro Inayama and Shigeo Nagano were both graduates from University of Tokyo, one in 1924, the other in 1927. Nagano began his career at the private steelworks Fuji, and Inayama at the state-owned steelworks Yawata. In 1935, the two corporations merged into Nippon Steel. Nagano became section manager of the purchasing department and Inayama received a position in the sales department. After the Second World War, US general MacArthur broke up the merger for antitrust reasons. Nagano advanced to chief executive of Fuji and Inayama to chief executive of Yawata. In 1963, Nagano was elected chairman of the iron and steel industry trade organization, and was succeeded by Inamaya some years later. The two again merged Fuji and Yawata into a new Nippon Steel with Nagano as chairman of the board and Inayama as CEO. Nagano later became the leader of Nissho, a powerful coalition of chambers of commerce. Ten years later, Inayama became head of Keidanren, another coalition between businesses. The two friends now headed one of the world's largest steelworks and the two mightiest business coalitions in Japan. Taira and Wada conclude that '...the two close friends ruled Japan's business community and indirectly governed Japan itself'. The behaviour of the whole steel market was controlled by the personal relationship between two school friends.

---

[7] This and the following paragraph are based on Taira and Wada (1987); the example of the steel industry is taken from p. 271.
[8] Delaryd (1989, p. 175).

'the global village' is built of tribes, people with the same ethnic and religious roots. Their bonds outrank national industry policies and traditions. He lists several such networks: Jewish families have since the Middle Ages engaged in trade and finance; the Anglo-Saxon tribe consisting of Calvinists who emigrated from the British Isles to America spread their accounting system and trade law, and English as the international business language; Japanese expatriates who left their resource-poor home country see loyalty to their countrymen as the number one priority; Chinese and Indian clans control global networks of finance, and manufacture and market textile products, jewellery, and IT products. The swift rise of the Chinese market economy during the 1990s has been made possible through relationships with Chinese expatriates. This 'bamboo network' favours relatives at the expense of Western investors.[9] Western business people getting into China are at a disadvantage as they lack social bonds with key informants and gatekeepers.[10] There is strong distrust toward strangers; they do not get access to information on potential customers, for example on upcoming tenders. The *'guanxi'* network is highly personal; social relationships come first – they are on a mega level – and they can be followed by market relationships.

Social relationships and personal networks also play an important role in the American society. In his study of trust, Fukuyama[11] says that:

> ...if Americans were traditionally as individualistic as they think they are, it would be hard to account for the rapid rise of giant corporations in the United States in the nineteenth century...These supposedly individualistic Americans have also been, historically, hyperactive joiners, creating strong and durable voluntary organizations from Little Leagues and 4H Clubs to the National Rifle Association, the NAACP, and the League of Women Voters.

Network membership can also fool you. Membership based on position alone is lost if the position is lost. Presidents of important corporations often draw their power solely on their position. I have met a number of ex-chief executives who have been forced to leave their job because of a merger or disagreement with the owners, sometimes also because of failure. They are forced to find a new job, or start their own business, or become consultants. They often claim that they have contacts everywhere, but their 'friendship' was based on their position. When the position is snatched away, the 'friends' quickly leave the sinking vessel.

US ex-presidents are asked for as advisers and board members as well as speakers. Former Secretary of State Henry Kissinger runs Kissinger Associates, Inc. The business mission is exploitation of Kissinger's experience and personal network and the unique knowledge and power that follows. His capital is personal access

---

[9] Wiedenbaum and Hughes (1996).
[10] Björkman and Kock (1995).
[11] Fukuyama (1995, pp. 270–2).

to government members and other key leaders throughout the world. He sells informed advice on international affairs, access to the powerful elite, and the opportunity of hobnobbing with Henry Kissinger.[12] Among his thirty customers, have been Coca-Cola, GTE, Volvo and Montedison.

The borderline between social and professional relationships is partly erased; work may become an around-the-clock-lifestyle. Membership in professional associations gives an opportunity to meet competitors and have informal discussions, sometimes of great significance. Playing golf has long been considered a key to informal but crucial business decisions.

Friendship is characterized by people speaking to each other, helping each other, trusting each other, and spending leisure time together.[13] This can also happen in a commercial relationship which gradually changes character into genuine friendship: 'In communal relationships, members have a special obligation to be responsive to one another's needs, whereas in exchange relationships they do not'.[14] It can, however, result in abuse, and 'the friendly thief' is born.[15] You buy from a friendly person or friend because you feel an obligation and the buying becomes part of the social protocol. Home-party selling thrives on this. The sales people are often housewives who arrange selling parties with invited neighbours. It can feel awkward to leave the party empty-handed. At the same time the party fulfils a social need which you as friend/customer may value and be willing to pay for.

It is hardly news for marketing practitioners that social networks exert influence. Sometimes they are critical, sometime of little significance. Their role has not been taken up in the marketing and economics literature, especially not when the focus is directed to anonymous mass marketing, which has characterized marketing and economic theory during the past decades.

Relationship 19 Mega marketing – the real 'customer' is not always found in the marketplace

Apart for the relationships between individuals in the seller's and buyer's organizations and their social networks, there are other relationships that open or close the presence in a market. This requires *mega marketing*, a term defined by Kotler as '...the strategically coordinated application of economic, psychological, political, and public relations skills to gain cooperation of a number of parties in order to enter and/or operate in a given market'.[16] It is marketing above the market

---

[12] *Newsweek* (1990, pp. 34–5).
[13] According to Goodwin (1994).
[14] Clark (1983, p. 282).
[15] Cialdini (1984, p. 163ff).
[16] Kotler (1986); Definition on pp. 117–18.

proper which addresses public opinion and political power. Without the initial megadecision there is no market to address.

Often the real battle for the market is not fought in the market. *The real battle is about being in the market at all.* Only after *mega decisions* have been taken in the *non-market network* – above the market relationships – is it wise to start building market relationships.

Through the lenses of economic theory, markets are seen as intensely competitive and rational. The invisible hand – the ability of the market economy to strive in the direction of equilibrium between supply and demand – is not always an abstract and self-regulating phenomenon. It is also a hands-on intervention by powerful agents whose influence is not visible from the outside.

For example, the market system in Japan is partly out of function through centralized control, disguised to give the impression of competition.[17] Former students from prestigious universities, industrial heads, and government representatives make the decisions. If you are not accepted by them, you have little chance of success. It is essential to exploit both the market mechanisms and the central control: 'Successful Japanese businessmen who are adept at utilizing the rules of the marketplace are also generally good at the use of the nonmarket network of kinship and marital ties'.

Case study

In the mid 1980s, the French government decided that the state-controlled manufacturing of telecom equipment should benefit from competition from a second source located in France. Candidates were American AT&T, German Siemens, and Swedish Ericsson. Their proposals had been compared by technical experts and all complied with the required specifications, albeit with differences. The final decision rested with politicians. It is rumoured that US president Ronald Reagan gave discreet support to AT&T; German Chancellor Helmut Kohl and the President of the EU Commission, Jacques Delors, to Siemens. Ericsson negotiated through its chairman and its CEO who met members of the French government on several occasions. Under French Premier Fabius, a decision was taken to award the contract to AT&T but this was undone by the new government under Premier Chirac. The new Secretary of Industry and the Secretary of Telecommunications recommended AT&T, whereas the Secretary of Finance recommended Siemens. Ericsson was ultimately awarded the contract, possibly because it could unite the two opinions and was politically harmless.[18]

---

[17] The paragraph is based on Taira and Wada (1987); quotation from p. 288.
[18] Based on Hallgren (1987).

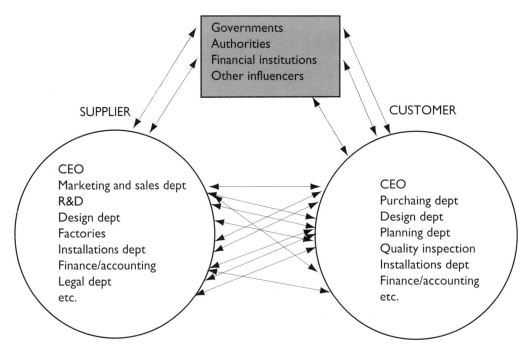

Figure 4.2 The real 'customer' can be found in a non-market network above the market

Mega marketing is often the most important part of marketing for companies producing goods and services of infrastructural character like telephone systems, military equipment, and nuclear power plants, but it can be the concern of any product and market.

The principal idea behind mega relationships is shown in Figure 4.2 which is an extension of Figure 3.5. The figure illustrates industrial marketing of a complex offering, but the same notion can be adjusted to consumer products.

Mega marketing is by no means new, but has not previously earned its way into marketing theory. One example is the financial wizard Ivar Kreuger who built an empire during the beginning of the twentieth century. By merging factories in many countries, Kreuger became the world market leader in safety matches and was granted a monopoly in several countries where he offered favourable credits to governments. At most he had an 80 per cent world market share. Despite the financial crisis that followed Kreuger's sudden death in 1932, the foundation was laid for a monopoly-like market status that has partly been sustained. The relationships on the mega level made marketing possible.

There are also general instances of locked networks on the mega level such as the 'military-industrial complex.[19] Buyers are national military organizations and suppliers are domestic and foreign manufacturers of weapons and defence

---

[19] See Arndt (1979).

Case study

Healon is injected into the eye during surgery and gently lifts and stabilizes the eye tissues. The substance dramatically enhanced the quality and productivity of common cataract surgery, but it required a revised surgical procedure. Healon could not be launched through the ordinary sales force, as the sales representatives did not have credibility among eye surgeons. Instead the ten most respected eye surgeons in the world were selected as the target group. If they converted to Healon, others would follow suit. Getting through to the megastars was not easy, it had to be achieved on a mega level. In one case, an effort was made to establish a relationship with a Spanish top surgeon who refused to meet vendors. A meeting was suggested with the Spanish Minister of Health, an ambassador, the president of Pharmacia-Upjohn, and the surgeon. The purpose of the event was to perform surgery together under the guidance of the surgeon – on eyes from dead cows, though. The status of the event was such that the surgeon agreed to participate.

systems. Within the military-industrial network there is an extreme need for mutual trust. Suppliers design specifications that must not leak to the enemy. The belonging of the seller and buyer countries to defence pacts can determine the outcome of the negotiations.

Mega marketing can be of a psychological and social kind and require communication with opinion leaders in the market. In order to reach difficult-to-access personalities, mega relationships are needed. The launching of a liquid for eye surgery, Healon, by Pharmacia-Upjohn provides such an example (see Case study above).[20]

Lobbying is part of mega marketing. The term lobbying comes from the US Congress and its lobby in which people waited to get an opportunity to speak to congressmen. Lobbying has developed into a profession. It is performed by trade organizations and interest groups as well as by single corporations. When Federal Express were about to start, changes in the regulations for postal services were needed, and the company managed to get these thanks to lobbying in Washington, DC The number of lobbyists in the United States is estimated to be 100,000 and Washington is the world capital of lobbyism. With the advent of the EU, Brussels, Belgium, became the European capital of lobbying.

The systematic and goal directed pursuit of an issue by means of lobbying is referred to as 'issues management'. There is a need for industries, companies and others to become involved in political decision processes at an early stage. If they become aware of a decision only through the news media, it is too late. Their knowledge of political decision processes are often superficial and therefore they need help from consultants. Lobbyists must belong to, or be able to access, a

---

[20] Based on discussions with the executives in charge of the launching of Healon.

network of relationships within the environments in which they operate. Presidents have these powerful networks; and ex-presidents relieved of their official duties have been called 'the ultimate lobbyists'.

Close relationships to a certain political group or individual politician can provide a strong marketing edge. If these 'friends' lose power and popularity, however, the intimate relationship can backfire. Business generally tries to be non-political and sell to everyone, irrespective of political colour. The skill of maintaining relationships with many political parties may be the ground for future business. Such a non-political strategy made possible the Iraq rearmament in preparation for the Gulf War in 1990.

In marketing terms, lobbying has been characterized as *a decision market*, the place (or space) where decisions are bought and sold. There is an evil and a good side of lobbying. In its good sense, lobbying conveys information and persuades politicians and others to consider the issues more carefully, using available knowledge. The need for lobbying is an effect of representative democracy not being, in practice, representative. It its evil sense, powerful economic interests can surpass the interests of society and citizens so that decision makers dare not act, or are misled. In order to prevent the misuse of lobbying, President Clinton introduced several regulations. For example, top officials and politicians are forbidden to work as lobbyists within five years of leaving office, thereby preventing them from 'selling' their administrative and political networks to external clients. Assignments must be registered in order to reduce the hush-hush surrounding lobbying.

The mega relationships involve customers, suppliers and others more deeply into the societal mega networks, not only in market networks. Approaching the customer with the marketing mix and the 4Ps is meaningless unless the basic conditions for marketing exist. There must be a stage to perform the play. In the examples above, the real 'customers' have been politicians, presidents, government members, and famed eye surgeons. None of these were accessible for a sales force. These real decision makers are not identified in marketing theory as being part of the market.

Marketing seems to be increasingly dependent on mega relationships as the following example indicates. It concerns complex products of importance for the buying country's infrastructure:[21]

- *1950s* – Direct exports and imports.
- *1960s* – Buyers stipulate that the sellers manufacture a small part of the delivery in the buying country.
- *1970s* – Demands on local manufacturing, national co-ownership, and support with financial solutions for the purchase.
- *1980s* – Additional demands include performing part of design and engineering in the buying country; supporting the exports of part of their production; establishing R&D projects together with the supplier; and barter.

---

[21] Based on the author's study of Ericsson.

■ *1990s* – Through deregulation in the industrialized world and the rapid development of technology the buying countries press their demands further. The Swedish defence negotiated the purchase of tanks from American General Dynamics. One stipulation was that the supplier should make sure that ABB would get a major order for rapid trains from Amtrak, the US railroads company. According to US law, a minimum of fifty per cent of the trains had to be manufactured in the USA, which was feasible through ABB's network of subcontractors.

A study of the relationships within Japanese business and between business and the public sector came to the conclusion that[22] '...business and government in Japan are like two major divisions of a well-run organization – Japan itself...the personal networks and contacts of the public officials and private business leaders render the formal structural distinction of government and business almost meaningless in Japan'.

As should be obvious from the examples, *mega marketing requires different skills than those usually existing in marketing and sales departments.* Marketers are not trained to play a political game on a mega level. Top management involvement with the aid of politicians, diplomats, lobbyists, and others is required.

Relationship 20 Alliances change the market mechanisms

Alliance is a designation for organized and agreed relationships between parties, for example between suppliers and customer and competitors. Companies can enter a large variety of dependencies which do not stand out in the traditional classification used in economics, such as monopoly and oligopoly. Alliances are part of corporate strategy and exist above the market relationships and the daily marketing routine.

While competition means that companies oppose each other, alliances mean collaboration. The incentives to enter into alliances vary. Alliances also vary in intensity and duration; they can be one-shot projects; imply limited but continuous collaboration; or take the parties so close that it is next to a merger. For Corning, alliances are so central that the corporation now describes itself as 'a network of organizations'.

Porter[23] defines five types of actors on the competitive arena: *present competitors, potential competitors, competitors that offer substitutes, customers* and *suppliers.* Between these, *competitive forces* develop as threats and power to bargain and influence. Interpreted within the spirit of RM, these *competitive forces* could also be perceived as *relationship forces*, giving birth to alliances.

Alliances appear in many costumes. Ohmae (1985) points to the necessity of global corporations to establish themselves in the triad of the world economy –

---

[22] Taira and Wada (1987, p. 264).
[23] Porter (1985, p. 5).

Case study

Another case is Apple Computer who established an alliance with Japanese Sony[24]. Apple made drawings and specifications for a new portable computer, Macintosh PowerBook, which Sony took from the design office to the factory and assembly line in just thirteen months. What were the advantages for the two partners? Apple could not mobilize enough designers to handle all the new products to be launched during 1991. Nor did Apple have experience in miniaturizing products, which Sony had; the PowerBook was to become a four pound (two kilo) variant of a sixteen pound (seven kilo) Macintosh. Sony wished to learn more about personal computers at the same time as it increasingly manufactured for others. It was also a strategic and prestigious assignment. Seven of the best designers were placed at their disposal and the CEO of Sony followed their progress personally.

North America, Western Europe, and South East Asia – and how this can be achieved through alliances with competitors. He gives examples from the auto, computer, and robotics industries which have formed alliances based on technology, marketing, and finance. In the UK, American Xerox has an alliance with Rank, marketing to Europe, Africa, the former Soviet states, and China. In Japan and India, Xerox has joined forces with Fuji and Modi. Thanks to these alliances, Xerox became the global market leader in the copier market. In Salisbury, England, visitors to the cathedral were offered a Pergamon roll as a token of their visit together with a discount coupon to McDonald's. The hamburger restaurant pays for the roll and gives a contribution to the restoration of the church. Body and soul have entered an alliance supportive to both of them. Disney and McDonald's have announced a promotional alliance; Disney products are going to be marketed through McDonald's 25,000 restaurants in 114 countries.

Collaboration *per se* is not new. It partly occurs in all buying and selling. When relationships are aiming for longevity and continuous development, outsourcing and imaginary organizations emerge and the relationship comes closer to formal alliances. The 'make or buy' choice has long been an issue in manufacturing, using different strategies. For example, GM manufactures 70 per cent of its components in-house, while Chrysler only manufactures 30 per cent. The rest is outsourced to others who increasingly deliver more composite modules and not just single components. Reebok develops and markets technically advanced and trendy shoes for sports and leisure. It has no factory of its own but outsources the manufacturing to Taiwan, South Korea and other Asian countries. The outsourcing of services is of more recent origin. Among the services that are contracted to

---

[24] See *Fortune* (Schlender, 1991).

other providers are transportation, cleaning, property maintenance, computer services, and canteens.

There is yet another link between companies that I have found little observed in the literature. We can call it *tacit alliances.* These emerge through industry consensus and mean that all industry members behave the same way. In an industry association, for example, good 'bedside manners' develop. These can grow slowly over a long period. A positive side is that they can instil ethical behaviour; a negative side is that they uphold the past at the expense of the future. Competitors – who have been converted to colleagues – protect each other and assume a hostile attitude to change, or at least pursue a wait-and-see strategy. Innovation then requires revolution, breaking with the tacit alliance.

I would like to introduce the concept of the *alliance market* with the following definition:

> An alliance market consists of companies which at a certain point of time are possible partners for an alliance.

The concept has similarities with a market for matrimony, with the difference that polygamy is allowed, even recommended. The alliance market operates at a corporate strategy level, above the market relationships. The first step is to find partners in the alliance market, the next to address the customer market.

When the major air carriers in Europe began to look for partners during the 1980s, only few attractive partners were available and everybody knew everybody else. SAS is one of the oldest alliances in the world; it has been in operation since 1946. It is made up of three companies from three countries – Denmark, Norway, Sweden – and owned fifty-fifty by the three states and private enterprise. In spite of this long experience of keeping an alliance together, SAS was not successful in extending it to other airlines. In 1997 a big step of welding an alliance was taken when SAS, Lufthansa, United Airlines, Thai, Air Canada and Varig announced the birth of Star Alliance covering 700 destinations and 95 per cent of all airports with regular passenger traffic. The alliance has since been expanded.

The expected outcome of airline alliances is improved competitiveness, increased sales, increased revenue and lower cost through coordination of destinations, timetables, reservations systems, ticketing and staffing.

In the USA, the number of formal business alliances increased by an average of 27 per cent per annum between 1985 and 1991 and the growth continued in the 1990s. The five US corporations which have most ardently pursued an alliance strategy put some 400 formal alliances together in the beginning of the 1990s: IBM (136 alliances), AT&T (seventy-seven), Hewlett-Packard (sixty-five), Digital

Equipment (sixty-three), and Sun Microsystems (forty-five).[25] In addition, these companies form an unknown number of informal alliances.

In a study of the globalization of hotels and restaurants, four groups of formal alliances were defined: strategic alliances, franchising, management contracts, and joint ventures.[26] *Strategic alliances* can vary from a common reservation system to complex networks including not only hotels but travel, holiday packages, and conference service. The European reservation system Amadeus and the American Sabre are of this character. *Franchising* is used by, for example, Holiday Inn with 1900 hotels offering 360,000 rooms. Those who run a Holiday Inn are independent firms but work strictly according to the concept of the hotel chain. The chain is entitled to a fee based on a percentage of the revenue. *Management contract* is an undertaking by someone to run a hotel for the owner, by applying skills, knowledge and systems but also to offer well-known names such as Hyatt or Hilton. SAS earlier expansion in the hotel market together with Intercontinental Hotels and Saison of Japan, is an example of *joint ventures*.

According to a study by McKinsey, out of forty-nine alliances, one third failed. Short-term alliances to reach quick results, such as cost reduction through downsizing, did not pay off; alliances should be strategic and long term. Alliances may look good on paper but may not work in practice. Another study showed that 70 per cent of all strategic alliances were discontinued or do not live up to expectations.[27] In an interview, the CEO of Whirlpool said that alliances are trendy but do not work. There follows comments on two issues, values and management, which are frequently reported to cause problems with alliances.[28]

Values

Making relationships between two corporate cultures work is known to be hazardous. Confrontations between value systems and cultural shocks are the rule rather than the exception. Time and patience are required to build relationships. There must be mutual trust. Trust cannot be assured through contracts and those who believe that lawyers can prevent the risks and hurdles of collaboration are bound to be disillusioned. As compared to many other cultures, the US business tradition seems to have a weakness in handling the more subtle aspects of relationships. The RM values discussed in Chapter 1 become clearly tangible in alliances. Alliances must be win–win, parties seeing each other as equals, as partners. Otherwise the parties will act covertly, trying to outsmart one another and thus pursuing hypercompetion strategies rather than RM strategies. It is not the formal structures – for example, that each partner owns equal shares of the

[25] See Forbes (Gumpert, 1992).
[26] Based on Tse and West (1992, pp. 126–32).
[27] Kanter (1989).
[28] See for example Lorange and Roos (1992).

alliance – which are crucial, but the spirit of the alliance. There are also obstacles in antitrust legislation, patent laws and the right to intellectual property, degradation of the other partner's ability, and the tradition to work alone rather than together.

Management

It is not easier to manage in a network of collaborating individuals and organizations than to manage a traditional hierarchical organization. Doz and Hamel[29] claim that 'Managing the alliance relationship over time is usually more important than crafting the initial formal design.' Management is definitely different although it offers more opportunities and varieties. If disputes arise, these cannot be settled by an executive in the same way as in the single enterprise. Managing an alliance jointly is not recommended; the risk of coming to a deadlock is pending. You either turn the alliance into a separate corporation which answers to its board, or you let one of the partners run it. The latter is recommended for an alliance where one partner possesses unique expertise which is crucial for future success. Giving the alliance full autonomy can be necessary for several reasons. The alliance must adjust to conditions prevailing in its market and not be drenched by its parent's financial control system and a standardized reporting format unfit for the operations of the alliance.

The advice provided by a marriage counsellor is surprisingly well suited for the advice needed for a company entering an alliance – choose your partner carefully, invest in a win–win relationship, stay attractive to your partner, develop a sound economy, and search for a division of labour that works for all parties. Good vibrations are needed, even if it is not passionate love. Still we know that decisions on cohabitation are taken under uncertainty with no guarantee whatsoever of the outcome.

Alliances lend opportunities for a company to achieve both *economies of scale* and *economies of scope* and yet stay lean and flexible; alliances are important elements of an imaginary organization. In order to cut down time to market and become more competitive – to create 'the fifteen minute advantage'[30] – companies can work together in constellations, concurrently performing several operations, and, via computer networks, do this in real time. Enchanted by the promises and potential of the electronic relationship (R12), however, it is easy to forget the importance of social relationships (R18) and the closeness to the customer (R8).

Alliances give birth to power networks which in themselves create partly locked markets. The complex networks of relationships which exist in markets create multifaceted interaction patterns between buyers, sellers, and others. These

---

[29] Doz and Hamel (1998, p. xv).
[30] The expression is taken from Skandia AFS.

patterns become institutionalized and limit the space for the market mechanisms. Within the spirit of RM and the marketing equilibrium, however, it is as equally important to utilize collaborative forces as it is to utilize competitive forces.

Relationship 21 The knowledge relationship

Knowledge can unite and divide. Established knowledge can inject stability and professionalism; if it gets obsolete it will stifle operations. New knowledge can initiate change, dissolve established industry definitions and create new ones, transcend geographical borders, and create novel technological conditions. Knowledge is often the basis for an alliance. The daily applications of knowledge may be part of the market relationships and the nano relationships, whereas new combinations of knowledge and new ways of commercializing knowledge largely exist on levels above market relationships.

In order to explore the knowledge relationship, we can ask the following question: 'If we look at the corporation from a knowledge perspective, what do we see that is pertinent to RM?'

Companies need knowledge to develop, produce, and market goods and services. Knowledge is progressively perceived as the core driver of competitiveness. In some organizations this is so evident that they are called knowledge-based organization or intelligent enterprises.[31] Current society is often referred to as the knowledge or information age. We hear more often these days that the future corporation is a learning organization – IBM presents this as one of its most prominent strategies for its reorientation – and its most eminent resource is intellectual capital.[32] The marketing of professional services has long been treated in the literature,[33] but a more general interest in knowledge and its meaning to organizations and profitability has grown over the past few years.

A company can be viewed as consisting of three knowledge processes:

1 the *generative* process in which knowledge is created;
2 the *productive* process transforming knowledge into products and services – or rather value-creating offerings;
3 the *representative* process handling the relationship to customers.[34]

In terms of traditional corporate functions, the generative process comprises R&D, design and engineering; the productive process production and purchasing; and the representative process marketing and sales. But emphasis is on knowledge, its content and significance. In alignment with modern thinking in

---

[31] See Sveiby and Risling (1986); Drucker (1988a); Quinn (1992); and Sveiby (1997).
[32] See Senge (1990); and Edvinsson and Malone (1997).
[33] See Wilson (1972); Gummesson (1977); and Ahrnell and Nicou (1995).
[34] According to Wikström and Normann (1994).

product development and the launching of new products – concurrent engineer-ing – the generative, productive, and representative processes are synchronous and reciprocal, not sequential steps. These processes embrace internal and exter-nal relationships that differ from those of the traditional hierarchical organization. The relationships are not tied to a certain structure or function; they constitute ele-ments of an imaginary organization.

According to Badaracco knowledge can either be *migratory* or *embedded*. This division has relationship consequences.[35]

Migratory knowledge is portable, it can emigrate and immigrate. In order to succeed in this transfer, the knowledge must be packaged in drawings, specifica-tions, books, videotapes, or databases. Furthermore, migratory knowledge can be a product which performs what an individual cannot; a computer and a crane are such examples. A product can be seen as 'frozen knowledge' and a skilled person can dismantle a machine and learn how it is constructed or make a chemical analysis of a substance. This is 'reverse engineering'; you start with the product and then make the drawing and specification instead of the other way around. Knowledge can also be moved when people leave one job and bring it to the next or start a new business. A necessary condition is that somebody can open the 'knowledge package' and has an incentive to do so. Patents and other methods of protecting inventions are insecure, particularly if the knowledge can easily migrate.[36]

Embedded knowledge cannot be transported as easily. It is embedded in '...spe-cialized relationships among individuals and groups and in particular norms, attitudes, information flows, and ways of making decisions...' Embedded knowl-edge is found in the skills of the master and the master's environment.

By being difficult to transfer, embedded knowledge offers a sustaining com-petitive advantage. In order to acquire this kind of knowledge, companies must have close access to those systems and relationships in which the knowledge is embedded. In their alliances with banks in the West, Japanese banks have insisted that the Western banks hire Japanese staff who can access the embedded knowl-edge of their allies. This is reported to have caused an asymmetric relationship. Instead of the mutually beneficial strategy of 'you show me, and I'll show you!' the strategy has become 'you show me, and I'll show my boss!'.[37]

Knowledge is not only embedded in an individual, group or corporation but also in the relationships between companies and – on a mega level – between companies and governments and between nations, and geography. Silicon Valley reached a critical mass of companies and innovative people within IT; knowledge was embedded in the community. In a similar vein Switzerland acquired fame for clocks and watches and Wall Street for financial knowledge. In Porter's extensive

---

[35] The following two paragraphs are primarily based on Badaracco (1991, pp. 79–81; quotation from p. 79).
[36] Porter (1980, p. 172).
[37] According to Wright and Pauli (1987, p. 63).

Case study

An example of embedded knowledge is Stradivari (1644–1737) who built violins with a sound quality and beauty that has not been surpassed since. This is not only explained by the skills of the master in using tools, wood, and varnish but also by his network within which others developed raw material, designed violins, experimented with new strings, invented techniques for treating wood, composed music, bought his instruments, and played on them. Stradivari worked in Cremona, Italy, where there was a century-long tradition of building violins, and he was the student of the master Nicolò Amati.

This way of working is not outdated or limited to the crafts and odd products like violins. It applies to all activities that require skills and knowledge, to high tech activities such as the design of software as well as the performing arts.

---

study of the competitiveness of nations, the geographically concentrated networks between companies in the same and supplying industries is emphasized:

> Once a cluster forms, the whole group of industries becomes
> mutually supporting. Benefits flow forward, backward, and
> horizontally…Entry from other industries within the cluster spurs
> upgrading by stimulating diversity in R&D approaches and providing
> means for introducing new strategies and skills…The cluster
> becomes a vehicle for maintaining diversity and overcoming the
> inward focus, inertia, inflexibility, and accommodation among rivals
> that slows or blocks competitive upgrading and new entry.[38]

Embedded knowledge can be moved by moving its holders and offering them a supporting environment.[39] French cuisine was created by Italian cooks. The technological and cultural development of the USA was partly the work of German intellectuals who fled the political persecutions during the 1930s and 1940s. Creative processes and knowledge advancement require interaction between individuals and professions in tightly knit networks. They need a meeting-place in order to interact. It is inherent in the nature of creativity that planned control in a rigid structure is not feasible and the meeting-places therefore are often informal. In Vienna and Paris people met in cafés, in Silicon Valley in bars, in Manchester, UK, at the Chamber of Commerce.

Embedded knowledge requires a different strategy than migratory knowledge. It requires extensive relationships and networks. These are influenced by the glob-

---

[38] Porter (1990, p. 51).
[39] This section is based on Törnqvist (1990, pp. 49–51).

alization of knowledge and its fragmented specialization to many individuals in many locations. The concept of *learning organizations* has been revived in the 1990s. Senge[40] lays stress on five 'disciplines' necessary to succeed in continuous learning: individual learning; guiding concepts and mental frameworks; leadership, shared values and visions; team learning; and finally the ability to see the whole, how everybody's contribution constitutes a system. Team learning makes possible knowledge development that individuals cannot achieve on their own, today like in the age of Stradivari: 'The discipline of team learning starts with 'dialogue'...To the Greeks, *dia-logos* meant a free flowing of meaning through a group, allowing the group to discover insights not attainable individually...Interestingly, the practice of dialogue has been preserved in many 'primitive' cultures...but it has been almost completely lost to modern society'. He further says that the requisite for team learning is the ability to interact.

Interpreted within RM, the team is more than the closest colleagues. It becomes a network of relationships which outgrows functional and hierarchical boundaries. It outgrows the organization, and extends to customers, competitors, suppliers, scientists, and others. It is a matter of handling the dialogue – the interaction – constructively in order to make the network stay alive. Dialogue means *availing oneself of existing knowledge* but also *creating new knowledge*; Einstein is reputed to have said that 'imagination is more important than knowledge'. Furthermore, you must teach others what you have created and the learning organization therefore has its counterpart in the *teaching organization*.

Knowledge not only creates and dissolves geographical and organizational borders, but also traditional industry borders. Cars, which are basically mechanical, contain more and more computer technology, and a new type of knowledge intrudes the auto industry. Until the end of the 1960s, offices could purchase purely mechanical calculating machines and these were supplemented with electromechanical machines. In the beginning of the 1970s these technologies were rapidly made obsolete by electronics, an entirely new concept which caused successful manufacturers to go bankrupt; they could not cope with the transfer from one technology to another.

Alliances between companies used to concern migratory knowledge, but the trend has changed[41]. From having been self-contained *citadels*, companies developed alliances through *product relationships* in order to transfer migratory knowledge and these then become *knowledge relationships* for the transfer of embedded knowledge. Knowledge relationships have four characteristics:

1 Learning and knowledge creation are increasingly the purpose of alliances.
2 Knowledge relationships need to be more intimate than product relationships.
3 Knowledge relationships require complex networks. Product relationships were usually established with competitors, whereas knowledge relationships are also estab-

---

[40] Senge (1990); quotation from p. 10.
[41] Badaracco (1991).

lished with universities, consultants, inventors, licensers, educators, customers, suppliers, and internally with functional departments.

4 Knowledge relationships have a greater potential, as knowledge is more general than a product which is one single application of knowledge.

Today, products are designed in minute detail and the design is meticulously documented. Despite this, there is *tacit knowledge* which has not found its place in the documents and is possessed by the master or a professional team. Lowe prefers the terms 'connoisseurship' and 'finesse' which epitomize the more subtle aspects of knowledge. Those properties belong to the master and are difficult to describe, they must be learnt through experience and socialization.[42] Not even computer programmers succeed in documenting all their knowledge about a piece of software, in spite of the thick manuals and the allegedly rational behaviour of computers. Instructions and signs are often hard to interpret, or are based on a logic which is different from the user's logic. We notice this as consumers when we try to install a VCR, or even worse try to use its timer function; we are brought into a jungle of instructions and industry jargon. Assembling furniture from IKEA can be quite an ordeal, but the customer-friendliness of the 'follow me' instructions – written in the international language of pictures – has been continually upgraded.

Gustavsson (1992) goes further below the surface by introducing *collective consciousness* as the substance of the organization. This is more than knowledge, it is the shared insights and wisdom which are revealed in the mode of operating, it is the activation of the deeper layers of our consciousness. Knowledge in this sense is more holistic and embraces not only the *knowledge* itself but also the *process* of creating the knowledge and the *personality* of the bearer of the knowledge. It is common sense in its broadest sense: 'common to all senses'.

Innovation networks can be established between suppliers and customers and other parties. The seller is usually described as the active driving force of the market through continuous change and innovation. According to one study,[43] however, innovations sometimes emerged among suppliers, sometimes among the future users, and sometimes in other organizations. Scientific instruments were developed in 77 per cent of the cases by customers; 90 per cent of ploughs were developed by suppliers; and of equipment for cable connections 56 per cent was developed by secondary suppliers, 33 per cent by primary suppliers, and 11 per cent by customers.

Intellectual capital, of which knowledge is part, is not visible in the balance sheet. It is not measured but exists all the same and may be the most crucial resource of the company. At Skandia, Leif Edvinsson is Corporate Director Intellectual Capital (Figure 4.3). The notion behind his title is expressed in the fol-

---

[42] According to a lecture by Andy Lowe at Strathclyde University, Glasgow, 1993.
[43] von Hippel (1988).

Leif Edvinsson
Vice President
Corporate Director
Intellectual Capital &
Skandia Future Centers

S-103 50 Stockholm, Sweden
Office: Sveavägen 44
Telephone +46-8-788 49 93
Telefax +46-8-788 34 64
Internet: edvlei@afs.skandia.se
Compuserve: 100433, 502

Skandia

www.skandia.se

Figure 4.3 Director of intellectual capital

lowing way:[44] 'While most companies appoint directors of finance and operations and focus company valuation on finance and operations, they lack a function to deal with hidden values…The mission of this function [Director Intellectual Capital] is to identify and improve the visibility of intangible and non material items, to capture and package these items for transfer to users, to cultivate and develop these items through training and knowledge networking, and to capitalize and economize on these items through rapid recycling of knowledge and increased commercialization.'

The work is performed in teams in order to secure the representation of all types of knowledge: 'Critical for this development is a federated global organization with competencies and alliances built on intellectual capital, information technology, and leadership around core cultural values.'

Relationship 22 Mega alliances change the basic conditions for marketing

In November 1994, Norway conducted a referendum about future membership in the European Union. In front of the TV screens, store owners along the Swedish side of the border watched the outcome with keen interest. It was also a referendum about their future, at that time a matter of some $400 million of consumer money. A yes to EU would reduce the border trade dramatically, a no – which was also the outcome – meant that Norwegians would continue to cross

---

[44] The quotations in this paragraph are taken from Buck-Lew and Edvinsson (1993). Intellectual capital will be treated further in Chapter 6.

the border to buy meat, tobacco, wine, liquor, gas, and other supplies at attractive prices.

In the previous mega relationships we have met social networks, mega marketing, alliances, and knowledge. *Mega alliances* are alliances above companies, industries and nations. They offer new conditions for business. Mega alliances are established through parliaments, governments and referenda, but also through resolutions taken on a supranational level. They give birth to new relationships and network constellations which become part of marketing.

All the same, the boundaries between corporate alliances and national alliances are partly blurred. Ohmae calls them the cartographic illusion of the interlinked economy. It is meaningless to proceed to view the world as a set of nations:[45] 'Put simply, in terms of real flows of economic activity, nation states have *already* lost their role as meaningful units of participation in the global economy of today's borderless world'. So it is not only the borders of organizations that become increasingly fuzzier, but also those between states. This is obvious in mega alliances where the objection often is that the member states lose their independence.

It is demanding to manage alliances between firms, but it is even more demanding to make alliances between countries work. Many national governments must come to agreements. Politicians are caught between considerations for national, local, party interests and their own re-election, and international cooperation. One of the dangers with the EU is the growing mammoth-like bureaucracies, another is the abuse of subsidies. According to one assessment, 9 per cent of the EU budget was awarded to fraudulent applications.[46] This cheating offsets the market forces for agricultural products in particular.

Building mega alliances is a long-term undertaking. The EU springs from the aftermath of the Second World War when British Prime Minister Winston Churchill proposed a United States of Europe. In 1947 the defence alliance NATO was formed and the US Marshall Plan brought new capital for the resurrection of Europe. In 1951, the Coal and Steel Union was formed with the purpose of preventing new wars. The Rome Treaty in 1957 established the European Economic Community, known as the Common Market, and it contained the seeds to the future mission of the EU: '...to work for a harmonious development of economic activity, continuous and balanced expansion, increased stability, faster increase of living standards, and closer relationships between the member nations.'

The four freedoms of EU provide new conditions for marketing. They offer free mobility across borders of *goods, services, people,* and *money*. Here are some examples of marketing consequences:[47]

---

[45] Ohmae (1995, p. 11).
[46] Based on reports in *European Times* (1994).
[47] These examples are partially based on Naisbitt and Aburdene (1990, pp. 49–50).

- The EU offers opportunities for specialists such as medical doctors, lawyers, and engineers to work in member countries without local authorization. Examinations which require at least three years of academic studies will be valid throughout the union, and later shorter specialist education will also be accepted, such as training for nurses. From 1993, six member countries had allowed free mobility of labour. In practice, however, language, nationalism, and local regulations for professionals will form barriers for many years.

- Competition for public contracts will change as governments on all levels are no longer allowed to favour domestic suppliers. This market may be worth as much as US$1000 billion, which is more than the GNP of several of the member states. In 1993, less than 20 per cent of all public tenders were open to competition from other countries; no member state had so far made legislation in its favour. Even if EU legislation takes precedence over national law, it will be difficult to apply unless national governments actively support the implementation.

- A series of IT-based services will simplify national borders for authorities and improve transportation planning, this in turn reducing pollution. SAD, a dismal acronym for Single Administrative Document, replaced some seventy documents needed to drive a truck through Europe. It means that the average speed of twenty miles per hour could be increased considerably.

- The next step is to establish a common currency in EU member states who will then abandon their national currencies. The 'ecu' is already used in special applications, but the 'euro' – when accepted by the member states – will render the 'bureaux de change' superfluous as well as the traveller's inconvenience of keeping track of a variety of coins and banknotes.

This all leads to faster distribution, more efficient logistics, simplified inventory, reduced capital employed, cheaper insurance, and simpler financial transactions. The cost of goods and services is reduced, marketing is facilitated, and competition is intensified.

Large multinational manufacturing companies, irrespective of national origin, have for decades been gradually adjusting to the new situation by establishing subsidiaries and alliances inside the EU. Domestic companies and smaller companies, particularly in the formerly protected service sector, are less prepared.

EU creates mega conditions which determine the rules of the marketplace. As was shown in R19 on mega marketing, companies and industries will try to influence the new conditions through lobbying at EU headquarters. The number of lobbyists has grown from 300 in the early 1990s to over 10,000. It is hard to tell how much the lobbyists can intervene, and how much is just keeping abreast with changes and sending home information for strategic marketing decisions. Close relationships to influential EU politicians and bureaucrats of course means informal power. There is the misgiving that rich corporations can buy the 'best' professional lobbyists – a full time lobbyist costs from US$300,000 per annum – while the less rich will be in a constantly inferior position.

EU demands adaptation in many details which has provoked consumers in member countries. Local lifestyles are challenged which offer new marketing opportunities and threats. The favourite cigarette of the French, Gauloise, became thinner to the great dismay of its fans, and French cheese made by non-pasteurized milk ('*lait cru*') was threatened with prohibition. The typical French citizen walking from the local 'boulangerie' with a fresh non-packaged 'baguette' under the arm will be history if unpackaged bread, as suggested, will be forbidden.

The North American continent has its corresponding mega alliance between USA, Canada and Mexico. The North American Free Trade Agreement, NAFTA, was signed in December 1993 and embraces 370 million consumers.[48] Canada, Japan and Mexico are the largest trade partners for the USA, and two of these are now integrated in the mega alliance. Already during the first quarter of 1994, the Mexican trade with the USA went up by 17.5 per cent and with Canada by 30 per cent. There are barriers for European and Asian companies to profit in NAFTA; 62.5 per cent of the components in manufactured products must come from NAFTA countries. This provided an obstacle for Mercedes who assembled cars in Alabama, USA, but manufactured the components in other countries. A series of non-tariff barriers and 20,000 tariffs will be abolished during a ten to fifteen year period, from the Canadian tariff on Mexican Tequila of 183 per cent to the US tariffs which on an average amount to 4 per cent. US retailing chains, such JC Penney, Dillards and Wal-Mart, can open up stores in Mexico where large-scale retailing has so far been absent. Before the year 2000, JC Penney plans to establish sixteen stores. Wal-Mart has entered an alliance with Mexico's largest retailer, Cifra, and in 1994 they had opened twenty-four stores together. Alliances are necessary as Mexican consumers have a low per capita income and other lifestyles, but expect more individual service. 'People greeters' wish you welcome to the store and accompany you inside and hand you a trolley; 'the 10-foot rule' states that customer contact must be established within the first 10 feet.

Through the larger market opened up by NAFTA, the possibilities increase for large-scale production and cost reductions on mass-produced goods and services. The bigger markets and deregulation also imply tougher competition. Banks, insurance companies, and telecommunications are other industries that see new opportunities. Mexico entered the mega alliance with only eight telephones per 100 inhabitants, while USA and Canada had over ninety. During the first NAFTA year, Detroit's three largest car manufacturers increased sales from 1000 to 60,000 cars. Through its presence in the USA, NAFTA enabled Skandia to found a subsidiary in Mexico, Skandia Vida. It offers 'unit linked insurance', which is an alternative to traditional life insurance and retirement plans. The customers decide themselves how their capital should be invested and consequently also take responsibility for the size of the returns.

Mega alliances are not only permeating business in the US and Europe and

---

[48] The text on mega alliances in America and Asia primarily builds on media reports.

changing the marketing conditions and relationships. The same is happening throughout the world. In 1994, Argentina, Brazil, Paraguay and Uruguay agreed to establish a common free trade area and tariffs union, Mercosur. In Middle and South America there is the Central American common market and the Andine Pact. From Latin America it has been proposed to turn the whole area into a free-trade zone within ten years. Asean (Association of South East Asian Nations) consisting of Thailand, Malaysia, Singapore, Indonesia, Brunei and the Philippines is developing into Afta (Asean Free Trade Association). Apec (Asia Pacific Economic Cooperation Forum), which includes fifteen countries on both sides of the Pacific, was in 1993 still a discussion club. Gatt (General Agreement on Tariffs and Trade) functions as a general promoter of free trade. In addition, there is a large number of bilateral trade agreements.

History shows that mega alliances have always been part of politics, defence and economy. The future value of mega alliances is even harder to evaluate. It is hard to evaluate even in retrospect as we do not know what would have happened without them. The outcomes of referenda in many countries – where yes or no has won with very small margins – exhibit insecurity and confusion among citizens. It is obvious though that the EU, NAFTA and the other mega alliances change the rules of the marketing arena and require new relationships and networks. They need to be treated as an integral part of marketing theory in the light of relationships, networks and interaction.

Relationship 23 The mass media relationship

Media report events from corporations, governments, and markets. Media have an impact on marketing, but exercise their influence primarily on the mega level, they are part of society rather than of the market.

According to one definition public relations, PR, is '...the management function that identifies, establishes and maintains mutually beneficial relationships between an organization and the various publics on whom its success or failure depends'[49]. PR comprises relationships to stakeholders with the purpose of maximizing the goodwill of the corporation or industry.

The relationships can embrace society at large, a town, a trade union, the investor market, and others. Often PR is primarily a marketing tool. Lobbying, which was treated in R19, can also be part of a PR function.

The term public relations is often associated with gimmickry and manoeuvring. Other terms are used to mitigate the negative connotation of PR, such as corporate communications and corporate affairs. Burson-Marsteller, the world's largest public relations consultants, see their work as 'perception management'. Its purpose is to influence perceptions – knowledge, attitudes, values, feelings – of

---

[49] Cutlip, Center and Broom (1985, p. 4).

customers and other stakeholders toward a company, a product, a service, new technology or a person.

The media relationship can be split into three types:

1 the relationship between an organization and media;
2 the relationship between media and their audiences;
3 the relationship between an organization and the media audience.

There are also intermediaries such as Reuters and United Press (UP) that select and distribute information. They are the wholesalers of the 'news' distribution networks, with television stations, radio stations, newspapers, and journals as the retailers. Some of the readers, listeners, and watchers are customers or prospective customers (the market relationship), some are politicians, legislators, or investors who can exercise influence over a company or industry (the mega relationship), and some are employees (the nano relationship)

The treatment of the media relationship will focus on the first and direct relationship, the one between an organization and the media. They are important to companies and customers whether a company is willing to interact with media or not. Therefore, it is part of a rational and proactive marketing strategy to pay attention to media relationships.

Even if companies and media need each other, there is a goal conflict. Companies want the good news to be published and the bad news to be held back. They want media space as free advertising, with the higher credibility that may be attributed to an editorial text than to a journal advertisement or a television commercial. Media want facts that make news and often preferably news that is sensational and even offer a scandal. The mission of media in democracies is to reflect society and analyse, interpret, and report events, and particularly hold misuse of power at bay. Editors and reporters have many incentives, such as passion for the truth, personal integrity, reaching a large audience, fame, esteem among colleagues, vanity, and revenge.

Corporations and media nurture a love–hate relationship; they have to stay married for better and for worse. It is essential to strike a balance between the value for both parties, so that both – at least over the longer term – perceive themselves as winners. If the relationship remains asymmetric – one party feeling exploited – the value of the relationship may become continuously negative for both, at the same time as divorce is no solution.

The ability of business leaders to create relationships with media can sometimes be their most importance marketing activity, the activity that determines a corporate image. In the 1980s Lee Iacocca of Chrysler made the headlines, in the 1990s Bill Gates of Microsoft.[50]

---

[50] See Iacocca (1984), Gates (1995).

Case study

A European example is Jan Carlzon. As president of Scandinavian Airlines (SAS) he became a media pet. Particularly in the beginning, he devoted ample time both to the media and to individual communication with employees on all levels. He skilfully used television to address existing and new groups of passengers as well as employees; much of his internal marketing went via the ordinary television networks. He could explain the role of leadership, the necessity of putting the customer in focus, and the advantages of service and quality. He made new market segments try air travel. He did it in a different and charismatic manner. Friendship with the media is not forever, though. When SAS failed to form strategic alliances with European and US major carriers – a necessity for marketing and survival – the media turned against Carlzon with headlines such as 'Are you finished now?' His private life was scrutinized. It all gave free publicity, but it is unclear whether it was beneficial to SAS or not. It certainly kept up the public interest in the company name – and the market needs continuous reminders.

When a critical and unexpected incident occurs, the relationship with the media can determine a company's future. Perrier, Bergene and Luby's provide examples:

- In 1990, a lab found traces of the carcinogen benzene in the French mineral water Perrier, a beverage which stood for a healthy lifestyle. It was the preferred drink of the young successful American business person, the yuppie. In the USA alone the yearly sales were $150 million. Perrier had no crisis strategy and was taken off guard. The firm behaved evasively, blaming the trouble on one cause after another. When a consumer telephoned Perrier to ask about benzene and the health risk they did not know what to say.[51] The brand name quickly lost its glamour and 160 million bottles worldwide were called back. In its home market France, people did not hesitate to go back to Perrier. In Britain and the USA the return was slow and gave competing waters such as Evian an opportunity.
- Bergene – a leading manufacturer of chocolate bars in Norway – followed another strategy. An outbreak of salmonella was located to the raw chocolate used in Bergene bars. The management chose to cooperate closely with media and health authorities and to be totally open. An internal task force, including representatives of the authorities, was appointed and no cost was spared to take necessary action. After an initial drop in sales and a bad year financially, Bergene recaptured its market position.
- Luby's, with 145 restaurants in America, had an emergency plan knowing that consumers, media and investors could react randomly and neurotically if a catastrophe or

---

[51] Popcorn (1992).

bad publicity occurred. In 1991, twenty-three people were shot down at one of their cafeterias, a killing which had nothing to do with Luby's as such. In one hour the company stopped all trade with its stock. The CEO was at the scene of the crime in two hours, arranging free hotel rooms for relatives of the victims, setting up a fund and guaranteeing that the employees would keep their jobs if the restaurant closed down.

The cases show different situations of the media relationship and different types of interaction. Perrier was ill prepared and reacted with evasiveness while Bergene, just as badly prepared, chose an overt and successful strategy forming a friendly alliance with media. Luby's was well prepared.

To gain media exposure when new products and services are launched is the dream of all companies. In 1948, Victor Hasselblad launched his new camera at a press conference in the USA.[52] He was unknown, but invited twenty reporters from the professional photo press. They hailed the camera as the perfect product. Hasselblad's relationship to this small group of opinion leaders was decisive for the rapid success of the camera. It became the natural choice for the first journey to the moon and fifty years after its introduction the Hasselblad camera holds its position among professional photographers as the king of cameras; it has a 20 per cent global market share in its niche. And it has kept its position as a media pet. In 1995, says a spokesperson for the company, the attention from the professional press was so high that there was no need to advertise the new products.[53]

Instant success through the media may be more difficult to achieve in today's escalated media noise. 'A weekday edition of *The New York Times* contains more information than the average person was likely to come across in a lifetime in seventeenth-century England', says Samuel Wurman in his book *Information Anxiety*.[54] Even if there is sometimes no response at all, media, including advertising, have a reinforcing role and can activate an interest that is already there. There is no doubt that mass media, not least for establishing and maintaining the parasocial relationship (R13), will remain important even if TRM advocates individualized approaches to both consumers and organizational customers.

An essential distinction must be made between investigative journalists, who are knowledgeable and apply systematic research techniques in long-term fact-finding missions, and the general reporter who is expected to cover any type of event and have an article or news flash ready in the next few hours. There are reporters and media specialized in certain industries, such as telecommunications or cars, which they follow continuously. There is even a special group of reporters and consultants around IBM – the IBM watchers – who focus singularly on IBM reporting and interpreting its decisions and activities.

Media can be approached through a variety of means: formal press conferences, informal meetings, press messages, interviews, etc. It is not just a matter of offer-

---

[52] Based on an article by Hemmungs Wirtén (1992).
[53] Interview with the Hasselblad information director (*Info*, 1996).
[54] Wurman (1989, p. 32).

ing news, but also of a personal and trusting relationship. It requires planning and stamina, just as all types of marketing. The media relationship is part of a total communications process, including internal marketing activities.

Virtual reality is an IT creation. Photos can already be manipulated with fairly ordinary computers; the dinosaurs of the movie *Jurassic Park* came to life through software; and in another movie Forrest Gump shook hands with President Kennedy, who died thirty years before the movie was made. Information and entertainment merge into infotainment.[55] Another unreal reality has long been around, the pseudo event and the pseudo news. *A pseudo event is engineered to be reported, it is not reported because it happened naturally.* Examples are the use of celebrities in the launching of a film, book, restaurant, sports game, or an art exhibition. Celebrities are add glamour to these events; in fact the events do not receive media coverage for what they are, but for the celebrities. These events build on the marketing of people: actors, authors, chefs, athletes and artists, and also CEOs and politicians. Media play a major role, maybe even *the* major role in their marketing. Talk shows with celebrities have become everyday programmes of television channels.

The following lines from a book on 'celebrity marketing' succinctly sum up the importance of the media relationship:[56] 'Because the media make up the most powerful of channels, they are crucial to winning high visibility. Other channels are capable of moving celebrity images out of the warehouse and into the marketplace, but none approaches the cost-effectiveness and audience impact of the mass media'.[57]

---

[55] See Postman (1987) who treats the confusion between reality and entertainment which above all television has contributed to.

[56] Rein, Kotler and Stoller (1987, p. 255).

[57] Inspiration to this relationship also comes from Karaszi (1991); and Hadenius and Weilbull (1993).

Chapter 5

Nano relationships

The previous chapter discussed relationships above market relationships. This chapter deals with the opposite, relationships below the market proper, that is inside an organization. These nano relationships (R24–30) are found in the suppliers' organizational structure, systems, and processes. They provide the antecedents for implementation of marketing activities and success with the market and mega relationships. They also provide a basis for handling mega relationships. The nano relationships show that there exists a market economy inside a company and that the boundaries between a company's external and internal work have become increasingly blurred.

Relationship 24 Market mechanisms are brought inside the company

Parallel to networks and alliances that curb the free market mechanisms outside the company, there is a long-term trend to install market mechanisms inside the company. The market mechanisms have partly replaced the internal planned economy, and it is not always clear who is the seller, buyer, or competitor. The boundaries between 'them' and 'us' become blurred. New marketing strategies are needed to handle the new internal and external market relationships.

In its purist form, a company can be seen as a planned economy where clearly defined activities are coordinated toward clearly defined objectives with the help of a business mission, goals, strategies, production systems, organizational structures, budgets, and financial control systems. Planned economies, as we know them from communism, have gigantic problems with productivity, quality and growth. They are known for rigidity, lack of initiative, and a general inability to manage their countries. In terms of number of employees, but not necessarily in terms of financial resources, corporations are tiny as compared to nations. Yet companies run into the problems of the planned economy, and have therefore constructed a dynamic internal market economy. This trend has been sustained since the 1960s. It is usually referred to as *decentralization* but within the concept of RM, I would prefer to see it as an expression for *internal deregulation and re-regulation*.[1]

This is pertinent to RM in so far as the relationships inside the organization change in two ways. First, market relationships are brought inside the company, constituting a new base for external market relationships. Second, from having had internal stability (at least in theory) via administrative routines, a market-like relationship is born between the internal supplier and the internal customer.

The introduction of a market economy inside the organization becomes visible in the organizational structure in several ways (Figure 5.1):

■ The company is organized in four types of units:
  1 top management and the board;
  2 operational units with production and marketing/sales as the core;

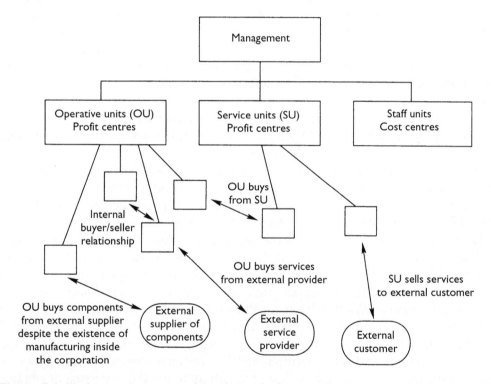

Figure 5.1 Market mechanisms are brought inside the organization

---

[1] An in-depth analysis of decentralization is found in Södergren (1987, 1992). In an anthology, Halal, Geranmayeh and Pourdehead (1993) have focused on the internal markets and their deregulation. They use an approach from organization theory and to some extent from economics. RM adds dimensions to this analysis by including services marketing, the network approach, and quality management together with the concepts of interactive and simultaneous production and consumption, the customer's role, internal marketing, internal and external customers, as well as new accounting theory (intellectual capital, balanced scorecard).

3 internal service units;

4 support or staff units.

■ The operative units and service units become profit centres: business areas, division, subsidiaries, and smaller profit centres within these. The most important units – strategic business units (SBUs) – are given considerable independence.

■ Separating staff units from internal service units is often not easy. Staff units are an extension of management at different organizational tiers. As such, they are treated as cost centres, even if they support and serve profit centres. With the purpose of utilizing the strength of the free-market forces, the strategy is usually to turn as many units as possible into service units. However, going too far in this direction may cause ineffectiveness through internal avoidance of the units, and a stifling and costly internal accounting system.

■ The original idea is that profit centres should enjoy autonomy. It means, for example, that a production unit can deliver to a marketing and sales unit, but the marketing and sales unit can use an external supplier if it does not find a brother or sister offering the right conditions. An internal service unit can deliver services together with an external provider and the specialists of an operating unit, but could also sell its services to external companies. The internal business requires an internal pricing system which should be competitive with the prices on the market.

There is no marketing theory treating the internal market mechanisms, despite the fact that decentralization and internal deregulation have gone on for so long. The notion of internal pricing indicates that the market has been let in, although less on market conditions than on accounting conditions.[2] During the 1980s, even the government sector began decentralization with profit centres.

Internal pricing may lead to inertia in relationships. If every cent must be accounted for – you can hardly talk to somebody in another profit centre without receiving an invoice – efficiency is arrested. It is possible for management to use regulations and interfere only when the market mechanisms are not adequate, thereby establishing internal marketing equilibrium. Internal pricing is important for core activities, less so for support functions. If a more rational and cost-effective mode of operations has been established with the assistance of internal pricing and competition during a period, continuous internal charging becomes less important. The practice of internal pricing is, however, an attempt to get away from arbitrary cost-plus pricing which has the character of internal taxation.

According to *transaction cost analysis,* the rationale for the existence of organizations is the notion that external information is less accessible and internal information is easily accessible.[3] The analysis assumes that internal relationships are well under control, and therefore the internal transactions become more efficient than transactions with external parties. It is consequently easier to operate inside

---

[2] There is a long tradition on internal pricing. The discussion here is partly influenced by an interview with Göran Arvidsson (Wennberg, (1994).

[3] Transaction cost analysis is further discussed in Chapter 7.

an organization than being dependent on market research techniques and other intelligence for learning about customers, competitors and others, some of them intentionally obstructing access to information. However, the assumptions of transaction cost analysis evaporate if we cannot clearly separate the organization from its environment, if there is interference with the external market mechanisms, and if market mechanisms are introduced inside the organization.

Corporations have been divided into profit centres for decades, but the early efforts created confusion about responsibility and authority. Although relationships between corporate headquarters and divisions are often strained, the ability to manage divisionalized organizations has improved and profit centres are common in all types of organizations.

The internal relationship market may be seen as a triad embracing two profit centres, one being the supplier and the buyer, and a relationship between each of the profit centres and corporate management.[4] The relationships are characterized by collaboration and competition, affinity and conflict. Corporate management enforces a certain amount of regulation. The three units – supplier, buyer, management – are in turn nested in a larger network within which their relationships are affected. In the relationships between supplier and customer, there is exchange between goods, services, money and information. Certain peripheral services can facilitate the relationships, such as computer-based ordering and invoicing systems.

By bringing the market into a company, new types of internal networks materialize. Management will still exercise governance through hierarchical power in the network. In an analogy with the external market, management is a government who can introduce regulations that limit free-market mechanisms:

Case study

A case study made by Hultbom will serve as an illustration to internal relationships in a profit-centre based organization. The members of the triad are Electrolux corporate headquarters (HQ) and its subsidiaries Husqvarna (selling sewing machines on the external market) and Mecatronic (internally selling components for sewing machines):

> In the study of the triad, it is not apparent that the relationship between Husqvarna and Mecatronic was affected by actions from HQ. The two profit centres were left alone. There were no signs that the internal interaction between the two was smoother and the transaction costs lower than if they had been totally independent companies and acted on the external

---

[4] This is based on Hultbom (1990, pp. 101); the case study quotation from pp. 136–7.

market. Both seller and buyer considered price negotiations cumbersome and information on deliveries was not easily available. Mecatronic found cooperation on R&D and manufacturing issues essential, but Husqvarna employees considered themselves on top of technology and claimed product development was best handled by them. There was an apparent risk for sub-optimization from the point of view of the corporation. The hierarchical power of HQ indirectly affected the selling–buying relationship. Husqvarna, being one of the world leaders on sewing machines, felt secure. Mecatronic on the other hand had been through a fundamental restructuring process. It had commenced the manufacturing of a new product which developed rapidly (as viewed from an engineering perspective). It gave rise to insecurity and a protective attitude. HQ demanded quick return on the investment which could disturb the long-term development of Mecatronic. The cumbersome price negotiations were probably caused by HQ's demand for rapid return. This demand and the internal competition created less satisfactory information flows in the buyer–seller relationship.

1 Management monitors the profit centres through financial reports.
2 The acquisition of financial resources is usually centralized, which means there is internal competition for capital. The independence of the operational units in allocating their profits is often limited, for example when new investment and development projects are planned.
3 Top management hire and fire the heads of business areas, subsidiaries, and divisions.
4 Everyone is expected to work in alignment with the corporate business mission, goals and strategies.
5 There is informal pressure.
6 The internal units may do business with any supplier or customer outside the corporation if they find this more profitable; but in practice, one cannot be certain that corporate management will support such freedom.

Within this framework, the internal units are allowed to act on market conditions in the relationships with one another. They often belong to different industries. Markets for goods and services exist inside the company and the internal units send invoices to each other. Consequently the relationships between the employees and functions will be different than in a traditional planned economy hierarchy. The difference between the internal operations of the corporation and the external market becomes less evident.

Internal exchange of information is often filled with conflict, while the exchange can be quite peaceful in external markets. As there is a defined hierarchical structure above the profit centre relationships in combination with market mechanisms, the relationships may even become more complex internally. Market mechanisms require that the interests of different parties are confronted and that goal conflicts are resolved.

The market system involves duplication of work. From an accounting perspective, this is not considered cost effective and is to be avoided through co-ordination. At the same time, coordination of human activity only works to a limited degree and if driven too far will cause inertia, low productivity and low flexibility.

Critics also claim that the profit centres are just shovelling money around inside the corporation and not adding value. The fact that companies keep decentralizing could be evidence that there are more advantages than disadvantages in the use of profit centres. The dynamics of the shorter and quicker decision routes and the opportunities for profit centres to develop their own relationships and networks outweigh the disadvantages. Inside the organization as well as in the market there is a trade-off between freedom and regulations.

> In the same way as we need to strive in the direction of marketing equilibrium externally – in the market and society – we must strive for marketing equilibrium inside the organization. This will be explained further in Chapter 7.

Relationship 25 Internal customer relationships

Lee Iacocca who took over as CEO of Chrysler, the third largest car manufacturer in America, described his first impressions in the following way:[5]

> Nobody at Chrysler seemed to understand that interaction among different functions in a company is absolutely critical: People in engineering and manufacturing almost have to be sleeping together. These guys were not even flirting...The manufacturing guys would build cars without even checking with the sales guys. They just built them, stuck them in a yard, and then hoped that somebody would take them out of there. We ended up with a huge inventory and a financial nightmare.

This quotation serves as a perfect introduction to relationships and dependency between different functions in a company, an aspect that is missing or only men-

---

[5] Iacocca (1984, p. 162).

tioned in passing in marketing theory. Here, I will borrow two concepts from quality management: the *internal customer* and *process management.*

In Figure 5.2 each ring represents an internal supplier and internal customer, beginning and ending with an external customer. It is a matter of *interfunctional dependency* and *horizontal interaction*, knocking down walls between specialist functions and organizational silos. It is also a matter of *interhierarchical dependency* and *vertical interaction* as there are also walls between the tiers of the organizational pyramid.

The relationship between operations management – R&D, engineering design, purchasing, manufacturing – and marketing is particularly important. It will be treated as a special case in R26, the reason being that modern quality management, TQM, is specifically addressing the gap between engineers and marketers.

Traditionally, there are conflicts between specialized functions and between organizational tiers. They form subcultures and tribes within the company and tribal warfare is common.[6] But organizations could be perceived as bundles of processes rather than piles of boxes. One such process is visible in Figure 5.2. *Process thinking* is gradually dominating the renewal of corporations. According to Harrington:[7] 'Everything we do today can be done better by concentrating on the process. Management has taken away our employees' ability to produce error-free output by saddling them with obsolete, cumbersome, bureaucracy-

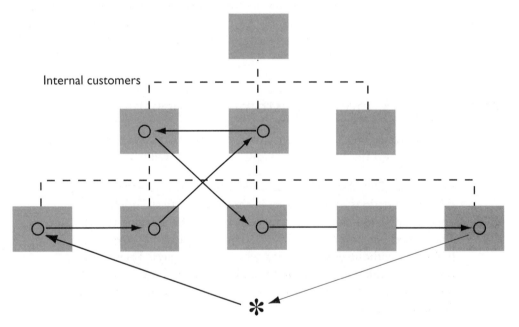

Figure 5.2 Relationships between internal customers, internal suppliers and external customers in a hierarchical structure

[6] See further Neuhauser (1988).
[7] Harrington (1991, p. x).

laden business processes.' Processes thinking is inherent in ISO9000, an international standard for purchasing and quality development. In order to acquire ISO certification, suppliers must document their processes. *Business process reengineering (BPR)* [8] is promoted as a dramatically new view on management. It requires rethinking the company from scratch without commitment to current structure and to reorganize around processes instead of specialist functions.

The arrows in Figure 5.2 indicate how a process can wriggle its way through an hierarchy. If we mentally erase the hierarchical structure we can visualize the relationships and the process more clearly. Principles of process management have been used for many years within manufacturing but recently they have also been applied to internal services and administration. Albrecht and Zemke have expressed this right to the point: 'If you're not serving the customer, your job is to serve someone who is.'[9] Expressions like 'white collar work', 'office work', and 'administrative routines' are no longer viable; they obscure more than they enlighten.

During the Second World War, the task force of the military became a new mode of operation. In order to reach an objective – beat the enemy at a defined location – a temporary collaboration between different organizational units was established within the allied forces. This way of organizing was introduced in business and it became common to work in projects. Projects were characterized by being *temporary* and focused on *solving a specific task*. They used *people from various parts of the extant organization*, sometimes supplemented with *consultants and other external suppliers*. With the task completed, the project organization was dissolved. Inside the project there was a certain hierarchy, usually a management group, a reference group, and work groups. Today projects are common in organizations, for example in product development where they can include people from design, engineering, manufacturing, purchasing and marketing. It is an organized way of achieving interfunctional cooperation.

The notion of the internal customer brings customer–supplier relationships into the company. It requires employees to see other employees as customers who receive deliveries of products, services, documents, messages, and decisions. The term *internal supplier* could be added as a companion to internal customer. Usually an employee fulfils the role of being both a recipient of something as an internal customer and to deliver something in a value-added state to another internal customer. Only when the customers are satisfied – and it is satisfied customers that count whether these are external or internal – a job is completed. Ishikawa, one of the fathers of TQM used the slogan 'the next process is your customer' back in the 1950s '...to resolve fierce hostility between workers from different production processes of a steel mill...' [and] '...still uses it today in his lifelong effort to break through the barriers of sectionalism in business organizations'.[10]

---

[8] Hammer and Champy (1993).
[9] Albrecht and Zemke (1985).
[10] Quotation from Lu (1985, pp. viii).

If a company does not consider the links between all functions, there will be 'broken chains', which are one of the 'invisible competitors', these are more obstructing to success than the visible competitors.[11] One of the messages in the network approach to industrial marketing is the interdependency between marketing and all aspects of operations management. This is particularly striking in the manufacture and assembly of complex, customized equipment. In services marketing it has been found that service delivery, production, marketing, and service development are largely handled by the same people, thus making interfunctional relationships indispensable.[12]

A process should not be perceived as if there was only one natural sequence of activities. The *value chain*[13] can give the impression that core functions such as R&D, manufacturing, and marketing must be performed in that very order. The *value constellation* (or *value star*),[14] puts emphasis on the simultaneous rather than the sequential, as well as on the importance of combining functions with regard to needs rather than to follow a uniform procedure. In the value chain, the customer is an external end-user of a firm's output; in the value constellation the customer is part of the process – a co-producer – and not just an end-user.

Like the external networks, the internal networks can be complex. A web is spun between the many-headed internal suppliers and the many-headed internal customers establishing both formal and informal links between everyone in the organization. Alliances, therefore, are not established only with external partners; there is also an *internal alliance market*. Purchasing may be handled by a profit centre on its own or through 'pooled purchasing', meaning that a purchasing department might achieve better conditions if buying larger quantities for several profit centres. 'Sourcing teams' may be used, consisting of members from different functions.[15]

Figure 5.3 shows interaction patterns between different departments in an R&D project. The development took place in an interfunctional project within the spirit of concurrent engineering, but most of the interaction took place within the R&D department. The interaction was also evaluated differently. For example, marketing people valued the interaction with designers higher than vice versa. In another case, the designers were highly negative to the marketers, but appreciated contacts with the buyers.

Complaints that boundaries between departments and tiers are a hindrance against efficient processes date long back. Yet these hindrances are maintained. Within quality management it has become obvious that quality and customer satisfaction cannot be achieved as long as processes are not operating smoothly.

Common sense tell us that the outcome to external customers cannot be satis-

---

[11] See further McKenna (1985, pp. 142, 143, 129).
[12] See Grönroos (1990) and Gummesson (1993).
[13] See Porter (1985).
[14] Wikström and Normann (1993).
[15] See Scheuing (1994).

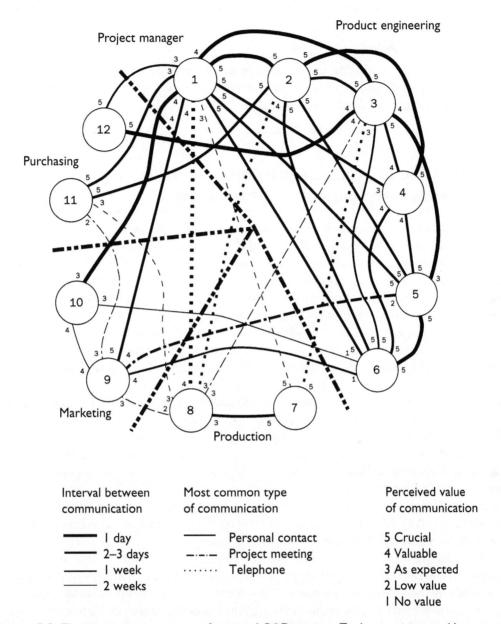

Figure 5.3 The interaction in an interfunctional R&D project. Twelve participants (drawn as circles) are connected through a line and the thickness of the line indicates the frequency of interaction. At the ends of each line a number shows the participant's evaluation of the interaction (5 is best). The participants include the project leader and representatives for design, purchasing, manufacturing, and marketing. (Source: Carlsson and Lundqvist, 1992; p. 9. Reproduced with permission)

factory if the internal customer relationships and collaboration are walking with a limp.

> By introducing the internal customer–internal supplier concepts, the nano view of an organization becomes a natural part of RM. The organization becomes a network of relationships, processes, and projects.

Relationship 26 Quality providing a relationship between operations management and marketing

Marketing literature often presents two opposite perspectives, *marketing orientation* and *production orientation*. R25 treated interfunctional dependency, and marketing and operations management are two mutually dependent functions. There are reasons to treat their relationship separately. First, they are the core functions of any company, and second, driving them closer together is the most noteworthy contribution of modern quality management.

Quality management can be approached *externally from the market* or *internally from the organization*. Together, these two approaches constitute *total quality management* (TQM). Externally oriented quality management is market driven, in contrast to internally oriented quality management which is technology or systems driven. The drivers in the market are found among a supplier's existing customers, those customer who buy from the competition, future customers who have not yet purchased, and existing and potential competitors.

In order to reinforce marketing orientation, changes in values and personal attitudes are necessary. Values change slowly and the new way of approaching the market must find support in business missions, goals, objectives, strategies, organizational structure, and management systems. This in turn requires changed leadership style. Much of the literature on quality today is focused on leadership and the development of employees.

Two frequently quoted definitions of quality emphasize the relationship between the market and operations management. Crosby[16] defines quality as *conformance to requirements*, meaning that companies must be able to produce a product or service according to drawings and specifications; deviation from these is 'non-quality'. If the drawings and specifications are correct, ideal conditions for quality exist. This is the core of *internal quality management*, which can also be expressed as *'Do things right!'*

A critical question for the marketer is whose requirements the offering shall conform with and how this generates value for the customer as well as for the supplier. In the second definition, Juran (1992) puts the emphasis on *fitness for use,*

---

[16] Crosby (1984).

which means that the supplier creates value by making certain that the offering is adjusted to customer needs. This is *external quality management* and its imperative is *'Do the right things!'*

Success is not the outcome of an either/or strategy, either production orientation and internal quality management or marketing orientation and external quality management. It is a both/and strategy, a trade-off between the two. We must understand both customer needs and be able to design offerings that satisfy needs, and organize for their fulfilment.

The most important conclusion from the recent unfolding of the quality concept, and which has vast implications for marketing is the following: Quality management in its modern form fortifies the relationship between operations management and marketing management.

I consider this a hitherto neglected but dramatic change in the management of a business. In Figure 5.4, characteristic features of the internal and external orientations are listed with TQM as the bridge. The quality concept has succeeded to do what marketing has strived to do for decades, unite production orientation with marketing orientation. From having been based on technical data and 'rational' and 'objective' statistics, quality management has moved to regard customer perceptions and the value for the customer as its touchstone.

The external part of TQM starts with *customer perceived quality* and market needs. The most comprehensive contributions are found in the marketing literature, often expressed in terms of needs, need satisfaction, and satisfied – and today even delighted – customers. Within market research, there is a long tradition of studying consumer satisfaction, consumer behaviour, organizational buying behaviour, and customer relationships to brands, but this literature almost exclusively deals with goods, not services. The quality concept from service research, is above all externally oriented, toward customers and revenue.

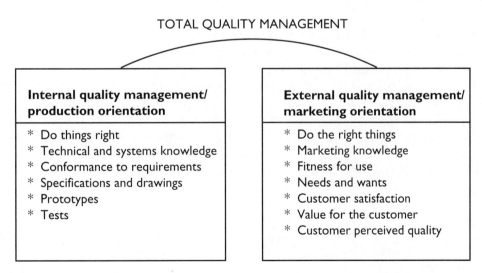

Figure 5.4 represents:

TOTAL QUALITY MANAGEMENT

Internal quality management/ production orientation	**External quality management/ marketing orientation**
* Do things right * Technical and systems knowledge * Conformance to requirements * Specifications and drawings * Prototypes * Tests	* Do the right things * Marketing knowledge * Fitness for use * Needs and wants * Customer satisfaction * Value for the customer * Customer perceived quality

Figure 5.4 TQM forging a relationship between marketing functions and technical functions

Case study

The IBM and Apple approaches to development can serve as an illustration. IBM had a reputation of being marketing oriented (or rather sales oriented), and to balance technical requirements and a tough and systematic salesmanship against an interest for customer needs. IBM has been on the top with regard to size, growth, and profits and has been the most admired company, the one university graduates wanted to work for. During the 1980s, IBM progress slowed down. Former CEO John Akers said in an interview that we '...took the eye off the ball', meaning that IBM lost sight of the customer.[17] He added that he thought IBM '...must become the world's champion in meeting the needs of our customers'. Apple Macintosh, competing with the IBM PC, had taken a different approach to the computer. A Mac should be user-friendly in the sense that *anyone* should be able to operate it, whereas a PC should be expert-friendly and be used by professionals. Computer experts saw the Mac as a toy; a real computer could not just work that simply! Apple focused on an inter-active relationship between the computer and the user. We now know that the Apple approach won and its software has largely been taken over by IBM and other PC manufacturers. As Apple expressed in an ad: 'Imagine a computer that is not based on the possibilities of technology, but of the possibilities of human beings'.[18]

Three efforts to design models for facilitating the technology–market link will be mentioned here. The first is *quality function deployment* (QFD). Its purpose is to unite customer requirements with the properties of goods and services. It is also referred to as 'the quality house' after the house-like form of its matrices. *What* customers want is found out in detail and linked with *how* the supplier shall achieve this technically in order to design an offering. The connections between the whats and hows are established and analysed, technical conflicts between properties are listed, and finally a specification is established.[19]

The second technique is based on process descriptions of services, already mentioned together with the service encounter in R5. They concentrate on the inter-action between the customer and the provider's front staff, and the interaction between front staff, support staff, and management. The vantage point is the 'customer's path', that is the customer's way of moving from considering to buy a service and to getting the service produced and delivered.[20]

---

[17] Quotations from *Fortune* (Dreyfuss, 1989, pp. 21 and 23).

[18] The quotation from an advertisement for Apple in *i Svenska Dagbladet*, June 10, 1992.

[19] Hauser and Clausing (1988).

[20] See also Gummesson (1993) pp. 198ff, and the discussion on contextual matrices, pp. 108–10.

The third effort consists of the widespread quality awards which demand integration between technical aspects, internal aspects, and customers (see further Chapter 8), and the quality standard ISO9000 which requires documentation of processes.

Certain services are performed at the customer's site, for example cleaning services. The cleaning company can focus on the customers' need for clean premises, their need for cleaning at a specific time, or on the amount the customer is willing to pay. If the cleaning company can influence the layout of an office before it is built, it can achieve better quality and productivity, which means better value for the customer as well as for the service provider. If a building is difficult to keep clean, efficient techniques and aids can facilitate, but only within the limits of the construction of the building. Improved quality then requires cooperation in an early stage between those who design, construct, and maintain the building.

Daily, we interact with deficiently designed and badly manufactured products. Bitner has drawn the following conclusion about the impact of the physical environment on service quality: 'Typically, decisions about employees and the design of physical evidence are not made by marketing managers, but rather by human resource managers, operations managers, and design professionals'.[21] The internal logic then takes over at the expense of the customer logic.

Psychologist Donald Norman has studied the psychopatholgy of everyday things, their 'mental' shortcomings. Let me end this section with his summary of the designer's dilemma:[22]

> Designing well is not easy. The manufacturer wants something that can be produced economically. The store wants something that will be attractive to its customers. The purchaser has several demands. In the store, the purchaser focuses on price and appearance, and perhaps on prestige value. At home, the same person will pay more attention to functionality and usability. The repair service cares about maintainability: how easy is the device to take apart, diagnose, and service? The needs of those concerned are different and are often in conflict. Nonetheless, the designer may be able to satisfy everyone.

Obviously there are many stakeholders with different needs: designers, suppliers, retail outlets, buyers, users, and those who handle the maintenance, plus, eventually, society and the environment. And which of these stakeholders should be considered the customers; for whom should the design be targeted? And how should we build relationships to them and interact with them?

---

[21] Bitner (1990, p. 79).
[22] Norman (1988, p. 28).

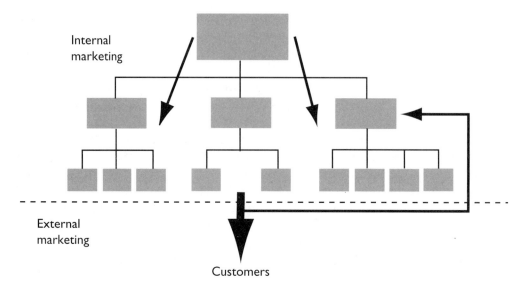

Figure 5.5 The difference between internal and external marketing and the link between them

Relationship 27 Internal marketing – relationships with the 'employee market'

So far we have encountered at least two phenomena which could be labelled internal marketing: the marketing between units in the same corporation (R24), and the relationships between internal customers (R25). However, the current marketing terminology reserves internal marketing for a third phenomenon, defined as follows: *Internal marketing is the application of marketing management knowledge – which was originally developed for external marketing – on the 'internal market', that is the employees.*[23]

Figure 5.5 shows that internal marketing is in-bound and directed to the personnel. External marketing can also have an impact on the internal market, which is shown by the arrow to the right. For example, advertisements for a company sometimes attract the employee's attention more than it attracts the consumer's attention, and if the CEO is interviewed on television the employees watch with particular curiosity.

Internal marketing in networks and imaginary organizations is much more complex than in the simple hierarchy shown in Figure 5.5: *not only own staff must be reached but also other actors in the network.* Reasons to apply internal marketing can originate from several sources, and people can belong to several networks.

---

[23] The concept internal marketing appeared at the end of the 1970s. It has been developed by several authors and has become part of management and marketing around the world (see e.g. Grönroos, 1990, pp. 221–39 and Varey, 1995).

The distinction between internal and external marketing becomes fluid. Internal marketing in the imaginary organization and the network has not been the object of research. Therefore the text will adhere to available knowledge of its application in the hierarchy, and it will focus on its general principles.

The objective of internal marketing within RM is to create relationships between management and employees and between functions. The personnel can be viewed as an internal market, and this market must be reached efficiently in order to prepare the personnel for external contacts; efficient internal marketing becomes an antecedent to efficient external marketing. Techniques from external marketing can be applied internally, mainly from the areas of promotion and communications. Internal marketing can be based on personal and interactive relationships as well as on a certain amount of mass marketing. Traditional activities to reach the employees have often been routinely performed and have built more on bureaucratic principles and wishful thinking than on professional marketing and communications know-how.

Internal marketing emerged from services marketing. Its purpose was to get the front-line personnel – who have interactive relationships with external customers – to handle the service encounter better and with more independence. It is essential that the contact people are well informed about a company's offerings, but also that they understand the business mission, goals, strategies, and organizational processes. It is equally important for support staff to be knowledgeable in order to be able to handle successfully the internal customer relationships.

In two classic articles on 'Mickey Mouse Marketing', the story is told of Disney's successful management of internal marketing (although it was not called so).[24] The staff was either *onstage* or *offstage*. On stage everyone participated in a show whether they were actors in the traditional sense or sold tickets, served hamburgers, or picked litter. Consequently, they should know their part and create satisfied customers. In the 'Ten Standards of Excellence' at Disneyland Paris hotels, 'Commandment no. 8' says: 'We're on stage and we know our role in the show. We're entertainers, we know our "script", we know our standards and we never miss a cue. We consistently give a good show – all the time.'

Even if internal marketing as a concept comes out of services marketing, it seems applicable to all types of organizations. This conclusion is based on the observation that companies in general have taken the concept to their hearts and use it.

The interaction between employees and external customers can be extensive. This was shown in R5 (the service encounter) and R6 (the many-headed customer and the many-headed supplier). Even if many employees have limited contact with customers, companies are looking – with some desperation – for better ways of preparing employees for changes in business missions and organizational structures. The launching of new offerings, new technologies, and new methods require participation and motivation. There can be a colossal gap between what

---

[24] Pope (1979a; 1979b).

management wants (and believes is happening) and what actually happens in the minds of employees and external customers. This is frequently observed in service organizations, and it has come out clearly in problem detection studies

Case study

The first example is from Ericsson's unit for components (formerly Rifa). They manufacture electronic components of strategic importance to Ericsson's telephone switches. There is a need for a certain amount of in-house manufacturing to protect and develop the core competence, but the company also wanted to exploit its knowledge on the external market. After a long life of internal deliveries without competition, the business area was required to prove its ability to meet the competition from other manufacturers, among them the successful Motorola. A transition to a more business-like and market-oriented culture was called for and internal marketing is *one* way of contributing to a new corporate culture. After a survey of possible means of reaching out to the personnel, a publication was made to explain the new situation. It was inspired by the SAS publication *Carlzon's Little Red*, a much hailed effort to inform the staff.[25] It became an unsophisticated pamphlet with short sentences and simple drawings which presented essential facts and strategies. Two pages from Rifa's pamphlet are shown in Figure 5.6.

Figure 5.6 Two pages from a pamphlet used in Rifa's internal marketing (Rifa, 1983; pp. 30–31. Drawing by Bengt Mellberg)

In internal marketing, as in everything else, management commitment is crucial. It was important for the head of the business area and his divisional managers to show that they stood behind the message. After discussions and tests it was concluded that the best way would be to appear in person, even if that would take time. How

---

[25] The SAS pamphlet is reproduced in Mårtensson (1984, pp. 118–35).

do you do this with 2000 people working in three towns far apart? Fifty-six appearances by the head of the business area and his management team were called for.

Most executives would claim they could not spare the time. Groups of forty employees participated in half-day programmes, which ended with lunch or dinner with management. Considering that many of them worked shifts, several programmes had to be performed at night, ending with coffee and cake. The management team presented ongoing changes and made comments followed by the participants working in groups around a number of themes with a subsequent plenary discussion. The publication was distributed as documentation when the participants left.

Case study

The second example concerns Karlshamns Oljefabriker, a factory making oil-based food products. At Christmas all employees were given a variant of Trivial Pursuit, one of the world's most loved quiz games. The mission of the factory of only supplying consumer cooperative stores, had been broadened to include the sales of its products to all types of retailers. A major organizational audit had been performed and the problems of informing everyone were massive. Of the 2000 questions in Trivial Pursuit, 500 were substituted. The new questions were of local nature, both of general interest such as 'Which year were the first winter Olympics held?' to direct questions regarding the company, for example, 'How many small soap bars for hotel rooms does the subsidiary in Stavanger, Norway, produce in one year: 2, 4, or 6 million?' and 'Which are the two most important ingredients in our margarine?'

The game was a hit. Employees played it over Christmas, in their spare time. That was also the idea; it was handed out during the last hours before the Christmas holiday. This way, its messages also reached family members and friends. Others who did not work in the factory asked for the game after it made the news in the local paper and radio station. So the internal marketing activity reached beyond the staff and had a positive mega communications effect, particularly in the home town of the factory.

(PDS).[26] In a PDS, the researcher makes an inventory of as many problems as possible. Customers are asked about the importance of these problems, and management is asked what they think customers will answer. The match between customer and management responses is invariably low.

---

[26] See the gaps model (Zeithaml, Parasuraman and Berry, 1990). The conclusions from PDS are based on my own participation in several studies and discussions with market researchers and their clients.

To a large extent, internal marketing must be interactive. Traditional ways of internal mass marketing – such as the distribution of formal memos and internal magazines – is insufficient. An intranet can help, but the social get-together is also important. At a kick-off before the sales season, large groups gather to learn, to be entertained, and to mix socially during a day or two. Or, as an airline did, all staff were gathered between midnight and 6 a.m. in a hangar, the only hours and space available to get everybody together.

Training and education can be seen as tools for internal marketing. Disney has its own university and McDonald's has its Hamburger University. Muzak's satellite system cannot only be used for commercial messages and music, but also for internal marketing. Taco Bell, one of the world's largest fast-food chains, deploys the Muzak system to communicate with staff in all their restaurants.

Two successful applications of internal marketing are presented above.

Internal marketing stresses human resources as key to the development and maintenance of a successful operation. Employees are best motivated to demonstrate service spirit and customer orientation if they are well informed; this effect is best achieved through a marketing approach. It requires both active learning and influence on attitudes.[27]

As was explained in R12 – the electronic relationship – the intranet offers a new medium for internal communications and for internal marketing. The extranet application can help to stretch internal marketing into a company's whole network and imaginary system. As with the internet, the technology itself is only of benefit when put to constructive use. The role of managers as well as the tasks of information departments may change, as much information is interactively available on the net. Despite this, and particularly when internal marketing is used in major changes, personal contact is critical. *High tech will never make the need for high touch obsolete.*

Relationship 28 The two-dimensional matrix relationship

The word hierarchy comes from the Greek *'hieros'*, holy, and *'archein'*, order or control. A hierarchical organization is based on clear ranking and absolute obedience. We know today that this holy order is not the best way of getting an organization to perform.

The hierarchy offers a one-dimensional relationship and the matrix organization offers a two-dimensional relationship. The matrix organization is an effort to get out of the rigid mould of the hierarchy and a step toward increased network thinking and improved interfunctional and interhierarchical relationships. The matrix has become commonplace and exists in many variants, often in an organization with product managers. It changes the relationships of the hierarchy.

---

[27] According to Grönroos (1990, p. 223).

Viewed in the light of RM, both the hierarchy and the matrix stand out as crude and naive. The former lives on the dream of *unity of command*, the latter on the acceptance of the somewhat more realistic – but not too realistic – *dual command*.

We are unwilling to endorse complexity and tend to see its existence as a failure, not having been able to get reality properly sorted out. The experience of most companies seems to be that the matrix is awkward to manage at the same time as they cannot live without it. At a closer look behind the neat facade of the matrix, there is a multi-dimensional, informal, complex and often contradictory network. It is a challenge to find oneself trying to manage such a network characterized by a series of negotiations, unstable balance of power, far reaching delegation of profits, and a variable structure. But reality provides this dynamic complexity whether we approve of it or not.

The matrix is limited to two dimensions, whereas the number of dimensions in the network are unlimited. We all know from experience that reality is not built on one or two dimensions, but both the hierarchy and the matrix offer appealing mental models of simplicity; we wish them to be true. Studying the matrix, however, may have an educational purpose. It helps us to foresee the complexity inherent in the networks of RM.

The matrix concerns relationships of principal interest to RM. There are many species of matrices:

- *Product/service group versus geographical area.* This is a combination of products on one side and districts, regions, countries or groups of countries on the other. In the beginning of the 1990s, Ericsson was divided in six product-based business areas while headquarter sales units and local subsidiaries throughout the world were in charge of sales. Ericsson Telecom, the biggest business area, had divided its geographical market in five country groups: Northern Europe, continental Europe and Australia, the UK, North America, and finally Asia, Africa, and Latin America. The areas reflected the importance of the markets.

- *Product/service group versus customer segments.* A simple matrix in food production consists of product lines on one side and two segments on the other: the retail market and the restaurant market. Sales can be direct or go via wholesalers. The buying behaviour of the two segments is different and so is often the design of the products and packaging, and the purchased volume, and price.

- *Product group/service versus function.* I have worked as product manager at a subsidiary of *Reader's Digest*, an international publishing and direct mail-order operation. As product manager, I was responsible for special books. This included development of the product line, production of the books, marketing, and profit centre responsibility. There were two more product managers, one for its magazine and one for music albums. I cooperated with a series of internal functions: editorial; production of books and promotion material; distribution of direct mail and the books; accounting with budgeting and follow-up of financial results; and some others. I was not in charge of any of these functions and I had to compete for their attention with other product managers. Moreover, in competition with some twenty subsidiaries, I utilized functions at the European headquarters in London and the international headquarters in Pleasantville, New York, for example in market research.

■ *Geographical area versus function.* The geographical representation, for example, of a chain of stores, restaurants, or hotels consists of a local unit and its customers. A chain of stores may have a central purchasing department with purchasers for different parts of their product line. The central purchaser of clothing must assess the fashion of the next seasons, prices, and expected demand, and the stores are then required to sell the garments.

■ *Key account management of strategic customers.* According to McDonald, Millman and Rogers:[28]

> Key account management (KAM) is...aimed at building a portfolio
> of loyal key accounts by offering them, on a continuing basis, a
> product/service package tailored to their individual needs. Success
> depends partly on...the degree of receptivity demonstrated by the
> customer to a partnership approach...To coordinate day-to-day
> interaction under the umbrella of a long-term relationship, selling
> companies typically form dedicated teams headed up by a 'key
> account manager'.

KAM was mentioned earlier in R6 (the many-headed customer and the many-headed supplier) pointing to the fact that this is not a new issue. But it is a special case of RM with increasing significance.

■ *Temporary projects versus the base organization.* The matrices that have been described so far are part of the fixed structure of the organization. This matrix variant is an ad hoc organization with projects on one side and a task force of people from different functions on the other. Projects are common in all types of organizations. As organizations change at a faster pace, even the 'fixed' structure becomes a project; it could be called the parent project. If an organization is a bundle of projects, it is already on the way to becoming a network and an imaginary organization.

It is obvious that the crossroads between two types of responsibility can induce constructive dialogue, but also head-on confrontation of strong egos. One product manager competes with another for the attention of a functional department. A store manager may feel that central purchasing orders the wrong articles at the wrong prices so that they cannot be sold. At the crossroad there are two views, but a joint decision is called for. Who shall yield? What happens if both drive ahead at full speed? Can we find a form for collaboration that allows both 'vehicles' to cross the junction in accord? The decisions must build on consensus, or the disputes are moved on to the executive level above the crossroad. The exercise in reaching agreements can be educational, or inertia and insecurity can grow. The internal relationships may take up more time than the external ones; they can be demanding on patience, personal maturity and social skills. Even if the matrix in

---

[28] McDonald, Millman and Rogers (1997, p. 112).

itself carries difficulties, there is an advantage in being able to address the product and the geographic market in combination.

Before its merger with Brown Boveri and the creation of ABB, Asea had an international product/country matrix. An executive vice president, Arne Bennborn, described its intricacies in the following way:

> The international matrix holds a potential for conflicts. We tell division and subsidiary managers that they have profit responsibility world wide, and country managers that they are responsible for everything inside their country. These are two completely different roles, both necessary in a multiproduct/multimarket organization. The roles need open-minded managers who can solve a problem together. If the matrix managers cannot agree on a solution they can come to us for help. If this is repeated time and again, we have to replace one or several of them. We need quick decisions in a flat organization with frequent interfunctional contacts within an overriding philosophy.[29]

Like all other organizational principles, the matrix must be deployed in the right situation. There are those who repudiate matrices as being unmanageable. They claim matrices engender controversies. An alternative interpretation is that they put the spotlight on existing but hidden conflicts.

In many major corporations, matrix designs supersede each other. In order to expose considerations in search of a working matrix organization, the Skandia matrix saga will be told.[30] In 1968, the insurance company was organized as a matrix with certain functions and product groups (groups of different kinds of insurance) on one side, and four geographical zones on the other. Two years later, the matrix became more market oriented. Its core became a matrix between zones and insurance to corporations, consumers, or groups, or specific applications named motor, sea, and air. In addition to the matrix, centralized corporate services were organized. The zones were expanded internationally. Finance was added (which broke the neat logic, as finance is a function) and the two dimensions of the matrix became less distinct. During the 1970s a gradual transfer took place toward a focus on customers and segmentation. An effort was made to avoid some of the problems with the matrix, particularly duplication of tasks and the abundant number of insurance types. The communications pattern of one of the units is reproduced in Figure 5.7. We can spot a dissolution of the matrix in something that looks like a network, albeit limited to employees and not including customers and other stakeholders.

In 1993, the organizational chart shows yet another design; it had been pre-

---

[29] Arne Bennborn quoted in Brandes and Brege (1990, p. 131).
[30] The Skandia case is based on Englund (1982) and discussions with Kjell Ångelia, Skandia. The matrices have been put at my disposal by Skandia.

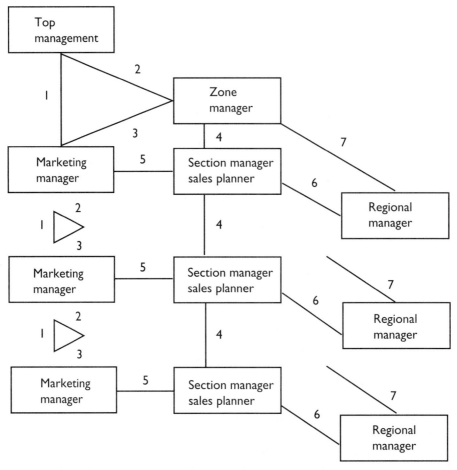

Figure 5.7 The communications pattern at Skandia in 1978. The numbers represent different decisions and types of communication. Channel 5, for example, represents issues on products, markets, and damages in everyday operations

ceded by several others since the 1970s. The insurance market has changed character – changed customer needs, changed competitive situation, deregulation, new types of insurance services – and the group structure of Skandia has also changed. Figure 5.8 shows the matrix for Northern Europe.

In summary, the advantages of the matrix organization are:

- The product managers 'own' the product and can work with all aspects of the product line. They can acquire a complete overview of the product, new technology, customers, competitors, volume, market share, profits, and other aspects.
- The geographical area managers 'own' their area and its customers. They have local closeness to the customer. But they also enjoy central support with a product line, advertising, and sales promotion through which experience from many local markets is shared and transferred between markets.

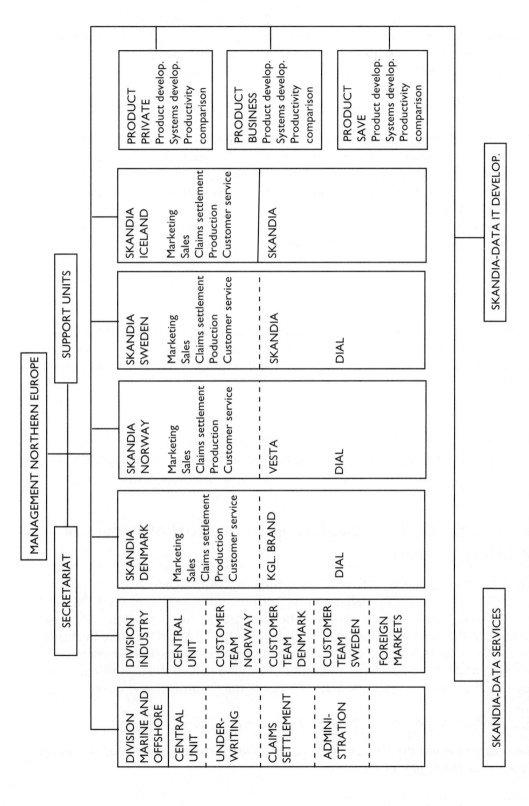

Figure 5.8 The matrix organization for Skandia Northern Europe in 1993

- There is less risk that an issue is abandoned and left in a vacuum. It is particularly important that the customers do not leave the supplier because of obsolete products, vanishing segments, or dissatisfied customers. Revenue, cost and profits are monitored both from a product and market view.

The disadvantages are:

- Managers must handle a large number of relationships, both externally and internally. Conflicts easily emerge at the matrix crossroads. For example, a product manager wants to replace a current product for long-term profit growth, while an area manager is first assessed by his or her ability to meet the current budget and prefers to bet on existing products.
- Management does not give enough support to the product managers but is still expecting superior performance. The responsibility placed on product managers is frequently not matched by their authority to make decisions and act. At the matrix crossroad, they run into area managers who are often empowered by a considerably larger organization and budget.

Constructive dialogue, lack of prestige, recognition of different roles, and a holistic view are required human properties in a matrix. Rapid resolution of problems, flexibility, and a willingness to change are needed without ending up in diluted compromises.

> But if we cannot manage the simplified two-dimensional network of the matrix, how then can we expect to manage the complex multi-dimensional networks of RM?

Relationship 29 The relationship to external providers of marketing services

Several marketing tasks are not performed by employees but by external providers. This was conceptualized in R4 with the introduction of the FTMs and the PTMs, the full-time marketers and the part-time marketers. External providers to the marketing function can be viewed as FTMs at the time the buyer pays for them. In these relationships, the providers become part of the customer's marketing and sales organization without belonging to it in the traditional sense. They become part of a network that transcends the organization–market boundaries.

The services of the external providers can be split into three groups:

I Services concerning the *physical distribution* of goods, such as those offered by haulage firms, wholesalers, and retailers.

2 Services primarily concerned with *selling and delivering*. Wholesaler and retailer services belong in this group. So do agents and brokers even if they never physically touch a product. So do telemarketing services. In some countries, including the USA and the UK, insurance to individuals is sold by brokers; in some countries they are primarily sold by the insurance companies' own sales organizations. These two approaches generate different market relationships. In both cases the insurance company has to keep up its image and the interest of the consumer. In the broker case, keeping up the spirit of brokers and helping them do good business becomes the number one priority. This can occur through frequent innovations, quality improvements, and supportive campaigns.

3 *Consulting* services of different kinds, such as those performed by advertising agencies, market research institutes, and head-hunters. These providers are primarily advisory – they are knowledge-based organizations – but they can also execute much of the craft such as the printing of brochures or field interviews.

The external providers reinforce and supplement the marketing function. They offer both strategic outsourcing and outsourcing of repetitive routine services. The providers become a hybrid between external firms and internal departments. If the customer interacts closely and continuously with them, they become in practice part of the customer's organization; they may even have permanent office facilities on the customer's premises. The buyer must ask two pivotal questions: 'What shall we do ourselves and what shall the independent provider do?' and 'Is this an occasional transaction or is it going to be a long-term relationship?'

The first two types of external providers connect with the physical distribution (R3) and the electronic relationship and its information-based services (R12). The rest of this section will focus on the third type, knowledge-based and advisory consulting services.

Today all companies use consultants in their marketing function, either on a continuous or ad hoc basis. The consultants provide expertise which is lacking or is in short supply at a specific moment. Several types of consultants are consequential for the success of the marketing function. These will be discussed together with the import of interactive relationships and the ability to obtain maximum support to the marketing function.

Consultants to the marketing function are listed below.[31]

Advertising agencies

The ad agency is perhaps the most common and ostentatious of all consultants to the marketing function. This is most likely so because marketing is still predominantly directed to mass communication to consumers, and consumer advertising has high public visibility. An ad agency is either hired until further notice and works continuously with its client, or the assignments are tied to specific projects.

---

[31] The rest of this chapter is an adapdation from Gummesson (1977).

The agency relationship is constantly under scrutiny, sometimes inspired by the latest invoice. With few exceptions, measurement of advertising effects on revenue are obscure, while fees, price of printed material, and media space are easy to measure. And how do you measure the value of creativity? In-house advertising production exists but is supplemented by agencies; complete in-house agencies are not often found any more. There must, however, be a defined flesh-and-blood client with whom the agency can interact, usually a marketing manager, product manager, or advertising manager. Many companies use several agencies and each profit centre has the right to make its own choice. Others request that all their units worldwide use the same advertising agency chain.

Consultants in marketing management

These can either represent a broad knowledge of marketing-oriented management or a deep expertise in a specific area. Sometimes their strength is the understanding of management and the marketing function, and they work directly under the CEO or marketing director. Their knowledge concerns marketing aspects of such areas as strategy, organization, planning, research, cost reduction and downsizing. Some are specialized in industries, such as retailing or IT. Regis McKenna has become known as Silicon Valley's marketing consultant; he began to work with Apple when it was still a garage operation. Consultants may also be specialized in a certain technique, such as the layout of stores or a computer application. Beginning in the 1980s, quality has become increasingly more important to management consultants. Since the current quality concept is strongly customer oriented, the job of the TQM consultant is closely knit to the marketing function. A series of consulting services have followed in the wake of quality awards and ISO9000.

Market research institutes

These are specialists in data generation[32] and the application of certain research techniques. They primarily research consumer attitudes to products, services and companies and compare competitors. They do this at regular or ad hoc intervals, collectively or as separate customized projects. Apart from proficiency in research techniques, their strength is the management of field interviewers and computer systems for the planning, processing, analysis and reporting of a study.

To some extent they also draw conclusions and recommend measures. In order to draw conclusions, two types of knowledge are required, but are rarely represented in one individual. One is the technical dexterity to investigate a phenom-

---

[32] I prefer the term *data generation* to the mainstream term *data collection*. Data in social contexts are usually not there to be collected but are generated through an interpretation process, governed by a preconceived notion of what is essential and what is not, or by total openness and sensitivity to what reality wants to tell the researcher.

enon, for example how customers behave and why. The second is institutional knowledge about the industry, the client company, its goods and services, competitive situation, and the more secluded mechanisms that can only be understood by those who live with them continuously: the power game, which decisions are possible to implement, and what financial risks are acceptable.

The first type of knowledge is best represented by the research institute, the second best by the client. The quality of the research will be the outcome of interaction between the research institute and the client and their ability to constructively coalesce their competencies. It is a frequent nuisance that the client does not attach enough weight to the contact with the researcher, but delegates the contact to a staff unit on a middle or lower management level. When the results are presented for decisions, the decision-makers lack in-depth understanding of the quality of the data; those who present it know too little about the whole context of the decision and have no power.

Speakers and educators

These are found among specialists on training and education, university professors, writers, management consultants, and successful business executives. Some have agents just like actors. They can embrace anything from formal training programmes on general and special aspects of marketing to speaking at kick-offs, business lunches, and conferences. The market for these types of services has grown continuously. There is need to lift the vision from the daily myopic routine and to be inspired by success stories, enthusiastic crusaders, and celebrities. Particularly, customer in focus themes, such as closer relationships to customers, measuring customer satisfaction, customer loyalty programmes, electronic markets, and quality management, catch the minds of marketing practitioners, which today also includes public sector representatives.

Recruitment consultants

Recruitment is handled both by niche firms and management consultants. The recruitment of sales people is a large business. Recruitment of executives and managers in marketing is handled by head-hunters, who search for individual candidates that fit a specification set up together with the client firm. They do not advertise, but approach candidates through personal contacts. Part of what the client is buying is an entry ticket to their network of relationships. They can approach a person without others knowing that a position is open and can guarantee confidentiality. They have experience in assessing a person's suitability for executive work. The cost of hiring the wrong marketing manager is excessively high, not least through lost opportunities and foregone revenue, so the recruitment procedure should be handled cautiously.

Some other consultants have already been mentioned. Among them are *public relations consultants*, specialized in external and internal relationships. They often compete directly with management consultants and ad agencies. Their services as lobbyists have grown, which is obvious in mega marketing (R19) and the mass media relationship (R23). *Lawyers* everywhere, and in the USA in particular, have become key players in the marketing arena (R16). Others specialize in small but critical niches, for example by helping firms *to design and present bids* on major contracts. Henry Kissinger was mentioned as *advisor on political risks* in international markets (R18). *Futurists* help to discern trends in consumption patterns and lifestyles.

We have focused on the consultant as an external provider of expertise. Another type is *management for hire* prompted by a need to substitute a position quickly to clear up a problem, or waiting for a permanent recruit. The consultants often stay for six to twenty-four months in the client organization. The borderline between employee and external provider is practically erased.

The text has shown the specific expertise that external providers can offer to bolster the marketing function. Their contributions can also be seen in a more general light. It is essential to apply our knowledge, from service production and service quality, on the relationship to the consultants as it was laid out in R5. The relationship needs to be interactive in the service encounters. It means a partial co-production between the client and the provider. It is not a matter of giving orders and obeying orders except in certain standardized instances, for example a print order for a brochure. To the ad agency it is a matter of understanding the needs of both their customer and their customer's customer (R7). The strengths of ad agencies include visualization, creative design, and the planning and execution of campaigns. Their knowledge on strategy varies considerably. At some agencies, individuals master a broader field than advertising and those can compete with management consultants.

The planning of an assignment must occur in close relationship between consultant and client. It is imperative that the real decision-makers participate. Intermediaries should be avoided; through them the information – which is often complex and subtle – will be filtered and sometimes distorted. Those who are going to implement the assignment need proper briefings, straight from the client's mouth.

The reinforcement to the marketing function is an example of outsourcing (or resourcing). It is not new, but it has become more significant and we are still learning how to handle the relationship.

Relationship 30 The owner and financier relationship

Not only loyal customers but also loyal owners exert influence on marketing success. A trusting and long-term relationship between owners (and other financiers) and management and the marketing function is a necessary condition for building long-term relationships with customers, suppliers, competitors, and others.

The owners' importance for finance is explored in the literature, but its importance for marketing is rarely mentioned. Investors appear in many shapes with diverse demands on short- and long-term return on capital. They can be active or passive, big or small, known or anonymous. Investors finance the operations of a company at the same time as a company has other financiers, primarily banks and other financial institutions but also customers, suppliers, and governments (through subsidies).

There is an irony that investors have been in the focus of management attention – not customers, not employees – as these have become less and less loyal.[33] However, investor relationships vary considerably between countries. Germany and Japan have long-term stable owner relationships. Compared to the United States, Japanese stockholding is four times more stable and seven times more likely to be reciprocated.[34] The loyalty of the American investor has been reduced as the turnover of investors has moved from 14 per cent in 1960 to 52 per cent in 1995.[35] This means that today the average investor holds shares for less than two years, albeit with a variation of a few minutes to several decades. Maximum short-term return on capital has taken priority over long-term survival and shares are bought and sold as transaction goods, much like ice-cream on a hot day on the beach. The relationship between a company and its investors has also become increasingly anonymous; it is sometimes even handled by computers programmed to search for the quickest buck of the day or the minute.

A countermove is the snowballing interest in *corporate governance* which stands for active, supportive and responsible ownership.[36]

Demonstrating success through a high and climbing share price can be the most important input to a favourable public image. If the share price is down, customers may feel insecure. This is especially true for equipment that requires spare parts, or motor vehicles for which the second-hand price is important.[37]

The customers' image of a firm may be affected by the image of its major owner but most often customers, especially consumers, do not know who owns a company or a brand name. If you stay at the illustrious Beverly Hills Hotel in California, you are a guest of the Sultan of Brunei, the richest man in the world. Of the shares of Disneyland Paris in 1995, 40 per cent were owned by Disney but the next major shareholder was Prince Al Waleed of Saudi Arabia with close to 24 per cent. The Prince arrived as a saviour in a financial crisis, which was basically caused by deficient customer proximity and excessive pricing resulting in a cultural clash and too few visitors. In 1996, he agreed to stay on as an owner for another five years, thereby bringing stability to the theme park and instilling belief in its future.

---

[33] Reichheld (1996).
[34] Gerlach (1992, p. xvii).
[35] Reichheld (1996).
[36] Carlsson (1997).
[37] See McKenna (1985).

The annual report has been directed to two groups: tax authorities and the stock market; monthly and quarterly reports are directed to the stock market. Indicators of the state and progress of a company primarily offer short-term financial information. In order to educate and inform investors, indicators are needed that show the importance of long-term goals. The balanced scorecard approach offers a framework for a more complete evaluation of a company (see further Chapter 6). I am not, however, a believer in the folklore of measuring everything. Investment decisions are taken out of strategic necessity and estimates of profits are not always possible, for example the change-over from one technology to another or a long-term product development project.

Figure 5.9 puts the marketing function in a financier and management context. Ownership affects marketing and the relationship between general management, marketing management, and major owners (who are often on the board of directors) becomes vital. Five types of ownership and financier relationships will be explained below.

Figure 5.9 Relationships between marketing, ownership/investors and other influencers

Private business run by core owners

The core owners are personally engaged in operating the enterprise; it is part of a lifestyle. This is typical of the small business like the mom and pop store, the restaurant, and the repair shop. The values of the founders and private owners are often strong and consistently applied.

Owner families often continue to run enterprises when they have grown large, and they know the operations in detail. In retailing there is a series of smashing successes, companies that have expanded through the founder's and owner's vision and perseverance. Examples of strong owner commitment are the Nordstrom department stores, known for superior quality of goods and services, and Feargal Quinn's consumer-focused and profitable supermarkets in Ireland. Another is IKEA. Its founder Ingvar Kamprad has three sons, one daughter, his wife, and his brother-in-law by his side. The retailing operation – the 130 IKEA furniture stores and seventy-nine Habitat stores in the UK, France, and Spain acquired in 1993 – are owned by a family controlled foundation in the Netherlands. Inter IKEA consist of the franchise division (comprising IKEA brand equity, copyrights, and concepts), the financial division, and the real estate division. The Ikano group includes banking, credit cards, and insurance. The corporate culture emerging from the founder is extremely strong:[38] '...Ingvar Kamprad is unquestionably "Daddy"...For those who have met him it is a great unforgettable moment. And there is a lot of talk about him in the store: "Kamprad would have liked that..." or "what would Ingvar have said about that"...Especially for the older Ikeans, Ingvar Kamprad represents an important symbol, an example of the true IKEA spirit'.

Even if these private companies should go public, core owners and subtle core values can continue to control the operations. The separation between the role of core owner and the role of manager is common in industry nations. A closer look at executives in Europe, however, indicated that they are often directly or indirectly linked to a network of owner families.

The reasons for going public are usually a need for cash flow but often also to reduce total family control. Family ownership has its hazards, especially when new generations take over. There are also cases when the best strategy should be to go from public back to private, provided that this were financially feasible, which it often is not. A viable strategy is actively to recruit investors and establish long-term relationships to those who constructively help build the future.

Founders and entrepreneurs are often not easy to please and an employee who does not comply with their leadership had better try another job. They may also be perceived as ruthless in their pursuit of their business mission and survival. The Roddick family, founders and owners of The Body Shop, have recently been accused of driving their franchisees too hard,[39] at the same time as Anita Roddick

---

[38] Quotation from Salzer (1994, p. 162).
[39] Entine (1996).

says: 'I have never been able to separate Body Shop values from my own personal values'.[40]

Single corporations and families can even keep a tight control over total markets and countries. An extreme case is De Beers and its owners, the Oppenheimer family.[41] They control 54 per cent of the stock value on the Johannesburg exchange in South Africa, that is one fourth of the financial wealth of the nation. De Beers are best known for their control over world sales of non-industrial diamonds; in all, their empire includes 1300 companies in various industries. Companies and countries have tried to break out of the influence of De Beers but with no apparent success. So the overriding production and marketing strategies of diamonds are globally determined by one owner family.

Long-term investors

The owners see their involvement as long term, but are engaged in different types of industries and do not directly take part in daily operations. The Wallenberg family, who exerts a controlling influence over such diverse multinationals as Ericsson, Atlas-Copco, Electrolux, SKF, and Saab, focus their investment on long-term industrial development, internationalization, and stability. There is a commitment, above all in financial and strategic issues, but the knowledge of the daily operations and industry-specific issues is limited.

Long-term ownership may put companies together even though they do not belong together for marketing reasons. It may be right at one time, but not at another. The Saab passenger car operation is now controlled by GM, but the Saab aerospace products and Scania, the world's fifth largest truck maker, have been owned by Saab for twenty-five years. They have the same roots but their products have grown apart. In 1996 they were demerged; there was absolutely no marketing synergy.

Warren Buffett and his company Berkshire Hathaway has been held up as a model of a long-term and extremely successful investment strategy.[42] Buffett invests in a few select companies, retains the investment and says that short-term stock price is not important. This type of owner is the best to make RM become successful. It allows a company to build long-term relationships with customers and others.

Short-term investors

The owners are investors looking for maximum short-term return on investment. Just as customers can be unprofitable even in the long-run, investors can be of little support, even be outright parasites. For these investors there is no responsibility,

---

[40] Roddick (1991, p. 123).
[41] See Kanfer (1996).
[42] Reichheld (1996, pp. 165–6).

only rights and demands; owning shares is an alternative to gambling in Las Vegas. Institutional investors, such as pension funds, have increased their role on the stock market. They have no sentiments for a specific company, merely for enhancing short-term investor wealth. Investment brokers are paid per transaction, meaning that the more frequently they can encourage big investors to buy and sell, the more they earn. So they are rewarded for transactions and owner promiscuity, not for long-term relationships and loyalty. This, of course, is counterproductive to RM.

The 1980s were characterized by changing ownership based on short-term speculation. Corporate raiders made hostile takeovers financed by junk bonds (high risk bonds with no collateral). Their strategy was cost reduction, downsizing, and asset-stripping; there was no intention of developing the companies over the long term and no emotional attachment to their products and services. No doubt a shakeup of complacent or inefficient management teams is necessary at times, but then the justification should be long-term survival. Some raiders became unbelievably rich, but many also had severe setbacks and were taken to court, even to jail.

In order to build a strong marketing function, a certain long-term stability is needed. Reichheld,[43] who puts as much emphasis on loyal investors and loyal employees as on loyal customers, suggests four active strategies for more stable ownership:

1 educate current investors;
2 shift to more stable investors;
3 attract the right type of core owners;
4 go from public to private.

When instability rules, management attention is directed to other things than the core activities of production and marketing. The top executives risk getting fired any day and it is meaningless for them to make a long-term commitment. They are driven to look at short-term results and discard investment in customer loyalty, product development and development of personnel.

Co-operative ownership

True co-operative ownership has the special commitment that characterizes the successful family firm, but it goes one step further – the owners and the customers are the same people. The customers own the supplying organizations and they do their purchasing in their own stores. Employees are owners and customers as well and sometimes co-ops are operated by unpaid volunteers. The relationship between co-op members and the personnel in the store is close. This is very well as long as the co-op is limited in size or split into small independent

---

[43] Reichheld (1996, pp. 160–70).

units. If it grows and functions become centralized and controlled from a distance, it becomes like any other company. The co-operations become corporations and the owners no more feel they are owners than I feel I own Ford, having bought a few Ford shares. The members become just customers and the authenticity of the membership is lost; the owner/customer becomes a pseudo member as was pointed out in R11. There are retailer co-ops, and producer co-ops are common in the agricultural sector. There are also voluntary chains such as Best Western Hotels. The co-ops as such have sometimes become so dominant as to imprison suppliers and customers in the way that was described in R10.

Government ownership

In most countries, but to a lesser degree in the USA, the state owns services like the post, telecom, railroads, and airlines. The health, education, and utilities sectors are often owned by state or local governments. These produce services of infrastructural nature and only in part do these services lend themselves to the forces of the market. Unfortunately, governments have based their management style and values on a bureaucratic–legal paradigm and not on a relationship and service paradigm. It means that these operations have lagged behind, not seeing themselves as a service to the citizens. They have become kingdoms of their own, closed off from the environment. They have been heavily criticized but learnt to accept that as the natural state of affairs. They have spent more time on 'explaining' why things do not work than on making them work. But they are not without competition. For example, Federal Express renewed US postal services as a private alternative, operating with service quality and customer in focus strategies.

The wave of deregulation and privatization that started in the 1980s has changed the scenery gradually. In the UK, former premier Margaret Thatcher's privatization included the Airport Authority, British Telecom, and British Rail. Regional and local governments have increasingly become involved in business-like operations. Governments have both a role as authorities and as service providers and a long tradition of muddling up the two by covering up for bad service with reference to legal authority. There is a risk that they compete successfully by establishing their own companies, beating private companies with lower bids made possible with taxpayers' money. This has been reported in construction and building, transportation, leisure activities, and other markets.

The ultimate owners of all government organizations are the citizens, that is the consumers. In modern terms: *They have outsourced certain activities to governments to make the production and delivery of them more efficient.* Unfortunately the owners' prospects of exerting influence through the democratic voting process is appallingly meagre. To influence a state-run mail operation, the citizens are supposed to vote for their candidates at the next election and hope that the right party wins; that the right person is appointed postmaster general; that the right people are recruited to perform to the customers' satisfaction; and that the needs and wants of the citizens are transmitted through leadership, business mission, strategies, organization, and systems. This chain of intermediaries is far too long, it is a distance relationship to the customer, so distant that that it is pre-empted of all muscle. The direct contact with the post – the citizen in the role of customer – is possible but the citizen has little clout; it is an unusually asymmetric relationship. The relationship between the citizen as an owner of the post and eventual responsibility for its bill via taxes – the same citizen as customer – and the state as administrator is not easily handled from a marketing point of view.

Should the sole goal of the company be to maximize shareholder wealth, counted in dollars? The short-term investors answer this question with a distinct yes. But could wealth also be to uphold a tradition of a certain industry, like retailing, car manufacturing, or film making, or to operate a business in a specific, town, region, or country, and be a good corporate citizen? For example, several of the film-making giants in Hollywood are neither owned by Americans nor are the owners knowledgeable about film-making. Metro Goldwyn Mayer was sold to an Italian swindler, backed by the French state-owned bank Crédit Lyonnais which was forced to take over the studio. Columbia was sold to Japanese Sony; Universal to Japanese Matsushita and later to Canadian Seagram; and 20th Century Fox to Australians. Since this was written, new ownership constellations have probably emerged.

If a company is being quoted on a stock exchange yet other relationships are born. New demands are put on its financial reporting and this is watched by a number of stakeholders: the big institutional investors as well as the little guy, the stock exchange, financial reporters, analysts, and public authorities. Managing *investor relations*, (IR), has become a profession in its own right.[44]

Ownership is an alternative to alliances. In the spirit of the imaginary organization it is one of a multitude of network formats of the organizational structure. When the Volvo–Renault alliance was preparing for a merger, the meaning of ownership was assessed in the light of Volvo's future prospects. Renault was a French state-owned company for which privatization had been suggested but had not been decided. There was a warranted fear that Volvo would be controlled by the French government. Even if Renault was privatized Volvo was likely to become powerless in its relationship to the considerably bigger Renault.

Doubts were raised about the purpose of the merger and then about its conditions. The Volvo president called it 'a new model' but it was uncertain how the model would function in a live test. The president was accused of playing a game in order to secure eternal power and that the merger proposal had no direct link to car manufacturing and car sales. Who would decide about new car designs, distribution networks, and other marketing strategies? A financial reporter called it 'a multinational monster'. In defence of the merger, cost reductions and coordination advantages were claimed to follow and furthermore

---

[44] See Tuominen (1996) for an investor relationship marketing framework.

Renault would place large orders with Volvo. The merger collapsed during the autumn of 1993 after protests from owner groups and executives.[45]

A board of directors represents owners, management, and other stakeholders. Criticism is often aired against the choice of board members who know little about the company and provide no functional expertise. It is obvious that support from knowledgeable owners and board members as well as a trusting relationship between them and the corporate and marketing executives is imperative in order to build a stable position on the market.

It is unfortunate if owners are seen by management as a necessary evil, which has to be soothed and cajoled. They should be partners. This requires the selection of the right owners, those who not only enhance their wealth through ownership but also add value to the companies in which they invest. It then becomes a win–win relationship within the RM spirit.

---

[45] See Sundqvist (1994).

Chapter 6

Does RM pay?

> Chapter 6 introduces return on relationships (ROR), that is the impact of RM on revenue, cost, capital employed, and eventually profits. The chapter treats customer satisfaction and ROR; duration, defection and retention; intellectual capital and the balanced scorecard; valuation of relationships; relationships and quality, productivity and profitability; return on the non-measurable; and finally, strategies for improved ROR. It ends with a section on a RM-inspired marketing plan and audit, and introduces the notion of the relationship portfolio.

Return on relationships (ROR)

Someone has said (I think it is Peter Drucker) that 'the language of management is money'. In business life, we want to know the financial impact of our activities; the 'bottom line' is a magic concept. Managers therefore must ask the question of the headline: Does RM pay?

We can broaden the question and ask: Is it possible to gauge *return on relationships* just like we gauge return on investment, return on capital employed, or even return on quality?[1] I would like to propose the following definition:

> Return on relationships (ROR) is the long-term net financial outcome caused by the establishment and maintenance of an organization's network of relationships.

Some statements pertaining to ROR have already been presented, for example, that an existing Cadillac-customer is worth $332,000 over his or her lifetime; and that it costs five to ten times as much to get a new customer as it costs to keep an existing customer.

Measuring ROR is in its infancy. The following sections offer a state-of-the-art review, suggest approaches, and show examples of applications.

---

[1] Return on quality is a concept developed by Rust, Zahorik and Keiningham (1994).

Satisfaction and ROR

A common assumption is that an improvement in customer perceived quality will increase customer satisfaction, loyalty, and profitability. A number of authors have suggested customer relationship lifecycles with virtuous circles or profit chains, all following a similar pattern:

good internal quality → satisfied employees → employees stay → good external quality → satisfied customers → customers stay → high profitability.[2]

There is also the opposite, the vicious circle and failure chain.

The logic seems indisputable; when everybody is happy we will do well. But the general validity can be questioned as the market logic sometimes follows other patterns.

Although the extensive studies by Fornell (1992) indicate that customer satisfaction is a predictor of future profits, it is not enough to ascertain that 73 or 86 or even 94 per cent of the customers are satisfied. Volvo, who started a long-term comprehensive RM programme, had previously considered satisfied customers to be loyal. There was considerable leakage, though. In the Volvo RM programme the next step has been taken actively to provide incentives for satisfied customers to remain loyal.

Most of those who leave a supplier say that they are satisfied but they switch for a variety of reasons, such as another supplier's marketing, being persuaded by friends, the desire to test something new, or mere coincidence. According to the exit-voice-loyalty choice from R9, many dissatisfied customers remain despite the fact that a supplier is charging more or offers lower quality than the competition. They do not switch for lack of time or knowledge or they remain loyal, for example, for nationalistic or ideological reasons. The switching cost can be considerable in the short run. However, retention coupled with dissatisfaction is a ticking bomb.

Some studies reveal that there is a sizeable difference in retention rate between those who say (in a questionnaire) that they are *very satisfied* and those who are just *satisfied*. Pitney Bowes, manufacturers of postage machines, found that 78.2 per cent of very satisfied customers said that they would remain customers in the future, whereas only 20.9 per cent of satisfied customers said they would remain. For Xerox the corresponding figures were 80 per cent and 14 per cent.[3]

A further analysis is found in the loyalty accounting matrix (Figure 6.1). The matrix combines the *attractiveness* of a supplier ('brain appeal') and the *strength of the relationship* ('heart appeal'). The most satisfied customers are called ambassa-

---

[2] See Grönroos (1990, pp. 129–33); Schlesinger and Heskett (1991); Normann (1991, pp. 153–63); and Schlesinger and Hallowell (1994). These 'chains' were developed for services but are also applicable for goods marketing.

[3] Quoted from Johansen and Monthelie (1996, p.17).

Strength of relationship

Risk	Loyal	Ambassador
Searching	Risk	Loyal
Lost	Searching	Risk

(left axis label: Attractiveness)

Figure 6.1 Loyalty accounting matrix. (Source: Johansen and Monthelie, 1996, p. 23, and the Loyalty Group International. Used with permission)

dors. They find the supplier highly attractive, have a strong relationship to the supplier, and recommend him to others. The next groups consist of loyal customers who are slightly less enthusiastic than the ambassadors. The diagonal represents risk customers who are easy prey for competitors. The last two groups are those who are actively searching for a new supplier and those who are already lost customers.

A study of one company showed the following pattern: ambassadors 32 per cent, loyal 30 per cent, risk 25 per cent, searching 9 per cent, and lost 4 per cent. Ambassadors and loyal customers constituted almost two-thirds of the customers, a result that might or might not be satisfactory, depending on the type of business.

It was less comforting to learn that ROR was not well correlated to loyalty. The ambassadors did not make the most profitable customers, those were found among the least loyal groups. The *service paradox*[4] states that the less profitable customers are, the more satisfied they are, while the more profitable customers are the less satisfied. This can be illustrated with the price of the return air fare from New York to continental Europe. An off-season economy class ticket might cost $250, a full business class ticket $3000 and a Concorde ticket $7000. The business traveller is highly profitable and highly demanding. The economy traveller contributes marginally to profits but is grateful for the low price and not as demanding. Value for the business traveller is primarily high quality: punctuality, comfort, the opportunity to work or rest. For the economy traveller, value is primarily low price. The likelihood is high that the business traveller is less satisfied than the economy traveller, although in objective terms the business traveller is offered a better service.

One ROR model further expands the links between satisfaction and profits (Figure 6.2).

---

[4] The service paradox is taken from an interview with Jan Lapidoth Sr and his experience from SAS.

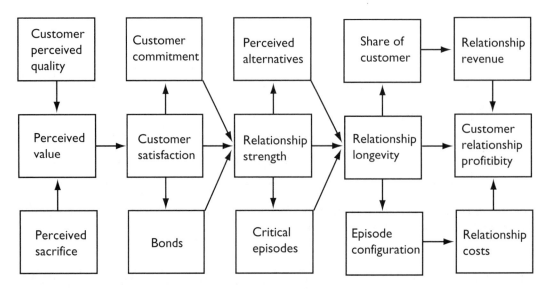

Figure 6.2 A 'relationship profitability model' (Source: Storbacka, Strandvik and Grönroos, 1994; p. 23. Reproduced with permission; © MCB University Press)

Figure 6.2 shows how stages and properties of the relationships between suppliers and customers are linked together.[5] Starting from the left, *perceived value* is defined as the outcome of customer perceived quality and the customer's sacrifice (cost in a wide sense). The perceived value is an antecedent to *customer satisfaction* which in turn influences customer commitment, bonds to the supplier, and *relationship strength*. The higher the relationship strength and the customer's feeling of loyalty toward the supplier, the fewer the perceived alternatives; when there is a monopoly, however, the customer is a prisoner. The number of alternative suppliers and their attractiveness impact on *relationship longevity*, which is also influenced by the positive, negative or indifferent interaction with the supplier (critical episodes). A long and beneficial relationship may lead to increased concentration of the purchases from a single supplier and share of customer goes up. A single-sourcing strategy pursued by the customer gives the supplier a 100 per cent share and maximum revenue. The length and strength of the relationship also affects the type of interactions that form the relationships (the episode configuration) which in turn determines costs. Finally, relationship revenue minus relationship cost establishes the *customer relationship profitability* or ROR.

Companies may dry out because business has become constant firefighting and eventually there is no water left to throw on the fire. RM promotes long-term thinking, but sometimes today's business has to be saved before the long-term

---

[5] Storbacka, Strandvik and Grönroos (1994). The model was originally designed for services but has been generalized here to embrace all sorts of commercial relationships.

aspects can be addressed. Certain decisions must be taken out of strategic necessity; they are market investments and cannot be financially assessed with simple indicators. They do not belong in the short-term profit and loss statement. You either do it, and stand a chance to survive, or you don't and you will disappear from the market. Declining customer loyalty often builds up in small steps which may not be discernible until it is too late to reverse the vicious circle.

The review of the 30Rs showed that relationships in marketing are not all consumer relationships. They are also relationships to intermediaries, competitors, own suppliers, and other players in the market. They are mega relationships to the media, politicians, and personal friends. They are nano relationships inside a company.

'What makes the economy of relationships so special is indeed that a relationship has functions (has economic consequences) for several actors and thus that the outcomes of different relationships are interdependent…Thus it is not enough for any actor to be concerned just about itself in order to be successful, as is suggested in all recommendations based on market theory'.[6] We can't just ask 'what's in it for me and my company?' we also have to ask 'what's in it for the other members of the network?' and 'how can we help to improve the competitiveness of the network as a whole?' 'Tomorrow's company will understand and measure the value from all its relationships', says a British report by an organization with the impressive name of The Royal Society for the Encouragement of Arts, Manufacture & Commerce (1994).

We are not there yet, but models and applications that have been suggested will be presented in the next sections.

Duration, retention and defection

Loyalty and ROR can be tied to several key indicators. Among them are the *duration* of a relationship, how long the customers remain customers; the *retention rate*, which is the percentage of customers who remain after one year, two years, etc.; and the *defection rate*, which is the percentage of customer who leave a supplier.

A central question in RM is how much should be spent on retaining existing customers and increasing the duration of the relationship, and how much should be spent on getting new customers. A study in the UK showed that 80 per cent of the managers of service operations felt they spent excessive resources on attracting new customers, and 10 per cent that existing customers occupied too much of their resources. Only 10 per cent were happy with the balance between resources spent on new and existing customers.[7]

It is also a matter of adjusting the RM strategy to the buyers' needs and wants. One supplier may badly want a relationship with certain customers, but the customers do not respond simply because they are unwilling or unable to make the

---

[6] Håkansson and Snehota (1995, pp. 284–5).
[7] Payne and Rickard (1994).

commitment. Conversely, suppliers may pursue a transaction marketing strategy without being empathic to the customer desires to establish a long-term relationship.[8]

A frequently cited study[9] shows that 68 per cent of customers who defected from a supplier did so because the supplier seemed indifferent and 14 per cent because of unsatisfactory complaints handling. These two failed relationships accounted for 82 per cent of the defection. Only 5 per cent were lost through competitor initiatives, and 9 per cent because of lower prices elsewhere.

In an article on 'zero defection', the authors draw the conclusion that a supplier could double net profit if the defection rate is reduced by as little as 5 per cent.[10] They advise companies to make defection analyses. These include interviews with lost customers but should also address the weak signals of a customer entering the risk zone.

Direct Tire Sales is specialized in tyres and brakes and makes three-quarters of their sales with regular customers.[11] These customers spend twice as much as the first-time customers who come through advertising ($173 against $90). First-time customers who come through the recommendation of a regular customer spend as much as $224 at the first visit. Credit card company MBNA America did a defection analysis and learned from it.[12] The defection rate went down from ten per cent to five per cent which was half the industry average and profitability was dramatically improved. An average cardholder who stays one year causes a loss of $51, one who stays for five years a profit of $55, and one who stays for twenty years a profit of $525. For industry laundry, the profit for Year 1 was $144 and for Year 5 $256; for auto repair, $25 Year 1 and $88 for Year 5. If defection rates go down from 20 per cent to 10 per cent per annum and then to 5 per cent, the duration will increase from five to ten to twenty years with a consequent increase in profits. If a customer is lost, the whole of the future profit potential goes down the drain. In a comparison between nine industries in which the defection rate was reduced by 5 per cent – among them insurance brokers, computer software and auto repair – profits grew by 25 to 85 per cent.

Reichheld (1996) presents an elaborate, yet practical system for assessing ROR. His research has shown that customer loyalty cannot be earned in isolation. It is closely dependent on the loyalty of two other stakeholders: employees and investors. Those who stimulate loyal relationships with both customers, employees and investors are amply rewarded. For example, the advertising agency Leo Burnett loses only 2 per cent of its customers per year and its productivity is fifteen to 20 per cent higher than that of its principal competitors. Chick-fil-A, a chain of 600 quick service restaurants, has a turnover of store

---

[8] Jackson (1985a).
[9] Research from the 1980s by Miller Business Systems.
[10] Reichheld and Sasser (1990, p. 105).
[11] Johnson (1992, p. 85).
[12] This and the following examples are based on Reichheld and Sasser (1990).

operators of 4 to 6 per cent per year while the industry average is 40 to 50 per cent. Moreover, its store operators earn 50 per cent more than those of competing restaurant chains. As compared to the industry average, State Farm Insurance agents stay twice as long, have 40 per cent higher productivity, and a 95 per cent customer retention rate. Lexus, Toyota's luxury car, has the highest repurchase rate in the premium car bracket; it is 2 per cent of Toyota sales but 33 per cent of its profits.

Market share is a traditional indicator in marketing management, showing the percentage of a total market or market segment that a supplier serves. Fewer and more select customers, each buying more during a longer period, could be a superior way to profits as compared to more customers with a small volume and shorter relationships.[13] *Share of customer* is recommended as an alternative ratio to market share. Milliken Company, a leader in textiles and winner of the Baldrige Quality Award, monitors share of customers. A bank can estimate what share of a customer's financial assets and transactions are handled by the bank. Taco Bell is a successful and rapidly growing fast-food chain with Mexican cuisine. The company does not measure market share but 'share of stomach', thereby establishing how much of the customer's intake is delivered by Taco Bell.

Intellectual capital and the balanced scorecard

As numbers from accounting exert a significant influence on decisions and practices, supportive accounting is an antecedent to sound RM applications. Marketers all too often find accounting rigid, traditional and bound by legal restrictions, seldom giving support to essential marketing strategies.

Employees represent different specialities and they could be classified into tribes with different vocational identities. The *accounting tribe* often does not get on so well with the *marketing tribe*, there is even the risk of civil war. But in recent years, a revolution has started. New accounting theories and practices, most notably the *balanced scorecard*, register indicators of other types of capital than financial capital. Among them are indicators concerning the customer base and retention. The original balanced scorecard contains indicators in four groups of capital:[14] financial, customer, internal business process, and learning and growth.

It has long been popular for executives to say that 'people are our most valuable resource'. The statement alludes to employees, not customesr, investors, or vendors even if most of these are human too and provide resources. In the spirit of RM, each and everyone who has an impact on the success of a company should be included, meaning each party in a network of relationships, not least the customers. It is only recently that the *customer capital* – the existing customer base and customer relationships – is being seriously approached.

Traditionally, the balance sheet consists of tangible, hard assets, above all

---

[13] Johnson (1992, p. 79).
[14] Kaplan and Norton (1996).

money, inventory, machines and buildings. The human being is worthless, while the chair on which they sit represents a value only to be slowly depreciated according to some accounting principle. The customer represents no official value. However, when a company is sold or its stock is traded on an exchange, buyers pay for intangible assets like goodwill, brands and expected future earnings.

Accounting systems do not catch the value of customer relationships although building relationships is an investment in marketing. The accounting tribe has often been suspicious against intangible, soft values, and sometimes for good reasons. When profits are down, it is tempting for management to misuse soft values and claim that book values are not telling the whole truth and that the situation is not all that precarious. These values have therefore acquired a bad reputation. However, the interest in human resource accounting, social audits, and the financial aspects of personnel is on the increase. More often these days we encounter such concepts as customer capital, relationship capital, human capital, knowledge capital, and social capital.

The traditional balance sheet is not particularly informative about service companies and knowledge-intensive companies. Efforts have been made to find procedures for presenting a more realistic value of these companies. As all companies – including manufacturing operations – to an increasing extent comprise services and knowledge, the issue is of general concern.

In new and broader accounting systems, the concept of *intellectual capital* is challenging the supremacy of short-term *financial capital* .[15] Financial capital must of course exist in every organization and in the balanced scorecard financial capital is assessed together with intellectual capital. When capital is defined as 'something of value' – a resource – we realize that money and other hard assets are not the only capital.

Intellectual capital is defined as follows: Intellectual capital is the total value of a company – the price of its shares – minus its book value. It means all the assets except those in the balance sheet.

A company's survival and growth is eventually determined by its financial outcome. The issue is to recognize the long-term importance of intellectual capital for the generation of financial capital, and to gradually convert intellectual capital into financial capital.

Intellectual capital can be divided into two major types: individual capital and structural capital.

Individual capital consists of employees and their qualities. It includes the individuals' knowledge, behaviour and motivation and also the individuals' network of relationships. This network consists of personal relationships which have been cultivated over a long period and the trust and confidence that an employee has established among customers and others. The power and prestige of individual

---

[15] The Swedish Coalition of Service Industries (1993); Edvinsson and Malone (1997); Sveiby (1997); Stewart (1997).

capital is evident for an advertising agency, or a partnership of lawyers who thrive on their personal interaction with clients. But it is also important for a retail store, a bank branch office, an car repair shop, or a manufacturing operation. This was pointed out in the service encounter (R5) and the many-headed customer and supplier relationship (R6).

There is also capital built into an employee who can quickly gain a customer's confidence, a quality which is particularly essential in a salesperson. In R1, the story was told about the top performing door-to-door salesman; he said that knocking on doors gives him twenty seconds to gain the confidence of the consumer.

If an employee leaves a company, the individual capital vanishes. You cannot own human beings, that would be slavery. They are '9 to 5 assets'.

In the knowledge relationship (R21), knowledge was presented as a prime reason for alliances. Two types of knowledge were discussed, migratory knowledge which is portable, and embedded knowledge which is inseparable from its environment. Embedded knowledge is part of the *structural capital*. It does not disappear if an employee leaves; it is owned by the company. In an RM sense, structural capital consists of relationships which have been established with a company as such and are tied to culture, systems, contracts, image, and the network to which a company belongs. The more successfully a company ties relationships to its structure, the less dependent it is on individual employees.

As all companies and marketing situations are unique in at least some aspects, applications must be adapted to each specific situation. Two cases will be presented below. The Skandia case is an application of the balanced scorecard, financial capital, and intellectual capital. The Bank case concerns the urgency of computing return on customer relationships.

Case study

For many years, Skandia has been experimenting with its own special variant of the balanced scorecard and intellectual capital indicators, the Skandia Navigator.[16] Skandia works actively to enhance the value of the customer base. In its fastest-growing operation, AFS (Assurance and Financial Services), a distinction has been made between different customer segments: all existing customers; those who are solely AFS customers; AFS customers who also buy from other providers; complete customers; part customers; lost customers; and young customers. Customers migrate between these groups.

The total customer capital is estimated as customer net revenue times duration. After the size of the customer capital has been established, four areas for enhancing the value of the customer capital are addressed:

---

[16] See Buck-Lew and Edvinsson (1993); and the Skandia Annual Report Supplements (1995, 1996, 1997).

1 improved customer relationships;
2 increased profits through longer customer relationships;
3 more sales;
4 a focus on profitable customers.

Questions to be asked in the marketing planning process are: How much can we increase both sales and the duration of the relationship? What will be the consequences of these increases? How will customer migration be influenced? What steps have to be taken?

Skandia has now developed a list of 111 indicators and a reserve of another fifty-five. This is certainly no short-list and it may scare off any executive as being too much and too complicated to report, let alone act upon. Of the total number of indicators, twenty have a financial focus and the others an intellectual capital focus. The following indicators have apparent relevance to RM.[17]

■ With the focus on customers: annual sales/customers, customers lost, average duration of customer relationships, rate of repeat customers, average customer purchases/year, average contacts by customer/year, points of sale, customer visits to company, days spent visiting customers, and a satisfied customer index.
■ With the focus on employees, but with consequences for customer relationships: motivation index, empowerment index, employee turnover, and average years of service with company.
■ With particular focus on customers and the electronic relationship: IT investment/customer, IT investment/service and support level, number of internal IT customers, number of external IT customers, and IT literacy of customers.

It takes time to make these indicators operational and practical and to select a manageable few that uncover useful information. It takes years before time-series are established and trends can be discerned. Among indicators that appear in Skandia's most recent annual reports are: availability on the telephone; an index of customer satisfaction; number of customers; retention rate; the ratio between cost for business development and total cost; the ratio between number of employees and IT investment; number of ideas for improvements; and revenue from new services.

---

[17] See Edvinsson and Malone (1997, pp. 151–8).

Case study

The Bank case will illustrate the critique that Johnson and Kaplan (1987) have pronounced against the lost relevance of accounting. It essentially concerns arbitrary distribution of cost. The way costs are distributed on products, services and departments is reminiscent of Russian roulette; the lucky one survives but you cannot influence the outcome. In a later book, Johnson (1992) revised and further developed the critique by blaming the problem on top-down management and remote control via ratios. Ratios offer simplistic and delayed information. They do not heed quality, neither the degree of customer satisfaction, nor the degree of employee motivation. They disregard the living processes of a company.

Activity based costing (ABC) offers certain new opportunities to assess cost. It is focused on activities and processes. This is particularly important for services which consist of activities, partly performed together with customers. Like most cost and revenue assessments, however, ABC has indulged in cost, but not in revenue and consequently not paid attention to the contributions of marketing. Despite its strengths, there is criticism claiming that ABC preserves industrial society features: mass manufacturing, top-down management, remote control, and preoccupation with cost. ABC needs to be expanded into D and E, 'demand' and 'effectiveness'.[18] In RM jargon it means that customers and quality need to get a place in the accounts.

Cooper and Kaplan (1991) consider ABC to give rise to better assessments than Pareto optimality or the 20/80 rule (stating that 20 per cent of customers or products account for 80 per cent of profits). They introduce the 20/225 rule, which claims that 20 per cent account for 225 per cent; consequently the majority of customers or products are unprofitable!

Storbacka's comparison between banks underscores this conclusion.[19] His 'Stobachoff curve' shows the distribution of profits from different customers. According to his bank study, profits can be a maximum of 100 per cent, which was reached with the help of 10 per cent of the most profitable customers. Twenty per cent of customers contributed 140 per cent of profits but 60 to 80 per cent of profits were erased by the remaining and unprofitable customers.

In making such assessments, one problem is the hidden links between the services offered by banks. These links imply that seemingly unprofitable services may be necessary requisites for cash cows and customer retention. Furthermore, the unprofitable services/customers carry allocated overheads. By abolishing these services/customers, the base for the overheads is narrowed, and currently profitable services/customers will become unprofitable.

Profit estimates have traditionally been tied to organizational units or products. Data on ROR of customers as consumer, family member, or a combination of con-

---

[18] Frenckner (1992).
[19] These data and the treatment of the Bank case are based on Storbacka (1994).

sumer and small business owners, are currently not retrievable from bank databases. Data are arranged to calculate the profits on a single transaction rather than the profits over a consumer's or business owner's lifetime.

ATMs, which handle bank transactions, are considered cost-effective. Studies claim that it costs three to four times as much to deliver the service via a person than via an ATM. It is, however, necessary to know how these estimates have been made and if all costs are included. Since ATMs were introduced, the number of transactions is reputed to have increased, therefore the estimates may be deficient. But it is evident that customer relationships are affected. Relationships to bank managers or clerks are personal and especially in small branch offices customers and staff know each other; it is a moderately high-touch relationship. Relationships to ATMs, telephone banking and internet banking are electronic, mechanical, and impersonal; they are high tech. How this transition in relationships will affect customer loyalty and retention, we do not know.

Customer interaction, triplets and tribes

The vantage point of this section is condensed in the statement that: 'Quality, productivity, and profits are triplets; separating one from the other creates an unhappy family'.[20]

The triplets are all concerned with the same issue: 'How well is the company doing?' They represent three different perspectives and tribes within the organization. We have already met the marketing tribe and the accounting tribe and we are about to meet the *quality tribe* and the *productivity tribe*. They represent different traditions and different cultures; each tribe's awareness of the total welfare of the company is limited.

Quality tribe members are devoted to revenue issues, they think of customers and revenue and are closest to the marketing tribe. Members of the productivity tribe are obsessed by costs; in practice, a productivity increase means cost reduction and downsizing. The accounting tribe deals with the annual report and its balance sheet and profit and loss statement. The tribes do not mingle well although they play in the same orchestra and should be playing the same symphony. They all contribute valuable expertise, but in order to get the best from each, top management must be conductors and lead them in the right direction.

Despite the balanced scorecard, intellectual capital, organizations being imaginary, and RM devising a new ground for marketing, there is a risk that the old ways of computing profitability continue. A particularly critical question in RM is: How shall the role of the customer be evaluated?

Both customers and suppliers have relationship costs. If the customer is a con-

---

[20] Gummesson (1991, p. 6).

sumer, costs are incurred in the consumer's spare time and are not part of the GDP. Grönroos[21] examines relationship costs and profitability in service operations and their connection to inferior quality. He makes a distinction between three types of costs that hit both consumer and companies. A consumer pays a certain price for a service, but in addition there are costs to correct mistakes caused by the consumer (direct costs), costs caused by the provider (indirect costs), and mental and social discomfort caused by the correction procedure (psychological costs). If the relationship between the customer and provider is perfect, these costs disappear. In conclusion, relationship costs and quality go in opposite directions – high service quality causes low relationship costs, and low service quality causes high relationship costs.

From other vantage points in the network approach to business marketing, relationship costs have been classified as the sum of activity costs (activities in a network) and structural costs (network investment and maintenance costs).[22] Furthermore, cost in a relationship is a matter of both static utilization of extant resources and dynamic development of the potential of new combinations that the resources of the network hold.[23] Changes in business networks occur every day. The imaginary organization is an expression of this dynamic aspect, the continuous resourcing in an enhanced 'opportunity space'.

Our research has brought to the fore the complications of defining the customer's role in service operations and the network of the imaginary organization. In service production and delivery, quality and productivity emerge from five sources:

1 the service provider as independent actor;
2 the customer as independent actor;
3 the interaction between the provider and the customer;
4 the interaction between customers;
5 service-supporting infrastructure.

Traditionally, quality and productivity are treated as the sole outcome of the first, the provider's independent work. Neither customer input, nor the contribution from the provider–customer interaction are taken into account. Service research has shown that the customer–supplier relationship may be a prime source of quality and productivity. Service production is interactive and the input from provider personnel and customers are partly substitutes (see R5).

Porter[24] acquired fame for the *value chain* which is composed of nine elementary internal activities. Primary activities are inbound logistics (incoming raw material), operations, outbound logistics (distribution of finished products), mar-

---

[21] Grönroos (1992, pp. 129–40). See also further elaboration of the financial dimensions of relationship quality, based on both service management and the network approach, in Holmlund (1997).
[22] Eriksson and Åsberg (1994).
[23] According to Håkansson and Snehota (1995).
[24] Porter (1985, pp. 36–43).

keting and sales, and service. Support activities are procurement, technology development (both technical and systems development), human resource management, and firm infrastructure (organization, systems). The value chain attempts to isolate individual activities and see their added value and costs. The chain is essentially sequential and each function is well delimited. To some extent it deals with interfunctional interaction, parallel activities, and alliances, which means that there is a slight affinity to RM. But even if value for the customer is given as a goal, the customer is not included in the value chain.

The *value constellation* (or *value star*)[25] has already been mentioned as an alternative to the value chain. In the value constellation, the relationships and interaction with the customer are viewed as part of a shared value creating process. Supplier and customer are co-producers, co-managers, and even co-developers of a product or service. For the customer, the value contributed by a specific provider is only one of a plethora of values that form his or her value constellation. Joint production through the service encounter is the key element of services marketing and management, but it is also being generalized to include the manufacturing sector. The value chain becomes a special case which is primarily valid in mass manufacturing. The value constellation highlights the integration between functions and concurrent activities, including customer contributions.

According to the value chain, marketing becomes the distribution of value to the consumer, who is a 'value destroyer'. The value constellation on the other hand recognizes that value is created through the concerted efforts of functions inside an organization, outsourced functions, and the customers. Making a product is one type of value creation, consuming it for a purpose is another or maybe the most important value creation.

If both the customer and the supplier are part of the same value-creating process, the role of price is altered: 'This means that both profits and losses…should be shared between supplier and customer. Instead of price-setting, it becomes a question of remuneration for participation in the creation of value. This kind of remuneration must be discussed in very open-minded negotiations between the two parties'.[26]

ROR can be enhanced by changing the balance between revenue, cost, and capital employed. Cost and capital employed can be increased in order to increase revenue even more. A revenue reduction – for example, eliminating unprofitable customers – can reduce cost even more. By myopic concentration on cost, the attractiveness of a company is reduced and customer relationships are jeopardized.

Return on the non-measurable – the Superquinn case

Particularly in the USA we hear: 'what gets measured, gets done.' There is a truth in this, but also a danger. Indicators are often selected because of tradition and

---

[25] Normann and Ramírez (1993); Wikström and Normann (1994).
[26] Wikström and Normann (1994, p. 62).

because they are easy to measure, not because they are useful. For example, it is easier to quantify short-term profits than the profits lost because of mismanaged relationships.

It may come as a shock to some, but the word 'measurement' is derived from the Sanskrit word *'maya'* which means *illusion* or *witchcraft*. But it can also mean *image*. Measurements should be images of reality whereas in practice they are often illusions or witchcraft.

Obsession with measurement means handing over the future of a company to the accounting tribe, abolishing vision and leadership. Many 'leaders' never become leaders, just grossly overpaid accountants.

There are marketers who suffer from measurement fright. They can neither count, nor analyse numbers. But there are also measurement fetishists and security seeking CEOs, accountants, and marketers. They cherish the illusions of measurement. Their fetish[27] is the bottom line and short-term profit ratios, which are often devastating to long-term stable development. When indicators are used to pinpoint certain phenomena with reasonable accuracy and validity, there is no problem. When indicators pinpoint the wrong things, employees will go for the indicators that promote their careers and not go for the real thing. Measurement becomes self-deception even if the tables and graphs look impressive.

Case study

Certain things must be measured in terms of money, others should never be associated with numbers. Fergal Quinn will serve as an example of the importance of the non-measurable. He is founder and president of Superquinn, a prosperous Irish chain of supermarkets. Quinn expresses his philosophy in the following way:[28] 'Most businesses focus on maximising the profit from current sales. Of course they are 'interested' in repeat business – who isn't? but often they see it as a bonus rather than the main pay-off. And so they tend to concentrate on what they see as the main pay-off, with the lesser part of the energy devoted to creating a bonus.'

According to Quinn, we should do it the other way around: 'If you look after getting the repeat business, the profit now will largely look after itself.' This is completely in line with RM; short-term profits are an outcome of long-term investment in relationships and consequently one should prioritize the long term.

Quinn found it difficult to prove long-term profit effects to his accounting tribe; confidence in his own judgement and gut feeling was necessary. He says that lead-

---

[27] Fetishes are objects – strangely shaped stones, animal teeth, claws, feathers – which are reputed to bring strength and success to its owners who are usually medicine-men, magicians, and shamans.

[28] This section is based on a book and an article by Quinn (1990 and 1994); the quotations are from the article.

ership is not to make all decisions based on numbers but also to make qualitative evaluations. Leadership is risk-taking, action and vision; it is consciousness about the situation, common sense and intuition. Numbers and accounting can be of assistance within leadership but they cannot replace leadership. Johnson (1992) says very distinctly in his assessment of activity based costing that it can improve accounting, but it is no substitute for marketing decisions.

Quinn offers the following examples.

- Example 1 – Superquinn stores introduced playrooms for children so that the mothers would be free to do purchasing. If the children enjoy the playroom, mothers were likely to stay longer, buy more and return. But it is not possible to measure the profitability of this investment in hard short-term figures.
- Example 2 – Sweets at the cash registers stimulates impulse buying, which gives easily measurable short-term income. While waiting to pay, children are tempted by the sweets and their parents get under fire. Irritation occurs, parents feel uneasy and may prefer to patronize another outlet. This effect cannot be figured out in accounting terms; it must be observed and the decision must feel right.
- Example 3 – When the Irish Post was restructured, it wanted the public to notice the change. The idea was suggested that the old postage cost from the last century, one penny for a letter, should apply during the day of celebration. It was agreed that this would be a costly campaign. To their great astonishment, the campaign paid off in a couple of weeks. People who used to write letters took the opportunity to write more and the number of letters increased dramatically during the cheap day. But return on investment came by return of mail as the recipients of letters replied and then at full postage. It was the ideal campaign; the pay-back was instant and the Irish Post reached the public with its message.

In all these examples, the activities are chosen to enhance revenue more than cost, and to achieve long-term and sustainable effects. Correct short-term costs are easy to forecast, whereas long-term revenue can only be assessed strategically and qualitatively.

If the supplier is handling relationships well, the customer comes back. Quinn sums up his philosophy in the *boomerang principle*: 'One of the beauties with the boomerang principle …is that you and the customer end up on the same side…So the relationship with your customer is not an adversarial one, it is a partnership.'

Strategies for improved ROR

A series of approaches to ROR have been presented. They help us understand aspects of RM but none of them offers the complete and ultimate solution.

Most of the text has dealt with return on customer–supplier relationships. Even if we primarily think of the relationship to our immediate buyer, customer–supplier relationships also include intermediaries, end-users, and our own suppliers. Furthermore, market relationships include relationships to competitors and their many faces, being first and foremost rivals, but often being customers, suppliers, and partners as well.

Return on non-market relationships – the mega and nano relationships – is not as obvious, especially in the short term. They are antecedents to successful market relationships. Mega relationships are often strategic and structural necessities; without them the supplier will be out of business. Nano relationships offer internal and necessary conditions for external relationships.

In summary, the following paragraphs will summarize consequences and strategies are essential for improving ROR.

Customer–supplier relationships

- Marketing costs go down when you do not have to recruit as many new customers as before.
- Both suppliers and customers become better partners, co-producers and even co-developers. As a consequence, quality defects go down.
- Suppliers get to know their customers better. They can build databases, become more sensitive to customer needs and wants, and target their offerings better.
- Customer frequently have several suppliers and especially new customers may be low users. If the relationships work out well, they are likely to favour fewer sources and the share of customer increases.
- Good relationships make customers better part-time marketers, adding marketing muscle without burdening marketing and sales budgets.
- Good relationships mean less hassle, for example, if delays occur and faulty goods or services are delivered. It is easier to sort out problems between 'friends' who trust each other.
- Loyal customers become less price sensitive – within limits – as they also value relationship dimensions such as trust, commitment, convenience, and easy access.
- New customers often have to be acquired with a special offer and a discount that make them initially unprofitable; such campaigns often attract 'junk customers' with no or little profit potential.

Competitor relationships

- Competitors have a tougher time when retention and loyalty increase; they are not served new customers on a plate.
- By collaborating with competitors in certain areas, both suppliers and customers gain advantages through, for example, cost reduction and joint development of products and services.

■ By collaborating in an industry, competitors can help each other to improve conditions for the industry as a whole.

Non-market relationships

■ Return on mega relationships is obvious when, for example, a lobbying campaign is successful or an alliance brings valuable knowledge to a product development project.
■ Nano relationships are partly internal market relationships, such as the supplier–customer relationship between profit centres. ROR then can be measured in the same way as an external market relationships. Other nano relationships are sometimes more difficult to assess, such as the value of cooperation between operations management and marketing through quality.

Recommendations

■ Watch out for unprofitable customers who hide among the profitable ones.
■ Establish a sound basis for estimates, making sure that relationships are properly evaluated, such as the customer's profitability over a lifetime, and that profitability links between different products, services, and customers are considered.
■ Watch out for senile accounting systems and indicators, which are geared to the mass manufacturing of the industrial era. They are not suitable maps in the value society.
■ Whenever possible, make sure that relationships become part of the structural capital as the individual capital is transient and less controllable. However, caring for the individual capital is also imperative.
■ Analyse the roles of the parties in a network such as the supplier role and the customer role. Who should do what and what should be done in interaction?
■ Measure what impacts ROR – if it is measurable! Do not fall into the trap of thinking the non-measurable – such as culture, leadership, vision, and long-term network building – is unimportant just because it can't be replicated in numbers. Numbers must be linked to common sense, sound judgement, vision, and endurance.

Words of caution

■ Satisfied customers are not enough.
■ High customer perceived quality is not enough.
■ Discriminate between 'very satisfied' and 'satisfied'.
■ Dissatisfied customers do not necessarily defect.
■ Customers have to be continuously encouraged to remain.
■ Satisfied customers are not necessarily profitable.
■ Satisfaction indicators must be interpreted, satisfied customers may just be 'happy slaves' who currently think there is no option.

Finally

- Pose the provoking question: How well are we handling our network of relationships? Do customers and other parties feel the same way as we do about the relationships, or is there a gap between our perceptions?
- RM is not a fundamentalist religion. Choose between a long-term bond and a short-term contact. Sometimes RM is not efficient and the strategy should be transaction marketing.

A RM-inspired marketing plan and audit

If we ask companies today how they practise RM, only very few are able to give adequate answers. This does not mean that RM is absent. It means that bits and pieces of RM are embedded in marketing, but they are not clearly discernible and they are called something else. In fact, companies are doing a lot of RM but for lack of concepts, models, a common language, and marketing planning and auditing tradition, the relationship activities are not openly acknowledged and put to use in a systematic and conscious manner.

It is particularly important to take a fresh look at the planning and evaluation of marketing efforts as RM offers new conditions. This should be done in two areas of marketing management, the marketing plan and the marketing audit.

The RM plan and the relationship portfolio

To carry weight, RM aspects must be introduced in the marketing planning process. Marketing in the light of relationships, networks and interaction becomes *marketing-oriented management*, and therefore the marketing plan must be an integral part of the *company's overall business plan*.

There is little research available on marketing planning in networks of relationships. One of the exceptions is Benndorf (1987) who studied relationships and networks in industrial marketing and their meaning for the marketing planning process. He concluded that companies in a network become dependent on each other's plans. Their resources and activities should ideally be co-planned with regard to network dependencies. Such co-planning is not easy to practice, however.

We know too little about how RM should best be integrated into the planning of a company. The only ways to find out are through trial and error in our companies and through research.

For lack of experience of RM planning, it seems reasonable to start by adding RM dimensions to the marketing plan in use, retaining its basic format.[29] A marketing plan which is focused on the opportunities offered by RM can include the relationships and networks that need to be built, maintained, or abandoned.

---

[29] For a review of systematic marketing planning procedures in use, see McDonald (1995).

Activity planning is a normal part of a marketing plan, and activities and inter-actions in relationships should also be the object of planning. Traditional goals of the marketing plan, such as sales volume and market share, must in part be sub-stituted or supplemented by ROR goals, such as customer retention and share of customer, in the spirit of intellectual capital and the balanced scorecard.

Activities in marketing are usually described as a marketing mix – the 4 or more Ps – including price, sales calls, physical distribution, and other activities and strategies. These are not replaced by the 30Rs, but the way RM has been pre-sented here, the relationships are the vantage point – what we see through the relationship eye-glasses – and the Ps and other activities can be supportive to the relationships. The relationships broaden the interplay between marketing and other functions such as production and internal services.

Instead of starting with mixing Ps, a company needs to define and review its *relationship portfolio*. I have chosen the word portfolio rather than mix to accentu-ate a novel perspective and novel values, a paradigm shift. A portfolio is a collec-tion of components and their total benefits should be greater than the sum of its parts; there should be synergy effects. The term financial portfolio is used for a combination of investments that fulfil chosen goals such as balanced risk, maximum short-term yield, or maximum long-term growth. In strategic manage-ment, portfolio is used for the choice of products to offer on the market (product portfolio) and the choice of customers to target (customer portfolio). The rela-tionship portfolio is a combination of RM activities to be performed during the planning period.

In summary, the following tasks should be added to the marketing plan:

1 *Select a relationship portfolio!* Analyse the currently interesting relationships and net-works and assess your ability to interact in these. Do this as an active part of the mar-keting planning and business planning processes. Use the 30Rs as a checklist. Each relationship must be defined to fit a specific company and its specific situation. Select relationships of particular importance which are currently not handled well enough but are gauged to have development potential.

2 *Set goals for ROR and their development!* Goals are an important part of the marketing plan, not only quantitative, short-term goals but also qualitative, long-term and strate-gic goals.

3 Monitor implementation and outcome! The implementation processes must be moni-tored and the outcome must be compared to the goals. If implementation is slow or weak, there will be no positive effect on financial results.

4 *Assess RM consequences for organization, processes, systems, and procedures!* RM puts new demands on the organization and its processes, methods, and procedures. In the next chapter, the importance of organizational structure and processes for RM are dis-cussed further.

The RM audit

Marketing is reviewed continuously during the working day and it is reviewed as part of the marketing planning process at least once a year. Marketing is also reviewed in management and board meetings; in meetings with others in a company's network; in special projects for new products, services, and marketing channels, and for assessing changes in the marketplace; in trouble-shooting missions by task forces; and at kick-offs and at marketing and sales conferences. It may be reviewed by our partners in networks. It may even be reviewed by the media. So what is really the use of a marketing audit?

The following definition of marketing audit has been suggested:[30] 'A marketing audit is a comprehensive, systematic, independent, and periodic examination of a company's – or business unit's – marketing environment, objectives, strategies, and activities with a view to determining problem areas and opportunities and recommending a plan of action to improve the company's marketing performance'.

A marketing audit is closely connected to marketing and business plans and reporting systems. The corporate business planning and marketing planning processes are recurrent events, but they primarily produce documents to guide the next planning period. Usually they do not include a systematic evaluation challenging fundamental strategic issues. According to McDonald:[31]

> Often the need for an audit does not manifest itself until things
> start to go wrong for a company, such as declining sales, falling
> margins, lost market share, underutilized production capacity, and so
> on. At times like these, management often attempts to treat the
> wrong symptoms....introducing new products or dropping
> products, reorganizing the sales force, reducing prices, and cutting
> costs...But such measures are unlikely to be effective if there are
> more fundamental problems which have not been identified'

This is where the marketing audit enters. It goes a step further than the marketing plan to analyse fundamental marketing issues. In contrast to the aforementioned review activities, the audit must also fulfil the four criteria of the definition. The audit should be:

1 *comprehensive*, thus covering all marketing aspects;
2 *systematic* by using an orderly method;
3 *independent* by being conducted by a person or team who do not have a stake in the company's marketing;
4 *periodic*, that is, be conducted regularly and not just on an ad hoc basis.

---

[30] Kotler, Gregor and Rodgers (1989).
[31] McDonald (1995, p. 28–9).

RM adds an extra and revolutionary dimension to marketing planning and the marketing audit. In viewing marketing as part of interaction and events in a network of relationships, we have to broaden the marketing function beyond marketing and sales departments and company boundaries.

Companies and consultants have developed various formats for marketing audits. Even if a company starts out with a general marketing audit checklist, it should adjust it to its specific needs as experience is gained with its application.[32]

Although the checklists may cover certain RM aspects, they do not have an RM focus; they are not based on observations made through the relationship eyeglasses. We are not yet ready to suggest a general RM checklist; the empirical base is too thin. In order to be practical, I will settle for suggesting RM additions to existing audit checklists. Therefore, look at each of the 30Rs and their parts and answer the following questions:

1 Is the composition of our relationship portfolio satisfactory?
2 How well are we handling specific relationships and their parts?
3 Are specific relationships or parts of them crucial for success?
4 Could specific relationships add to our performance if we improve them?
5 Should certain relationships be terminated?
6 Do we measure ROR in the best possible way?

---

[32] See marketing audit checklists in McDonald (1995, pp. 30–2); and Kotler (1997, pp. 777–84).

Chapter 7

RM and the new organization

The dependency between RM and novel ways of approaching organizational structures — imaginary organizations — have been noted in previous chapters. This chapter deals with this intriguing issue at more length and ends with a discourse on the significance of RM for both corporations and the market economy.

Introducing the new organization

In working with RM, marketing and organization began to stand out as two expressions of the same thing. My conclusion became that *RM can be perceived as a marketing perspective of the new organization, the imaginary (or virtual) organization.* The direction of cause and effect is not evident. It may rather be that there is a circular causality, a reciprocal, constructive dependency between the two – a symbiotic relationship.

In this chapter I will share my view of the connection between a company's organization, market, and marketing. The reason for treating organization separately and more at length is to give the marketer a better understanding for its significance.

RM lives in three environments: the *market, society,* and the *organization.* The RM approach means that these three are woven together into a network. The nano relationships show the importance of the internal environment. The notion of imaginary organizations has been used in the book as an umbrella for new organizational thinking, but the following is also drawing on other efforts to reproduce an image of the new corporation.[1]

---

[1] The new organizational thinking offers a rich fauna of concepts and terms. Among them are Handy's 'federative organization' (1990,p. 117ff) and 'Triple I' organization – 'intelligence, information, ideas' – (p. 141ff); Quinn's (1992, p. 120ff) 'spider's web organization' which is a network and the 'starburst organization' (p. 148) which is a continuously budding organization; Mills' (1991, p. 31) 'cluster organization' consisting of clusters of teams; and Tjosvold's (1993) 'team-based organization'. Although they will not be referred to further in the text, I like to give recognition to them here as they all have affinity with imaginary organizations.

According to Hedberg et al.[2] an imaginary organization is '...a system in which assets, processes, and actors critical to the "focal" enterprise exist and function both inside and outside the limits of the enterprise's conventional "landscape" formed by its legal structure, its accounting, its organigrams, and the language otherwise used to describe the enterprise'.

The imaginary organization is a construct with the purpose of making the invisible visible and to acquire new frames of reference, to 'imaginize'. The organization is looked at through new lenses, and a new business logic for entrepreneurship and renovation of existing companies emerges.

The imaginary organization consists of an *own base* which in turn consists of a *leader company* and an *imaginator* (the leader, the entrepreneur) and their *strategic map*; a unique *imaginary culture*; a *customer base* which is tied to the leader company through systems for *production, delivery, market communications,* and *payment; partnering companies* and others that contribute resources; and a *business mission* that keeps the network of internal and external relationships together.

As a consequence of the definition and its core elements, imaginary organizations are characterized by being larger than they seem from the organizational chart. They are more resourceful than the balance sheet reveals, as their core is intellectual capital and external resourcing (or outsourcing).[3] IT often helps to create totally new organizational solutions but not a condition per se; customers are involved in co-production and thus joint value creation, customers are treated as temporary members of the organization; and they are based on processes rather than functional structures.

Organizational and imaginary properties have emerged in the 30Rs. Among them are the full-time and part-time marketers (R4); the electronic relationship (R12); the market mechanisims being brought into the organization (R24); interfunctional and interhierarchial dependency and internal and external customer relationships (R25); the two-dimensional matrix (R28); and relationships to external providers of marketing services (R29). In several of the other Rs, organizational aspects have played a role.

My guess is that imaginary organizations just like RM have been there a long time, perhaps always. Our way of approaching marketing and organization in the textbooks and education leads us astray. The books begin to look like nostalgic albums with black and white picure postcards from a bygone industrial society: factories with smoking chimneys, mass manufacturing, huge companies, hierarchies, clearly defined roles and positions, and blue collar workers as opposed to white collar workers. We have come to a point where the new – or rather the old but newly uncovered – is commencing to be visible and is developing with more zest. It is the outcome of the service society, the information society, the knowl-

---

[2] Hedberg, Dahlgren, Hansson and Olve (1997, p. 13).

[3] In the language of the imaginary organization, *resourcing* is preferred to outsourcing. It refers to the company adding resources to its core competency rather than abandoning responsibilities such as investment, personnel and cost.

edge society, the neoindustrial society, the postmodern society, all dimensions of what I prefer to name the value society.

In the next few sections, my personal interpretation of imaginary organizations will be unfolded in the light of RM.

Nobody has seen a corporation!

The heading may seem absurd, but when we talk about a corporation we refer to something abstract although it has certain tangible features. When the CEO is interviewed on TV or when the new model of a car is shown, we catch a glimpse of the being of the corporation. We cannot take a photograph of a business, but we can produce pictures of its elements: a photograph of a building or a group of employees, an organizational chart, a logotype. The goods and services of a company are tangible evidence of its existence. We see the tracks of the elusive animal in the snow, we surmise its presence, we may even catch a quick glimpse before it slips away.

Morgan (1997) approaches the organization with a series of metaphors. The organization is looked upon as if it were a machine, biological organism, brain, culture, political system, psychic prison, flow and change, and finally a tool to dominate society. Metaphors draw our attention to certain qualities of an organism, but they only provide fragments, not the whole. They should not be stretched too far; if they do, they lose their value.

Gustavsson (1992) talks about 'objectification' when we compare an organization to something tangible, and 'reification' when we mistake the phenomenon for its tangible representation. This may lead to myopia and imprisonment in existing concepts and definitions. Our perceptions about organizations take over, and we become their slaves instead of making them our servants. Inferior quality, disinterest in the customer, erroneous decisions, and inertia are blamed on the organization and the system: 'I'm sorry, I can't do anything about it.' This has been called 'learnt helplessness'. Such a state of mind makes lousy marketing and lousy customer relationships. It can be found among companies, but above all among those government organizations which have become a 'reality' separated from us – the impersonal system, the authority, the computer, the state, society, public opinion – and which we ultimately cannot or dare not affect. The map takes over and the landscape gets lost. The renowned painting of a smoking pipe by Belgian artist Magritte, with the inscription 'Ceci n'est pas une pipe' (This is not a pipe), is named 'La trahison des images' (The treachery of images). The artist makes us understand how easily we can mistake an image of an object for the object itself.

According to Weick[4] organizations are relationships and interaction:

> Most 'things' in organizations are actually relationships, variables tied
> together in a systematic fashion. Events, therefore, depend on the

---

[4] Weick (1979, p. 88).

strength of these ties, the direction of influence, the time it takes
for information in the form of differences to move around circuits.
The word organization is a noun, and it is also a myth. If you look
for an organization you won't find it. What you will find is that
there are events, linked together, that transpire within concrete
walls and these sequences, their pathways, and their timing are the
forms we erroneously make a substance when we talk about an
organization.

Consequently, management cannot take for granted that the boundaries of their
corporation are clear. They are expected to defend a moving fortress which continuously changes character and has different boundaries depending on whose
vantage point is prevalent, that of the owners, the customers, the authorities, production, or whatever.

The company and the market – two phenomena, or two perspectives of the same phenomenon?

It has already been said that company boundaries are fuzzy. This dilemma will be
further explained in this section by means of systems theory and transaction cost
analysis, both with the aspiration of establishing boundaries.

Applied to the company and the market, *systems theory* assumes that the *system*
(the organization) can be delimited from the *environment* (the market and society),
and that it comprises *subsystems* and *components* (the inner functions of the orga-

Case study

When a deal between Volvo and Procordia was announced, there was reason to ask
what the corporations and the market really were. Volvo owned already 43.5 per
cent of Procordia stock. Procordia was going to buy Volvo, but the new corporation
was going to be called Volvo. Procordia produced tobacco, lozenges, and hamburgers; Volvo passenger cars, trucks, buses, and aircraft engines. There was no product
synergy in sight. The smoker could not care less if the plants were owned by Volvo
and some 100,000 anonymous stockholders who change from day to day. The relationship existed between the consumer, the brand, and the store where the cigarettes were bought. Moreover, the two companies owned stock in other companies.
There was partial ownership between Volvo and Renault, although Volvo was primarily owned by private investors, and Renault primarily by the State of France. A
large number of subcontractors were tied to their customer Volvo, and from an
operations point they were part of the Volvo empire. Where actually were the
boundaries between these two companies, their markets, and society?

nization). This approach helps to recognize the whole and its parts. In a network, however, boundaries are many and ever changing. The difference between the company and its market, as well as its functions, is a matter of grade, transitions, and difference in species. If decisions are the outcome of negotiations, consensus, or power through interaction in a network, clear systems boundaries cannot be upheld. The traditional image of the atomistic market, populated by a large number of independent companies who act against relatively passive buyers, is still promoted in the textbooks, however.

The dichotomy of *open* and *closed systems* from systems theory is eluded by the properties of the networks and the imaginary organization. A network is a more open system than the corporation in its classic 'citadel' sense. Networks, however, can also be closed, with openness inside the network, but closeness toward those who do not belong to the network.

The company as an open system means that it interacts with the environment. Today, it may be more appropriate to describe the company as *both interacting with the environment and being integrated with it*. The customer also becomes part of the company which has stood out most clearly in services marketing. One example of both interaction and integration is Ernst & Young, one of the world's largest firms of accountants. Their office in Chicago was transformed into a 'virtual office' for 500 of its 1360 employees. The accountants work in the clients' offices and conference rooms, in hotel rooms, at airports and in airplanes, in their cars and at home. If they plan to work in their office they call in and book a room the day before ('hotelling') and a room is prepared for them with their telephone connection. From a daily, operative view, the boundaries between the accounting firm and the client do not stand out as particularly important.

Transaction cost analysis [5] claims to be able to guide the establishment of boundaries between a company and its market. The analysis has received extensive exposure as a synthesis between economics, organizational theory, and contract theory from law. Unfortunately, the analysis is based on simplified assumptions about the industrial society and manufacturing, and does not pay attention to the service-based economy. It is limited to the 'pure' company and does not treat hybrids such as franchizing and alliances. General marketing management has not been included, nor services marketing and the ideas of RM. The assumptions, therefore, seem obsolete and simplistic.

Its basic tenets, however, embrace some elements that can shed light on the differences between RM and the traditional perceptions of organizations and marketing. In neoclassical economic theory there are no transaction costs so transaction cost analysis, in spite of its shortcomings, adds a new element of realism. The analysis sets the business deal – the transaction – in focus, and postulates that companies strive to minimize transaction costs. These concern the

---

[5] Transaction cost analysis is treated by Coase (1937, 1991) and Williamson (1975, 1985, 1990). In Johanson and Mattsson (1987) there is a comparison between transaction cost analysis and the network approach to industrial marketing.

costs of peforming business transactions, meaning in practice marketing and pur-chasing costs. It is cost effective to perform certain activities inside the own orga-nization, and to handle others via the supply–demand mechanism of the market economy by purchasing from external suppliers. According to transaction cost analysis, the cost comparison between own production and purchasing explains the boundaries of the company.

Transaction cost analysis is based on three assumptions about the emergence of a company:

1 by organizing a company under the same owner and management, they can plan the work so that dual tasks and suboptimization are avoided;
2 as an organization consists of a number of coordinated units under one management it is easier to solve problems and disputes than it is in a market with a number of inde-pendent actors;
3 inside their own organization, access to information is better.

These, however, are a theoretical conjecture and are not based on real world data.

So there are two possibilities to handle transaction costs: inside the organiza-tion if that is the more cost effective (Figure 7.1a) or in the market if that is cheaper (Figure 7.1b). RM, however, offers a third option which is a combination of the first two, namely to handle transaction costs through a deeper relationship with an outside supplier (Figure 7.1c). In this way, a company can reduce its transac-tion costs without increasing its size or ownership.

According to transaction cost analysis it is difficult to analyse and measure rela-tionship aspects, and therefore they are disregarded. The analysis does acknowl-edge two hazards, though: the *bounded rationality* of human beings, and *opportunistic behaviour*. To put it more simply: stupidity, selfishness, greed, and dishonesty are such important components of human nature that they affect the applicability of transaction costs analysis.

Every company must both have a strategic core and supporting, ancillary activ-ities. The core is the remainder of the citadel. Transaction cost analysis talks about *asset specificity*, the specific resources which constitute the core. Part of the core

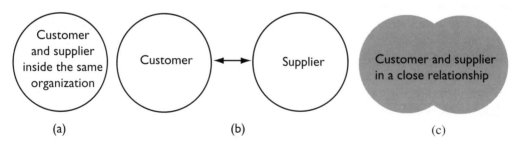

(a)   (b)   (c)

Figure 7.1 Three cases of transaction costs. Cases (a) and (b) are treated by transaction cost analysis. Case (c) is becoming more frequent and is characteristic of RM and imaginary organiza-tions

must be kept intact to preserve the unique competence of the firm. Other activities can be handled through resourcing, the reason being that external resources can be better equipped to add value, provided transaction costs are not prohibitive.

According to Quinn[6] ancillary activities are not the only object of outsourcing which is often claimed, but so are certain core activities. He recommends that own production be focused on a very select number of internal resources based on knowledge and services where the company has muscle to maintain a sustaining competitive edge. The company must, however, protect its core competency by building moats around the remainders of the citadel. This is argued by the proponents of hypercompetition who claim that the core competency must be continuously remodelled; you do not survive and prosper by protecting the extant regime, you do it by continuous disruptions of status quo.

Many have worked in this spirit of imaginary organization for a long time. In this respect the 'new' organization is not new. Publishers rarely have authors in their employ; these have an independent relationship to the publisher and obtain a certain percentage of the book sales revenue in royalties. Movie companies do not usually have their own actors and directors, and there are theatres with employed artists and those who audition for each new show. Building and construction can be organized according to many different models, usually around a large number of subcontractors and consultants, for example independent architects. Building projects have always been imaginary organizations, set up for a specific job and limited in time. Some projects are small, others are huge and long term such as the construction of the Eurotunnel under the English Channel.

In economics, however, the market and the company are seen as two clearly delimited entities. The market is governed by supply and demand with the help of price and competition. The corporation is an anonymous black box to the economist who studies aggregates of companies in industries, regions, and nations. In a basic book on management from the 1950s, the following definition was found 'a company is a unit within which a planned economy rules'; the ideal model being all employees marching like soldiers in good order toward a clearly set destination. In R24 – market mechanisms are brought into the company – it was shown that this model is false and furthermore that the external deregulation of markets has its internal consequences. Decentralization and the split-up of companies in subsidiaries, business areas, and other profit centres have expedited the dissolution of the internal planned economy.

Which boundaries we choose depends on the purpose of the boundaries. A company thus becomes many different organizations. The desire to draw generally valid boundaries is not possible to fulfill if we require the boundaries to be sharp; generally seen companies are fuzzy sets. Several boundaries co-exist:

---

[6] Quinn (1992, pp. 47 and 53).

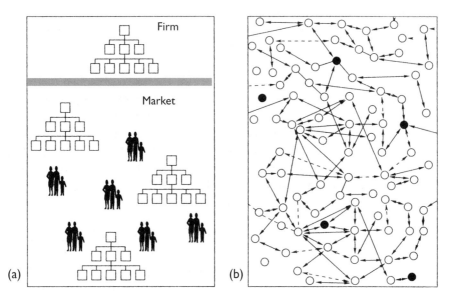

Figure 7.2 The traditional image of the firm and the market in systems theory, transaction cost analysis and economics (a) versus the complex network reality (b)

1 Law based, concerning the establishment of a specific corporate format, taxes, and annual reporting.
2 Financial, concerning the procurement of money.
3 Operative, concerning the daily work with partners, customers, suppliers and others.
4 Strategic, such as a joint development project with competitors, research institutes and consultants.
5 Ecological, concerning the environmental impact of the operations. Customers are found both outside and inside the organization, depending on how the boundaries are drawn.

Looking at business as relationships, networks and interaction makes it difficult to pinpoint the beginning and the end of a company. We need new concepts and models in order to obtain mental access to reality. Figure 7.2a shows the traditional terminology, the company as a clearly defined, hierarchical structure and the market consisting of distinctly identifiable customers, both other organizations and consumers. In Figure 7.2b, we see a network of relationships which contains all types of actors. In this network, we can more or less distinctly delimit clusters of relationships and call them organizations for a specific purpose. The black dots represent core competencies.

We move from the *exclusive* organizational structure – one that excludes and delimits – to the *inclusive* structure – one that includes and unites.

Paradoxes of organizations

A paradox is a *seemingly* absurd or contradictory statement; it is not absurd or contradictary if you dive under the surface. Naisbitt (1994) has defined a number of global paradoxes. One of these claims that the more integrated the world economy becomes, the more important become the small actors. In other words, the larger the global corporations, the more important the small local firms. If this paradox is valid, the atomistic division of companies in either/or – either large or small or maybe medium – becomes meaningless. It may be acceptable in colloquial language, but does not apply in financial assessments and statistical classifications, or in forecasts.

Companies today strive to unify things that we have learnt to be contradictions. They try to be both *local* and *global*, both *small* and *big*, both *centralized* and *decentralized*, both *stable* and *dynamic*. They want to become *bigger without growing*. They want to offer both *standardized mass manufacturing*, *customized mass manufacturing*, and *individually designed goods and services* simultaneously. These are oxymorons in the mechanically and sequentially formatted brains of Western civilization, but within the logic of RM and the imaginary organization they provide realism.

In an advertisment, German corporate giant Siemens describes its telecom business with the words 'Local Presence – Global Player' and the headline of the ad is 'Connecting the Global Village'.[7] It is an example of trying to be both local and global, or 'glocal'. It does not mean that you can necessarily sell the same product or run a company with standarized techniques throughout the world. In some cases this is feasible – American soap operas and McDonald's are the same everywhere – while in other cases it does not work as well. It did not work for Disneyland Paris. IKEA sticks to its core concept but makes local adjustments. Sensitivity is needed to exploit the same offering, and sensitivity is needed to make amendments. Standardization and customization unite.

ABB tries to combine the best of the alleged opposites. The corporation was formed through a merger of Swedish Asea and Swiss Brown Boveri. In 1991 ABB had 215,000 employees, and was divided into eight major segments, sixty-five business areas, 1300 subsidiaries, 5000 profit centres, and innumerable teams. The management at headquarters is kept down. The head of operative units and their assistant staff units should, according to former ABB CEO Percy Barnevik '...function on a self co-ordinating basis...in a continuing process of contact, information exchange, priority setting and correction cycles'. According to an executive at the ABB competitor General Electric, employees must have '...networking skills, and be able to work in a boundaryless organization'.[8] The desire

---

[7] Advertisement in *International Management* (July/August 1993, pp. 20–1).
[8] Quotations from interviews in *International Management* (Lester, 1992).

ORGANIZATION	BODY	BRAIN
Dinosaur organization	Big	Small
The imaginary organization	Small	Big

Figure 7.3 The 'dino organization' versus the imaginary organization

is to unite the best of the big corporation with the best of the small firm.

The giants of the business world have borrowed their muscle from size. In the same way as the dinosaurs, extinct sixty-five million years ago, they risk becoming too clumsy to proact, act and react swiftly and efficiently. The planned economy of the totally integrated company is replaced by a modular company, which preserves a few core competencies inside and buy goods and services from other suppliers.

The new imaginary organization could be contrasted against an old dinosaur organization (Figure 7.3). The 'dino organization' has a big body but a small brain, the imaginary organization has a small body but a big brain. The dino organization is a reflection of the industrial society when a company was composed of a few skilled and powerful people who ruled over hordes of blue and white collar workers.

High tech–high touch – balancing IT and HRM

IT has gradually influenced the structures and processes of companies. IT can contribute to glue together activities which are taken from different parts of an organization, from different legal units with different owners, and from different geographical locations. IT can mean enhanced ability to act and reduced cost of customer contact. This may only be the overture to a new type of company where the future possibilites of electronics are now being explored: databases with rapid access to customers, rapid networks of communication, and standards that allow rapid application of new knowledge. The spot market for oil was once established in Rotterdam, the Netherlands. Today it exists in an electronic network. It's spread around the world and operates around the clock. It's everywhere and nowhere. It's a marketspace, not a marketplace.

> Technology offers a potential, but *it is the people who make it work.*

The more I hear from enthusiastic representatives of IT and virtual organizations, the more cautious I get. They lack history; many of them are young and seem completely intoxicated and blindfolded by technology. They claim IT drives the development of business. From the late 1950s computer technology has been allowed to boast about excellence and abilites that never existed. It used to turn obsolete administrative routines into rigid computer systems which, faster than ever before, produced useless data under the deceptive euphemism 'information'. They never understood what they speeded up; speed was everything. They continue to overrate their importance. Compared to the human being IT is not very smart, but it can enhance our performance in the same way as the fork-lift truck can save our backs and the car can shorten a trip.

IT was treated in R12, the electronic relationship, a contrast to R18, the personal relationship and the social network. Both are needed, that is the message in the expession *high tech–high touch*, the advanced technology combined with the human touch. HRM, human resource management – human being both employees, customers and others in a network – cannot be replaced by IT.[9]

Combining high tech and high touch is a matter of attitude. Rod, manager at a Stew Leonard's fresh food store expressed this very distinctly to us in explaining the three causes of success: 'The first is attitude! The second is *attitude*! And the third is ATTITUDE!' The attitudes, perceptions, and paradigms – our way of facing reality and identifying problems and opportunities – are more essential than IT and sophisticated measurement techniques. Zohar and Marshall express it in this way: 'For the phycisist, *measurement* is a way of looking at the situation...*Attitude*...is the human equivalent of measurement'.[10] Within these human frames, IT may hopefully thrive and contribute.

When a company grows and becomes physically dispersed, personal contact is easily lost. Relationships are maintained via IT with no face-to-face encounters. The system of life-long employment facilitates what the Japanese call '*mimikosuri*', the ability to massage somebody's ears. The massage simplifies decisions and execution, it mitigates conflict and prevents collegues from losing face. A personal relationship, established over decades provides security and support even in the era of IT. IT without personal trust as a ground is a management hazard.

Mimikosuri also has an important role in companies in western countries, as long employment is still not uncommon. Companies are often held together through personal contacts irrespective of organizational boundaries. When problems arise between the European headquarters and overseas subsidiaries, the personal relationship between a subsidiary president and corporate management could be decisive for the outcome. In some subsidiaries, the presidents are natives of the country where the subsidiary is located. These have better local knowledge about the market, the culture and the management of local business than their European collegues. However, they miss the deeper relationship with corporate

---

[9] On HRM, see further Schneider (1994).
[10] Zohar and Marshall (1993, p. 100).

management – language, values, cultural references, school experiences – a relationship that has been built up from childhood.

The possibilities of distance work increase thanks to IT. Traditionally, most employees are expected to be at the same location at the same time. Flexible working hours have been introduced and employees are only present simultaneously part of the time. Instead of travelling from their home to the office, employees can travel mentally via the computer and a telephone connection. The hardships of commuting which include waste of time, waiting lines, pollution, and noise are reduced as well as the need to live where the employer is physically established. The disadvantage is a thinner social relationship to colleagues; belonging to a group can be an important motivational factor. On the other hand, not all people like to work closely together. Conflicts are common, and their extreme manifestations in mobbing and sexual harassment are currently causing more and more concern.

The human resource ratio – internal and external 'employees'

In the imaginary organization it is not so evident who is employed and who is otherwise engaged. Skandia AFS describes its organization as consisting of one million customers; alliances with 65,000 active and independent insurance brokers and banks; 2000 employees; and a core management group of sixty.[11]

Hedberg, Dahlgren, Hansson and Olve[12] suggest the use of the I/E ratio. It stresses the fact that more human resources (people involved, I) are available for the company than the people employed (E). In AFS the ratio is high:

$$65,000/2060 = 32$$

If we classify customers as people involved, the ratio will grow to 517!

'The shamrock organization' has been proposed as a metaphor for the different roles in a company.[13] A shamrock normally has three leaves. These symbolize three types of human resources. The first leaf is the *employees*, those who work with the core activities of the company. The second leaf is the *suppliers* who supplement the corporation with resources. The third leaf is the *part-time employees and temporary workers*. But a special shamrock may have four leaves, the fourth leaf being the *customers*. In service management, customers have long been treated as part-time employees during the service production, delivery, and marketing process. The customers can be seen as the professional representatives of the need and use of the service without whom a service often cannot be produced. The customer base is also increasingly accepted as the most crucial resource of a company.

Although suppliers are not employees, the boundary between suppliers and

---

[11] Edvinsson and Malone (1997, p. 50).
[12] Hedberg, Dahlgren, Hansson and Olve (1997, pp. 124–8).
[13] Handy (1990, pp. 87ff).

own employees is fuzzy. 'Cottage industries' in manufacturing have a long history, particularly in textile production. The workers provide flexibility, add resources when sales peak, but cost nothing when sales go down. The 'knowledge industry' employs intellectuals who need to be organized, but is strategically dependent on free intellectuals such as poets, authors, and reviewers. The former are officially part of the organization, the latter are part of the external network. The search for the organization of the knowledge-based company partly concerns the form of affiliation for those who generate revenue: employment, full- or part-time work, ownership or shared ownership, and legal design. Financial and tax considerations may influence the structure of the organization. Freelance workers are common in certain industries, for example in journalism and the performing arts. A freelance can have his or her own firm which can grow through partnering or employees. This is commonplace among consultants and craftsmen. Companies who arrange for temporary secretaries or other staff, for example through International Manpower, are growing rapidly as a consequence of increasing outsourcing of internal services. Computer consulting firms have often earned the major share of their revenue from renting programmers on long-term contracts. When visiting a corporation today, we may be met at the reception desk by personnel provided by a security company.

Finally, an interesting observation and paradox is that *while relationships between suppliers and customers are becoming closer, relationships between employers and employees are becoming looser and more flexible.*[14] This is further evidence of the imaginary properties of an organization and that the distinction between the company and the market is being blurred.

From delimited structures to boundaryless processes

Hierarchy means 'holy management', a designation that may fit the egos of many executives. Its next of kin is *bureaucracy*, which means 'management from the desk'. The dawn of the dissolution of hierarchy is found in the establishment of profit centres and the introduction of the market mechanism inside the company (R24). *Heterarchy*, 'multidimensional management', and *adhocracy*, 'management to fit a temporary state of affairs', are better designations for today's organization and management.

Bureaucracy and adhocracy are extremes; the demand for rule-based governance is confronted with the demands for flexibility and adaptability to individual situations. The *project organization* – which was dealt with in R25, in connection with the internal customer and interfunctional and interhierarchical dependency – used to be a temporary supplement to a relatively fixed hierarchical *base organization*. Today the base organization is increasingly dynamic and becomes more of a *parent project* for a series of *subsidiary projects.*[15] Perhaps the

---

[14] Root (1994).

[15] Compare the dichotomy parent company – subsidiary which applies to stable base organizations related to each other through formal and legally obliging decisions.

imaginary organization can be characterized as a sophisticated and timely version of the project organization.

The variability of adhocracy is also part of culture and lifestyle. Adhocracy is characterized by sensitivity for the unexpected, quick action, high degree of freedom, support from management and colleagues, generosity, accepted and necessary messiness, and only the sky is the limit. Bureaucracy stands for the planned and repressive where the rule and ritual are give priority to the actual issue and the outcome. Bureaucracy both in the government sector, industrial companies and consulting firms have a proven record of suffocating adhocratic tendencies.

In its extreme application adhocracy leads to chaos. Again paradoxically, a great deal of discipline is required to make adhocracy work. The knowledge-based organization therefore needs a dash of bureaucracy. In the language of Tao, *yin* is the adhocratic property and *yang* the bureaucratic. The dynamism is in the tension and oscillation between yin and yang. If yang is given too much rope, the organization is petrified. If yin takes over, chaos and destruction follow. The extremes are companions, not adversaries. The combined outcome is *dynamic stability*.

Chaos and ambiguity are central concepts in Peters and Watermans' classic book *In Search of Excellence* (1982) and later in Peters's books *Thriving on Chaos* (1985) and *Liberation Management* (1992). Ehrlemark (1978) said that 'to consciously keep the firm unmanaged and unmanageable to such an extent that its stability and development is created out of disturbances and disorder is perhaps the true skill in management'. Stacey (1993), in *Strategic Management and Organisational Dynamics*, takes chaos research from physics as his vantage point. The concept *dissipative structures* was used by Nobel laureate and chaos scientist Ilya Prigogene. Dissipative structures are spawned in volatile processes in systems which are in disequilibrium:[16] '...most of reality, instead of being orderly, stable and equilibrial, is seething and bubbling with change, disorder, and process.' Disorder and order co-exist and become conditions for each other. Chaos theory in its popular form has become known for the 'butterfly effect': 'When a butterfly flaps its wings in Beijing it affects the weather in New York.' Teeny-weeny episodes have an impact in the spirit of the adage 'the straw that broke the camel's back'. When networks become complex and interactions are countless, a small episode can propagate in the network with an unpredictable and significant impact.

The staff of a knowledge-based organization consists largely of intellectuals and professionals. Independence and opportunities to develop are conditional for their performance. Managing intellectuals is 'institutionalized anarchy', it is managing the unmanagable: 'Managing them is a craft or trade, maybe even an art. It is definitely not a science'.[17] Or in Drucker's terms:[18] 'As the business organiza-

---

[16] Prigogene and Stengers (1985).
[17] Donovan (1989).
[18] Drucker (1988a, p.3).

tion is restructuring itself around knowledge and information, it will increasingly come to resemble nonbusiness – the hospital, the university, or the opera – rather than the manufacturing company of 1920, in which there were a few generalists called "managers" and a great many unskilled and unknowing "hands" doing as they were told'.

The mechanical mode of operation from manufacturing which contaminated – and still contaminates – life in many organizations, is obsolete even for its original application. But hospitals, universities and operas also face gargantuan hardships and are searching for new structures. Health care in most countries is in a state of flux and transition, and university bureaucracies are notorious.

The need to flatten organizations has been pointed out by several authors. Former SAS president Jan Carlzon originally entitled his book *Knock Down the Pyramids*.[19] Zuboff (1988) calls hierarchies obsolete and dysfunctional in an era when real power is IT-based knowledge. But there are also proponents for hierarchies, and hierarchies are common in practice. Jaques claims that '…35 years of research have convinced me that managerial hierarchy is the most efficient, the hardiest, and in fact the most natural structure ever devised for large organizations.'[20]

Peters and Waterman (1982) provided an expressive epithet for an informal phenomenon: *skunk works*. In R&D and engineering, skunk works are guerrilla operations; they are the outlaws of the formal organization. The skunks are passionate technicians and hackers obsessed with an idea. They hide their work from management who may be too remote from the pulse of the market and new technology. Some of the most successful innovations were skunk products in a period of their development. Among them the Saab Turbo, the first commercially successful application of the turbo engine on a passenger car; and Losec, an ulcer medication, which has made Astra one of the world's richest pharmaceutical companies. We do not know how many excellent ideas have been systematic victims of abortion. One should not forget, however, that many of the skunk products fail in the market even if the technology is supreme.

Skunks are adhocrats but illegitimite adhocrats. They can be punished and rejected. They can be tacitly tolerated, thus giving innovative minds and entrepreneurs opportunities to realize ideas with support of company resources, without being burdened by internal red tape; they become *intrapreneurs.* A passive skunk tolerance seems to be quite common. The global corporation 3M – best known to consumers for Scotch tape – allows its R&D people to set aside 15 per cent of their time for own projects. There are also *extrapreneurs* who leave as employees but continue to collaborate with the 'parent' or take over some of its customers.[21]

The imaginary organization has affinity to the *transcendent organization*. It is an organizational format which exists deep in the consciousness of the members of

---

[19] The book was published in English under the title *Moments of Truth* (1986).
[20] Jaques (1990, p. 127).
[21] Johnsson and Hägg (1987, pp. 64–74).

the organization, its base is *collective consciousness*. It goes deeper than the observable signs and activities of a corporate culture, its formal and informal structures and do's and don'ts. It is manifested in our intuitive and spontaneous reactions.[22] Zohar and Marshall who talk about the quantum society, an approach inspired by the quantum theory of physics, say:[23] 'Persons are not quite the same as solitary individuals, nor are they a crowd. Persons are living networks of biology and emotions and memories and relationships. Each is unique, but none can flourish alone. Each in some way contains others, and is contained by others, without his or her personal truth ever being wholly isolated or exhausted.' This is a fitting description of the Russian relationship doll, which was used to demonstrate the existence of intertwined market, mega, and nano relationships in Chapter 1.

A daring metaphor is provided by quantum physics in approaching reality as either particles or waves. 'The wave aspect is associated with our unstructured potential, with our spreading out across the boundaries of space, time, choice and identity. The particle aspect gives us our structured reality, our boundaries, our clearly defined selves, our ordered thoughts, our social roles and conventions, our rules and patterns', say Zohar and Marshall. They say that atomism rejects relationships and gives rise to confrontation whereas we need 'relational holism'. This holistic view of society is akin to both RM and imaginary organizations and the statement from Chapter 1 that society is a network of relationships. We can let the particles be the well defined, the individual, the formal organization, the buildings, the equipment, that is everything visible and tangible. The waves then represent the relationships, the collective consciousness and the organizational culture, the coherent processes and the dynamics.

In conclusion, dynamic processes receive a progressively larger role and fixed hierarchies play a diminishing role. 'Organization design should be made up of processes that emit sequences of ceaselessly changing solutions', according to Nystrom, Hedberg and Starbuck.[24] Organizations go from structure in focus and processes in the periphery to processes in focus and structures in the periphery (Figure 7.4). The understanding of processes expands which was pointed out in R25. The whole company can be regarded as a coherent business process and not as insulated activities which occur in functional compartments and hierarchical tiers. The processes extend beyond the corporation and unite it with the market. The network is boundaryless and inside the network there is interaction. The sequential has lost in importance and the simultaneous has gained, as has been shown in concurrent engineering and the value constellation.

---

[22] See Gustavsson (1992) and Harung (1996 and 1999).
[23] Zohar and Marshall (1993); quotation from p. 64; the following quotations from pp. 82, 6 and 85.
[24] Nystrom, Hedberg and Starbuck (1976, p. 226).

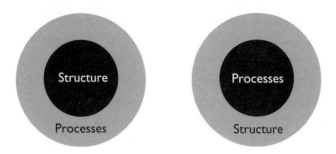

Figure 7.4 Shifting from structure in focus supported by processes, to processes in focus supported by structure

Synthesis

The theme for the last twenty pages or so has been RM and the imaginary organization as reflections of one another. With a certain amount of graphic playfulness, the treatment of this theme can be summarized in five images of the corporation (Figure 7.5). The first image (a) is the fortress, the *clearly delimited hierarchical structure*. The second (b) is the *matrix organization* that was treated in R28 as an expansion of the hierarchy and a rudimentary network. Both are traditional images even if the matrix signals the dissolution of the hierarchy. The third image (c) shows a *multi-dimensional network.* Its core, the unique competency which empowers the organization, is marked in black. We recognize the characteristic features of RM, the network of relationships within which the parties interact. We surmise the imaginary organization in which other actors than employees are let in, among them customers. The fourth image (d) accentuates the *boundaryless and amorphous features* of the imaginary organization, the corporation as a *fuzzy set.* The last image (e) takes a full step toward the *process organization,* a series of harmonious waves and completely concerted processes.

The new is often presented as an extreme alternative, an opposite to old. The imaginary organization as the completely flexible organization with low transaction costs and rapid adjustment to new conditions is an idealized and absurdly simplistic image. The same can be said for RM, which may seem too benign and harmonious to gain credibility in a greedy and imperfect business environment where hypercompetition is lurking around the corner. The new images may appear as mirages in the wilderness; perhaps they can even erect a new mental prison. We may be conned into 'seeing' something in the same way as we 'see' the magician sawing someone in half. RM and the imaginary organization are rather directions and intentions, emphasizing properties in marketing and organization which have been neglected and must now be given more prominence.

In Figure 7.6, the hierarchy, the matrix, the network, the amoeba, and the process have been superimposed on each other into one single image but without merging their structures. All these structures co-exist in various proportions. But the proportions are being re-examined; the role of the hierarchy is reduced in favour of

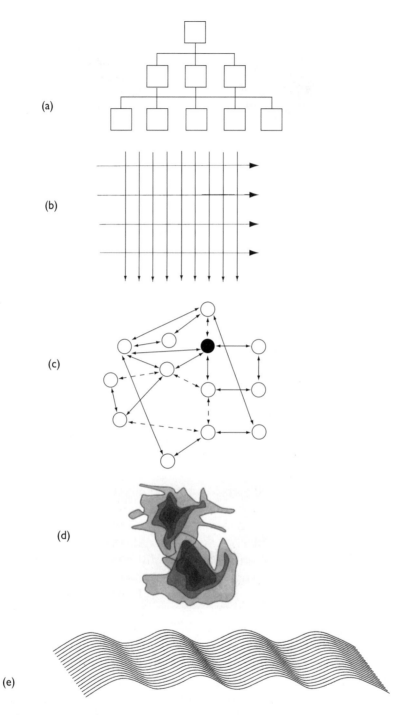

Figure 7.5 Organizational structure transitions: (a) the hierarchy with clear boundaries; (b) the matrix, the two-dimensional network; the imaginary organization first reproduced as a network (c), then as an amoeba with fuzzy boundaries which dissolve from a core competency (d); and last, the process organization (e), the corporation as a series of processes or waves

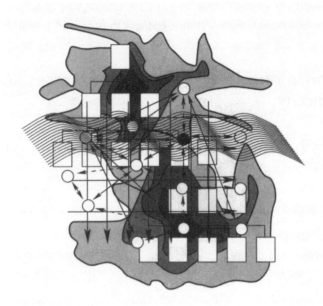

Figure 7.6 The corporation as many images at the same time: hierarchy, matrix, network, amoeba and processes

dynamic changes and processes. As the figure shows, it is hard to visualize all of this at the same time; we risk seeing nothing at all, or we just see a mess.

In summary, these are the characteristics of the link between RM and imaginary organizations:

■ According to RM, marketing consists of networks of relationships in which we interact. They embrace markets, society and the organization. The imaginary organization adds dimensions, which enhance our understanding for the evolution and functions of RM.

■ The organization exists, but not in a physical and tangible body. Its most important resources – its intellectual capital and core competency – do not show in the balance sheet.

■ The boundaries between the company and its markets are fuzzy and people engaged are not the same as people employed. A larger part of those engaged, sometimes the greater part, are found outside the organization. The customer is integrated with the organization and the customer base is a central resource, sometimes the most important resource. In this way, the roles of supplier and customer, become less obvious; value is created through their interaction.

■ The increasingly ubiquitous and flexible IT offers new opportunities for RM and the imaginary organization to develop. The electronic relationship must however be balanced against social and human relationships. High tech needs high touch.

■ The company becomes a parent project and what is traditionally known as a project becomes a subsidiary project. The organization becomes a series of dynamic and coherent processes rather than a stable, compartmentalized hierarchy.

The significance of relationships for businesses and the market economy

Two phenomena will be treated in this section. The first is the *need for security in an insecure world.* The second is the expansion of marketing equilibrium (treated in R2) from *partial* to *complete* equilibrium.

Our need for security

In Chapter 1, the rationale for RM was defined as:
1 enhanced retention and duration in order to improve financial performance;
2 a way of creating better conditions for efficient marketing and management.

In the most militant of cases – hypercompetition – competitors turn into lethal adversaries and marketing warfare breaks loose. In the most benevolent case, competitors turn into colleagues and buddies. Or maybe they try to be a bit of both: 'Businessmen and industrialists who on the one hand fight for radical freedom of the *laissez-faire* market none the less find themselves clubbing into lobbies and cartels'.[25] History also shows that relationships and collaboration have always been in the centre of business activity. Why is this so? Let me venture an explanation.

Both consumers and companies need *a basic level of security.* Security is associated with words such as *promises, honesty, trust, reliability, predictability, stability, fear of being swindled or let down, and reduction of uncertainty and risk.*

Promise is a core concept in all relationships.[26] Only in exceptional cases are promises legal promises – contracts, which can be forcibly honoured with the help of courts. Most promises are made without written contracts, they are moral and ethical promises to perform a service, deliver goods, or collaborate in a development project. The quality of certain suppliers and their offerings are easy to assess in advance (search qualities), whereas others must be tried (experience qualities). For customers it may often be difficult to assess what they got even after the purchase; they are left to trust the promises of the supplier (credence qualities).[27]

The market as well as society in general offers so much insecurity and risk that only what is by nature unpredictable should be left pending. What can be

---

[25] Zohar and Marshall (1993, pp. 73–4).

[26] The promise comcept is little treated in marketing literature; see Levitt (1983) and Calonius (1987).

[27] 'Search qualities' and 'experience qualities' are terms borrowed from Nelson (1970) and 'credence qualities' from Darby and Karni (1973).

planned should be planned. What cannot be planned can best be handled through preparedness for the unexpected. Companies must make certain that promises are fulfilled, both in their role of suppliers and customers. The supplier must be reliable and deliver the right thing at the right time to the right place; JIT (just in time) is the most advanced manifestation of those requirements. The customer should be reliable and not cancel an order or dodge payment. Companies need predictability so that, for example, production can be planned and performed with high productivity and quality.

If society offers a weak infrastructure, companies cannot work efficiently. Frequent electricity failures, unreliable airlines and airports, and a corrupt and unpredictable government sector make it difficult to compete with more reliable societies. When US Mail could not promise delivery, a market was opened for Federal Express, DHL, and others who took responsibility for delivery promises. Also the internal market must be reliable and predictable. There is the story about a New York company that sent internal letters and parcels, addressed to people in the very same building, via Federal Express. The mail first went to the Federal Express hub in Memphis, Tennessee, and then back to the building in New York. Delivery within twenty-four hours was guaranteed, whereas the internal mail needed a couple of days and offered no guarantee. Having experienced the internal mail of large corporations, this anecdote could very well be true.

Companies can obtain security through several sources:

1 *Relationships* can create security. People trust each other and plan to make future business with each other. The relationships open up for a plus sum game, for win–win. This is what the whole book is about; it is the soul of RM.
2 Security may also be created through *laws* and other *formal regulations* as well as *institutions* that secure compliance. Its unique properties and consequences were discussed in R16 and R17, the law-based relationship and the criminal network. But law is no automatic source of security: 'Formal contracts are often ineffective in taking care of the uncertainties, conflicts and crises that a business relationship is bound to go through over time'.[28]
3 *Knowledge* as a relationship driver was treated in R21. If the customers' knowledge is high, they can rest securely in their knowledge. For most consumers it is a problem to buy medical services or a used car; consumers rarely possess the expertise to assess their quality. The used car trade seems to remain an industry where customer ignorance is a natural part of its business mission. In today's society – which is frequently referred to as the knowledge-based society – knowledge is fragmented. We are dependent on more and more products and service systems, which we only understand to a limited degree. We may be able to use them, but we do not know what is underneath the surface. We become dependent on intermediaries – brokers in knowledge

---

[28] Håkansson and Snehota (1995, p. 8).

and insecurity[29] – to help us, especially if something goes wrong. Even if we gain more knowledge in absolute terms, the need for knowledge grows faster and we become increasingly ignorant in relative terms. We are left to base our decisions on symbols such as corporate identities and brand names and what we believe they represent. The image and the parasocial relationships from R13 become important substitutes for knowledge.

4 *Business culture and ethics* – the *informal regulations/institutions* – can also contribute to security. The culture can be very distinct with clear rules and a clear ethical code telling us what is right and wrong. It can work like the parlour game where the rules are not negotiable; if the dice shows five dots, you move five steps. The culture can comprise clear rewards and punishments and those who misbehave are excluded from the business community. If it is a commercial predatory culture as in Russia today, insecurity rules. As is emphasized by transaction cost analysis, the rational behaviour of organizations is impeded by human opportunism.

The four ways of achieving security are not mutually exclusive. Even strong relationships and excellent knowledge may need a dash of formal law. A strong business culture includes social relationships and personal proximity. The USA is an example of a culture with legal dominance and weaker relationships with Japan as its opposite. Even inside a country there may be differences in cultures between industries and places. Global competition and mass markets create anonymity and insecurity about the rules of the game, which can explain a growing need for trust. Con artists are successful in business life through their ability to instil trust and confidence.

My conclusion is that long-term and close relationships best satisfy the need for security, albeit with some support from the other sources. The ratio between the importance of the four sources can vary. If you are highly knowledgeable in one field, this may be enough to instil security. If the business culture is strong and no one breaks the rules and the law, security also becomes high.

From partial to complete marketing equilibrium

A conclusion from R2 (the customer–supplier–competitor relationship) was that the market is governed by competition, collaboration, and regulations/institutions. Together, these three forces strive for balance – marketing equilibrium – without ever reaching this heavenly state, though. The tension creates a dynamic state as long as no single force becomes excessively dominant.

The conclusion will be carried further in this section by integrating it with the imaginary organization. Marketing equilibrium concerned the state of the *external market*, whereas the same notion can also be applied on the *internal market* of a company. Each of these two instances will subsequently be referred to as a *partial equilibrium*.

---

[29] Giarini and Stahel (1993).

	COMPETITION	COLLABORATION	REGULATIONS & INSTITUTIONS
Traditional perception of a firm's internal operations	No	Yes	Yes
Traditional perception of the operations of the market	Yes	No	No
New perception of the firm and the market	Yes	Yes	Yes

Figure 7.7 Today the company and the market are controlled by the same forces

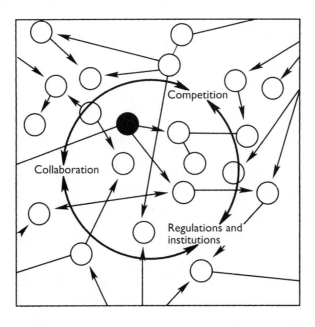

Figure 7.8 Complete marketing equilibrium in the network, both 'outside' and 'inside' the organization

The circle that showed the three forces of partial marketing equilibrium in Figure 2.1 is equally needed as a balancing force inside an organization. The corporation is regulated by its control systems, both hard and soft ones. Among the hard ones are the financial control system, production planning, and marketing planning; among the soft ones business missions, values, and collective consciousness. These control systems correspond to regulations/institutions. Competition and the price mechanism have been brought inside the company according to R24, and many of the other Rs support that notion.

The market and the company are thus governed by the same three mechanisms: competition, collaboration, and regulations/institutions (Figure 7.7). The proportions between the forces as well as their content can vary between markets and companies, between companies, and within markets. Each specific marketing situation – both inside and outside the company – struggles to reach its own specific marketing equilibrium.

Figure 7.8 combines partial marketing equilibrium from R2 (Figure 2.1) with the image of the complex network reality from Figure 7.2 where the clear boundary between the company and the environment has been dissolved. We can then speak about *complete marketing equilibrium.*

This chapter has dealt with the consequences of RM for organizational structure and also its effect on society. The organizational consequences of RM and the RM consequences for imaginary organizations have been analysed. The emphasis that RM puts on security through relationships, with collaboration as one of the three forces that make the market economy work, and attempts to reach complete marketing equilibrium have been explained. This is a tentative synthesis between several trends in today's management, made visible through the mental images provided by RM and the imaginary organization.

Chapter 8

The genesis of RM

This chapter is about the evolution of RM and its theoretical and practical foundation. The synthesis toward a more general theory of marketing is presented, contained in the notion of total relationship marketing.

Contributions to total relationship marketing

The word *theory* has the same roots as *theatre*. Both theory and theatre present mental images or scenes, which show something of interest to an audience.

It is considered an old truth that nothing is so practical as a good theory. The quality pioneer W. Edwards Deming has said that 'experience tells nothing unless it is related to theory'.[1] Robert Pirsig, in his philosophical novel *Lila*, says that 'Data without generalization is just gossip'.[2]

These statements imply that data are of no value unless they can be structured and organized in a category, model or theory, which can later be applied in more than a single case. Theory is a tool to derive meaning out of interviews, observations, statistics, advice and ideas, thus helping to generate usable knowledge. The most burdensome task is not to collect – or rather generate – more data, but to interpret and combine what is already there and make some sense out of it. Theory provides a context, a map that offers guidance.

This requires theory to be good theory. In an applied discipline like marketing, good theory must be grounded in the real world. The maps must be well drawn, or they will lead us in the wrong direction and lure us into morasses or make us drive straight into a rock.

If the marketing that is presented in textbooks and seminars should only build on the fragmented contributions from scholarly research, it would be lightweight. It is necessary to fill the gaps – consisting of areas which have not (yet) been scientifically surveyed – with the best available knowledge, namely the knowledge from 'those who were there when it happened'. It is not evident what should be counted as theoretical contributions, and what are contributions from practition-

---

[1] Quoted at the Ninth World Productivity Congress, Istanbul, June 1995.
[2] Pirsig (1992, p. 70).

ers. In scholarly research, theory is escorted by *empirical data*. Empirical comes from the Greek *empeiria* meaning *experience*. In the language of science, empirical refers to real-world data generated with certain methods and techniques. Note that the language of many business schools has been impoverished by limiting the term empirical to quantitative data and statistical processing.

It is therefore imperative to add the knowledge and experience of *reflective man*. Many business executives, marketing managers, consultants and others are *reflective practitioners* who demonstrate their experience in managing successful companies, but also convey their experience in lectures, interviews, memoirs, articles and manuals. Every one of us continuously gains experiences as consumers, at best as *reflective consumers*. One should, therefore, not discard one's own personal knowledge and experience – one's *pre-understanding* – as a source to developing understanding of marketing. Common sense and experience are usually not 'clean' in the academic world but a growing trend recognizes *tacit knowledge* – knowledge that has no language – which is deployed both in practical work and in scientific research.[3]

If scholarly research in marketing was more of reflection and less of 'administration of research techniques', we would have more *reflective scholars* devoting themselves to incorporating all types of knowledge into better techniques, concepts, models, theories and applications, thus making themselves more useful to society.

It was mentioned in Chapter 1 that total relationship marketing is inspired by many sources. Traces of these sources are found in the description of the 30Rs. The sources are: traditional marketing management and the 4Ps; services marketing; the network approach to industrial/business marketing; and TQM. It is also inspired by current RM literature. A review of these sources is given below. Two other sources of inspiration, new accounting and new organizations, were treated in previous chapters.

Marketing management, marketing mix and the 4Ps

Textbooks and teaching in marketing management are primarily structured around the marketing mix theory.[4] The core of this theory is the use of various means to influence the market. The best-known variant is based on four parameters which all start with a P: product, price, promotion, place. It is popularly known as the 4Ps.

The definition of marketing suggested by the American Marketing Association – and which tends to become official and authoritarian – is based on marketing

---

[3] The notion of the reflective practitioner is discussed by Schön (1983); preunderstanding and understanding are central concepts in hermeneutics, see Gummesson (1999); on tacit knowledge, see Polanyi (1962).

[4] Those who wish to study the marketing mix theory further can turn to any book with 'marketing management' in the title. See also a review of the marketing mix approach by Grönroos (1994) and the discussion by Brownlie and Saren (1992).

mix thinking: 'Marketing is the process of planning and executing the conception, pricing, promotion, and distribution of ideas, goods, and services to create exchanges that satisfy individual and organizational objectives'.[5]

Suppliers are perceived as independent units in the market. Using various means, the supplier exercises an impact on the market. This may occur under conditions which are more or less uncontrollable by a single firm, such as consumer tastes, the general economic situation, and legislation. How much of these conditions the supplier can influence depends on its size, power, creativity, persistence and not least coincidence.

In Chapter 1 the marketing concept, which puts customer needs and customer satisfaction in focus, was described. The thought behind the marketing mix is that marketing, by handling a series of activities, should persuade the consumer to buy a product. If a supplier feels capable of satisfying a need, the supplier must go for it and make sure that the consumer buys their products.

In practice, however, the 4P approach has led to a manipulative attitude to people.[6] If we just select the right measures in the right combination and with the right intensity, the consumer will buy; it is a matter of putting pressure on the consumer. The consumer is a locked black box, maybe with a tiny peep-hole. We often know little what is in the mind of consumers, how they think and feel and what their motives are. It is more of a stimulus-response model, it is similar to the fisherman's relationship to fish. If we improve the bait, the fish will bite and it is hooked. The supplier and its salespeople are the active party. Sometimes the consumer is pig-headed and rejects an offering. Conclusion: we used the wrong bait. To face such a challenge – 'Never take no for an answer!' – and turning it to our advantage is part and parcel of an aggressive sales culture.

Instead of being customer oriented, I will contest that marketing management in practice is *supplier oriented*. There is ample experience behind the use of the marketing mix and it is often functional as seen from the supplier's perspective. The marketing mix contains problems, however. One is how to mix the activities. What will be the effect of a certain mix and what happens to the other measures if the value of one of them is altered? What will happen if we reduce the price by 10 per cent? If we invest more in advertising? If we launch a new product for a new segment?

The marketer tries to find an *optimal mix* – or more realistically a *satisfying mix* – which gets a superior response on the market and at the same time creates profits. Because of the complexity in the interaction between different factors and the uncertainty in a competitive market, the mix will be the outcome of the availability of data, analytic rationality, experience, opinions, emotions, intuition and visions.

---

[5] AMA (1985).

[6] Anthony Cunningham, Ireland's first marketing professor, has pointed out to me that consumer manipulation was not the intent when marketing thinkers began to teach need orientation and the 4Ps. It may, however, in practice have turned out otherwise.

We would prefer clear guidelines about the rights and the wrongs of marketing management. We would prefer strict, scientifically proven links between what we do and the outcome. The PIMS project (profit impact of marketing strategy) was an effort to establish these links. It deploys some thirty parameters and the data are retrieved from a comprehensive base which is continuously renewed. The installation of PIMS in a business unit, however, is a costly affair and it does not give the whole answer. Rather than establishing cause and effect it establishes covariation between marketing strategies. For those who do not participate directly in the project, certain general conclusions are available.[7]

The marketing mix theory is founded on studies of the marketing of consumer goods, not of services, not of industrial marketing. The literature usually zooms in on the narrower concept of consumer and shows less interest in the generic concept of customer. However, a large share of the studies concern distribution channels, thereby including a part of both services and business marketing, namely wholesalers and retailers. The channel companies are service producers, but they are treated from a goods perspective.

Marketing mix concerns mass marketing and standardized consumer goods. Such goods are usually packaged and piled on shelves in self-service stores. The relationship between the personnel of the store and the consumer is minimal and left to brief encounters at the cash register. The stores are 'service factories' and the service consists of a convenient location of the store and opening hours; goods available on the shelves; packaging and signs that display information about product and price; several checkout points; and aids such as trolleys, baskets and bags. Consumer goods also include capital goods such as freezers and CD-players. The sales through independent small stores and stores with manual service is frugally treated in the literature. They rely more heavily on personal contact whereas supermarkets require more of an impersonal mass marketing approach.

The 4Ps have been widely exposed after their introduction in a textbook by McCarthy, first published in 1960. The 4Ps structure is a role model for globally circulated textbooks, all with very similar content. The Ps have also been expanded into more Ps in order to cover the marketing domain more completely.[8]

Even if the 4Ps form the hard core of the marketing mix theory, a number of other areas are covered in marketing management textbooks. These include marketing strategy and its link to business mission, goals, objectives and corporate strategies; market segmentation; market research techniques; marketing planning procedures; and the design of the marketing and sales organization. At the same time the marketing mix theory excludes or treats marginally such things as complaints handling, invoicing, design and production. The 4Ps approach is narrowly limited to functions and it is not an integral part of the total management process. It is marketing management, but not marketing-oriented management.

---

[7] Buzzell and Gale (1987).
[8] See, for example, Booms and Bitner (1982), Kotler (1986), Judd (1987), and Baumgartner (1991).

	Dominating production	Dominating marketing
Industrial society	Mass production	Mass marketing
Value society	Customized (mass) production	Customized (mass) marketing

Figure 8.1 Marketing and production in the industrial and value societies

The marketing mix theory is a child of the standardized mass production of the industrial society and its dissociation from the individual consumer. The contemporary value society – or if we prefer to call it the service society, information society, knowledge-based society, postindustrial or even post-modern society – clamours for another type of production. Even if mass production and mass marketing will always play a significant role in economic life, it should not be the reigning godfather. Instead, the centre of attention should be customization of offerings and a more individualized marketing, often in a combination expressed by the paradoxial concept of *customized mass marketing* (Figure 8.1).

Marketing management and marketing mix theory particularly treat four phenomena connected to relationships, networks and interaction.

1 The relationship between the *supplier and the customer* (R1). In the marketing mix theory, this is 'personal selling', a sub-category to promotion. It deals with the face-to-face encounters between a salesperson and a customer with the purpose of persuading the customer to buy.
2 The treatment of competition, here defined as the relationship between *the buyer, the current supplier and the competitors* (R2).
3 This is found under the fourth P, place, as the *network of distribution channels* (R3).
4 Within the marketing mix theory, image and brand equity are treated and they have contributed to the *parasocial relationships* (R13).

Services marketing

In the beginning of the 1960s, the service sector share of GDP and employment got ahead of the industrial sector. The reactions to this have been slow and it took until the second half of the 1970s for services marketing and management to gain attention. Services marketing had been treated by occasional writers during the 1960s, but obviously 'the time was not ripe' (whatever that means). During the

1980s, services marketing became the fastest growing field of marketing and together with RM it will probably continue to be so. Contributions came from researchers in many countries, above all from the USA, UK, France, and the Nordic School (primarily Sweden and Finland).[9]

In the early days, much of the effort was devoted to show differences between goods and services and to prove that services need their own type of marketing. Still, however, nobody has in a more fundamental and generic way been able to understand what goods and services are and how they relate to each other. Usually four properties are mentioned in the literature in order to show the differences:

1 services are *intangible* whereas goods are tangible;
2 services are *less standardized* than goods;
3 services *cannot be stored*;
4 finally, *simultaneity and inseparability*, meaning that the production and consumption of services are partly simultaneous and that customers partly participate in the production process.

I mention these alleged differences as they are continuously repeated in the literature as the rationale for separating goods marketing and services marketing. The properties may seem attractive at first glance – they have face validity – but what are their operational consequences? The first three can easily be dismissed. Let me explain by presenting a few examples.

Airlines are classified as service companies. But the aircraft, the food, the drinks and the staff are very tangible. The airports and the view from the aircraft window and the feeling when there is turbulence are tangible, and if you are fortunate to fly by Concorde you feel the vibrations when the speedometer on the wall says '1 mach' and the aircraft breaks through the sound barrier. If I am operated on at the hospital I am myself the 'machine', the object of 'repair and maintenance'. It is unpleasant, it may hurt. I can get better, worse, or die. Can it be more tangible?

Services and goods alike can be standardized and be produced in factories but yet include customized elements. The pizzeria and the retail bank offer highly standardized services while knowledge-intensive services from management consultants, lawyers and architects are highly customized (although they also contain standardized modules).

The claim that services cannot be stored is nonsense. Services are stored in

---

[9] For the history of services marketing, see Berry and Parasuraman (1993), and Fisk, Brown, and Bitner (1993); for the Nordic School see Grönroos and Gummesson (1985). For a general overview of services marketing, see Grönroos (1990); Woodruff (1995); Zeithaml and Bitner (1996); and Lovelock, Patterson and Walker (1998). The developement of RM within services marketing is described by Berry (1995); Nordic School contributions to RM are discussed in Gummesson, Lehtinen and Grönroos (1997).

systems, buildings, machines, knowledge, and people. The ATM is a store of standardized cash withdrawals. The emergency clinic is a store of skilled people, equipment and procedures. The hotel is a store of rooms. Fresh bread, milk, fruit, fish, and meat are quickly perishable, not to talk about an oyster and an opened bottle of Mumm's Cordon Vert. But food can be treated to last longer, some treatments keeping the quality well, whereas others are just preserving cosmetic dimensions, or jeopardizing the health of the consumer by adding chemicals, radiation and gene manipulation with unknown effects.

The last of the four properties is different. The simultaneous production and consumption process, the presence of the customer, and the customer's role as co-producer form the pivotal distinguishing properties between goods and services. These are also salient features of RM and they require interaction in a customer–provider relationship, sometimes also in a customer–customer relationship. The interaction can be face-to-face but it can also take place via IT and other equipment.

Services have more impact on a nation's economy than was previously recognized. The classifications used in statistics, for example the manufacturing industry with such subgroups as the auto or electronics industries are production and product oriented and say little of interest to marketing. In the future, less then 10 per cent of the working population of a mature industrialized nation will work on the shop floor.

To make a total offering to customers' competitive and value adding, both goods and services must comply with the requirements of the customers. Services are also used as a means to differentiate an offering and are thereby allotted a strategic marketing role. Moreover, work in an office is now being seen as internal services, not as administrative routines or white-collar bureaucracy. Internal services are broken up and given their own identity and profit centres are instituted. The data processing department becomes a computer consulting company, the real estate is taken over by a maintenance company, and a financial company manages cash flow, credits and pension funds. The services then must be marketed and sold internally and they become support to external marketing.

Prompted by dissatisfaction with services, much of the development of services marketing has focused on service quality in the sense of customer perceived quality, customer satisfaction, and value for the customer. A large number of service quality models have been designed.[10] Lists of quality dimensions – essential properties of a service with which customers are satisfied or dissatisfied – have been established. The dimensions could also be interpreted as factors which enhance or reduce the likelihood of customer loyalty. The most quoted dimensions are

---

[10] For an overview of service quality models, see Gummesson (1993); and Edvardsson, Thomasson and Øvretveit (1994).

■ *reliability* (the ability to correctly perform a service according to promises);
■ *responsiveness* (willingness to serve customers);
■ *assurance* (the ability and credibility of service provider staff);
■ *empathy* (a sensitive, understanding and personal care for every customer);
■ *tangibility* (the goods and people that are part of the service delivery).[11]

Interaction has stood out as a central concept in services marketing and it also stands out in its contributions to RM. Most literature on services marketing is focused on the *service encounter*, the interaction between the customer and the service provider (R5). The fact that marketing and production must work hand in hand is in the core of services marketing theory and so is quality. The concepts of the service encounter and service quality support the effort of *modern quality management to bridge the gap between marketing and technical functions* (R26). Services marketing is the mother of *internal marketing* (R27) which subsequently has earned the status of being generally applicable. As many services consist of data processing and transmission, the *electronic relationship* (R12) is of primary importance for service companies.

Services marketing has added emphasis to several other relationships. Among these are the:

■ notion that marketing is performed by each and every one, not only by the *full-time marketers* but also by *part-time marketers* (R4);
■ *non-commercial relationship* which is usually about services (R14);
■ need for being *close to the customer* (R8);
■ *relationship to dissatisfied customers* and how recovery should be handled (R9);
■ *introduction of the market economy inside the organization*, among other things the internal trade of services (R24);
■ *interaction between internal customers* and the transcendence of traditional functional and hierarchical boundaries (R25).

The network approach to industrial/business marketing

Industrial marketing is marketing to other organizations (in contrast to consumers and households). The term has a limiting connotation; it leads the thought to manufacturing industries selling to each other. *Business marketing* or *business-to-business marketing* are other terms which aim to broaden the application and include, for example, consumer goods sold to intermediaries. A large part of industrial marketing is selling to the government sector. It is no doubt necessary to stick to terms that have a certain acceptance, but at the same time it is neces-

---

[11] The five dimensions are suggested by Zeithaml, Parasuraman and Berry (1990). Many others have suggested general service quality dimensions, e.g. Grönroos (1990, p. 47); see also an overview and an integration between goods quality, service quality, and computer software quality dimensions in Gummesson (1992, pp. 51–9).

sary to be alert to their content, even if the words as such do not wholly cover the phenomenon we want to communicate.

The *network approach*[12] is a designation for developments in marketing thought from the IMP Group (International/Industrial Marketing and Purchasing Group). The group has its roots at Uppsala University, Sweden, but has spread to include major universities throughout Europe, on to Australia, and also to a lesser extent to Asia and USA. Beginning in the 1970s, comprehensive studies, which are reported in numerous articles and books, have been conducted. Its work is a reaction against the marketing mix theory, a reaction documented in a book by Håkansson and Snehota in 1976.

A similar approach to industrial marketing was taken by Jackson in the late 1970s and early 1980s in the USA. Her findings are close to those of the IMP Group but she used a different language (relationship marketing versus transaction marketing), and her theoretical and empirical foundation was different. IMP research gave birth to a school of thought and their members have continuously grown in number. Curiously enough, in the era of globalization, Jackson had not encountered IMP research until 1996 when I told her about it.

According to the basic beliefs of the network approach, a company:

> ...can be viewed as a node in an ever-widening pattern of interactions, in some of which it is a direct participant, some of which affect it indirectly and some of which occur independently of it. This web of interactions is so complex and multifarious as to deny full description or analysis. Indeed, the interaction between a single buyer and selling company can be complex enough...[13]

The network approach sees industrial marketing as interaction in a network of relationship. Even if the research has been primarily directed to dyadic relationships, it has successively broadened its scope to more complex networks. In addition to networks and interaction, its core variables are *activities*, *resources* and *actors* as was mentioned in Chapter 1.

The character of relationships varies between companies. They are influenced by product type, degree of standardization, complexity, frequency, and technological conditions. Sometimes business aspects prevail, sometimes technological aspects. The relationships between two companies are subsystems of larger networks. The larger networks are inhabited by the customers' customers, the suppliers' suppliers, intermediaries, and various other collaborating parties. National relationships are usually more extensive, informal and intimate than international relationships. The network approach accentuates the:

---

[12] For presentations of the network approach and its research programs, see anthologies edited by Ford (1990), Iacobucci (1996), and Möller and Wilson (1996); and books by Håkansson and Snehota (1995), and Ford *et al.* (1998). For a critical discussion on the appropriateness of RM in industrial marketing, see Blois (1996).

[13] Ford, Håkansson and Johanson (1986, pp. 26–7).

- longevity and stability of relationships;
- importance of collaboration as a means to an efficient market economy;
- importance of transaction costs and switching costs;
- active participation of the parties;
- importance of power and knowledge;
- importance of technology, procurement, and logistics.

The network approach is based on case studies of industrial marketing and therefore the theory only qualifies for industrial marketing, unless further studies
widen its field of application. By comparing its results with other theories and
data, I see three indications of generality. First, its emphasis is on market-oriented
management rather than marketing management. Just like in service research, it
has been found that marketing cannot be isolated as an independent function but
is rather an attitude to management. Second, its results give food for rethinking
both consumer goods marketing and services marketing. Finally, marketing situations are seldom clear-cut. Almost all companies sell both to consumers and
organizations, and offer both goods and services.

The Nordic School of Services in particular has benefited from the network
approach, whereas representatives of the network approach to a lesser degree
have exploited the results of service research. Although IMP members are increasingly presenting at RM conferences and are being quoted in RM texts, many have
not found RM to be an extension of or a possible partner to the network approach:
'...it is futile to say what comes after [the network approach], if there is anything'.[14] Prominent IMP representatives are dismissing the broader RM concept
by claiming that RM deals with consumer marketing; does not heed networks but
rather multiple dyads; ignores actors outside the dyad; and even that RM does
not make the existence of the relationship phenomenon credible.[15]

This, however, should not dishearten others from making their interpretations
and using IMP research as an input to RM. In my opinion, the network approach
offers a unique contribution to marketing thought which has received international acclaim – with the exception of the USA and US textbooks. No other salient
theory of industrial marketing has come forth during the past twenty years. Its
contribution to RM is beginning to receive more attention during the 1990s. The
network approach is also influenced by interorganizational theory, transaction
cost analysis and other theories, but above all it is the outcome of the network
researchers' own empirical studies.

I have made my own interpretation of the network approach and I see it in the
light of its contributions to RM. This interpretation does not necessarily comply
with everybody else's interpretation, but on the other hand there are also several
perceptions of the approach within the IMP Group.

The network approach is using interaction in networks of relationships as the

---

[14] Johanson (1994, p. 9).
[15] Easton and Håkansson (1996, pp. 411–12).

vantage point. It has contributed to the 30Rs by showing that the *customer and the seller are many-headed* (R6) and that *mega relationships* are influential (R18–R23). The emphasis on technology and purchasing has contributed to the interfunctional and interhierarchical dependency and the *relationships between internal customers and suppliers* (R25). The concept of quality is not used in IMP research but their research has put the spotlight on the *need to bridge the gap between technology and marketing* (R26).

Quality management – rejuvenating marketing orientation

Quality management is the fourth theory that inspired the 30R approach. Modern quality thinking is not only a revolution in quality management but also a *rejuvenation of marketing orientation*. In marketing, quality was long used in a general and loose sense. It became a cliché, which was routinely appended to advertising copy, which sales people allowed to litter their talk, and which CEOs boasted about at conferences and dinners. Quality became an empty word.

To some extent this is still true but during the 1980s, quality began to dress up in new clothes. Today, the word quality is interpreted as *customer perceived quality*, meaning that it is marketing-oriented and focused on customer satisfaction. The customer side of quality, however, should not be promoted at the expense of the technology aspect of quality. Prior to the quality revolution during the 1980s, technology aspects were in the driver's seat, and a bias toward customers was called for in order to restore balance. The customer approach to quality management is of course directly pertinent to marketing although in the long run, I advocate a balanced view.

Systematic approaches to quality management grew out of operations management with limited or no base in marketing until the 1980s.[16] The contributions to service quality became an integral part of service research and practice and consequently part of services marketing theory.

The quality perspective has successively moved from the shop floor to the management of the whole corporation. This is evident in the now widespread quality awards. The Malcolm Baldrige National Quality Award, which was established in the USA and handed out for the first time in 1988, has become a role model for international and national quality awards. In Japan the Deming Quality Prize was established as early as in 1952 but was designed differently from today's awards.

Baldrige regulations provide a comprehensive list of criteria which an organization must consider to make quality happen. It is my contention that these awards have given rise to the most comprehensive approach to quality that had hitherto seen the light. It could even deserve to be called a *meta theory of quality*. The perspective is holistic; the theory consists of quality factors as well as a discussion of links between them.

---

[16] For an overview of quality management, see e.g. Crosby (1979), Deming (1986), and Juran (1992).

A brief description of the Baldrige Award will give an idea of the structure of quality prizes.[17] Baldrige offers seven categories of criteria. A total of 1000 points are divided between the following categories:[18]

1 Leadership (110 points);
2 Strategic Planning (80);
3 Customer and Market Focus (80);
4 Information and Analysis (80);
5 Human Resource Development and Management (100);
6 Process Management (100);
7 Business Results (450).

This is nothing less than a list of criteria for a complete company audit! It shows that quality cannot be achieved unless all activities inside a company are directed toward quality; it points to interfunctional and interhierarchical interaction. This does not mean that the quality concept has taken over all management, only that quality development requires contributions from each and everyone. It would of course be surprising if badly managed internal work would end up in quality excellence.

Just over half of the points concern activities and the rest business results. The points cover both internal activities and those directed toward the market and society. In several of the points, the link between quality and relationships are emphasized.

The most conspicuous contribution from quality management to RM was treated in R26, namely the creation of a *relationship between operations management – technical functions – and marketing*. Quality management has contributed to R25 with the concepts of the *internal customer* and *process management*, which aim to establish *interhierarchical and interfunctional collaboration*. Quality management has added weight to *customer satisfaction*. In doing so, it underscores both the general *supplier–customer relationship* (R1) and the *relationship to dissatisfied customers* (R9).

The concept of *relationship quality* was introduced in the Ericsson Quality Program in 1985.[19] The purpose was to call attention to the fact that relationships are part of customer perceived quality. This quality concept is a long way from the traditional engineer's logic. Relationship quality has stood out as a pivotal issue in services marketing, where the interaction during the production and delivery process affects the quality of the service. In every corner of a company there are people who influence the quality of customer relationships. There are *part-time marketers* (R4); they become visible in the *service encounter* (R5); and in the *many-headed relationship in industrial marketing* (R6).

---

[17] This is based on the Malcolm Baldrige Regulations (1997) and interviews with former Baldrige executive Curt Reimann: see also an overview of Baldrige in Hart and Bogan (1992).
[18] Malcolm Baldrige (1997, p.2).
[19] See Gummesson (1987a); see also Storbacka, Strandvik and Grönroos (1994), Holmlund (1997).

Relationship quality concerns both *professional and social relationships* and both are important. In order to establish credibility, suppliers must know their industry and be able to show it. But often the human aspect, to be liked by the customer, is the differentiating factor in customer perceived quality. R18 – *personal relationships and social networks* – is therefore also linked to the concept of relationship quality.

Current RM literature – a comparison with the 30R approach

The review of the four theories, as well as the theories treated in Chapters 6 and 7, has revealed the major antecedents of the 30R approach. None of these theories use relationship marketing (or RM) as their key term although the term was introduced both in services and business marketing during the 1980s.

Throughout the book, ample references have been made to those who have furnished inspiration and illustrations. To review everything being presented on RM in the expanding number of journal articles, books, conference papers, and applied cases, is simply not feasible, not even if we limit ourselves to the English language.

RM is given different meaning by different authors. The influx and vitality of the current research and debate about RM, although mostly fragmented and addressing special issues in terms of traditional marketing management theory, has become an extra impetus to the evolution of my approach. These sources have modified and broadened my understanding. At the same time they have strengthened my conviction to stick to the path laid out by the 30R approach.

This section first points to the distinction between the *term* relationship marketing and the relationship marketing *phenomenon*, a greatly misunderstood issue. It proceeds to make reference to influential books and articles on RM and to compare a selection of definitions and multi-relationship approaches.

The term and the phenomenon

There is an unfortunate mix-up between the term RM and the understanding of the actual phenomenon, a mix-up that should be avoided. A term is only a label of the phenomenon, it is not the phenomenon *per se* (recall the discussion on objectification, reification and Magritte's pipe in Chapter 7). In order to avoid an intellectual *Titanic* disaster, scholars are expected to consider the whole iceberg (the phenomenon), not just its tip (the term). *RM is a new term, but it represents an old phenomenon.*

The phenomenon of RM is as old as trade itself but it has gone unnoticed by most marketing professors, economists, marketing textbook writers, and business school educators. Since the 1970s, many terms have been used to catch the phenomenon, among them the network approach and the interaction approach (IMP Group), long-term interactive relationships and a new concept of marketing (Gummesson), and interactive marketing (Grönroos). Other terms are database marketing, direct marketing, niche marketing, one-to-one marketing, wrap around marketing, dialogue marketing, and client management.

The term relationship marketing was used by Barbara Bund Jackson in her project on industrial marketing from the late 1970s, and published in a seminal book and a Harvard Business Review article, both in 1985. She used the term as an opposite to transaction marketing. The term was used by Len Berry in a conference paper in 1983, but exclusively for services. In other words, the term appeared simultaneously in industrial marketing and services marketing. In the 1990s the term is increasingly becoming a general marketing term although most of the seminal writings on the phenomenon so far have used other terms. Considering its long history in the practice of marketing management, the diversity of terms used to pinpoint the phenomenon in theory and literature, it is pointless to ascribe the 'discovery' of the phenomenon of RM to a specific date or individual. The phenomenon was part of indigenous knowledge in business cultures around the world.

Many have contributed to make the phenomenon of RM visible which is evident from the description of the various theories earlier in this chapter. In a number of books, researchers and consultants have developed their own approaches to RM. Some have used the term in the title.[20] For others the term is central in their text although it is not in the titles of their books.[21] Most of the authors have not used the term but are zooming in on customized marketing and relationships in an innovative and informed way.[22] Similar books have been published in many languages in many countries. Most likely, the phenomenon of RM has also been treated in now forgotten texts. An upsurge in RM articles and conference papers present different ways of approaching RM. Some of these references have been used in this book. Others are found in overviews, which show that different roads lead to RM.[23]

Definitions

Short definitions are never complete or unambiguous but they can hint at the core of a phenomenon and thus provide initial guidance. Several authors propose RM definitions and a selection of these are listed in Table 8.1.

The definitions vary in scope and emphasis. Berry's definition is developed within services marketing. He explains his concern to be customer retention and the allocation of resources to keep customers and strengthen relationships, and not just attract new customers. Jackson's definition involves industrial customers and individual accounts as compared to mass markets and segments. Her concern is to make the business-to-business supplier choose whichever is the best strategy for each individual customer in each specific situation, either RM or transaction mar-

---

[20] Christopher, Payne and Ballantyne (1991); McKenna (1991); Cram (1994); Payne *et al.* (1995); Buttle (1996); and Halinen-Kaila (1997).

[21] Jackson (1985); Berry and Parasuraman (1991).

[22] Sewell (1990); Rap and Collins (1990, 1995); Peppers and Rogers (1993, 1997); Treacy and Wiersema (1995); Scheuing (1995); Daffy (1996); and Reichheld (1996).

[23] Webster (1992), Sheth and Parvatiyar (1993), and Morgan and Hunt (1994) – all with a US perspective – and Gummesson, Lehtinen and Grönroos (1997) with a Nordic School perspective.

Table 8.1 Selected definitions which emphasize different aspects of RM

Source	Definition
Berry (1983, p. 25)	'Relationship marketing is attracting, maintaining and – in multi-service organizations – enhancing customer relationships.'
Jackson (1985a, p. 165)	'Relationship marketing is marketing to win, build and maintain strong lasting relationships with industrial customers.'
Gummesson (1994, p. 5)	'Relationship marketing is marketing seen as relationships, networks and interaction.'
Grönroos (1996, p. 11)	'Relationship marketing is to identify and establish, maintain, and enhance relationships with customers and other stakeholders, at a profit, so that the objectives of all parties involved are met; and that this is done by a mutual exchange and fulfilment of promises.'
Ballantyne (1994, p. 3)	'An emergent disciplinary framework for creating, developing and sustaining exchanges of value, between the parties involved, whereby exchange relationships evolve to provide continuous and stable links in the supply chain.'
Morgan and Hunt (1994, p. 22)	'Relationship marketing refers to all marketing activities directed to establishing, developing, and maintaining successful relational exchanges.'
Sheth (1994)	'The understanding, explanation and management of the ongoing collaborative business relationship between suppliers and customers' and '... an emerging school of marketing thought.'
Porter (1993, p. 14)	'Relationship marketing is the process whereby both parties – the buyer and provider – establish an effective, efficient, enjoyable, enthusiastic and ethical relationship: one that is personally, professionally and profitably rewarding to both parties.'

keting. The messages of the two definitions are similar, but they are grounded in two different types of marketing, services marketing and industrial marketing.

The Gummesson definition is founded on three core variables – relationships, networks, interaction – that have emerged out of research. The variables are common to both goods/services and consumer/industrial marketing. Whereas the other definitions list activities or properties, this definition provides core variables as vehicles for thought and action. The definition is based on a relationship perspective, hence the notion of the relationship eye-glasses. It is the only definition that includes the concepts of networks and interaction.

Grönroos provides a broad definition comprising relationships between a series of stakeholders, not just supplier–customer relationships. He excludes not-for-profit organizations and thus most of the government and voluntary sectors.

Morgan and Hunt as well as Ballantyne also offer broad definitions. Together with Grönroos, Porter and Ballantyne stress win–win aspects (fulfilment of promises, rewarding both parties, value exchange) and in alignment with Jackson and Sheth includes the long-term aspect (continuous and stable, lasting, ongoing).

Five of the eight definitions use terms such as creating and maintaining relationships, but no one points to the need to divest in a relationship, although this is also a necessary and continuously applied option.

Sheth defines relationships as collaborative in contrast to competitive or adversarial, and adds a more scholarly approach by speaking about the understanding and explanation of relationships. Both he and Ballantyne claim that RM is an emerging school of thought. This rings true with reference to the term, but not with reference to the phenomenon. Relationships not only go far back in the history of business practice but they are in the core of both services marketing theory and the network approach, even if the term RM was not used.

Porter adds important social elements. Relationships should not only be efficient and effective but also enjoyable, enthusiastic, ethical, and personally and professionally rewarding. Marketing theory seems to forget the importance of social interaction and personality dimensions in a business relationship: Business is fun! Furthermore, ethical aspects are at the core of RM, which is reflected in the importance that many authors place in trust, for example Morgan and Hunt.

Multi-relationship approaches

The definitions showed that some limit RM to the supplier–customer dyad while others include several parties or stakeholders. In Table 8.2, the 30R approach is com-

Table 8.2 Comparison between categories in multi-relationship approaches. The number of relationships included in each subcategory is shown in brackets

Source	Categories	Subcategories
Christopher, Payne and Ballantyne (1991)	6 markets	Customer markets (1)
		Supporting markets (5)
Kotler (1992)	10 players	Immediate environment (4)
		Macroenvironment (6)
Morgan and Hunt (1994)	10 partnerships	Buyer partnerships (2)
		Supplier partnerships (2)
		Lateral partnerships (3)
		Internal partnerships (3)
Gummesson (1994)	30 relationships	Market relationships:
		• Classic (3)
		• Special (14)
		Non-market relationships:
		• Mega relationships (6)
		• Nano relationships (7)

pared to three other approaches which go beyond suppliers and customers and see marketing relationships as embedded in a network of multiple relationships.

Christopher, Payne and Ballantyne[24] propose a 'six markets' model' consisting of *customer markets* (existing and prospective customers) surrounded by *supporting markets* which are *referral markets* (satisfied customers who recommend the supplier to others); *supplier markets* (to be a partner rather than an adversary to their suppliers); *employee markets* (making certain that the right employees are recruited and promoted); *influence markets* (such as financial analysts, journalists, and governments); and *internal markets* (the organization and its staff).

In his concept 'total marketing', Kotler says that '...there are at least ten critical players in a company's environment, of which the immediate customer and the ultimate customer are only two'.[25] He makes a distinction between four players in the *immediate environment* of the firm – *suppliers, distributors, end-users, and employees* – and six in the firm's macroenviroment – *financial firms, governments, media, allies, competitors,* and *the general public.*

Morgan and Hunt[26] suggest ten relationship exchanges with four partnership groups: *buyer partnerships (ultimate customers, intermediate customers); supplier partnerships (goods suppliers, service providers); lateral partnerships (competitors, non-profit organizations, governments);* and *internal partnerships (functional departments, employees, business units).*

The fourth classification, the 30Rs, has been presented in the previous chapters. It goes further than the others and involves not only parties but also certain properties of relationships. In that respect it is less consistent than the other classifications but it is more comprehensive. Generic relationship properties that were listed in Chapter 1 are inherent in the relationships, and other properties have been added to form their own Rs. Some are based on content, such as the green relationship, the law-based relationship and the criminal relationship; others on form, such as alliances; and on conduit, such as the electronic relationship.

In a comparative analysis it became evident that the relationships of all four approaches can be classified as market or non-market relationships and can further be sub-grouped into both mega and nano relationships. There is a good match between the approaches although the emphasis and scope vary. There are no obvious contradictions or conflicts.[27]

Concluding comment

This presentation of a selection of RM approaches shows that there is a rich literature searching for an RM identity. The growth rate is currently exponential. The approaches have varied emphasis and scope, all the way from market relationships based on a consumer–seller dyad to a series of supportive, non-market

---

[24] Christopher, Payne and Ballantyne (1991, pp. 21–30).

[25] Kotler (1992, p. 4)

[26] Morgan and Hunt (1994, p. 21).

[27] The communication-based marketing model by Duncan and Moriarty (1998, p. 9) also includes a series of stakeholders, in essence covered in other multi-relationship approaches.

relationships. Some limit RM to specific applications, such as services marketing or a technique such as the use of databases and IT. The 30R approach is the broadest, also aiming to reach a high degree of generality.

Toward a total relationship marketing theory

The theories which have been presented above are substantive or *specific theories*; they concern a specific area, such as services. The next step in theory generation is to extend these theories in the direction of *formal* or *general theories* which cover a greater domain, if possible all marketing.[28] But this is an ultimate goal which will never be reached. It is not scientifically acceptable to generalize one substantive theory to other substantive areas. Empirical data and empirically grounded theories from each substantive area must be 'heard'. Unfortunately, this very mistake has been made in marketing, most noticeable in the nomination of marketing mix theory to the status of a general marketing management theory.

RM becomes a vehicle for generalization in two respects:

1 Generalizing above the traditional dichotomies of goods/services and consumer/industrial marketing. On this higher level the *total offering and its value to the customers, suppliers and society are in focus.*

2 Generalizing to a management theory with a marketing perspective, meaning that *marketing management is converted into marketing-oriented management.*

My road to generalization will be laid out below. It is not claimed to be the only road, just the road I travelled.[29]

Figure 8.2 shows that the *first stage* of modern marketing management was based on real world data from the mass marketing of standardized consumer goods. The marketing management and mix theory emerged as a substantive theory. It has *per se* no direct application on anything but the domain from which the data were derived. It has conceptualized the raw real world data and made them applicable within its substantive area.

In the *second stage*, this thinking – in a deductive way and with little additional real world data – was superimposed on services and industrial marketing (Figure 8.3). Thereby, marketing mix theory invaded services marketing and industrial marketing. When the theory was confronted with real world data and practice, anomalies occurred. These were explained away on purely theoretical and deductive grounds. More Ps and tools were added which enhanced the value of the marketing mix theory, but only temporarily. It became a patchwork, and the theory became increasingly strained. To use a term from telecommunications, it became a spaghetti system; it was full of cables and nodes and finally

---

[28] For a discussion on substantive and formal theories, see Glaser and Strauss (1967) and their grounded theory.
[29] This a further development from Gummesson (1983 and 1987b).

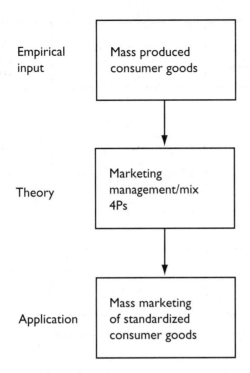

Figure 8.2 The marketing management and mix theory

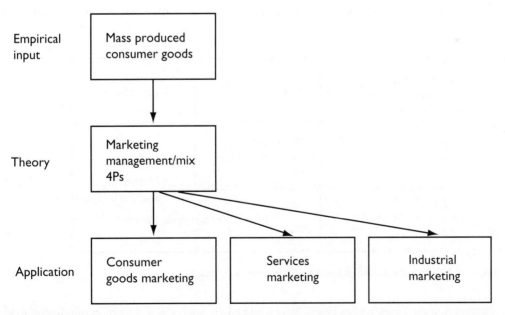

Figure 8.3 The forced transition of the marketing management and mix theory to other types of marketing

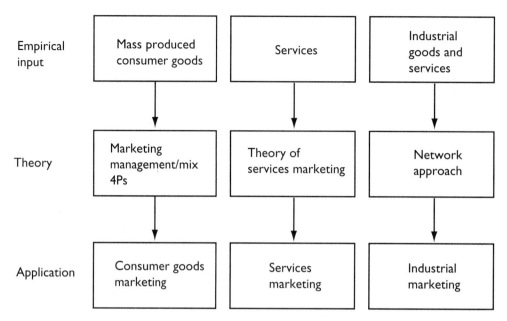

Figure 8.4 Real world data as the basis for three substantive marketing theories

so entangled that no one could use it. Marketing management also became procrustean science,[30] meaning that reality was forced into boxes where it did not fit. If a box was not filled the theory was stretched, if the box was flooded overflowing material was cut away.

In the *third stage*, service marketing and industrial marketing were studied on

Type of product \ Type of buyer	Consumers	Organizations
Goods	Marketing management/mix 4Ps	Network approach
Services	Services marketing theory	

Figure 8.5 The substantive domains of the marketing theories

---

[30] Named after the Greek robber Procrusteus who had the kindness of offering accommodation for travellers, but demanded that they fit exactly the bed size. If they were too short, they were put on a stretcher; if they were too tall, their feet were cut off.

their own terms in their own environment. Two theories emerged from inductive, empirical studies of services marketing and industrial marketing. The foundation was no longer marketing mix but reality was allowed to shape its own concepts and connections (Figure 8.4). The procrustean science was replaced by sensitivity for what reality tried to tell us – if we were willing to listen to its story.

The three marketing theories presented above can be classified by type of product (goods or services), and type of customer (consumer or organization). How the theories match marketing situations can be seen in Figure 8.5.

In the *fourth stage*, the foundation was reinforced from two directions. First, beside the three marketing theories, contributions came from quality management, organization theory, and accounting theory. Second, we enter practical experience and common sense, from our roles as reflective marketers, consumers, and scholars. The extended model is shown in Figure 8.6.

We are now arriving at the *fifth stage* in which contributions from all theories and experience converge toward a more general marketing theory, total relationship marketing. The TRM theory is not restricted to type of product or customer; it can be brought to bear on all marketing situations (Figure 8.7). Please note that this does not mean that it should be applied in the same way to all companies and all occasions; *the uniqueness of each marketing situation must be taken into account*. The general and the specific must enter into constructive dialogue.

I can, however, visualize a *sixth stage* concerning marketing applications that have hitherto been seen as peripheral but which may be equally significant. We have caught glimpses of them in the 30Rs, but they have a less solid theoretical base than the major theoretical contributions that have been presented above. Among these are:[31]

- markets created by *exchanges* (stock, bonds, metals) which offer – in a split second – prices, delivery times and payment through electronic relationships;
- *public sector* and its marketing of public services and also the marketing of authorities;
- marketing of the *voluntary sector* and other non-commercial corporations and organizations such as universities' fund-raising and recruitment of students;
- marketing of *culture and events* such as films, theatres, and the Olympic Games;
- marketing of *people* (actors, politicians);
- *place marketing* (tourism, immigration, attracting industry);
- the recent *marketing of nations*.

These have had some influence on RM but too little considering the amount of revenue they control and their growth. RM is to an extent applicable to them but we must be sensitive to the fact that they have not been the object of systematic studies for my RM concept.

---

[31] Several of these are treated in special literature. Kotler and co-authors, for example, have done groundbreaking work in applying marketing management theory on celebrities, education, non-profit organizations, museums, places, and even whole nations.

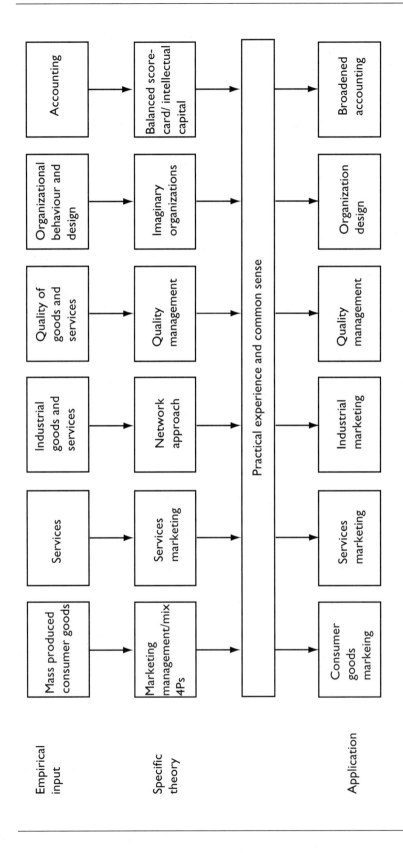

Figure 8.6 Contributions to RM from marketing theories, other theories and practical experience

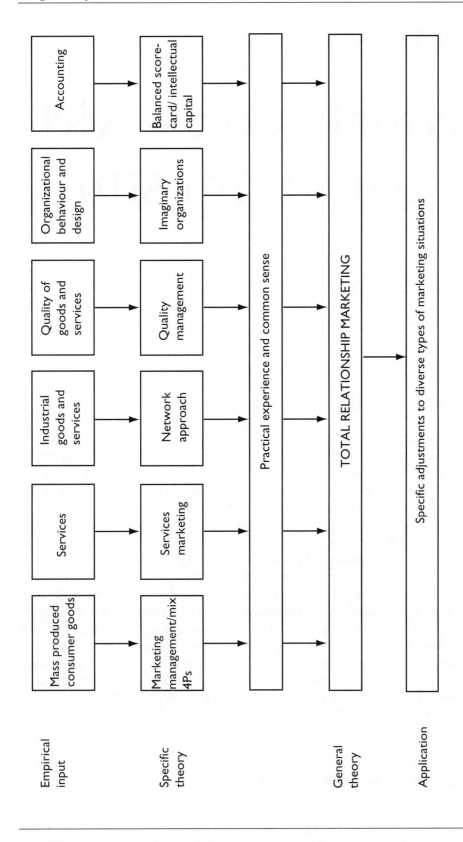

Figure 8.7 Synthesis of specific theories and experiences into TRM

Chapter 9

In conclusion – RM is a paradigm shift!

This final chapter sums up total relationship marketing. It claims that RM is a paradigm shift. In a sense we have come to the end. In another sense we are only at the beginning of exploring the consequences of a new marketing paradigm.

RM as a paradigm shift

A paradigm shift implies that a science or discipline is given a new foundation, with new values, new assumptions, or new methods. The accepted and established must be set aside. It either disappears completely, succumbs to the new, or takes the role of one of several co-existing paradigms. An established paradigm can be a springboard, but it can also be a mental prison.

The American automotive industry is a case in point. When the small car came from Europe and Japan it was not taken seriously by US manufacturers, but it was taken seriously by the consumers. Morgan offers an explanation: 'American auto industry in the early 1970s was a prisoner of its early success. And numerous firms in other industries have shared a similar experience, declining and decaying as a result of policies that made them world leaders in earlier stages of development'.[1]

Organizations get caught in mental traps, 'knowing' how everything is and erecting monuments over their prejudices. 'Group think' is hubris linked with the security in the power group, such as a corporate or marketing management group. No one dares openly challenge the conditions for decisions and action. Snug in 'The Yesmen Choir' the singers are sheltered by the perceptions that might have once been realistic, but in a changed market are nothing but shared illusions.[2]

---

[1] Morgan (1997, p. 201).
[2] For a discussion on the yesman, see Ortmark (1996).

Some claim that RM is just a marginal variant of established marketing management with one or two add-ons. With such a view, RM is brutally forced into the old and will never be allowed to display its qualities. Paradigm shifts break existing patterns. A small car is not a shrunk limousine, a tanker is not a blown-up rowing-boat. They are based on different concepts and obey different laws. In the same spirit, I see RM as a paradigm shift in marketing.

At the end of Chapter 1, total relationship marketing was given a brief definition. The ensuing chapters spelled out the concept in more detail. Table 9.1 now sums up total relationship marketing and its contribution to a paradigm shift.

Table 9.1 TRM as a paradigm shift in marketing

Definition	RM is marketing seen as relationships, networks and interaction.
Characteristics	Value for the parties involved – of which the customer is one – is created through interaction between suppliers, customers, competitors and others; the parties in a network of relationships are co-producers, creating value for each other.
Making RM tangible	Specification of thirty relationships, the 30Rs, both operational market relationships, and mega and nano non-market relationships.
Relationship portfolio	As part of the marketing planning process, a selection of focal relationships is made for the planning period.
Values	Collaboration in focus; more win–win and less win–lose; more equal parties; all parties carry a responsibility to be active in the relationship; long-term relationships; each customer is an individual or a member of a community of likeminded people.
Theoretical and practical foundation	Built on a synthesis between traditional marketing management, marketing mix (the 4Ps) and sales management; services marketing; the network approach to industrial marketing; quality management; imaginary organizations; new accounting principles; and the experiences of reflective practitioners.
Links to management	RM is more than marketing management, it is rather marketing-oriented management – an aspect of the total management of the firm – and not limited to marketing or sales departments; the marketing plan becomes part of the business plan.
Links to accounting	The balanced scorecard and intellectual capital provide tools for measuring return on relationships.
Links to organization structure	RM is the marketing manifestation of the imaginary organization and vice versa.

Table 9.1 TRM as a paradigm shift in marketing (*continued*)

Advantages to a firm	Increased customer retention and duration; increased marketing productivity and thus increased profitability; and increased stability and security.
Advantages to the market economy	RM adds collaboration to competition and regulations/institutions; the symbioses between these three contributes in the direction of a dynamic marketing equilibrium.
Advantages to society, citizens, and customers	RM is the marketing of the value society and the postmodern society; increased focus on customized production and one-to-one marketing, diminished focus on standardized mass manufacturing and anonymous mass marketing.
Validity	By focusing on relationships, networks and interaction, RM offers a more realistic approach to marketing than is currently prevailing in marketing education. In practice, business is largely conducted through networks of relationships.
Generalizability	RM can be applied to all kinds of organizations and offerings, but the relationship portfolio and the application is always specific to a given situation.

The paradigm shift has partially taken place in the real world of marketing, but the shift is not properly echoed in theories, textbooks and education. Students bring theoretical knowledge – marketing maps – to their current or future jobs. This knowledge must be usable knowledge, representing the terrain. This year's marketing reality cannot be tackled with previous years' theories.

New concepts

New thinking requires new concepts – reconceptualization – so that the new will be allowed to live on their own terms.

Several new concepts have been introduced in this book or they are developments of concepts I have used before. I believe I have innovated some of them or used them with a novel touch; if I am mistaken I would appreciate being corrected.[3]

Among these concepts are the relationship eye-glasses; the full-time marketer and part-time marketer, the FTMs and PTMs; mega and nano relationships; face-

---

[3] As has been pointed out before, it is vital to make a distinction between a phenomenon and the term used to catch the phenomenon. I have not invented any of the phenomena, I have conceptualized some of them and given them names.

less relationships; alliance markets; decision markets; service collision; horizontal and vertical interaction; power company and power industry; the pseudo-personal relationship and pseudo membership; the value society; the bureaucratic–legal paradigm; return on relationships; relationship portfolio; and not least the marketing equilibrium.

Several of the relationships are under-represented in current 'general' marketing literature, such as the many-headed customer and the many-headed supplier (R6), the customer or supplier as prisoner (R10), the electronic relationship (R12), the parasocial relationships (R13), the green relationship (R15), the law-based relationship (R16), the criminal network (R17), the knowledge relationship (R21), mega alliances (R22), quality management sponsoring the relationship between marketing and technology (R26), and the owner and financier relationship (R30).

Other concepts and terms are other people's innovations, such as mega marketing, internal marketing, internal customer, the service encounter, imaginary organizations, the knowledge-based organization, migratory and embedded knowledge, and value monopoly. But the concepts have been given a more central role here than in other general marketing presentations and they have been looked at through the relationship eye-glasses.

RM and the 4Ps

If RM takes the place of traditional marketing management and marketing mix theory as a basic new structure for marketing thinking, the question comes up: Are the 4Ps (5Ps, 6Ps, etc.) dead? The answer is – No! Product, price, promotion, place, and the other Ps will always be important – and they have their role in RM – but their role changes. In short, I see it this way.

I would like to dissolve the 4Ps and just talk about Ps as symbols for supplier controlled activities for managing customers and persuading them to buy. A certain element of persuasion and influence will always be needed in marketing. But the role of the Ps should be a supporting role instead of a leading role; a focus shift should take place (Figure 9.1). In practice, the Ps became too manipulative – even if this was not the original intention – and this has damaged the credibility and functionality of the marketing discipline. The Ps are also directed to mass marketing, which is becoming less dominant, but will always be part of marketing. Goods and services will be treated as a way of creating value together with individual customers, and the customer's role in the production will be more important.

The industrial society and the value society, modernism and post-modernism

The transition to imaginary organizations represents a paradigm shift with close affinity to RM, as spelled out in Chapter 7. RM can also be a sign of other para-

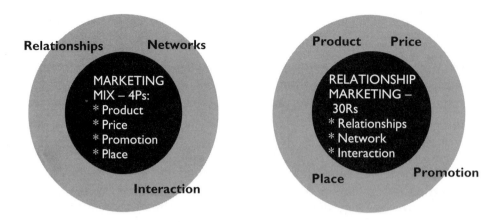

Figure 9.1 A shift from the 4Ps to relationships, networks and interaction

digm shifts on a more general level. Two such shifts will be considered here – the shifts from *modernism* to *post-modernism*, and from *the industrial society* to *the value society*. These represent *megaparadigms,* a term that may cause cardiac arrest for those who are already at war with the terms of paradigm and post-modernism.

Even if the phenomena of the modern and the post-modern are nebulous, they tease our brains. They attempt to uncover essentials in a long-term passage from certain governing values and behaviour to others. Modernism coincides with the industrial society, post-modernism with the new economy which I designate the value society.[4]

Modernism is characterized by a belief in progress and unbounded trust in science, the rational and the expert; by our ability to take charge over nature and social behaviour; by finding universal laws and absolute truths. Everything is measurable, and if it is not, it does not exist. Common sense and experience are degraded to superstition and opinions to be replaced by facts and objective knowledge. Society will become neatly ordered by means of social engineering, and social equality is infused through planning, regulations and institutions.

Post-modernism turns these tenets upside down. We live in an age of uncertainty.[5] The expert becomes 'a broker of uncertainty', not the sage and assured expert who knows 'how it is' with reference to 'scientific proof'. We have seen that the organization, the supplier, the customer and the competitor are ambiguous phenomena. Companies can be suppliers, customers, and competitors and they can own one another. The supplier and the customer are recognized as co-producers of services, and increasingly as co-producers also of goods and eventually of experiences and value. Service customers become temporary workers in

---

[4] The discussion on postmodernism and marketing is primarily inspired by the creative work of Brown (1995).

[5] See further Giarini and Stahel (1993).

the provider's service factory. The physical marketplace is challenged by the marketspace of internet technology. Personal and organizational relationships, which contain both technical rationality and emotions, are central to marketing. It is accepted that we deal with fuzzy phenomena with a unique core, but with blurred boundaries; perspectives that are multiple and overlapping; and knowledge that is incomplete and variable.

The imaginary organization is post-modern, it flows and changes. Complexity, ambiguity and change are natural, not inconvenient and nerve-racking. Chaos is part of everyday marketing, but even if *chaos cannot be managed* we can learn to *manage in chaos*. There is lack of equilibrium, but there is an aspiration to reach a balance which will never be reached. Trends are not continuous and many trends appear simultaneously and move in different directions; they carry the hallmark of the paradox but not of the oxymoron. The profound transformation – the discontinuity, the quantum leap, the paradigm shift – can be released suddenly, like the oil crisis in the 1970s, the Soviet perestroika and the fall of the Berlin Wall in the 1980s, and the internet breakthrough in the 1990s.

To a large extent, successful marketing has always been post-modern and value-creating. But the issue is not being either post-modern or modern, viewing society as either a value society or an industrial society. The issue is where to place the emphasis. RM is a tool and an attitude, not a fundamentalist religion. RM does not exclude transaction marketing or anonymous mass marketing when those are justified. RM does not throw the 4Ps overboard, just change their position.

A note on research method – approaching the end – or the beginning?

Peter Drucker has said that '...we are prone, both in academia and in management, to...mistake the surface gloss of brilliance for the essence of performance. But it is so easy to fall for sophistry – to mistake clever techniques for understanding, footnotes for scholarship, and fashions for truth...'.[6] This needs to be observed both by those who appear as attorneys for the defence of the established and those who advocate the new.

Heeding current issues is not the same as being faddish. The phenomena of RM caught my interest because I believe they are there to stay. When my attention was first drawn to relationships back in 1968, I had no idea what I was getting into. It took until the script of this book was ready to realize that I had opened the lid to a deep well – and could not see its bottom. RM became a black hole theory, it seemed endless. Although stars are shining here and there, most is still darkness.

My original reason for treating RM was to contribute to a more realistic understanding of marketing through the generation of a new and more general theory.

---

[6] Drucker (1988b).

In search of this theory, relationships, networks, and interaction have stood out as the core concepts, the foundation. My most important criterion in selecting and defining the 30Rs has been the pinpointing of phenomena which are of prime importance to practitioners and scholars alike. Observations of current issues in companies, and the study of literature and research, together with interpretations of these sources, have given birth to total relationship marketing.

As the Rs emerged – without my having a clue how many they would be – I tried to find a unifying logic. The failure to find that logic felt embarrassing until I realized I was misguided. It is unjustified to demand that the relationships in some rationalistic mode should yield to established patterns and a simplistic logic. Eventually, the Rs formed a pattern of classic and special market relationships, and mega and nano non-market relationships.

Behind the emergence of total relationship marketing is a strong influence from inductive research, and especially from grounded theory as developed by Glaser and Strauss.[7] It puts relentless demands on sensitivity, openness and an absence of preconceived notions. Glaser says: 'The researcher must have patience and not force the data out of anxiety and impatience... *He must trust that emergence will occur and it does* [italics added].' Finding categories and core variables is a continuous process of creatively comparing data and phenomena, letting categories and core variables emerge without forcing. In an inductive approach the data are sperms and eggs and their interaction determine the birth of new life. The final outcome in a grounded theory study is a core category which contains the whole of a phenomenon. Here, the core category became total relationship marketing.

This book has come to an end, but it is meant to be a springboard for something better. I possess boxes of material which I have not yet been able to benefit from and which have not been given a fair chance in this text. Better RM approaches will hopefully advance our understanding of marketing. Personal and scholarly reflections and a constructive dialogue around total relationship marketing and its 30Rs – and I consider reflections and dialogue the most viable scientific principles – are respectfully invited.

---

[7] Glaser and Strauss (1967); Glaser (1992), quotation from p. 4. For further elaboration on my approach to science, see Gummesson (1999).

References

Ahrnell, Britt-Marie and Nicou, Monica, *Kunskapsföretagets marknadsföring*. Malmö: Liber, 2nd revised edition, 1995.

Albinsson-Bruhner, Göran, 'Den rationella välfärdsstatens kollaps'. *Svenska Dagbladet*, 4 September 1993.

Albrecht, Karl, and Zemke, Ron, *Service America!* Homewood, IL: Dow Jones-Irwin, 1985.

Alderson, Wroe, *Dynamic Marketing Behavior*. Homewood, IL: Irwin, 1965.

AMA, 'Board Approves New Marketing Definition'. *Marketing News*, 1 March 1985.

Anderson, James C. and Narus, James A., 'Partnering as a Focused Market Strategy'. *California Management Review*, **33**, Spring, 1991, pp. 95–113.

Andreassen, Tor Wallin, *Dissatisfaction with Services*. Stockholm: Stockholm University, 1997.

Arndt, Johan, 'Toward a Concept of Domesticated Markets'. *Journal of Marketing*, **43**, Fall, 1979, pp. 69–75.

Arndt, Johan, 'The Political Economy Paradigm: Foundation for Theory Building in Marketing'. *Journal of Marketing*, **47**, Fall, 1983, pp. 44–54.

Badaracco, Joseph L. Jr., *The Knowledge Link: How Firms Compete through Strategic Alliances*. Boston, MA: Harvard Business School Press, 1991.

Baker, Michael J., 'Evolution of the Marketing Concept', in Baker, Michael J. (ed.), *Marketing: Theory and Practice*. London: Macmillan, 1976.

Baker, Michael J., 'Marketing – Philosophy or Function?' in Baker, Michael J. (ed.), *Companion Encyclopedia of Marketing*. London: Routledge, 1995a.

Baker, Michael J., 'The Future of Marketing', in Baker, Michael J. (ed.), *Companion Encyclopedia of Marketing*. London: Routledge, 1995b.

Ball, Robert, 'Brand Old, Brand New'. *Time*, 11 November 1991, p. 53.

Ballantyne, David (1994), 'Marketing at the Crossroads'. Editorial, *Asia-Australia Marketing Journal*, **2**(1), August, pp. 1–7.

Bannon, Lisa, 'Latin Outrage. A Milan Investigator Opens Pandora's Box of Italian Corruption'. *The Wall Street Journal Europe*, 12–13 June, 1992, pp. 1 and 24.

Baumgartner, Jim, 'Nonmarketing Professionals Need More Than 4Ps'. *Marketing News*, 22 July 1991, p. 28.

Benndorf, Hans, *Marknadsföringsplanering och samordning mellan företag i industriella system*. Stockholm: MTC/EFI, 1987.

Berry, Leonard L., 'Relationship Marketing', in Berry, L. L., Shostack, G. L. and Upah, G. D. (eds.), *Emerging Perspectives in Services Marketing*. Chicago: AMA, 1983.

Berry, Leonard L., 'The Service Quality Agenda for the 1990s'. *Distinguished Papers*, no. DP 89F–2. New York: St. John's University, December 1989.

Berry, Leonard L., 'Relationship Marketing of Services – Growing Interest, Emerging Perspectives'. *Journal of the Academy of Marketing Science*, **23**(4), Fall, 1995, pp. 236–245.

Berry, Leonard L. and Parasuraman, A, *Marketing Services*. New York: The Free Press, 1991.

Berry, Leonard L. and Parasuraman, A., 'Building a New Academic Field – The Case of Services Marketing'. *Journal of Retailing*, **69**(1), Spring 1993, pp. 13–60.

Bitner, Mary Jo, 'Evaluating Service Encounters: The Effects of Physical Surroundings and Employee Responses'. *Journal of Marketing*, April 1990, pp. 69–82.

Björkman, Ingmar and Kock, Sören, 'Social Relationships and Business Networks: The Case of Western Companies in China'. *International Business Review*, **4**(4), 1997, pp. 519–535.

Bliemel, Friedhelm W. and Eggert, Andreas, *Relationship Marketing under Fire*. Kaiserslauten, Germany: University of Kaiserslauten, Schriftenreihe Marketing, Heft 4/97, 1997.

Blois, Keith, 'Relationship Marketing in Organizational Markets: When is it Appropriate?' *Journal of Marketing Management*, **12**, 1996, pp. 161–173.

Blomqvist, Ralf, Dahl, Johan and Haeger, Tomas, *Relationsmarknadsföring: strategi och metod i servicekonkurrens*. Gothenburg: IHM, 1993.

Blumberg, Paul, *The Predatory Society*. New York: Oxford University Press, 1989.

Booms, Bernhard H. and Bitner, Mary Jo, 'Marketing Strategies and Organization Structures for Service Firms', in Donnelly, James, and George, William R. (eds.), *Marketing of Services*. Chicago: American Marketing Association, 1982.

Boissevain, Jeremy, *Friends of Friends*. Oxford: Basil Blackwell, 1976.

Bradford, Hugh, 'A New Framework for Museum Marketing', in Kavanagh, Gaynor (ed.), *The Museums Profession: Internal and External Relations*. Leicester, UK: Leicester University Press, 1991.

Brandenburger, Adam M. and Nalebuff, Barry J., *Co-opetition*. Boston, MA: Harvard Business School Press, 1996.

Brandes, Ove and Brege, Staffan, *Marknadsledarskap*. Malmö: Liber, 1990.

Brodie, Roderick J., Coviello, Nicole E., Brookes, Richard W. and Little, Victoria, 'Towards a Paradigm Shift in Marketing? An Examination of Current Marketing Practices'. *Journal of Marketing Management*, **13**, 1997, pp. 383–406.

Brown, Stephen, *Postmodern Marketing*. London: Routledge, 1995.

Brownlie, Douglas and Saren, Michael, 'The Four Ps of the Marketing Concept: Prescriptive, Polemical, Permanent and Problematical,' *European Journal of Marketing*, **26**(4), 1992, pp.34–47.

Buck-Lew, M. and Edvinsson, L., *Intellectual Capital at Skandia*. Stockholm: Skandia, 1993.

Buttle, Francis (ed.), *Relationship Marketing: Theory and Practice*. London: Paul Chapman, 1996.

Buzzell, Robert D. and Gale, Bradley T., *The PIMS Principles: Linking Strategy to Performance*. New York: The Free Press, 1987.

Calonius, Henrik, *The Promise Concept*. Helsinki: Swedish School of Economics and Business Administration, 1987.

Cang, Stephen, 'Organisational Change and the Doctor-patient Relationship as the Model for Client-consultant Relationships'. Paper presented at *The Seminar on Client-Consultant Relationships*. Groningen: University of Groningen, The Netherlands, November 1976.

Carlsson, Rolf H., *Ägarstyrning*. Stockholm: Ekerlids Förlag, 1997.

Carlsson, Matts and Lundqvist, Mats, *Work with and Implementation of New Concepts for Management of Product Development – Some Emperical Findings*. Gothenburg: Chalmers, 1992.

Carlzon, Jan, *Moments of Truth*. Cambridge, MA: Ballinger, 1987.

Christopher, Martin, Payne, Adrian and Ballantyne, David, *Relationship Marketing*. Oxford: Butterworth-Heinemann 1991.

Cialdini, Robert B., *Influence*. New York: Quill, 1984.

Clark, Margaret S., 'Reactions to Aid in Communal and Exchange Relationships', in *New Directions in Helping*. New York: Academic Press, vol. 1, chapter 11, 1983, pp. 281–304.

Coase, Ronald H., 'The Nature of the Firm'. *Economica*, 1937, pp. 387–405.

Coase, Ronald H., 'The Institutional Structure of Production'. Stockholm: The Nobel Foundation, *Prize Lecture in Economic Science in Memory of Alfred Nobel*, 9 December 1991.

Cooper, Robin and Kaplan, Robert S., 'Profit Priorities from Activity-Based Costing'. *Harvard Business Review*, May–June 1991, pp. 130–135.

Cova, Bernard, 'Relationship Marketing: A View from the South', in Meenaghan, Tony (ed.), *New and Evolving Paradigms: The Emerging Future of Marketing*, Conference Proceedings. Chicago, IL: American Marketing Association and University College Dublin, 1997, pp. 657–672.

Cowles, Deborah L., 'Relationship Marketing for Transaction Marketing Firms: Viable Strategy via Command Performance', in Sheth, Jagdish N. and Parvatiyar, Atul (eds.), *Relationship Marketing: Theory, Methods and Applications. 1994 Research Conference Proceedings*. Atlanta, GA: Center for Relationship Marketing, Emory University, 1994.

Cram, Tony, *The Power of Relationship Marketing*. London: Pitman, 1994.

Crosby, Philip, *Quality Is Free*. New York: McGraw-Hill, 1979.

Crosby, Lawrence, Evans, Kenneth, and Cowles, Deborah, 'Relationship Quality in Services Selling: An Interpersonal Influence Perspective.' *Journal of Marketing*, **54**, July 1990, pp. 68–81.

Cutlip, S. M., Center, A. H., and Broom, G. M., *Effective Public Relations*. Engelwood Cliffs, NJ: Prentice-Hall, 1985.

Czepiel, John A., 'Managing Relationships with Customers: A Differentiating Philosophy of Marketing', in Bowen, D., Chase, R. and Cummings, T. (eds.), *Service Management Effectiveness*. San Francisco: Jossey-Bass, 1990, pp. 299–323.

Daffy, Chris, *Once a Customer, Always a Customer*. Dublin: The Oak Press, 1996.

Darby, M. R. and Karni, E., 'Free Competition and the Optimal Amount of Fraud'. *Journal of Law and Economics*, April 1973, pp. 67–86.

Davidow, William H. and Malone, Michael S., *The Virtual Corporation*. New York: Edward Burlingame Books/Harper Business 1992.

D'Aveni, Richard A., *Hypercompetition*. New York: The Free Press, 1994.

Davenport, Thomas H., *Information Ecology: Mastering the Information and Knowledge Environment*. New York: Oxford University Press, 1997.

Davis, Stanley M., *Future Perfect*. Reading, MA: Addison-Wesley, 1987.

DeBono, Edward, *Sur/Petition: Going Beyond Monopolies*. London: Fontana, 1992.

Degan, James M., 'Warehouse clubs move from revolution to evolution'. *Marketing News*, 3 August 1992, p. 8.

Delaryd, Bengt, *I Japan är kunden kung*. Stockholm: Svenska Dagbladet, 1989.

Deming, W. Edwards, *Out of the Crisis*. Cambridge, MA: MIT, 1986.

Donovan, Hedley, 'Managing Your Intellectuals'. *Fortune*, 23 October 1989, pp. 103–106.

Doz, Yves L. and Hamel, Gary, *Alliance Advantage*. Boston, MA: Harvard Business School Press, 1998.

Dreyfuss, Joel, 'Reinventing IBM.' *Fortune*, 14 August 1989, pp. 20–27.

Drucker, Peter F., *The Practice of Management*. New York: Harper & Row, 1954.

Drucker, Peter F., 'The Coming of the New Organization'. *Harvard Business Review*, January–February, 1988a, pp. 45–53.

Drucker, Peter F., 'Teaching the Work of Management'. *New Management Magazine,* **6**(2), Fall, 1988b.

Drucker, Peter F., *The New Realities*. Oxford: Heinemann, 1989.

Drucker, Peter F., *Managing the Nonprofit Organization*. New York: HarperCollins, 1990.

Duncan, Tom and Moriarty, Sandra E., 'A Communication-Based Marketing Model for Managing Relationships'. *Journal of Marketing*, **62,** April 1998, pp. 1–13.

Dwyer, F. Robert, Shurr, Paul H. and Oh, Sejo, 'Developing Buyer and Seller Relationships'. *Journal of Marketing*, **51,** April 1987, pp. 11–27.

Easton, Geoff and Håkansson, Håkan, 'Markets as Networks: Editorial Introduction'. *International Journal of Research in Marketing*, **13**(5), 1996, pp. 407–413.

Economist, 'BSN Who?' 14 May 1994, p. 7.

Edfeldt, Åke W, *Påverkan*. Stockholm: Proprius, 1992.

Edvardsson, Bo, Thomasson, Bertil and Øvretveit, John, *Quality of Service: Making It Really Work*. London: McGraw-Hill, 1994.

Edvinsson, Leif and Malone, Michael S., *Intellectual Capital*. New York: Harper Collins, 1997.

Ehrlemark, Gunnar, *OTOM Paper*, 7 November 1978 (as quoted in *The ForeSight Entrepreneur*, no. 3, 1989).

Englund, Karl, *Försäkring och fusioner*. Stockholm: Skandia, 1982.

Entine, Jon, 'Let Them Eat Brazil Nuts'. *Dollar and Sense*, March–April 1996, pp. 30–35.

Eriksson, Ann-Kristin and Åsberg, Maria, *Kostnadseffekter av affärsrelationer*. Uppsala: Uppsala University, Department of Business Studies, 1994.

Falcone, Giovanni and Padovani, Marcelle, *Cosa Nostra: Domarens kamp mot maffian*. Stockholm: Forum 1991.

Faltermayer, Edmund, 'Does Japan Play Fair?' *Fortune*, 7 September 1992, pp. 22–29.

Feurst, Ola, *Kost och hälsa i marknadsföringen*. Stockholm: Stockholm University, School of Business, 1991.

Fiorentini, Gianluca and Peltzman, Sam (eds.), *The Economics of Organized Crime*. Cambridge, UK: Cambridge University Press, 1995.

Fisk, Raymond P., Brown, Stephen W. and Bitner, Mary J. 'Tracking the Evolution of Services Marketing Literature', *Journal of Retailing*, **69**(1), Spring, 1993, pp. 61–103.

Ford, David (ed.), *Understanding Business Markets: Interaction, Relationships and Networks*. London: Academic Press, 1990.

Ford, David et al., *Managing Business Relationships*. Chichester, UK: Wiley, 1998.

Ford, D., Håkansson, H. and Johansson, J., 'How Do Companies Interact?' *Industrial Marketing & Purchasing*, **1**(1), 1986.

Fornell, Claes, 'A National Customer Satisfaction Barometer: The Swedish Experience'. *Journal of Marketing*, **56**, January 1992, pp. 6–21.

Fornell, Claes and Wernerfelt, B., 'Model for Customer Complaint Management' *Marketing Science*, no. 7, Summer, 1988, pp. 271–286.

Fornell, Claes and Westbrook, R. A., 'The Vicious Circle of Consumer Complaints'. *Journal of Marketing*, no. 48, Summer 1984, pp. 68–78.

Forrester, Jay W., 'A New Corporate Design', in Halal, William E., Geranmayeh, Ali and Pourdehead, John (eds.), *Internal Markets*. New York: Wiley, 1993.

Frankelius, Per, *Kirurgisk Marknadsföring*. Malmö: Liber, 1997.

Frenckner, Paulsson, 'ABC-kalkylen: vad behövs mer?' *Ekonomi & Styrning*, no. 2, 1993, pp. 26–29.

Fukuyama, Francis, *Trust*. New York: The Free Press, 1995.

Gabbot, Mark, 'Relationship Marketing and IT'. Paper presented at *The 6th Colloquium of Relationship Marketing*, Auckland: University of Auckland, December 1998.

Gadde, Lars-Erik, 'Developments in Distribution Channels for Industrial Goods', in Baker, Michael (ed.), *Perspectives on Marketing Management*. Chichester: Wiley, vol. 4, 1994.

Gates, Bill, *The Road Ahead*. New York: Viking, 1995.

Gerlach, Michael L., *Alliance Capitalism: The Social Organization of Japanese Business*. Berkley, CA: University of California Press, 1992.

Giarini, O. and Stahel W. R., *The Limits of Certainty: Facing Risks in the New Service Economy*. Dordrecht: Kluwer, 1993.

Glaser, Barney G., *Basics of Grounded Theory Analysis*. Mill Valley, CA: Sociology Press, 1992.

Glaser, Barney G. and Strauss, Anselm L., *The Discovery of Grounded Theory – Strategies for Qualitative Research*. New York: Aldine Publishing Co., 1967.

Goleman, Daniel, *Emotional Intelligence*. New York: Bantam Books, 1995.

Goodwin, Cathy, 'Private Roles in Public Encounter: Communal Relationships in Service Exchanges', in *Proceedings from the 3rd International Research Seminar in Service Management*. Aix-en-Provence: Institut d'Administration des Entreprises, Université d'Aix-Marseille, May 1994, pp. 312–332.

Granovetter, Mark, 'The Strength of Weak Ties. A Network Theory Revisited.' *American Journal of Sociology*, **78**(3), 1973, pp. 3–30.

Granovetter, Mark, 'Economic Action and Social Structure. The Problem of Embeddedness.' *American Journal of Sociology*, **91**(3), 1985, pp. 481–510.

Gray, Barbara, *Collaborating*. San Francisco, CA: Jossey-Bass, 1989.

Grönroos, Christian, *Service Management and Marketing*. New York: Lexington/Macmillan, 1990.

Grönroos, Christian, 'Facing the Challenge of Service Competition: The Economies of Service', in Kunst, Paul and Lemmik, Jos (eds.), *Quality Management in Services*. Assen/Maastricht: Van Gorcum, 1992.

Grönroos, Christian, 'Quo Vadis, Marketing? Toward a Relationship Marketing Paradigm'. *Journal of Marketing Management*, **10**, 1994, pp. 347–360.

Grönroos, Christian, 'Relationship Marketing Logic'. *Asia-Australia Marketing Journal*, vol. 4, 1996.

Grönroos, Christian and Gummesson, Evert (eds.), *Service Marketing – Nordic School Perspectives*. Stockholm: Stockholm University, School of Business, Research Report R 1985:2.

Gruen, Thomas W. and Ferguson, Jeffery M., 'Using Memberships as a Marketing Tool: Issues and Applications', in Sheth, Jagdish N. and Parvatiyar, Atul (eds.), *Relationship Marketing: Theory, Methods and Applications, Proceedings from the Second Research Conference on Relationship Marketing*. Atlanta, GA: Center for Relationship Marketing, Emory University, June, 1994.

Gummesson, Evert, *Marknadsföring och inköp av konsulttjänster*. Stockholm: Akademilitteratur/MTC/University of Stockholm, 1977.

Gummesson, Evert, 'A New Concept of Marketing'. Proceedings from the *European Marketing Academy (EMAC) Annual Conference*, Institut d'Etudes Commerciales de Grenoble, France, April, 1983.

Gummesson, Evert, *Marketing of Public Telecommunications*. Stockholm: Ericsson, 1984.

Gummesson, Evert, *Quality – The Ericsson Approach*. Stockholm: Ericsson, 1987a.

Gummesson, Evert, 'The New Marketing: Developing Long-term Interactive Relationships', *Long Range Planning*, **20**(4), 1987b, pp. 10–20.

Gummesson, Evert, 'Service Quality: A Holistic View', in Brown, S.W., Gummesson, E., Edvardsson, B. and Gustavsson, B. (eds.), *Service Quality*. Lexington, MA: Lexington Books, 1991, pp. 3–22.

Gummesson, Evert, 'Quality Dimensions: What to Measure in Service Organizations', in Swartz, Teresa A., Bowen, David, E. and Brown, Stephen W. (eds.), *Advances in Services Marketing and Management*. Greenwich, CT: JAI Press, 1992.

Gummesson, Evert, *Quality Management in Service Organizations*. New York: ISQA, 1993.

Gummesson, Evert, 'Making Relationship Marketing Operational'. *Service Industry Management*, **5**(5), 1994, pp. 5–20.

Gummesson, E., 'Implementation Requires a Relationship Marketing Paradigm' *Journal of the Academy of Marketing Science*, **26**(3), July, 1998, pp. 242–249.

Gummesson, Evert, *Qualitative Methods in Management Research*. Newbury Park: Sage, revised edition, 1999.

Gummesson, Evert, Lehtinen, Uolevi, and Grönroos, Christian , 'Comment on Nordic Perspectives on Relationship Marketing', *European Journal of Marketing,* **31**(1–2), 1997, pp. 10–16.

Gumpert, David E., 'Big Company, Small Company: The New American Partnership.' *Forbes*, 20 July 1992, pp. 225–240.

Gustavsson, Bengt, *The Transcendent Organization*. Stockholm: Stockholm University, 1992.

Hadenius, Stig and Weibull, Lennart, *Massmedier*. Stockholm: Bonnier Alba, 1993.

Håkansson, Håkan and Snehota, Ivan, *Marknadsplanering – Ett sätt att skapa nya problem?* Lund, Sweden: Studentlitteratur, 1976.

Håkansson, Håkan and Snehota, Ivan, *Developing Relationships in Business Marketing*. London: Routledge, 1995.

Halal, William E., Geranmayeh, Ali and Pourdehead, John (eds.), *Internal Markets*. New York: Wiley, 1993.

Halinen-Kaila, Aino, *Relationship Marketing in Professional Services*. London: Routledge, 1997.

Hallén, Lars and Widersheim-Paul, Finn, 'Psychic Distance and Buyer-Seller Interaction'. *Organisation, Marked og Samfunn*, **16**(5), 1979, pp. 308–324.

Hallgren, Mats, 'Spelet kring en order'. *Veckans Affärer*, no. 20, 14 May 1987.

Hamel, Gary and Prahalad, C.K., *Competing for the Future*. Boston, MA: Harvard Business School Press, 1994.

Hammer, Michael and Champy, James, *Reengineering the Corporation*. New York: HarperBusiness, 1993.

Handy, Charles, *The Age of Unreason*. Boston, MA: Harvard Business School Press, 1990.

Harper, Ross, 'Hunt for Holy Grail of Dispute Mediation'. *Scottish Gazette*, 20 October 1993, p. 10.

Harrington, James H., *Business Process Improvement*. New York: McGraw-Hill, 1991.

Hart, Christopher W. L. and Bogan, Christopher E., *The Baldrige*. New York: McGraw-Hill, 1992.

Hartley, Robert F., *Marketing Successes*. New York: Wiley, 1985.

Harung, Harald S., 'A World-Leading, Learning Organization: A Case Study of Tomra Systems'. *The Learning Organization*, **3** (4), 1996, pp. 22–34.

Harung, Harald S., *Invincible Leadership: Building Peak Perfomance Organizations by Harnessing the Unlimited Power of Consciousness.* Fairfield, Iowa: MUM Press, 1999.

Hauser J. R. and Clausing D., 'The House of Quality'. *Harvard Business Review*, no. 3, May–June, 1988.

Hawkins, Leonard S., *How To Succeed in Network Marketing.* London: Piatkus 1991.

Hedberg, B., Dahlgren, G., Hansson, J. and Olve, N.-G., *Virtual Organizations and Beyond: Discover Imaginary Systems.* London: Wiley, 1997.

Heidenry, John, *Theirs Was the Kingdom.* New York: W.W. Norton & Co., 1993.

Helling, Jan, *Världsmästarna.* Stockholm: Sellin, 2nd revised edition, 1992.

Hemmungs Wirtén, Eva, 'Mannen som var en kamera'. *Tur & Retur*, no. 3, 1992, pp. 42–47.

Heskett, James L., Sasser, W. Earl and Hart, Christopher W. L., *Service Breakthroughs.* New York: The Free Press, 1990.

Hessling, Torbjörn, *Att spara eller inte spara – vilken fråga!* Stockholm: Sparfrämjandet, 1990.

von Hippel, E, *The Sources of Innovation.* Oxford: Oxford University Press, 1988.

Hirschman, Albert O., *Exit, Voice and Loyalty.* Cambridge, MA: Harvard University Press, 1970.

Holmlund, Maria, *Perceived Quality in Business Relationships.* Helsinki: Swedish School of Economics and Business Administration, 1997.

Howard, Philip, *The Death of Common Sense: How Law Is Suffocating America.* New York: Random House, 1994.

Hultbom, Christina, *Intern handel: köpar/säljarrelationer inom stora företag.* Uppsala: Uppsala University, Department of Business, 1990.

Hunt, Shelby D., and Morgan, Robert M., 'The Comparative Advantage Theory of Competition'. *Journal of Marketing*, **59**, April 1995, pp. 1–15.

Iacobucci, Dawn (ed.), *Networks in Marketing.* Thousand Oaks, CA: Sage, 1996.

Iacocca, Lee (with Novak, W.), *Iacocca.* USA: Bantam Books, 1984.

Info, 'Hon har kameran i fokus', no. 1996, p. 53.

International Management, Advertisement for Siemens. July/August 1993, pp. 20–21.

International Management, 'Black market turns importer to Iran for caviar'. June 1994, pp. 12–13.

Jackson, Barbara Bund, *Winning and Keeping Industrial Customers.* Lexington, MA: Lexington Books, 1985a.

Jackson, Barbara Bund, 'Build Customer Relationships That Last'. *Harvard Business Review*, November-December 1985b, pp. 120–128.

Jakobsson, Peter, *Internet.* Lund, Sweden: Studentlitteratur, 1995.

Jaques, Elliott, 'In Praise of Hierarchy'. *Harvard Business Review*, no. 1, January–February 1990.

Johansen, Jon Ivar and Monthelie, Caroline, *Lojalitetsredovisning.* Gothenburg: InfoNet Scandinavia, 1996.

Johanson, Jan, 'Marknadsnätverkens uppväxtår och framtid'. *MTC-Kontakten*, 1994.

Johanson, Jan and Mattsson, Lars-Gunnar, 'Interorganizational Relations in Industrial Systems: A Network Approach Compared with the Transaction Cost Approach'. *International Studies of Management and Organization*, **XVII**(1), Spring 1987, pp. 34–48.

Johnson, Thomas H., *Relevance Regained.* New York: The Free Press, 1992.

Johnson, Thomas H. and Kaplan, Robert S., *Relevance Lost: The Rise and Fall of Management Acounting.* Boston, MA: Harvard Business School Press, 1987.

Johnsson, Thomas and Hägg, Ingemund, 'Extrapreneurs – Between Markets and Hierarchies'. *International Studies of Management & Organisation*, **XVII**(1), 1987, pp. 64–74.

Jones Yang, Dori and Warner, Joan, 'Hear the Muzak, Buy the Ketchup'. *Business Week*, 28 June 1993, pp. 40–42.

Judd, V. C., 'Differentiate with the 5th P: People'. *Industrial Marketing Management*, November, 1987.

Juran, J. M., *Juran on Quality by Design.* New York: The Free Press, 1992.

Kahn, Sikander and Yoshihara, Hideki, *Strategy and Performance of Foreign Companies in Japan.* Westport, CT: Quorom Books, 1994.

Kaikati, Jack G., quoted in *Strategic Direction*, December 1993, pp. 20–22.

Kanfer, Stefan, *The Last Empire: De Beers, Diamonds of the World.* New York: Farrar Straus Giroux, 1996.

Kanter, Rosabeth Moss, *When Giants Learn to Dance.* New York: Simon and Schuster, 1989.

Kaplan, Robert S. and Norton, David P., *The Balanced Scorecard.* Boston, MA: Harvard Business School Press, 1996.

Karaszi, Peter, *Använd pressen.* Stockholm: PK FinInformation, 1991.

Karpesjö, Anders, *Miljöprofilering.* Malmö: Liber Ekonomi, 1992.

Kingman-Brundage, Jane, George, William R., and Bowen, David E., 'Service Logic: Achieving Service System Integration.' *International Journal of Service Industry Management*, **6**(4), 1995, pp. 20–39.

Kirkpatrick, David, 'Breaking up IBM'. *Fortune*, 27 July 1992, p. 120.

Kotkin, Joel, *Tribes.* New York: Random House, 1993.

Kotler, Philip,'Megamarketing'. *Harvard Business Review*, March-April 1986, pp. 117–124.

Kotler, Philip, 'Total Marketing'. *Business Week Advance*, Executive Brief, **2**, 1992.

Kotler, Philip, *Marketing Management.* Englewood Cliffs, NJ: Prentice-Hall, 9th edition, 1997.

Kotler, Philip and Andreasen, Alan R., *Strategic Marketing for Non-Profit Institutions.* Englewood Cliffs, NJ: Prentice-Hall, 1991.

Kotler, Philip, Gregor, William and Rodgers, William, 'The Marketing Audit Comes of Age'. *Sloan Management Review,* Winter 1989, pp. 49–62.

Lappalainen, Tomas, *Maffian.* Stockholm: Forum, 1993.

Laurelli, Rolf, *TOTAL-säljaren.* Lund: Studentlitteratur, 1979.

Lehtinen, Jarmo R., 'Improving Service Quality by Analysing the Service Production Process', in Grönroos, C., and Gummesson, E. (eds.), *Service Marketing–Nordic School Perspectives.* Stockholm: Stockholm University, School of Business, Research Report R 1985:2, pp. 110–119.

Lehtinen, Uolevi, Hankimaa, Anna, and Mittilä, Tuula, 'On Measuring the Intensity in Relationship Marketing', in Sheth J. N., and Parvatiyar, A. (eds.), *Relationship Marketing: Theory, Methods and Applications*, 1994 Research Conference Proceedings. Atlanta GA: Center for Relationship Marketing, Emory University, 1994.

Lester, Tom, 'The Rise of the Network'. *International Management*, June 1992, pp. 72–73.

Levitt, Theodore, *The Marketing Imagination.* New York: The Free Press, 1983.

Liljander, Veronika and Strandvik, Tore, 'The Nature of Customer Relationships in Services', in Swartz, Teresa A., Bowen, David E. and Brown, Stephen W. (eds.), *Advances in Services Marketing and Management.* Greenwich, CT: JAI Press, vol. 4, 1995.

Liljegren, Göran, *Interdependens och dynamik i långsiktiga relationer.* Stockholm: MTC/EFI, 1988.

Linn, Carl Eric, *Metaprodukten och marknaden.* Malmö: Liber, 1985.

Lorange, Peter and Roos, Johan, *Strategic Alliances.* Oxford, UK: Blackwell, 1992.

Lovelock, Christopher H., 'Classifying Services to Gain Strategic Advantage'. *Journal of Marketing*, **47**, Summer 1983, pp. 9–20.

Lovelock, Christopher H., Patterson, Paul G., and Walker, Rhett H., *Services Marketing: Australia and New Zealand*. Sydney: Prentice-Hall, 1998.

Lowe, Andy, 'Small Hotel Survival: An Inductive Approach'. *The International Journal of Hospitality Management*, **7**(3), 1988, pp. 197–223.

Lowe, Andy, 'Managing the Post-merger Aftermath by Default Remodelling'. *Management Decision*, **36** (3), 1998, pp. 102–110.

Lu, David J., 'Translator's Introduction', in Ishikawa, K., *What Is Total Quality Control? The Japanese Way*. Englewood Cliffs, NJ: Prentice-Hall, 1985.

Lunn, Terry, 'Customer Service: The Joshua Tetley Experience'. Dublin: *Third National Conference of the NSAI*, 1990.

Macneil, I. R., 'Relational Contract: What We Do and Do Not Know'. *Northwestern University Law Review*, **78**, 1983, pp. 340–418.

Macneil, I. R., 'Values in Contract'. *Winsconsin Law Review*, 1985, pp. 483–525.

Malcolm Baldrige National Quality Award, *1997 Criteria for Performance Excellence*. Gaithersburg, MD: United States Department of Commerce, 1997.

Mårtensson, Rita, *Marknadskommunikation*. Lund, Sweden: Studentlitteratur, 1984.

Martin, Michael H., 'Why the Web Is Still a No-Shop Zone'. *Fortune*, 5 February 1996, pp. 67–68.

Mattsson, Lars-Gunnar, 'Relationship Marketing and the Markets-as-Networks Approach'. *Journal of Marketing Management*, **13**(5), July 1997, pp. 447–462.

Mattsson, Lars-Gunnar and Lundgren, Anders, 'En paradox? – konkurrens i industriella nätverk'. *MTC-kontakten*, no. 22, 1992/93, pp. 8–9.

McCarthy, Jerome E., *Basic Marketing: A Managerial Approach*. Homewood, IL: Richard D. Irwin, 1994 (1960).

McDonald, Malcolm, *Marketing Plans*. Oxford, UK: Butterworth-Heinemann, 1995.

McDonald, Malcolm, Millman, Tony and Rogers, Beth, 'Key Account Management: Theory, Practice and Challenges'. *Journal of Marketing Management*, no. 13, 1997, pp. 737–757.

McKenna, Regis, *The Regis Touch*. USA: Addison-Wesley, 1985.

McKenna, Regis, *Relationship Marketing*. Reading, MA: Addison-Wesley, 1991.

McKinsey, *A Career with McKinsey & Company*, 1991.

Michels, Antony J., 'Customers Drive Company Tie-Ups'. *Fortune*, 27 January 1992, p. 8.

Mills, D. Q., *Rebirth of the Corporation*. New York: Wiley, 1991.

Möller, Kristian and Halinen-Kaila, Aino, 'Relationship Marketing: Its Disciplinary Roots and Future Directions', in Tikkanen, Henrikki (ed.), *Marketing and International Business: Essays in the Honour of Professor Karin Holstius*. Turku: Turku School of Economics and Business Administration, Series A–2, 1998, pp. 171–198.

Möller, Kristian and Wilson, David (eds.), *Business Marketing: Interaction and Network Approach*. Boston, MA: Kluwer, 1996.

Moore, James F., *The Death of Competition*. Chichester, UK: Wiley, 1996.

Morgan, Gareth, *Images of Organization*. Newbury Park: Sage, revised edition, 1997.

Morgan, R. M. and Hunt, Shelby D., 'The Commitment-Trust Theory of Relationship Marketing'. *Journal of Marketing*, no. 58, July, 1994, pp. 20–38.

Nader, Ralph, *Unsafe at Any Speed*. New York: Grossman, 1965.

Naisbitt, John, *Global Paradox*. New York: William Morrow, 1994.

Naisbitt, John and Aburdene, Patricia, *Megatrends 2000*. New York: William Morrow, 1990.

Nakane, Chie, *Japanese Society*. New York: Penguin, 1981.

Nelson, Philip, 'Advertising as Information'. *Journal of Political Economy,* July–August 1970, pp. 729–754.

Neuhauser, Peg C., *Tribal Warfare in Organizations.* Cambridge, MA: Ballinger, 1988.

Newsweek, 'The Black Economy'. 30 June, 1986, pp. 20–26.

Newsweek, 'The Kissinger Clique'. 27 March 1990, pp. 34–35.

Newsweek, 'Eyes on the Future'. 31 May 1993, pp. 35ff.

Nilson, Torsten H., *Värdeladdad marknadsföring.* Malmö: Liber-Hermods, 1993.

Nilsson, John Peter, 'Disney à go-go'. *Nobis Nyheter,* no. 3, 1993, pp. 25–28, 40.

Nocera, Joseph, 'Fatal Litigation'. *Fortune,* 16 October 1995, pp. 40–57.

Norman, Donald A, *The Psychology of Everyday Things.* New York: Basic Books, 1988.

Normann, Richard, *Service Management.* Chichester, UK: Wiley, 1991.

Normann, Richard and Ramírez, Rafael, 'From Value Chain to Value Constellation'. *Harvard Business Review,* July–August 1993, pp. 65–77.

North, Douglass C., 'Economic Performance Through Time', Stockholm: The Nobel Foundation, *Prize Lecture in Economic Science in Memory of Alfred Nobel,* Stockholm, 9 December, 1993.

Nystrom, Paul C., Hedberg, Bo and Starbuck, William H., 'Interacting Processes as Organization Designs', in Kilmann, Ralph H., Pondy, L. R. and Slevin, D. P. (eds.), *The Management of Organization Design.* New York: American Elsevier, 1976, pp. 209–230.

Ohlson, Johan, 'Interview with Ove Sjögren'. *Upp&Ner,* no. 6, 1994, pp. 6–9.

Ohmae, Kenichi, *Triad Power–The Coming Shape of Global Competition.* New York: The Free Press, 1985.

Ohmae, Kenichi, *The End of the Nation State.* New York: The Free Press, 1995.

Olsen, Morten, *Kvalitet i banktjänster.* Stockholm: Stockholm University/CTF, 1992.

Ortmark, Åke, *Ja-sägarna.* Stockholm: Gedins, 1996.

Ottman, Jacquelyn A., *Green Marketing.* Lincolnwood, IL: NTC Business Books, 1992.

Palmer, Adrian and Bejou, David, 'The Effects on Gender on the Development of Relationships between Clients and Financial Advisers'. *Bank Marketing,* **13**(3), 1995.

Parlour, Richard, 'Europe's Fight Against Dirty Money'. *European Business Report,* 3rd Quarter, 1993, pp. 63–66.

Pattinson, Hugh and Brown, Linden, 'Metamorphosis in the Marketspace'. *Irish Marketing Review,* **6**, 1996, pp. 55–68.

Patton, Michael Quinn, *Qualitative Evaluation and Research Methods.* Newbury Park, CA: Sage Publications, 1990.

Paulin, Michèle, Perrien, Jean, Ferguson, Ronald, 'Relational Contract Norms and the Effectiveness of Commercial Banking Relationships'. *Service Industry Management,* **8**(5), 1997, pp. 435–452.

Paulsen, Mats, 'Statoil rustar mot maffian'. *Dagens Industri,* 3, November 1994, p. 15.

Payne, Adrian, *The Essence of Services Marketing.* London: Prentice-Hall, 1993.

Payne, Adrian and Rickard, John, *Relationship Marketing, Customer Retention and Service Firm Profitability.* Cranfield: Cranfield School of Management, 1994.

Payne, Adrian, Christopher, Martin, Clark, Moira and Peck, Helen, *Relationship Marketing for Competitive Advantage.* Oxford: Butterworth-Heinemann, 1995.

Pelton, Lou E., Strutton, David and Lumpkin, James R., *Marketing Channels: A Relationship Management Approach.* Chicago, IL: Irwin, 1997.

Peppers, Don and Rogers, Martha, *The One to One Future.* New York: Currency/Doubleday, 1993.

Peppers, Don and Rogers, Martha, *Enterprise One to One.* London: Piatkus, 1997.

Peters, Tom, *Thriving on Chaos*. New York: Macmillan, 1985.

Peters, Tom, *Liberation Management*. New York: Alfred A. Knopf, 1992.

Peters, Tom and Waterman, Robert J. Jr., *In Search of Excellence*. New York: Harper & Row, 1982.

Pirsig, Robert M., *Lila: An Inquiry Into Morals*. London: Corgi Books, 1992.

Polanyi, Michael, *Personal Knowledge*. London: Routledge & Kegan Paul, 1962.

Popcorn, Faith, *The Popcorn Report*. London: Century Business, 1992.

Pope, N. W., 'Mickey Mouse Marketing'. *American Banker*, 25 July 1979a.

Pope, N. W., 'More Mickey Mouse Marketing'. *American Banker*, 12 September 1979b.

Porter, Clive, quoted in *The Marketing Strategy Letter*, May 1993, p. 14.

Porter, Michael E., *Competitive Strategy*. New York: The Free Press, 1980.

Porter, Michael E., *Competitive Advantage*. New York: The Free Press, 1985.

Porter, Michael E., *The Competitive Advantage of Nations*. New York: The Macmillan Press, 1990.

Postman, Neil, *Amusing Ourselves to Death*. New York: Penguin Books, 1987.

Price, Linda, Arnould, Eric and Tierney, P., 'The Wilderness Servicescape' in *Proceedings of the 4th International Research Seminar in Service Management*. La Londe, France: Université Aix-Marseille, 1996.

Prigogene, Ilya and Stengers, Isabelle, *Order out of Chaos*. London: Fontana/Flamingo, 1985.

Quinn, Fergal, *Crowning the Customer*. Dublin: O'Brien Press, 1990.

Quinn, Fergal,'The Boomerang Principle'. *European Business Report*, Spring, 1994, pp. 36–39.

Quinn, James Brian, *The Intelligent Enterprise*. New York: The Free Press, 1992.

Ramsey, Richard David, ''It's Absurd': Swedish Managers' Views of America's Litigious Society'. *Scandinavian Journal of Management*, **6**(1), pp. 31–44, 1991.

Rapp, Stan and Collins, Tom, *The Great Marketing Turnaround*. Englewood Cliffs, NJ: Prentice-Hall, 1990.

Rapp, Stan and Collins, Tom, *The New MaxiMarketing*. New York: McGraw-Hill, 1995.

Rayport, J. F. and Sviokla, J. J., 'Managing in the Marketspace'. *Harvard Business Review*, November-December, 1994, pp. 142–150.

Reichheld, Frederick F., *The Loyalty Effect*. Boston, MA: Harvard Business School Press, 1996.

Reichheld, Frederick F. and Sasser, W. E. Jr., 'Zero Defections: Quality Comes to Services'. *Harvard Business Review*, September–October 1990.

Rein, Irving J., Kotler, Philip and Stoller, Martin, R., *High Visibility*. London: Heinemann, 1987.

Reynoso, Javier F. and Moores, Brian, 'Internal Relationships'. In Buttle, Francis (ed.), *Relationship Marketing: Theory and Practice*. London: Paul Chapman, 1996.

Rice, Faye, 'Be a Smarter Frequent Flyer'. *Fortune*, 22 February, 1993, pp. 56–60.

Rifa, *Vi skapar framtidens Rifa*. Stockholm, 1983.

Robèrt, Karl-Henrik, *Det nödvändiga steget*. Stockholm: Affärsförlaget Mediautveckling, 1992.

Roddick, Anita, *Body and Soul*. New York: Crown Publishers, 1991.

Root, Paul H., 'Relationship Marketing in the Age of Paradox: What Do We Know? What Do We Need to Know?' Presentation at the *14th American Marketing Association Faculty Consortium*, Emory Business School, Atlanta, GA, June, 1994.

Rossander, Olle, *Japanskt ledarskap*. Stockholm: Svenska Dagbladet/ Affärsvärlden, 1992.

Rowan, Roy, 'The 50 Biggest Mafia Bosses'. *Fortune*, 10 November 1986, pp. 20–32.

The Royal Society for the Encouragement of Arts, Manufacture & Commerce, *Tomorrow's Company: The Role of Business in a Changing World*. London, 1994.

Rust, Roland, T., Zahorik, Anthony J. and Keiningham, Timothy L., *Return on Quality*. Chicago, IL: Probus, 1994.

Salzer, Miriam, *Identity Across Borders: A Study in the IKEA-World*. Linköping: University of Linköping, 1994.

Saren, Mike J. and Tzokas, Nikos X., 'The Nature of the Product in Market Relationships', in Bloemer, J., Lemmik, J. and Kasper, H. (eds.), *Marketing: Its Dynamics and Challenges, Proceedings from the 23rd EMAC Conference*. Maastricht: European Marketing Academy, May, 1994.

SAS, *The Quality Book*. Stockholm: SAS, 1987.

Scheuing, Eberhard E., *The Power of Partnering*. New York: Amacom 1994.

Scheuing, Eberhard E., *Creating Customers for Life*. Portland, OR: Productivity Press, 1995.

Schlender, Brenton R., 'Apple's Japanese Ally'. *Fortune*, 4 November 1991, pp. 95–96.

Schlesinger, Leonard A. and Hallowell, Roger H., 'Putting the Service Profit Chain to Work', in Scheuing, Eberhard E. and Christopher, William F., *The Service Quality Handbook*. New York: Amacom 1994.

Schlesinger, Leonard L. and Heskett, James L., 'Breaking the Cycle of Failure in Services.' *Sloan Management Review*, Spring, 1991.

Schlossberg, Howard, 'Frequent mileage club sends consumers running to shoe stores'. *Marketing News*, 3 August 1992, p. 12.

Schlossberg, Howard, 'Home Club discounts give renters reason to stay'. *Marketing News*, 15 February 1993, p. 15.

Schneider, Benjamin, 'HRM–A Service Perspective'. *Service Industry Management*, **5**(1), pp. 64–76, 1994.

Schön, Donald A., *The Reflective Practitioner – How Professionals Think in Action*. New York: Basic Books, 1983.

Scott, John, *Social Network Analysis*. London: Sage, 1991.

Senge, Peter M., *The Fifth Discipline*. New York: Doubleday/Currency, 1990.

Sewell, Carl, *Customers for Life*. New York: Doubleday, 1990.

Shamir, Boas, 'Between Gratitude and Gratuity'. *Annals of Tourism Research*, **11**, pp. 59–78, 1984.

Sheth, Jagdish N., 'The Domain of Relationship Marketing', handout at the *Second Research Conference on Relationship Marketing*. Atlanta, GA: Centre for Relationship Marketing, Emory University, 1994.

Sheth, Jagdish N. and Parvatiyar, Atul, 'The Evolution of Relationship Marketing'. Paper presented at the *Sixth Conference on Historical Thoughts in Marketing*, Atlanta, GA, May 1993.

Shostack, G. Lynn, 'How to Design a Service'. In Donnelly, J. H. and George, W. R. (eds.), *Marketing of Services*. Chicago, IL: American Marketing Association, 1981.

Sisula-Tulokas, Lena, *Dröjmålsskador vid passagerartransport*. Helsingfors: Finlands Juristförbund, 1985.

Skandia Annual Report Supplements. Stockholm: Skandia, 1995, 1996, 1997.

Smith, Craig, 'The New Corporate Philanthropy'. *Harvard Business Review*, May–June 1994, pp. 105–116.

Smith, P. G. and Laage-Hellman, J., 'Small Group Analysis of Industrial Networks', in

Axelsson, Björn and Easton, Geoffrey (eds.), *Industrial Networks*. London: Routledge, 1992.

Snehota, Ivan and Söderlund, Magnus, 'Relationship Marketing – What Does It Promise and What Does It Deliver?' in Andersson, Per (ed.), *Proceedings from the 27th EMAC Conference, Track 1, Market Relationships*. Stockholm: EMAC, May, 1998.

Södergren, Birgitta, *När pyramiderna rivits*. Stockholm: Timbro/Affärsledaren, 1987.

Södergren, Birgitta, *Decentralisering: Förändring i företag och arbetsliv*. Stockholm: EFI, 1992.

Solomon, Robert C., *Ethics and Excellence*. Oxford: Oxford University Press, 1992.

Stacey, Ralph D., *Strategic Management and Organisational Dynamics*. London: Pitman, 2nd edition, 1996.

Stern, Louis W., and Reve, Torger, 'Distribution Channels as Political Economies: A Framework for Comparative Analysis'. *Journal of Marketing*, **44**, Summer, 1980, pp. 52–64.

Stern, Louis W., El-Ansary, Adel I., and Coughlan, Anne T., *Marketing Channels*. Upper Saddle River, NJ: Prentice-Hall, 1996.

Stewart, Thomas A., *Intellectual Capital*. New York: Doubleday/Currency, 1997.

Storbacka, Kaj, *The Nature of Customer Relationship Profitability*. Helsinki: Swedish School of Economics and Business Administration, 1994.

Storbacka, Kaj, Strandvik, Tore and Grönroos, Christian, 'Managing Customer Relationships for Profit: The Dynamics of Relationship Quality'. *Service Industry Management*, **5**(5), 1994, pp. 21–38.

Strandvik, Tore and Törnroos, Jan-Åke, 'Discovering Relationscapes – Extending the Horizon of Relationship Strategies in Marketing', in Meenaghan, Tony (ed.), *New and Evolving Paradigms: The Emerging Future of Marketing*, Conference Proceedings. Chicago, IL: American Marketing Association and University College Dublin, 1997.

Sundqvist, Sven-Ivan, *Exit PG*. Stockholm: T. Fischer, 1994.

Sveiby, Karl Erik, *The New Organizational Wealth*. San Francisco, CA: Berret-Koehler, 1997.

Sveiby, Karl Erik and Risling, Anders, *Kunskapsföretaget*. Malmö: Liber, 1986.

Svengren, Lisbeth, *Industriell design som strategisk resurs*. Lund: Lund University Press, 1995.

Swedish Coalition of Service Industries, *Tjänsteföretagens värde*. Stockholm, 1993.

Taira, Koji and Wada, Teiichi, 'Business-Government relations in modern Japan: a Todai-Yakkai-Zaikai complex?', in Mizruchi, Mark S. and Schwartz, Michael (eds.), *Intercorporate Relations*. Cambridge: Cambridge University Press, 1987.

TARP, *Consumer Complaint Handling in America: An Update Study*. Part II, assigned by US Office of Consumer Affairs, 1 April 1986, p. 50.

Teutenberg, Penny, 'Renaming the Kiwi.' *New Zealand Marketing Magazine*, April 1997, pp. 28–34.

Thorelli, Hans B., 'Networks: Between Markets and Hierarchies'. *Strategic Management Journal*, no. 7, 1986, pp. 37–51.

Time, 'Corruption 101'. 10 May 1993, p. 16.

Tjosvold, Dean, *Teamwork for Customers*. San Francisco: Jossey-Bass, 1993.

Törnqvist, Gunnar, 'Det upplösta rummet – begrepp och teoretiska ansatser inom geografin', in Karlqvist, Anders (ed.), *Nätverk*. Stockholm: Gidlunds/Institutet för framtidsstudier, 1990.

Tuominen, Pekka, 'Investor Relationship Marketing', in Tuominen, Pekka (ed.), *Emerging Perspectives in Marketing*, Turku, Finland: Turku School of Economics and Business Administration, 1996, pp. 185–210.

Treacy, Michael and Wiersema, Fred, *The Discipline of Market Leaders*. Reading, MA: Addison-Wesley, 1995.

Tse, Eliza C. and West, Joseph, 'Development Strategies for International Hospitality Markets', in Teare, Richard and Olsen, Michael, *International Hospitality Management*. London: Pitman, 1992.

Vandermerwe, Sandra, *From Tin Soldiers to Russian Dolls: Creating Added Value Through Services*. Oxford: Butterworth-Heinemann, 1993.

Varey, Richard J., 'Internal Marketing: A Review and Some Inter-disciplinary Research Challenges'. *Service Industry Management*, **6**(1), 1995.

Vedin, Bengt-Arne, *Elektroniska marknader – dagligvara eller vision*. Teldok Info no. 15, December 1995.

Verbeke, Willem and Peelen, Ed, 'Redefining the New Selling Practices in an Era of Hyper Competition'. Paper presented at the workshop *Relationship Marketing in an Era of Hypercompetition*, Erasmus University and EIASM, Rotterdam, May 1996.

Waksberg, Arkadij, *Sovjetmaffian*. Stockholm: Norstedts, 1992.

Waksberg, Arkadij, 'Rysk prostitution går över alla gränser'. *Svenska Dagbladet*, 13 June 1994.

Walsh, James, The Triads Go Global'. Cover Story, *Time*, 1 February 1993, pp. 36–41.

Ward, Tony, Frew, Edwina and Caldow, Debra, 'An Extended List of the Dimensions of 'Relationship' in Consumer Service Product Marketing: A Pilot Study', in Meenaghan, Tony (ed.), *New and Evolving Paradigms: The Emerging Future of Marketing*. Conference Proceedings. Chicago, IL: American Marketing Association and University College Dublin, 1997.

Webster, Frederick E., 'The Changing Role of Marketing in the Corporation'. *Journal of Marketing*, no. 56, October 1992, pp. 1–17.

Weick, Karl E., *The Social Psychology of Organizing*. Reading, MA: Addison-Wesley, 1979.

Weitz, Barton A. and Jap, Sandy D., 'Relationship Marketing and Distribution Channels'. *Journal of the Academy of Marketing Science*, **23**(4), Fall 1995, pp. 305–320.

Wennberg, Inge, interview with Göran Arvidsson, 'Internpriser behövs', *Ekonomi & Styrning*, no. 2, 1994, pp. 18–20.

Wiedenbaum, Murray and Hughes, Samuel, *The Bamboo Network*. New York: The Free Press, 1996.

Wikström, Solveig and Normann, Richard, *Knowledge and Value*. London: Routledge, 1994.

Wilkinson, Ian F. and Young, Louise C., *Business Dancing – Understanding and Managing Interfirm Relations*. Asia-Australia Marketing Journal, **2**(1), 1994, pp. 67–79.

Williamson, Oliver E., *Markets and Hierarchies: Analysis and Antitrust Implications*. New York: The Free Press, 1975.

Williamson, Oliver E., 'The Economics of Organization: The Transaction Cost Approach'. *American Journal of Sociology*, **87**(3), 1981, pp. 548–577.

Williamson, Oliver E., *The Economic Institutions of Capitalism*. New York: The Free Press, 1985.

Williamson, Oliver E., 'The Firm as a Nexus of Treaties: an Introduction', in Aoki, Masahiko, Gustafsson, Bo and Williamson, Oliver E (eds.), *The Firm as a Nexus of Treaties*. London: Sage, 1990.

Wilson, Aubrey, *The Marketing of Professional Services*. London: McGraw-Hill, 1972.

Winai, Peter, *Gränsorganisationer*. Malmö: Liber, 1989.

Womack, James P., Jones, Daniel T. and Roos, Daniel, *The Machine that Changed the World*. New York: Macmillan, 1990.

Woodruffe, Helen, *Services Marketing*. London: Pitman, 1995.

Worthington, S. and Horne S., 'Charity Affinity Credit Cards – Marketing Synergy for Both Issuers and Charities?' *Journal of Marketing Management*, **9**, 1993, pp. 301–313.

Wright, Richard W. and Pauli, Gunter A., *The Second Wave*. London: Waterlow Publishers, 1987.

Wurman, Richard Samuel, *Information Anxiety*. New York: Doubleday, 1989.

Yunus, Muhammad, *Grameen Bank: Experiences and Reflections*. Bangladesh: Grameen Bank, 1992.

Zeithaml, Valerie A., Parasuraman, A. and Berry, Leonard L., *Delivering Quality Service*. New York: The Free Press, 1990.

Zeithaml, Valerie A. and Bitner, Mary Jo, *Services Marketing*. New York: McGraw-Hill, 1996.

Zohar, Danah and Marshall, Ian, *The Quantum Society*. London: Bloomsbury 1993.

Zuboff, Shoshana, *In the Age of the Smart Machine*. New York: Basic Books, 1988.

Index

Marketing Plans
How to prepare them, how to use them

Malcolm McDonald
Professor of Marketing Strategy, Cranfield School of Management

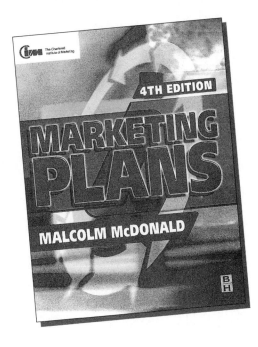

Kenneth Simmonds, Professor of Marketing and International Business, London Business School

Warren J. Keegan, Professor of International Business and Marketing Director, Institute for Global Business Strategy, Pace University, New York

- ● Thoroughly revised
- ● New material on key new areas of theory including key account management and electronic marketing
- ● An international marketing bestseller
- ● Two colour internal design and new page layout and design for maximum clarity

John D. Ryans, Jr, Bridgestone Professor of International Business and Professor of International Marketing, Kent State University, Ohio

With the new edition of **Marketing Plans**, marketing managers and business executives concerned with profitability and sustained growth of their organisation have at their fingertips a practical guide which tells them how to prepare and use a marketing plan.

May 1999 : Paperback : 0 7506 4116 9

Butterworth-Heinemann, Linacre House, Jordan Hill, Oxford OX2 8DP
Tel: +44 (0)1865 310366
Fax: +44 (0)1865 310898

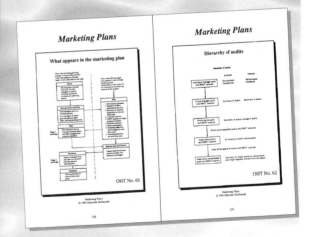